JAPANESE VIEWS ON ECONOMIC DEVELOPMENT

Do markets work in any developing country?

Should government be as small as possible?

Japan – a major provider of development aid – is challenging conventional wisdom in economic development. This book is the first systematic exposition of the Japanese approach to economic development and systemic transition in the English language. Eminent development economists who shape Japan's massive economic aid policy are assembled in this one essential volume.

Japanese economists generally believe that long-term vision and phased real-sector strategies are lacking in the policy recommendations of the World Bank and International Monetary Fund. They argue that development of a market economy requires many conditions which do not automatically arise by hands-off economic policy; these conditions must be built by conscious efforts of the government with international help. Therefore to promote a market economy, development economists should design a comprehensive and long-term development strategy tailored to the realities of each country.

This book will be a revelation to those who thought that the Japanese approach was simply to recommend universal industrial policy; they will be surprised by the broad scope of *Japanese Views on Economic Development*, touching on history, economic anthropology, and political development. Students of development economics, Asian studies, international relations as well as professional policy makers will find this perspective both controversial and stimulating.

Kenichi Ohno is a professor at the National Graduate Institute for Policy Studies, Saitama University, Japan, and former economist at the International Monetary Fund. He is the author of *Strategy for Transition to Market Economies* (1996, Japanese), and co-author of *Dollar and Yen* (1997).

Izumi Ohno is senior economist of Japan's Overseas Economic Cooperation Fund. She was formerly a public sector management specialist at the World Bank and a project coordinator at the Japan International Cooperation Agency. She and Kenichi have written *IMF and the World Bank* (1993 in Japanese).

ROUTLEDGE STUDIES IN THE GROWTH ECONOMIES OF ASIA

JAPANESE VIEWS ON ECONOMIC DEVELOPMENT

Diverse paths to the market

*Edited by Kenichi Ohno
and Izumi Ohno*

London and New York

First published 1998
by Routledge
2 Park Square, Milton Park, Abingdon, Oxon, OX14 4RN

Simultaneously published in the USA and Canada
by Routledge
270 Madison Ave, New York NY 10016

Transferred to Digital Printing 2006

© 1998 Editorial matter, by Kenichi Ohno and Izumi Ohno; individual chapters, the contributors

Typeset in Times by Keystroke, Jacaranda Lodge, Wolverhampton

British Library Cataloguing in Publication Data
A catalogue record for this book is available from the British Library

Library of Congress Cataloging in Publication Data
Japanese views on economic development: diverse paths to the market / edited by Kenichi Ohno
and Izumi Ohno.
p.   cm.
Includes bibliographical references and index.
1. Development economics—Japan. 2. Economic development.
3. Developing countries—Economic conditions—Case studies.
I. Ohno, Kenichi.   II. Ohno, Izumi.
HD75.J36 1998
338.952—dc21   97–29027
CIP

ISBN 0–415–15639–4

Publisher's Note
The publisher has gone to great lengths to ensure the quality of this
reprint but points out that some imperfections in the original
may be apparent

CONTENTS

CONTENTS

CONTENTS

FIGURES

TABLES

CONTRIBUTORS

Masahiko Aoki is a Professor of economics at Stanford University, California and Managing Director, Research Institute of International Trade and Industry, Ministry of International Trade and Industry.

Yonosuke Hara is Professor of economics at the Institute of Oriental Culture, University of Tokyo.

Shigeru Ishikawa is emeritus Professor of economics, Hitotsubashi University, and was a chairperson of the Japan International Cooperation Agency Study Group on Viet Nam.

Japan International Cooperation Agency is a government agency responsible for technical cooperation and grant aid.

Tatsuo Kaneda is Professor of economics in the Faculty of International Studies, Suzuka International University and a former advisor to the President of the Kyrgyz Republic (1992–5).

Hirohisa Kohama is Professor of economics in the Faculty of International Relations, University of Shizuoka.

Keiji Maegawa is Associate Professor of anthropology in the Faculty of Humanities and Social Sciences, Shizuoka University.

Yasusuke Murakami (1931–93) was a Professor of economics, University of Tokyo.

Yoshiaki Nishimura is Professor of economics at the Institute of Economic Research, Hitotsbashi University.

Izumi Ohno is a senior economist with the Overseas Economic Cooperation Fund in Tokyo.

Kenichi Ohno is Professor of economics at the National Graduate Institute for Policy Studies, Tokyo and Saitama.

Overseas Economic Cooperation Fund is a government agency responsible for concessional financial aid, and the Research Institute of Development Assistance is its research organ.

Masaki Shiratori is a senior advisor of the American Family Life Assurance Company, Japan, and a former Japanese executive director of the World Bank and Vice President and Member of the Board of the Overseas Economic Cooperation Fund.

Toshio Watanabe is Professor of economics in the Graduate School of Decision Science and Technology, Tokyo Institute of Technology.

Toru Yanagihara is Professor of economics in the Faculty of Economics, Hosei University of Tokyo.

PREFACE

Problems that development economics must deal with are becoming increasingly complex as East Asian newly industrializing tigers and their followers roar, while many countries in Sub-Saharan Africa, in particular, continue to stagnate. Former socialist economies in their bold jump from plan to market have had winners and losers. The widening gap between the successful minority and the struggling majority in the developing world is striking and calls for rethinking existing development strategy.

From the 1980s to date, the dominant idea in the global development scene has been neoclassical economic liberalism as practiced by the international financial organizations, led by the World Bank and the International Monetary Fund. This Washington consensus – featuring stern macroeconomic restraint and rapid economic liberalization and privatization – has come under attack from several quarters, not least from the countries which are themselves going through structural adjustment with Bank and Fund technical and financial assistance.

Meanwhile, in Japan, which now is the number one provider of official development assistance (ODA), a new approach to economic development and systemic transition has emerged. This approach, though still in its infancy, has come to be accepted by officials and scholars shaping Japan's ODA policy in the last several years. Unfortunately, many of its key writings are in Japanese and have been inaccessible to foreign researchers. This volume translates them into English and makes them available to a wider, non-Japanese speaking audience for discussion and constructive criticism. For those who have naively thought that the Japanese approach is simply to recommend industrial policy to any late-comer country, this book will be an eye opener.

The authors contributing to this volume are each well known to Japanese ODA policy-makers – if not to the Japanese economics profession at large or to scholars and practitioners outside Japan. We have selected essays which are frequently quoted, present key concepts, or illustrate unique Japanese prefer-ences. Except for the newly written overview chapter, all chapters in this volume are chosen from the body of literature existing in the first half of the 1990s. Thus, style and target audience vary from one chapter to another. Some originals are cleanly-edited published works, while others retain a certain unfinished quality.

Despite this, the main idea that each author is striving to convey should be clear. In translation, we have adhered to the Japanese originals as closely as possible. However, when a previous English translation existed, we did not hesitate to correct grammatical errors and stylistic awkwardness. For convenience, a reading guide for the entire volume is included at the end of Chapter 1.

This combined effort to translate and publish Japanese writings was prompted by our decade-old work experiences as regular economists at major aid organizations – the World Bank, the International Monetary Fund, the Japan International Cooperation Agency, and the Overseas Economic Cooperation Fund of Japan – and as consultants and advisors to these and other national and multinational institutions. Our trans-Pacific commuting has convinced us that the emerging Japanese view can play an important role in reshaping the global development strategy – and yet, the information on it is pitifully lacking outside Japan.

We have been very fortunate to have Ms. Anne Emig as an editorial advisor to our project. She is well acquainted with Japanese and American development philosophies and highly proficient in development economics and the Japanese language. Without her intense professional assistance, we would have hardly been able to publish this volume in the present form or in such a timely manner.

We would like to thank the authors and publishers who granted us the permission to translate and reprint the original works, and Ms. Alison Kirk of Routledge for her efficiency and helpful advice in publishing this volume. Last but not least, our gratitude goes to the many colleagues in Japan – and East Asia – who have morally supported us in the execution of this project. We hope that the finished product lives up to their expectations.

Kenichi Ohno
Izumi Ohno

1

OVERVIEW: CREATING THE MARKET ECONOMY[1]

Kenichi Ohno

I Introduction

In recent years, the Japanese government has begun to advocate strategies for economic development and systemic transition which are significantly different from those traditionally supported by the International Monetary Fund (IMF) and the World Bank. Particularly since the early 1990s, there have been numerous workshops and conferences in Japan leading to a broad consensus on the alternative strategy within the Japanese development aid circle.

Japanese officials and economists also began to broadcast their views abroad. The first clear voice of official dissent was raised in a short paper by the Overseas Economic Cooperation Fund (OECF, implementing body of the massive Japanese official development assistance (ODA) loan program) against the structural adjustment policy of the World Bank (OECF 1991; see also Chapter 3). This paper contained in the OECF Occasional Paper No. 1 (alternatively known as the "Shimomura Paper" because it was drafted by Yasutami Shimomura, then Director of the OECF's Economics Department) was based on recommendations of a study group composed of OECF officials and academic experts. The paper has been frequently quoted by analysts abroad.[2] Since then, Japanese essays criticizing the Bank–Fund orthodoxy have proliferated.

The increasing assertiveness of the Japanese aid community results from the convergence of four factors during the last several years. First and foremost, Japan's emergence as the largest ODA donor has naturally made it more confident and outspoken. Second, the recent experiences of systemic transition in Eastern Europe and the former Soviet Union – perceived to be generally less than satisfactory, especially in the latter, by many Japanese observers – stimulated the debate. Third, the dynamism of East Asian economies compared with the rest of the developing world has generated much interest in the Asian approach to economic development. Fourth, from the doctrinal perspective, the extremely negative view on government intervention which swept the global development scene in the 1980s began to correct itself in part in the early 1990s, paving the way for a wider acceptance of the Japanese view, which emphasizes the role of government.

In Japan, the dramatic collapse of the command economies around 1990 did not lead to all-out support for *laissez-faire* development strategy. On the contrary, the consensus among Japanese economists is that there will be less political support for American-style democracy and market capitalism now that the postwar ideological confrontation is over; instead, differences among market economies based on the diverse structures of individual societies will become the major cause of future international friction (Nihon Keizai Shimbunsha 1993). As a non-Western society that has embraced Western technology, democracy, and market capitalism, Japan believes that its intellectual contribution should come not by the refinement of Western values but from its non-Western origin. The rising Japanese – and more generally, East Asian – voices are perceived to be part of a process of relativization of the hitherto dominant free-market, free-society doctrine.

Compared with the neoclassical orthodoxy that stresses macroeconomic stability and free markets, the emerging Japanese view is distinct in its primary pursuit of long-term real targets; recommendation of fundamentally dissimilar policies for different initial conditions and stages of development; emphasis on the active role of government as an initiator of change; and – though not explicit in official documents but nonetheless real – the acceptance of authoritarian developmentalism in the early stages of development. These ideas strongly influence Japan's official development aid and advisory activities. Moreover, in the policy making processes of the governments of Eastern Europe and the former Soviet Union, China, Viet Nam,[3] Mongolia, etc., the Japanese (and other East Asian) views are routinely in contest with the Fund–Bank orthodoxy. The feeling is that the idea will have further impact on the future policies of the international financial institutions.

The Japanese aid community is generally unhappy with neoclassical development economics. We feel that its methodological scope is too narrow to handle a total social change – such as economic development or systemic transition. We are also uncomfortable with outsiders' views on the success of East Asia, which tend to oversimplify very complex matters (World Bank 1993; Huntington 1993; Krugman 1994; Sachs and Woo 1994). However, so far, Japan has not systematically explained its distinct view to a non-Japanese audience.

This chapter summarizes discussions currently taking place among officials and academic researchers responsible for the formulation of Japanese aid policy. This is not a historical survey of how Japan became an industrial economy, of which many excellent studies already exist (Komiya *et al.* 1988; Itoh *et al.* 1988; Minami 1992; Teranishi and Kosai 1993; Yanagihara and Sambommatu, 1997). Nor is the "Japan model" presented here one that indiscriminately promotes industrial policy and "priority production" to all countries as an antithesis to the neoclassical ideology. While a few overzealous Japanese officials do exist, most of us would strongly disapprove such a simple-minded approach. Rather, our focus is on *methodology*: when a developing country calls for our policy recommendations, how should we diagnose the underdevelopment of its market economy, and what should be done to overcome it, and in what sequence?

The view presented below is by no means Japanese monopoly. We know of many sympathizers in East Asia and elsewhere. It is not called the "East Asian Model" or "Asian Way" only because the present author is not sufficiently acquainted with the intellectual landscape of other countries to make the claim. However, the overall thrust – if not details – of our ideas has strong support among officials and students in many developing and transition economies.

It is also useful to remember that the orthodox and Japanese approaches share many common ideas, and that we are not disagreeing with every aspect of World Bank and IMF operations. Macroeconomic stability, managing global financial flows, human resource development, environmental protection, poverty alleviation, rural development, institution-building, good governance, etc. are serious concerns for both parties. In execution of aid programs and information exchange, the Japanese aid community is benefiting greatly from deepening interaction with these international financial institutions.

Nevertheless, we believe that there also exist fundamental differences between us that cannot be simply papered over. This chapter – and the entire book – addresses these differences, rather than the common ground which is taken for granted. We may at times oversimplify and criticize too much. But that is how heretical ideas are brought into the world of established beliefs – until a profitable synthesis of the old and the new is achieved. We certainly hope that such a synthesis will emerge in the future.

II How Japanese policy recommendations differ

By now the major differences between the IMF–World Bank orthodoxy and the Japanese approach are fairly well known to those engaged in development and aid. They are summarized in Table 1.1, and explained in detail below.

Real-sector concerns

The first major difference is the highest policy priority. The government of a developing or transition country faces a large number of grave issues, while its budget, time, and number of competent officials are severely limited. Advising such a government to solve all problems simultaneously is no advice at all. As a matter of highest priority, international financial institutions – especially the IMF, which plays the catalytic role in mobilizing external financial assistance – advise macroeconomic stability and "structural adjustment" (typically, rapid and comprehensive liberalization and privatization) to a country in economic crisis. For instance, IMF Managing Director Michel Camdessus had this to say to the Russian newspaper *Izvestia* on the faltering Russian reform in early 1993:

3

Table 1.1 Comparison of development and transition strategies

	Neoclassical approach	*Japanese approach*
Highest priority	Financial and macroeconomic (fiscal and BOP deficits, money, inflation, debt)	Real (output, employment, industrial structure)
Time scope	Short-term (solving problems as they arise)	Long-term (long-term targets and annual plans)
Basic attitude toward market	*Laissez-faire*; minimal government intervention	Active support by government
Speed of systemic transition	As quickly as possible	Will take long time even with maximum effort

the Directors [of the IMF Executive Board] regretted two major failures in the implementation of commitments made by the Government in July [1992]. First, several measures to increase the budget revenues, which had been pledged in July, have not yet been taken. Also the budget deficit has been allowed to grow rather than shrink. Second, and more important – and here the Executive Board [of the IMF] was quite emphatic, I should say – they regretted the substantial loosening of monetary and financial policies. . . . We believe, and the Executive Board has made the point very strongly, that hyperinflation must be stopped at all costs.

(*IMF Survey*, February 22, 1993)

It should be noted that the strong accent on budget, money, and inflation is not taken out of context; in fact, this is Camdessus's main message in the interview – as seen from the title of this newsletter article ("Russia's Hyperinflation Must Be Prevented, Says Camdessus").

Most Japanese aid officials find such obsession with finance and the macro-economy narrow and unbalanced. True, inflation must be dealt with, but not *at all costs* to the society, especially when the country is distressed by collapsing output, joblessness, political instability, ethnic conflicts, lawlessness, and public discontent. Under such adverse circumstances, the highest priority for Japan would be the *real* economy and *not* the financial side: how to arrest the fall in output, how to secure jobs, how to initiate revival and industrial restructuring, etc. These real concerns take precedence over money, budget, and inflation.

Historically, this was most vividly illustrated in 1946–48 when, following the war defeat, Japan itself was in deep economic crisis with output collapse and triple-digit inflation. The famous report "Basic Issues of Japanese Economic

Reconstruction" (Ministry of Foreign Affairs 1946) is full of these real-sector discussions, analyzing the status quo, proposing concrete measures to overcome obstacles, and suggesting prospective exports, industry by industry.

Also, in Japan around 1947, there was an intense debate as to how to stop the postwar inflation. Three major views were contested: (i) "Quick Stabilization" (i.e., shock approach) advocated by Member of Parliament Kihachiro Kimura, to eliminate inflation as quickly as possible by drastic monetary measures; (ii) "Conditional Quick Stabilization" advocated by Tokyo University Professor Hiromi Arisawa, to adopt the shock approach only after output had recovered to 60 percent of the prewar level; and (iii) "Intermediate Stabilization" (i.e., gradualism) advocated by the Economic Stabilization Board, to gradually lower inflation while receiving foreign aid and implementing recovery measures. The remarkable thing is that, despite the intensity of the debate, everyone agreed that securing output and employment was primary. Contestants differed only regarding the best way to achieve that common goal. Sacrificing production for the sake of inflation stabilization was out of the question.[4]

Long-term targets and concrete annual plans

The second salient characteristic of the Japanese approach is its long-term orientation. In a sense, this is a natural consequence of the priority given to concern for the real economy. Financial policies – money supply, budget, interest rates, the exchange rate – can be altered drastically in the short run (as long as the political will exists). But real targets – growth, saving, industrial structure, export base, technology – cannot be achieved overnight by official decrees. Inevitably, a strategy which emphasizes real targets must also be a long-term development strategy.

Typically, this takes the form of (i) setting long-term national goals (e.g., creating a certain number of new jobs within five years, doubling income in ten years, building certain industries from scratch, achieving industrialization by 2020, etc.); and (ii) designing comprehensive and concrete annual steps toward these goals, identifying bottlenecks, appropriating budgetary resources, and establishing implementing bodies. Working backwards from long-term goals thus determines action required today. The process often materializes in five-year plans and similar indicative official blueprints.[5] These plans are not rigid but remain quite flexible, allowing modifications as circumstances change. These long-term visions and accompanying official guidance are deemed necessary for underdeveloped countries in order to concentrate available resources in a few key sectors which can bolster overall growth. Igniting economic growth requires such resource concentration. The free market mechanism based purely on individual economic incentives tends to dissipate limited human and non-human resources over too many projects and sectors.

In 1946, Japan recognized the need for long-term planning and downplayed the market mechanism in order to initiate its own postwar recovery:

> To rebuild the Japanese economy from complete devastation, we need comprehensive and concrete annual reconstruction plans for the coming years. To speed up the reconstruction timetable, limited resources must be selectively used for starting an expansionary reproduction cycle. A liberal economy wastes economic resources and thus should not be adopted.
>
> (Ministry of Foreign Affairs 1946: 92)

Half a century later, in 1996, essentially the same advice is offered to the Vietnamese government by the official Joint Japan–Viet Nam Research Project (see Section 6 below). Viet Nam is a poor agrarian country devastated by three decades of war and a failed experiment of socialist planning. After the adoption of Doi Moi policy featuring market mechanisms and openness in 1986, the economy began to register robust growth. However, Viet Nam's market economy remains severely underdeveloped. Japanese economists urge Vietnamese policy makers to draw up a "blueprint" for strengthening its market economy and industrial base, listing specific target years and interim benchmarks. Selective industrial intervention is regarded as an important ingredient of this strategy. The blueprint should evolve as more experience is gained and circumstances change.

This approach, with long-term real vision, contrasts sharply with the IMF's current negotiating procedure which relies on short-term performance criteria and a large number of variables to be monitored quarterly and monthly. Problems are dealt with as they arise. Government budgets for this year and next are intensely discussed, but those for outer years are simply extrapolated. Even the World Bank, which is more directly involved with the real sector than the IMF, rarely recommends mobilization of limited resources to a few vital sectors in order to transform the national economy; Bank reports tend to cover many issues across many sectors without prioritization. The only routine long-term exercise at these institutions is the financial projection of debt relief operations. Long-term targeted, industrial intervention is never put on the negotiating table because, according to these institutions, it is the market, and not the government, that determines future industrial structure.

The positive role of government

The third characteristic of the Japanese approach is its pragmatic attitude toward market and government. Market and government are not antonyms in the ideological war between capitalism and socialism, but something that must always be blended in any society. The appropriate mix differs from one society to another, and also from one stage of development to another. The role of economic advisors is to find that particular mix. The question is not *whether* government should play a role in economic development in the abstract, but *how* it should do it in the context of each individual society. True, we have witnessed many cases of failed development attributable to incompetent and corrupt government.

Based on these experiences, some say "remove government," while the Japanese would say "improve government." Economic success depends on the quality of government intervention, and not on its absence.

The active role of government is particularly important in the early stages of development and in economic crisis. Without wise government, an underdeveloped economy will not take off. Government intervention is a necessary – although definitely not sufficient – condition for starting and sustaining economic growth. This was already recognized clearly in the nineteenth century when Japan began its transformation from a feudal samurai society to a modern, industrialized one. Returning from the two-year official mission to America and Europe,[6] the Meiji government's high official Toshimichi Okubo wrote in his back-to-office report:

> The strength of a country depends on the prosperity of its people which, in turn, is based on the level of output. To increase output, industrialization is essential. However, no country has ever initiated the process of industrialization without official guidance and promotion.
>
> (Okubo 1874)

More recently, the Japanese aid community has been watching policy trends at the World Bank closely. During the 1980s, the Bank appeared to be excessively preoccupied with spreading the free-market ideology. In a number of Bank publications, it even attributed East Asian economic success to the absence of government intervention, confounding many observers, particularly officials of East Asian governments. However, beginning with the 1991 *World Development Report* which presented the "market-friendly approach," the Bank's faith in the supremacy of the market seems to have begun to weaken (World Bank 1991). It listed what government should do and should not do more even-handedly. In *The East Asian Miracle* report of 1993,[7] the Bank further admitted that financial intervention did seem to work in a few East Asian countries (especially Japan and Korea), and that "contest-based" competition with official guidance may be a viable alternative to market-based competition (World Bank 1993). The 1997 *World Development Report* recognized that targeted industrial intervention may be effective if institutions are strong. It then proposed a two-part strategy to (1) match intervention to current institutional capacity; and (2) build institutional capacity over time – see the Afterword for our evaluation of this strategy.

However, other recent Bank publications seem to have reverted to the more traditional neoclassical line in promoting divestiture of state-owned enterprises (World Bank 1995) and fast liberalization in transition economies (World Bank 1996). We in the Japanese aid community have read, analyzed, and debated these principal Bank publications intensely. We are still dissatisfied with the Bank's remaining bias toward the market, but we also find some of the current directions of change desirable. (However, no clear sign of such policy change has been detected in IMF publications.)

Quick transition is impossible

Fourth, partly because of its long-term orientation, the Japanese aid community accepts the fact that fostering a market economy requires patience. The time span that is appropriate for this endeavor is not years, but decades and generations. Marketization is a total social process involving economy, polity, culture, class, ethnicity, international relations – and not just a technical problem to be solved by economic principles only. The path is fraught with many shocks and conflicts from within and without, and temporary setbacks are the rule rather than the exception. From this viewpoint, Russia's proposed 500-Day Plan for creating a market economy, or the claim that Russia has already become a market economy, is incomprehensible.

Tatsuo Kaneda, former advisor to the President of the Kyrgyz Republic (see Chapter 12), summarizes the problems of the Russian "shock-therapy" reform in the early 1990s as seen from the Japanese perspective (Kaneda 1995). He declares that "no overnight victory is possible for a large change involving the entire society, like transition to a market economy." According to Kaneda, the Russian policy design was defective because (i) no long-term target vision of the market economy was provided; (ii) marketization was thought to be a socio-engineering task to be completed within a few years; (iii) marketization was incorrectly assumed to induce immediate change in the behavior of individuals and firms; (iv) output was assumed to recover automatically after a few years, for no reason; and (v) political aspects of the reform were ignored. It may be added that his views are shared not only by other Japanese but by many researchers the world over. We sometimes hear that systemic transition in EE/FSU has been unexpectedly prolonged and severe in terms of output losses. However, few Japanese analysts are surprised, since they never expected the transition to be over so soon.

The need for country-specific long-term strategy

In sum, the Japanese view is based on the belief that a market economy does not grow automatically in developing countries even if the macroeconomy is stabilized, prices and economic activities are liberalized, and state-owned enterprises are privatized. More is required for the development of the market economy. What is additionally needed is well-designed activism by the government in the production sphere. While incompetent government will surely stunt growth potential, withdrawal of government will not solve the problem either. The ability to formulate appropriate long-term development strategy is the key to economic development – and there is no way around it.

Japanese development economists believe that the "appropriate" development strategy differs fundamentally from one country to another, and from one stage of development to another. Thus we reject generalization at the level of individual policy measures. The validity of import substitution, agricultural price support, industrial policy, privatization – and thousands of other policies – cannot be ascertained in the abstract. They are good or bad depending on the particular situation of the country in question. The path to the market is unique to each individual country. Hence, the main task of the economist is to uncover the relevant unique characteristics of the country and propose a set of comprehensive and concrete policy measures suitable for its initial conditions. What is common across countries is the operational procedure for doing this research (i.e., methodology), and not final policy recommendations (i.e., conclusions).

For this reason, the Japanese aid community is extremely ill at ease with the universal policy orientation of the international financial institutions, which can be summarized as the simultaneous pursuit of macroeconomic stability and "structural adjustment" (liberalization and privatization). Although these institutions argue that all adjustment programs are designed differently, the difference only extends to the intensity of individual measures in the preset menu of policies – tight budget, subsidy cuts, monetary restraint, positive and internationally competitive real interest rates, exchange rate devaluation, price and trade liberalization, higher public utility charges, etc. The original menu does not change. This approach ignores the fact that each country requires a different menu and the effectiveness of each policy is case-dependent. Careful diagnosis is needed before treatment. The same medicine can cure or kill depending on the condition of the patient.

The next four sections will present the political and economic ideas that underlie the distinct characteristics of the Japanese approach expounded above.

III The meaning of "marketization" for latecomers

Before we get into the technical question of how to create a market economy where it did not exist previously, it is worthwhile to present a broader perspective from economic anthropology.[8] Specifically, we ask the question: what is the historical significance of "marketization" in today's underdeveloped and (formerly) socialist countries? This will provide a useful reference point from which the process of economic development and systemic transition can be understood. It will also explain why the Japanese approach takes the particular form explained above.

The resource-transfer model of development and transition

To begin with, let us first clarify the meaning of *marketization*. Assume that the economy is composed of three production sectors:

1 *customary-economy sector:* typically, subsistence agriculture and family businesses in the developing world. It is characterized by low productivity, small scale, vulnerability to weather, limited scope of commodity exchange,

9

member survival as the principal goal, and clan or village organization as a social core;

2   *state-economy sector*: made up of state-owned enterprises and collective farms where the central authority directs production and distribution at publicly-owned production units on a command basis; and

3   *market-economy sector*: resource mobilization and allocation are regulated mainly through prices determined by competition among individuals and firms possessing economic freedom.

The resource-transfer model is useful for discussing various aspects of economic development and systemic transition (Figure 1.1). Within this frame-work, marketization is defined to be the process in which resources (labor, capital, land, etc.) previously engaged in the first or second sector are transferred to the third sector, increasing the share of the market economy in GDP. Two types of marketization should be distinguished: "economic development" which is a resource transfer from the first to the third sector; and "systemic transition" which is a resource transfer from the second to the third sector. The process of economic development is usually accompanied by "industrialization," that is, an increasing

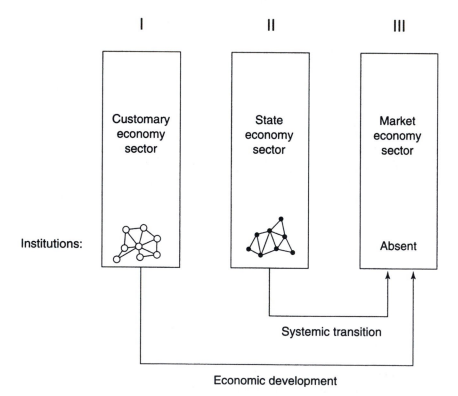

Figure 1.1 Resource-transfer model of development and transition

share of manufacturing industries in GDP. In either case, the economy's long-term productive capacity will rise significantly because of superior informational and incentive characteristics of the market economy. Indeed, this is the primary reason why governments wish to marketize their economies.[9]

The center and the periphery

From the anthropological perspective, the process of marketization cannot be analyzed independently from international relations and politics. It inherently entails power relationship between the center and the periphery.

Ever since the ascent of the West (Western Europe and, later, the United States), modern history has been characterized by the dominance of the center (the West) over the rest of the world. In the language of historians, "internationalization" is a politically loaded word. It implies the process by which the militarily and economically superior West has subjugated other peoples in the periphery, absorbing them into its own cultural universe, positioning them as inferior, and exploiting them, if necessary, to the benefit of its own development. Through this process, sometimes also called "modernization," the geographical domain of Western civilization has expanded. The West was the activator while the non-West was a passive entity to be "internationalized." The most prominent incident of internationalization was the colonization of Asia and Africa in the late nineteenth–early twentieth centuries.

The age of colonialism and naked military invasion is over, and almost all developing countries have now achieved political independence. Thanks to the rise in cultural relativism, traditional cultures of the developing world are no longer considered inferior to Western art, music, and literature. However, "internationalization" is still alive today, albeit in a more subtle form. There still exist certain Western values that are deemed superior; therefore, the rest of the world should emulate them. Though politically emancipated, developing countries are still subsumed into the global system which promotes these desirable values. The two Western creations thus revered today are *market* and *democracy*. The United States, as the leader of the postwar world, has vigorously promoted these values. In the 1990s, with the demise of socialism, these values have been even more aggressively advocated as the norm of international society.

It is not entirely correct to assert that these Western values are being imposed on non-Western countries against their own will. The market mechanism is genuinely attractive because it promotes economic growth. That the market mechanism based on individual freedom and incentives raises production in the long run is now an indisputable historical fact. Like it or not, latecomers who wish to improve living conditions and catch up technologically and economically with the West must inevitably – and often very willingly – embrace the market mechanism. In many countries, marketization, industrialization, modernization, joining the rank of the developed countries, etc., are the most common national slogans, not without the support of the population.[10]

Within this framework, the role of international organizations like the IMF and the World Bank can be interpreted as a formalized multilateral mechanism to promote economic "internationalization" – i.e., marketization of latecomer countries. Western countries which dominate the decision-making process of these organizations prod novices to convert to proven values. In turn, willing developing and transition countries knock on their door soliciting financial and technical assistance. Conditionalities attached to IMF credit and World Bank structural adjustment lending are the carrot-and-stick for accelerating this process. Similarly, in the political area, the peacekeeping and election-monitoring operations by the United Nations can also be construed to have comparable effects in advancing democracy in the periphery. Thus, global propagation of accepted Western norms has become a major *raison d'être* for international organizations during the last half century.

One very important aspect of countries in the periphery converting to the market mechanism is the internal conflict between westernization (modernization) and nationalism (local culture). As the foreign value system starts to invade the indigenous social fabric, the country is thrown into a split identity. On the one hand, new things are welcomed as the harbinger of better, more civilized life and old customs are abandoned as obsolete. On the other hand, sweeping materialism, inability to adapt to the speed of change, and the sense of lost traditional values will engender cultural chauvinism and hostility toward foreign imports, whether material or spiritual. This inner conflict occurs within the minds of individuals as well as at the family, community, and national levels. This is an inherent feature of the peripheral society in ascent. It happened in Japan in the late nineteenth century as it tried to catch up with the West economically and militarily (Sakamoto 1994).[11] It is also happening, for example, in Vietnamese society today under Doi Moi policy. This cultural sensitivity must be taken into account in the formulation of strategies for marketization.

Translative adaptation

Are countries in the periphery really passive? Do they accept the market mechanism wholeheartedly while the existing socio-economic structure is simply destroyed, replaced, or abandoned? Does indigenous culture cease to exist, with the non-Western society completely overtaken by the foreign system? According to economic anthropologist Keiji Maegawa, the answer is No. In any country which succeeds in marketization, the structure of the base society remains surprisingly intact even after a drastic change in the economic mechanism.

From the outside, marketization may appear to be a process of passive subsumption of a non-Western society into the dominant international system. But from the viewpoint of the "subsumed," it is not at all abandonment of the old system and all-out importation of the new. The base society remains active in the adaptation process and survives the systemic transformation. The society conveniently reinterprets and selectively accepts the foreign system. This is not a hijacking of one culture by the other, but rather a genuine merger of two systems – at the initiative of the indigenous.

> Except for the case of sudden destruction of the internal system by an external force, . . . the indigenous system is not as vulnerable as might have been thought. The process of transformation, if closely examined, can be seen in terms of the interaction between the two systems; the indigenous system should be recognized as prior and fundamental, with the external system being a later addition.
>
> (Maegawa 1994a: 193)

The purpose of Maegawa's anthropological research is to explain how each individual non-Western society, with its own historically unique conditions, interprets and accepts Western culture without discontinuity in the cultural system of the base society. Here, the roles of the superior and inferior cultures are paradoxically reversed; the "subsumed" is no longer passive but becomes a positive actor accepting the foreign culture on its own terms, adjusting it if necessary. Maegawa explains further:

> many nations and societies have adopted Western institutions and objects from without in order to survive (or by their own choice). However, it is important to recognize that they did not accept Western inventions in their original forms. Any item in one culture will change its meaning when transplanted to another culture, as seen widely in ethnography around the world. Not only cosmology, religious doctrine, rituals, but also the family system, institution of exchange, and even socio-economic organizations like the firm exhibit the property of adapting to external institutions and principles with the existing cultural system maintaining its *form* of structure. The essence of what has been called "modernization" is the adaptive acceptance of Western civilization under the persistent form of the existing culture. That is, actors in the existing system have adapted to the new system by reinterpreting each element of Western culture (i.e., "civilization") in their own value structure, modifying yet maintaining the existing institutions. I shall call this "translative adaptation."
>
> (Maegawa 1994b, emphasis in the original; see also Chapter 9)

Similarly, Yonosuke Hara, one of the most influential economists in the Japanese aid community today, argues that the process of economic development in Southeast Asia should also be understood as an interaction between the old and new systems:

> The rapid economic growth of Southeast Asian countries . . . is taking place in the heavy presence of unique values, social institutions, and customs of each country, even though technology and economic

organizations invented in the advanced market economies are being introduced to enhance efficiency. The internal dynamism of their economic development should be analyzed as an interactive process of "foreign" elements which improve economic efficiency on the one hand, and "indigenous" elements unique to that country on the other. When the internal dynamism of economic development is understood as such, the crucial issue is compatibility between indigenous elements (unique values and social institutions) and foreign elements (imported technology, enterprise organization, etc.) introduced to raise economic efficiency. If the indigenous and foreign elements are not too different, they can be merged and the economy will develop by absorbing these foreign elements. If, on the contrary, the two are irreconcilable, the only possible outcome will be either the rejection of foreign elements or the tragic destruction and dismantling of the unique social institutions by foreign elements.

(Hara 1985)

The fundamental realization made by Maegawa and Hara is twofold: (1) the market economy does not stand alone but is strongly conditioned by the existing social structure – "economy is embedded in society" (Karl Polanyi); and (2) social structure is unique to each country, and some societies may even be incompatible with the imported market economy. These observations lead to the policy conclusion that the path to a market economy must be unique to each individual society, and that the government must ensure, in its own way, that the newly introduced market mechanism is accepted by the base society (Chapter 7).

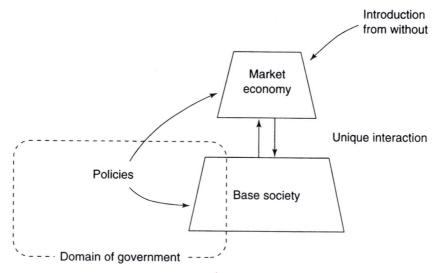

Figure 1.2 Systemic interaction in the marketization process

14

This, in essence, is key to adopting Western technology and institutions without losing national self-identity. According to Hara, Japan has been the most successful country to achieve this feat. And many other East Asian countries are now on the verge of achieving it. Maegawa's and Hara's ideas are summarized graphically in Figure 1.2.

Because the indigenous social structure is only modified, never abandoned, a successfully marketized latecomer will retain its dual character even after it has been industrialized. On the one hand, the country grows to be a full-fledged member of civilized international society, equipped with democracy and the market mechanism; on the other hand, it still appears to be an outsider laden with premodern legacies hopelessly incompatible with Western institutions and customs. This is not an aberration, but quite normal. Again, Japan provides the best example. Even after 130 years of translative adaptation and after a quarter century of being an "advanced" country, Japan is still regarded as "fundamentally different" by many observers in the West.

Market underdevelopment and the role of government

The process of economic development in the non-Western world is characterized as a deliberate attempt, perhaps only once in the history of any such country, to implant a system from without that does not arise automatically from inside the existing society. This is a very different situation from the British Industrial Revolution in the eighteenth and nineteenth centuries, which was driven from within and not by deliberate official initiatives. It is also different from the subsequent industrialization of Germany or the United States where the Western value system was already in place.

Marketization of non-Western latecomers entails two grave problems that are peculiar to them. First, there is a serious risk that the existing society is unready for or incompatible with the requirements of the newly introduced market economy. If inconsistencies are left unattended, the market economy may well remain underdeveloped. Second, the government must act first to start the process of marketization, since the existing society does not necessarily possess the dynamism for creating the market economy. Unlike the British Industrial Revolution where private inventors and entrepreneurs were homegrown, the role of government becomes crucial in today's less developed countries where the private sector is very weak. How to overcome this disadvantage will be the main subject of the next two sections.

IV The market economy and its underdevelopment

The sharp contrast in policy orientation between the neoclassical orthodoxy and the Japanese dissent, as reviewed in Section 2 and summarized in Table 1.1 above, stems fundamentally from different concepts of the market economy and its development process.

Economic theory evolves not only in response to the changing external environment (i.e., the economy itself) which is the object of its analysis; it is driven by its internal dynamics, with its established methodology and academic institutions. Because of this, the type of economics practiced widely at any time may or may not be suitable for solving the most urgent real-world problem of that age. When political and economic transformation in the (former) socialist countries began in earnest at the beginning of the 1990s, the most influential doctrine in the international financial institutions happened to be neoclassical development economics. The new challenge of systemic transition was met by extending and adjusting the existing neoclassical paradigm, rather than devising a completely new approach. Thus, the policy design of the IMF and the World Bank has remained essentially the same – aside from a slightly wider scope and variation in the intensity of its components – from Sub Saharan Africa in the 1980s to Russia and Kyrgyzstan in the 1990s. The emphasis was – and still is – on the rapid liberalization and privatization of the entire economy. The IMF's preoccupation with macroeconomic stability also remains intact. Policy matrices are similar from one country to another.

We feel that the methodology of neoclassical economics is inherently unsuitable for guiding the historical task of systemic transition. Certainly, it can deal with many other problems – consumer behavior, production and investment decisions, portfolio investment, etc. – when the fundamental social structure remains unchanged. On the other hand, neoclassical economics is incapable of analyzing a total social change of the nature of systemic transition because of its basic logical structure.[12]

"Market" in neoclassical economics

According to Hara (1994), neoclassical economics "can neatly demonstrate the efficiency of the market economy, but offers little to those wishing to properly understand the dynamic process of development of the market economy." In the history of economic theory, neoclassical economics is a very unusual doctrine. Let us summarize its characteristics which are relevant to our inquiry.[13]

The concept of "market" in neoclassical economics is closely related to the concept of "perfect competition." The latter is a state in an abstract multi-dimensional space with goods, prices, and "representative agents," and where all of the following technical conditions are met:

- All goods are identical
- Consumers are identical from the viewpoint of sellers
- A large number of both sellers and buyers exist
- Information is perfect
- Each firm maximizes profit
- Each consumer maximizes utility
- Free entry and exit are assured

Obviously, these are not derived from the careful observation of actual economies but are assumed for the sake of subsequent deduction (i.e., construction of models). In the neoclassical research program, it is customary to first build a mathematical model from axioms and assumptions, and its implications are later tested by statistical methods ("econometrics").

It is also well known that utilitarianism and individualism provide the philosophical basis of neoclassical economics. Efficiency ("Pareto optimality") is the principal criterion for value judgment. The two fundamental theorems of welfare economics mathematically prove that competitive equilibrium is efficient, and any efficient economy can in turn be supported by competitive equilibrium with appropriate initial endowments. Competition and market (where competition takes place) are deemed good because they promote allocative efficiency. Desirability of a state of the economy is measured by the distance from the ideal state of perfect competition. The research program of neoclassical economics typically asks: when each economic agent maximizes its objective function (utility, profit, etc.) subject to the budget constraint and under the prescribed states of information, competition, and organization, what will be the final result and how will it be achieved?

The following three features of neoclassical economics are particularly problematic when applied to the investigation of developing and transition economies:

1 *market as an ideal type*: as noted above, neoclassical economics analyzes a hypothetical market with perfect competition and various partial deviations from it. The existence of a market is presupposed; the market is the rule and non-market economic activities are the exception. Generalization and mathematical formulation are common, and deduction (model building) precedes induction (hypothesis testing by econometrics);

2 *abstract time*: time in neoclassical economics is mathematical and not historical. Economic dynamics studies the existence and uniqueness of equilibrium and possible paths from one equilibrium to another. It does *not* deal with the problem of how various classes, institutions, and spirits in support of the market economy arise, develop, and interact within each individual society;

3 *disregard for non-economic factors*: aspiring to be a pure science, neoclassical economics separates the technical problem of efficiency from all other value systems – politics, religion, education, ethnicity, morality, culture, etc. "Good" models explain events solely by the internal logic of economics (i.e., maximization principle) without recourse to these non-economic factors.

All these features deliberately ignore the uniqueness of each society and seek the universal applicability of a single principle to all societies across all ages. Since the marketization process is critically dependent on the existing structure of each individual society (Section 3 above), we believe that the marriage of the neoclassical paradigm and development economics is a theoretical mismatch.[14] Neoclassical development economics would automatically rule out the most important topic for investigation from the outset. Where deductive logic reigns supreme and empirical diversity is relegated to secondary status, it is difficult to even ask the question: how do the inheritances of each society from its own unique past affect the formation process of the market economy?

Biological analogy

Perhaps a better way to study marketization is to view it not as a mechanical process analogous to interstellar gravity or chemical reaction, but as a process similar to biological growth and evolution – featuring individuality, self-identity, internal dynamism, external shocks, mutation, adaptation to environment, and the role of parents and community. Fostering a market economy is like rearing a human child, which requires guidance and protection of the parents (government) in the early stages. A few eminent Japanese scholars have been inclined to propose an evolutionary approach to marketization.

Political-economist Yasusuke Murakami expresses such a view in his posthumous book, *Outline of Anti-Classical Political Economy*:

> Evolution is a serial process where the world which seemed constant is suddenly jolted by a totally unexpected discontinuity, creating a new world which is maintained awhile, but is again shocked by a sudden and discontinuous jump, etc. Roughly speaking, the world of biological evolution is characterized by instability which leads to discontinuity and divergence. It is fundamentally different from the world of physical dynamics where continuity and stability of equilibrium are the norm. Now consider human history. Viewed objectively, human history is a repeated process where social patterns with self-preserving tendency are nonetheless forced to change. In this sense, it is truly an evolutionary process. Industrialization is a historical process, and this is the reason why economics of industrialization must be "evolutionary."
>
> (Murakami 1994: 121)

In the same spirit, Masahiko Aoki, Masahiro Okuno, and other researchers in comparative institutional analysis have advanced a theory of evolutionary games for the comparison of different economic systems and the analysis of their dynamics. In this literature, the two opposing aspects in evolution – continuity versus change – are also featured. "Strategic complementarity," "institutional complementarity," and "path-dependency" provide the theoretical basis for explaining the continuity of society. (See below for more discussion on institutional complementarity.) However, social equilibrium resistant to minor shocks may jump to another equilibrium if sufficient force is applied to overcome the "transition cost":

> Theoretically, one mechanism that can relax the constraint of history is the successive and stochastic occurrence of vacillation in the "bounded rational" strategy (i.e., duplication of the socially optimal strategy) or mutants ... evolutionary equilibrium is an equilibrium which is stable against a few minor strategic vacillations or invasions by alien elements. More than one such equilibrium exist in our Darwinian dynamics. However, the evolutionary equilibrium will move to another evolutionary equilibrium if mutations occur collectively and simultaneously, covering a fairly large population.
>
> (Aoki 1995a: 86)

Aoki and Okuno (1996) consider the economic system to be an institutional Nash equilibrium in a random-matching evolutionary game. Forces underlying social continuity and discontinuity in their model are summarized in Table 1.2.

Methodological question

At this point, let us consider the basic methodological question in social sciences in general and in the study of the marketization process in particular.

On the one hand, there is a popular orientation in economics toward simplicity and parsimony, explaining all phenomena by a single tool – i.e., the maximization principle in a choice-theoretic framework. Ideally, one model with a small number of common variables should explain and predict all behavior across space and time. Case-by-case, *ad hoc* analyses are to be resisted. This is a pursuit of general theory. In policy recommendations, it produces a uniform policy package for all. Researchers intentionally disregard the individuality of each case and take formalization to the extreme.

On the other hand, there is also an entrenched research attitude in area studies, which respects individuality. Its proponents contend that understanding a society requires long-term participation and assimilation. Researchers from an outside world need to learn its language, customs, culture, values, and *become as a member of that society* before they can even ask – and eventually answer – the right questions, consistent with the internal structure of the society. Borrowed

Table 1.2 Causes of systemic inertia and mutation under imperfect information and bounded rationality (from the viewpoint of evolutionary game theory)

Sources of systemic continuity	Sources of systemic discontinuity
Strategic complementarity	Emergence of idiosyncratic individuals
Institutional complementarity	Social experimentation
Multiple equilibria	Government intervention
Path dependency	Contact with foreign culture

Source: Summarized from Chapter 11, Aoki and Okuno (1996).

19

yardsticks – such as Western individualism or rationalism – cannot be used to evaluate non-Western societies.

These opposing academic attitudes are respectively called the "hate and love of empirical diversity" by Hara (1985) and "transcendental reflection versus interpretative reflection" by Murakami (1992). Essentially, this is the classical deduction-versus-induction debate. Should we choose the first approach, or the second?

Our view is that researchers should not be ensconced in either of them but must continuously go back and forth between the two approaches. Endless abstraction is as unattractive as uniqueness without comparability. The two approaches should not be thought of as mutually exclusive. We need to generalize if we are to practice science, but we also need to recognize the uniqueness of each society. The neoclassical resurgence in the 1980s imparted too much deductive bias to development economics. The pendulum has swung too far, and it is time to regain balance.

Specifically, as argued in Section 2, we need to shift the level of generalization from a concrete policy menu to a common analytical procedure. The new paradigm should consist of an accepted methodology, but not concrete policy conclusions – unlike neoclassical development economics which imposes both methodology and conclusions (Ohno 1996b). The key is to formalize the common procedure to identify the idiosyncracy of the underdeveloped market economy in a particular country. Each time we are confronted with a new case, we should start a similar analytical process from scratch. At present, no such procedure has been clearly established in development economics – but we will see some efforts by the Japanese aid community later in this section, as well as in Section 6.

The methodological eclecticism proposed here may be uncomfortable for those who have adhered to only one approach, whether deductive or inductive. However, the sense of methodological security derived from the traditional practice may well be deceptive. If one model fitted all situations, or if no model were required, the task of social scientists would be too easy. Reality is complex, and forcing a methodology on complex reality because it is convenient will inevitably sacrifice analytical power and relevance. Instead of lamenting, methodological complexity should be happily accepted.

To implement the new approach, far more information will be required than filling in the standardized tables in the IMF's *Recent Economic Development* (GDP, budget, money, and the balance of payments). Investing more time and effort on the uniqueness of each country would be a healthy change in development economics. Before building any model, we should look harder at empirical reality than the neoclassical research program allows.

Underdevelopment of the market economy

The discussions above show why Japanese development economists take the underdevelopment of the market economy very seriously.[15] Highly advanced industrial economies apart, we do not believe that the socially integrated market economy is ubiquitous in every human society and only suppressed by inappropriate state control and bureaucratic meddling. We do not subscribe to the view that, in *any* country, removal of government intervention alone will immediately release the potential of the market. That may happen in some countries, but not all. Unlike other systems such as self-sufficiency, customary economy, feudalism, or mercantilism, the market economy is a very demanding economic system. Its proper operation requires a large number of conditions to be satisfied: property rights, contract system, economic freedom, firms and entrepreneurs, labor and capital markets, transportation and communication, technical absorptive capacity, and so on. Provision of these conditions is not automatic, and only those societies which happen to be equipped with them – or those that deliberately adapt themselves to be compatible with the market mechanism – can successfully adopt it.

The argument can be put in a slightly subtler way. Consider the debate on whether "institutions" (the social structure supporting the economic system) can adapt flexibly to the requirements of the economic system. The most extreme view in this regard was historical materialism championed by Karl Marx. He argued that "superstructure" (non-economic systems) is critically dependent on "infrastructure" (economy), and when the economy (production force and production relations) changes, superstructure will also change.[16] A similar but much weaker view currently in vogue is the idea of induced institutional change, which says that institutions respond to the needs of the economic system over time. Without any official help, by trial and error, incentives and optimizing behavior of private agents are able to alter existing institutions which no longer contribute to economic efficiency. Neoclassical development economists must have something like this in mind when they advocate big-bang liberalization and privatization.

We reject induced institutional change, at least for low-income and systemic transition countries. True, institutions may have the ability to adapt, but in many underdeveloped economies, the speed and scope of automatic institutional change are very limited. Instead, we generally observe that institutional rigidity is the main obstacle to introducing the market mechanism. These economies remain underdeveloped precisely because they lack the internal dynamism to create necessary institutions. In such cases, government must take the initiative to marketize the economy or it will not be marketized. Laissez-faire policy will not work.

The concept of underdevelopment of the market economy has been most forcefully presented by Shigeru Ishikawa, a China specialist who is unquestionably the most influential development economist in the Japanese aid community today (also see Section 6). In his words,

> If the market economy automatically develops as productivity and income levels rise, there is no need to investigate the matter any further.

21

By contrast, if the development of a market economy is a necessary condition for the rise in production capability and income levels, we will be confronted with the practical need to understand how the development of a market economy becomes possible.

(Ishikawa 1990: 16)

More recently, Ishikawa introduced the distinction between two types of economic distortions to make the same point. In the JICA report included in this volume, which he drafted, Ishikawa argues thus:

Market economies are underdeveloped in most developing countries. Dirigiste economic systems, of which centrally planned economies are one variety, are one factor distorting the market economy in these countries. However, removing that factor alone will not cure the underdevelopment of the market economy when other pre-existing distortions are present. We term these "innate distortions" and distinguish them from "artificial distortions" attributable to state control. In such instances, efforts must be made to create and enhance the market economy itself, if that system is to take root.

(JICA 1995; see also Chapter 14 of this volume)

Thus, unless both innate and artificial distortions are overcome, the economy will not be marketized. But what specifically are innate distortions? Ishikawa classifies the basic conditions for the market economy – whose absence leads to innate distortions – into the following three categories (Ishikawa 1990; Chapter 6 of this volume):

1   *social division of labor in production*: a market economy cannot be started unless a fairly large geographical area has been integrated under its mechanism, with specialization in production and exchange of products among its subregions. Village self-sufficiency, hunting and gathering, slash and burn, and a nomadic way of life – with very limited exchange among subregions – are inconsistent with the development of a market economy;

2   *infrastructure for merchandise distribution*: this includes such physical facilities as roads, railways, ports, airports, railway wagons, and trucks, as well as organizations handling commerce, transportation, storage, communication, finance, and insurance. Unless distributional "hardware" and "software" are sufficiently developed, the market economy cannot operate properly; and

3   *observance of rules for market exchange*: the minimum required here is the effective protection of property rights and commercial contracts. In addition, more complex business institutions like an anti-monopoly law, corporate laws, rules of financial transactions, trade unions, etc., will have to be created. Furthermore, morals and sentiments which support these laws and

rules must be engendered in people's minds. These are institutions and spirits that impart order and stability to the market mechanism.

Others may want to reclassify or add to Ishikawa's list of basic conditions for the market economy. In fact, Ishikawa's own list seems to be evolving over time. Identification of these conditions to the satisfaction of the majority of development economists is certainly a very important topic for future research.

While the state of market underdevelopment is unique to each society, some typology may be possible and even useful. For Ishikawa, the *stage of development* is one crucial factor which determines appropriate policy design. For example, Laos and the remote provinces of Viet Nam which are barely monetized (as measured by the M_2/GDP ratio, commercial bank deposits, use of trade credits, etc.) must adopt more elementary financial policies than the rest of Southeast Asia where financial sectors are better developed. The fact that some countries are farther from the market economy than others may be obvious, but its recognition provides a good departure point from the neoclassical assumption of the ubiquitous market.[17]

Another typology proposed by Ishikawa is based on the *state of relative factor endowments* such as labor, land, and natural resources. He often evokes two distinct development models: Arthur Lewis' famous model of rural–urban labor migration under industrialization which is suitable for densely populated agricultural countries; and the vent-for-surplus model of Hla Myint where development depends on finding overseas markets for domestic natural resources, which is suitable for sparsely-populated resource-rich countries. In either case, the dominant economic mechanism makes an irreversible transformation at some "turning point," and the government's role is to prepare conditions for such a transformation. Of course, there may be other models that could be employed. Matching development models with each actual economy is another important research task.

Ineffective liberalization: cases from China

If underdevelopment of the market economy is not properly recognized, policies may fail to achieve their intended results. Ishikawa points out that, even in China where marketization is generally more successful than other transition economies, there have been many instances where liberalization policies did not work well because the actual market economy was less developed than was required by the policies. He gives five examples (Ishikawa 1990, 1994; see also Chapter 6 of this volume):

1   while the liberalization of Chinese agriculture since 1978 raised output and productivity, the lack of an inter-provincial distribution system proved to be a serious bottleneck. Archaic merchant networks could not handle bumper crops or crop failure. Uncertain supply and the inability to ship, led to the food crisis in 1984;

2   dismantling of people's communes did restore market incentives to family farms, but it also terminated the productive services that those communes used to provide – construction and maintenance of irrigation facilities, communal procurement and shipment, finance, control of fertilizers and pesticides, etc. Private enterprise substitutes did not emerge as quickly as the Chinese government had hoped;

3   the autonomy granted to state-owned enterprises (SOEs) since the early 1980s did not automatically lead to the emergence of vigorous private markets due to the lack of marketing skills and distribution system;

4   the management autonomy of SOEs was often abused to please workers who demanded wage increases comparable to those at other SOEs, regardless of productivity. Work ethic was still based on equity and job security, not hard work and performance;

5   decentralization of state finance allowed local governments to sharply increase bank loans to SOEs under their jurisdiction, leading to the accumulation of bad debt and inflation in 1984–88. This was the result of premature liberalization, occurring before the central government had put effective macroeconomic control mechanisms and financial discipline in place.

The EPA report: international comparison of market underdevelopment

The report on an alternative development policy, commissioned by the Economic Planning Agency and edited by the Japan Research Institute, is one of the products of ongoing research initiated two years ago (Japan Research Institute 1996). Not only does it introduce the current thinking of several distinguished contributors but, even more important, the report constructs a matrix of (mostly qualitative) indicators of market underdevelopment for four developing and transition countries – the first such attempt as far as we know.

The study group co-chairs, Toru Yanagihara and Yonosuke Hara, each wrote a theoretical overview to the report. Yanagihara summarizes the "economic system approach" (ESA) which directs the entire report. Unlike the neoclassical approach with anonymous, atomistic agents on the one hand and the market as a neutral playing field on the other, ESA emphasizes the middle ground where the organizational structure of enterprises and industries matters. The market is not an impersonal environment but a relational structure among clearly identifiable players – e.g., *keiretsu*, main banks, parent firms and their subsidiaries, etc. The market is created and developed by inventing or altering relationships among these economic agents, and the role of the government is to promote that process.[18]

Hara, in turn, asserts that the development of a market economy is dependent on the homogeneity of its economic agents. When information is imperfect, institutions affect the actual working of the market. Market transactions can expand only if agents willingly adhere to contracts and agreed transaction rules, but this cannot always be taken for granted. Hara argues that such market-preserving behavior is easy to obtain in highly homogeneous societies like Japan or Korea, but not so in more divided societies like India. As in his previous writings, Hara is deeply concerned with the organizational structure of the base society and the way it affects the development of the market economy. The degree of social homogeneity can serve as another criterion for classifying societies, in addition to Ishikawa's stages of development and relative factor endowments.

However, what is even more remarkable about this report is its attempt to assemble a set of common indicators to gauge the underdevelopment of a market economy. Osamu Nariai constructed the indicator matrix while four country specialists (for Kenya, Malaysia, China, and Poland) filled the provided cells for each country and additionally wrote essays explaining each item. The matrix has the following structure (each heading is divided into further details which are not reproduced here):

1   General status of state and society
2   Governance and administrative capacity
3   Development of the market economy (general)
4   Development of the market economy (specific)
     4–1 Financial and capital markets
     4–2 Labor market
     4–3 Foreign exchange market
     4–4 Land market
     4–5 Final goods market
     4–6 Market for intermediate inputs
5   Summary and further remarks on market development
6   Implications for development and aid policy

The completed matrix, five pages long, permits cross-country comparison of underdevelopment of various markets. Although still crude, this matrix provides a good starting point. In the future, the overall design of the matrix should be improved, more quantitative indicators should be added, and the number of countries should be increased. Eventually, the exercise may lead to the compilation of market economy status report for each country, with identical chapters and similar statistical tables. This would be a real-sector equivalent of the IMF's *Recent Economic Development* report or the World Bank's *Country Economic Memorandum* and *Country Assistance Strategy* reports.

Institutional complementarity

One economic school that can supply the theoretical background for the Japanese approach to development and transition is comparative institutional analysis.

Japanese economists, including Masahiko Aoki and Masahiro Okuno, are major contributors to this new school.

Why do the two market economies of the United States and Japan not converge over time despite close interaction? Why do almost all American firms – regardless of industry and size – hire and promote workers based on individual qualification and performance, while almost all Japanese firms continue to value loyalty and devotion in their workers? Once established, a web of institutions remains resilient against external shocks, and enormous social energy would be required to change it. Aoki (1995a) explains such inertia by the concept of "institutional complementarity." This concept is useful for comparing not only different types of market economy but non-market economies as well.

According to Aoki, the emergence of incompatible institutions within each society is deterred because existing institutions (contracts, corporate governance, laws, regulations, systems of transaction, merchandise distribution, employment, finance, education, morals, etc.) are interdependent and mutually reinforcing. These institutions are common to all domestic industries and no single firm can select them randomly.

Since information is imperfect in the real world, economic agents must make decisions based on "bounded rationality." In collecting information and acquiring skills, they must orient their effort toward the needs of existing institutions. For example, college students may wish to obtain professional qualifications if their society values them; but they may cultivate team spirit and general communication skills if these are the primary societal requirements. In time, this will lead to multiple evolutionary equilibria in different countries which are history-dependent and resilient to minor shocks. Once a certain type of organizational principle – whether individualistic or relational – becomes dominant, rules will also emerge that impose acceptable behavior on economic agents in order to avoid wasteful human capital investment and protect the existing institutions from intruders. For example, the postwar Japanese society based on long-term relations was supported by such customs as the seniority-based wage system and lifetime employment, laws that protected workers from lay-offs, and company ethics which promoted attachment to one's organization.

Individuals with bounded rationality will never achieve unconditional rationality (i.e., Pareto optimality) even when they are united to form an organization (firm). No principle which is actually adopted is optimal under *all* circumstances. Different institutions will exhibit strength or weakness depending on the task to be performed and the external environment. Thus, Japanese firms dominate in consumer electronics where incremental remodeling and quality control are key, whereas U.S. firms excel in finance and computer software where creativity is the crucial factor.

The concept of institutional complementarity can also be used to analyze systemic transition from plan to market. It can explain why reform processes have been slower and more difficult than initially anticipated. Consider a former socialist country with three production sectors – customary economy, state economy, and market economy – as was shown in Figure 1.1. At the outset, institutions that support the first two sectors co-exist without much interaction, while institutions that can support the market economy do not yet exist. To marketize such a society, four more or less independent actions are required: (1) building new institutions for the market economy; (2) dismantling the institutions supporting the customary economy and releasing resources therefrom; (3) dismantling the institutions supporting the state economy and releasing resources therefrom; and (4) rendering incentives neutral by abolishing commands, regulations, and subsidies.

Given the inertia of institutions, these are demanding long-term tasks which must be pursued patiently. The important thing is to release resources gradually from existing sectors to match the speed of creation of the new market economy. Destroying the old sectors will only lead to a collapse in output and massive unemployment unless institutions in support of the market economy have already been constructed. According to Aoki, the big-bang privatization of Russia failed because reformers ignored the weight of history:

> The privatization programs of state-owned enterprises (SOEs) in Russia and Central Europe, which were modelled after the Anglo-American system, did not produce the structure of corporate governance by outside shareholders. On the contrary, they led to the phenomenon of "insider control," i.e., capture of the majority of shares by the management and workers of the former SOEs. In the last years of the communist rule, enterprise managers had already secured a large degree of autonomy and SOEs were providing workers with communal welfare benefits. These were the historical initial conditions of these transition economies, and they severely constrained the outcome of the privatization process.
>
> (Aoki 1995: 5–6)

Aoki contends that the widely observed spontaneous privatization (misappropriation of state assets by enterprise managers) was the result of the "inherent difficulty in trying to transplant the Anglo-American system which has a different historical background, like affixing bamboo to a tree" – on this point, also see Chapter 8 of this volume.

Similarly, Russia specialist Yoshiaki Nishimura reviews the first few years of the Russian privatization program in detail and concludes that what had emerged was far from a market economy. There were many irregularities in the process, eventually leading to dominant insider control. Russian privatization proceeded as an "enclosure" mechanism by which assets were transferred from the poor to the rich, from pensioners and public employees to the manager-worker groups in the enterprises (Nishimura 1994; Chapter 13 of this volume). Russia's tenacious social structure based on power and human connection was not transformed by the privatization process. Instead, it hijacked the privatization process. According to Nishimura, this was because economic agents with the proper interest and management skill to use and maintain enterprise assets rationally, were absent.

V Government as creator of the market economy

For obvious diplomatic reasons, Japanese aid officials remain less vocal about the desirable path of political development in latecomer countries. Perhaps there is less consensus in the Japanese aid community on this matter than on appropriate economic strategies. Even so, in Japan, we detect greater acceptance toward restrictions on political freedom and human rights in the early stages of development than is found in the United States and Western Europe. This section attempts to explain the origin of this attitude.

We believe that, like the economy, the political system cannot jump. Its development is a long social process fraught with shocks and temporary setbacks. Like economies, political systems evolve as institutions and spirits supporting them change. While we generally agree that democracy should be the ultimate goal of all societies, each society must find its own unique path to achieve it.[19] Appropriate policies must differ depending on the initial social conditions and stage of political development. Furthermore, political development interacts with economic development; politics and economics cannot be separated. Finally, it is extremely important to recognize that the governments of developing and transition countries face unique constraints that make the task of economic reform extremely difficult.

Government as the initiator of change

The fundamental difficulty of government in the developing world stems from its dual role as the subject and object of reform. The situation is analogous to a sick doctor, or a management consultant who himself is facing bankruptcy.[20] Each has a duty to help others, but each also faces its own problems which interfere with the execution of that duty. Without proper action, a vicious circle will set in and the society will remain poor and stagnant.

The first thing we must recall is that a market economy will not automatically grow in developing or transition countries, a point that has been made at length above. In those countries, the market mechanism is intentionally introduced by the government to raise productivity and living standards. There are no internal dynamics within the existing social structure which will generate the institutions and attitudes needed to support the market economy. Hence, the role of government becomes crucial; the initial impulse for marketization must come from government (assisted by the international donor group). Active government is absolutely necessary because without it, the base society will not turn into a market economy.

There is another reason why government action is essential. Marketization is a process that must be undertaken with the nation-state as the implementing unit.

It requires the enforcement of laws, rules, and standards consistent with market exchange; scarce resources must be mobilized into selected projects on a nation-wide scale; geographically integrated markets with supporting infrastructure must be built; personal and regional income inequality must be corrected by taxation, subsidies, and public investment; and foreign diplomatic and economic relations must be managed properly. The private sector, ethnic groups, and local governments are incapable of handling these tasks. The central government, with concentrated political authority for mobilizing people and resources, is the only viable alternative at an early stage of development.

As the initiator of change, the government must implement policies that create the necessary institutions and attitudes for the market economy. It must recognize the society's unique initial conditions, identify bottlenecks and potential obstacles, deal with unexpected shocks, set long-term targets, and design comprehensive and concrete annual plans to achieve them. But even before all this, the government may have to face a more urgent issue: how to unite diverse people within its border and create the "nation" and the "state" whose existence is the fundamental prerequisite for the execution of development policy (see the next section).

However, at the same time, government itself is part of the problem. Like the economy, the government is also "underdeveloped." In too many corners of the world, the government has been the main obstacle for economic development – with incompetence, inefficiency, corruption, formalism, nepotism, red tape, bloated bureaucracy, chronic budget deficits, white elephant projects, inconsistent policies, arbitrary enforcement, and the rest, all too well known. Even when government officials are fairly competent and uncorrupt, they are constantly pressured into undesirable action – or inaction – by despotic rulers, politicians, privileged groups, etc.

Typical governments in the developing world are so impaired that they cannot make proper policies to address the unique development problems of their society even if they know what they are – and often times they do know. This is perhaps the main reason why the international financial institutions have come to regard government as the prime enemy of development and advocate its reduction – although Japanese aid officials do not subscribe to such a view.

So this is the dilemma: the doctor is ill. Under such policy paralysis, offering a long conditionality list or huge policy matrix to be implemented within a year or so – as the Fund and the Bank routinely do – is not very productive. More fundamental thinking about the interplay between economics and politics is called for. How can we break this impasse? How can the government, with its intrinsic handicaps, reform itself and the society simultaneously?

Creating an imagined community

We have said that the nation-state is the only effective implementing unit for economic development of latecomers. But the nation-state is not something that naturally emerges in any society.[21] Rather, it is often an "imagined community" created artificially by government for the pursuit of certain goals. Nationalism and technological progress have played key roles in its formation process (Anderson 1983).

In reality, there is no presumption that "nation" and "state" would coincide; ethnic boundaries rarely conform to political borders. Still, the state – not localities or ethnic groups – must be the implementing unit of marketization. The primary task of government therefore is to unite diverse people within its political boundary into one contrived group, and become the legitimate leader of that group for the purpose of implementing economic policies.

When a country is about to undertake a total social change like marketization, with inevitable pains and adjustments, maintenance of centripetal force in the society is indispensable. Otherwise, the country will break up along the ethnic lines and political crisis, even civil war, may ensue. Success in this area determines not only whether the reform will succeed but whether the country itself will survive – consider the tragedy of Yugoslavia (Abe 1993). But how can we keep people, who have never seen each other, speak different languages, and have irreconcilable cultural backgrounds, united within artificially drawn national borders?

That this is not impossible has been proved by historical facts. Many countries have successfully created "something" that diverse people can identify themselves with. If there is a dominant language or religion, that can be used to mobilize the entire country. The traditional family system or village community can also be extrapolated to invent a contrived national community, with the royal family or president as the symbol of unity. But the ultimate technique to rally diverse people is to adopt the goal of economic development itself as the identity banner; to deliberately create the social ambience that we are in the same boat from poverty to economic prosperity – and reinforce it daily through propaganda and education. Whether real or imaginary, the convergence of people's identity is absolutely necessary for marketization to succeed.

Here are some examples. Malaysia unites its Malay, Chinese, and Indian citizens in the national aspiration to join the ranks of developed countries by the year 2020 (Vision 2020). Indonesia similarly unites its even larger population with the goal of economic development – along with an officially-imposed national language, national anthem, national flag, and President Suharto as the Benevolent Father. In Thailand, with a large number of ethnic minorities, the unique regime featuring Buddhism and the Royal Family has been in place since 1957, promoting economic development despite chronic political instability not seen elsewhere in Southeast Asia. And in Peru, President Fujimori has succeeded in mobilizing the impoverished population with his effort to deliver the country out of the extreme crisis of the late 1980s and toward economic prosperity. In 1995, he was re-elected with overwhelming support – by whites, *indios*, and *mestizos*.

Birth of authoritarian developmentalism

The East Asian answer to the problem of weak government and economic backwardness is authoritarian developmentalism. It is a temporary but very effective political and economic regime for latecomers who wish to catch up with the West. This regime should be evaluated not by the standard of advanced democratic market-economies but in the historical context of the countries that actually adopt this regime.

Yasusuke Murakami argues that "developmentalism" is a valid alternative to classical economic liberalism. The former is suitable for latecomers while the latter is appropriate for mature industrialized countries:

> Developmentalism is an economic system based on private property and the market economy (i.e., capitalism) whose aim is to achieve industrialization (i.e., sustainable growth in per capita output) and where the government is permitted to intervene in the market from the long-term perspective as long as it is consistent with this aim. Clearly, the state (or a similar political entity) is the founding unit of developmentalism as a political and economic system. This regime often restricts the operation of parliamentary democracy – as seen under royalism, one-party dictatorship, and military dictatorship.
>
> (Murakami 1992: 5–6)

According to Murakami, official intervention is justified because modern industry in developing countries exhibits dynamic increasing returns (see Chapter 11). Production costs decline rapidly as technology is absorbed and industry expands. However, left unattended, the market structure of such industry will be very unstable due to fierce competition, overcapacity, and monopolies that come and go. The vital role of government is to let industry enjoy ever lower costs without such "excess" competition. (Murakami calls this policy of eliminating excess competition "industrial policy," which is his unique definition.) In addition, certain supplementary policies must be implemented to sustain rapid industrialization. The most important among them is income redistribution policy to deal with the emerging gap between rich and poor, without which social stability will be lost. Other supplementary policies include universal education and the creation of a modern bureaucracy.

Similarly, Asia specialist Toshio Watanabe defines authoritarian developmentalism as:

> a system in which the military or political elite who seize power advance development as the supreme goal, assign the responsibility for designing and implementing economic policies to bureaucratic–technocratic institutions created for the very purpose of development, and derive legitimacy from the success of economic development

31

itself. Under this system, popular participation in decision making is inevitably limited.

(Watanabe 1995; see also Chapter 11 of this volume)

Watanabe declares that the adoption of a state-led development strategy is unavoidable for any country wishing to industrialize rapidly. He argues that many East Asian countries adopted authoritarian developmentalism because of external security threats. The Meiji government of Japan in the late nineteenth century believed that building a strong military and economy was the only way to escape colonization by Western powers. The governments of Korea and Taiwan during the Cold War period were forced by external communist threats to implement strong economic policies. When national survival is at stake, it is easier for the government to mobilize human and non-human resources.

One thing that is clear is that authoritarian developmentalism is a special kind of authoritarianism not frequently found outside East Asia. Critics of East Asian development strategy sometimes point to the dismal performance of authoritarian rulers in Africa or Latin America and argue that authoritarianism is neither necessary nor sufficient for rapid development. But this is off the mark. No one has ever argued that *any* authoritarian state will do. Simply corrupt and oppressive government – the most common type – will surely destroy the economy. Nor does the dictatorship whose sole governing legitimacy is personal charisma and ideology – regardless of actual economic performance – do any good, as in the cases of Stalin and Mao. Watanabe's definition above should clarify the unique nature of East Asia's authoritarian developmentalism. Arguments which fail to distinguish the Singaporean authoritarianism and the pre-1991 Soviet regime are hardly convincing.

Dissolution of authoritarian developmentalism

Authoritarian developmentalism is *not* the ideal regime that all societies should ultimately realize. As is clear from the definition above, it is a transitional regime for the purpose of rapid industrialization. When this purpose is achieved, it must be dismantled – just like the booster must be detached at a certain altitude in a Space Shuttle launch.

Figure 1.3 schematically depicts the East Asian catch-up process. The successful adoption of authoritarian developmentalism puts the country onto the path of rapid economic growth. If high growth is sustained for several decades, the society will be transformed into a well-developed and diversified economy. After this, authoritarian developmentalism must be replaced by a freer and more open system. There are two critical turning points in this process: initiation and graduation. At both junctures, properly designed official actions are required; otherwise, social transformation is doomed to failure. Thus, the success of East Asian authoritarian developmentalism is by no means guaranteed. To succeed, it must be supported by appropriate regime shifts.

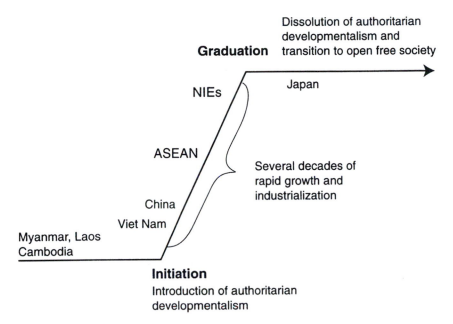

Figure 1.3 East Asia's catch-up process

Watanabe argues that authoritarian developmentalism contains an internal mechanism where its very success causes its undoing over time: "if development under an authoritarian regime proceeds successfully, the authoritarian regime will sow the seeds of its own dissolution" (Watanabe 1995; see also Chapter 11 of this volume). He cites Korea and Taiwan as the prime examples of not only well-executed authoritarian developmentalism but its successful dissolution as well. It does not mean, however, that the dismantling is going to be orderly and peaceful. On the contrary, democratization processes in Korea and Taiwan since the late 1980s have been replete with political turmoil and social confrontations.

As for Japan, measured by per capita income, it had already caught up with the Western industrial economies by the early 1970s. The problem with Japan is that the political regime featuring power concentration and bureaucratic intervention, which worked so marvelously during the 1950s and 60s, remains more or less intact to this day, constituting a barrier for further development. This "institutional fatigue" problem is widely recognized among Japanese officials and ordinary citizens alike.

These experiences indicate the existence of natural forces working to undermine authoritarian developmentalism, but its dissolution is far from automatic. It is not quite like sunshine melting ice. Three factors contribute to its successful dissolution.

First, as living standards rise, society will develop diverse needs and values, as clearly observed in Japan during the 1960s and the Asian NIEs and ASEAN countries today. With industrialization, close-knit rural communities gradually give way to urbanization. Social strata diversify and a new middle class emerges. Workers demand higher wages and more rights. The educated and well-informed population now want to think and act on their own rather than being forced to accept government dictates. Materialism is criticized, and the quality of life – clean environment, comfortable transportation, social welfare, etc. – are promoted. As society matures, popular demand for economic and political liberalization will accelerate. This is the force undermining authoritarian development from within.

Second, the open-door policies adopted for the purpose of industrialization also contribute to the ultimate demise of authoritarian development from without (Hara 1996b). As productive capacity rises, a previous primary-commodity exporter will gradually be drawn into the intricate international networks of production, commerce, and investment. As the international division of labor intensifies, free economic agents know no national boundaries. One by one, trade and investment privileges enjoyed during earlier years will be withdrawn as participation in regional or global free trade becomes obligatory. The very success of outward-oriented growth will invalidate the nation-state as a unit of economic development. It no longer is possible to maintain economic isolation in an increasingly integrated world economy.

Third, to graduate successfully, domestic and international pressure for a more liberal system must be matched by appropriate government actions at the critical moment: private forces alone are not enough. Necessary policies include deregulation, decentralization, promotion of competition, enforcement of anti-monopoly laws, downsizing of the government, external market opening, transparency of political and administrative processes, and political liberalization toward full democracy. Since all these imply denial of elite interventionism, the impetus for reform is unlikely to emerge from inside the existing strong and centralized bureaucracy. It takes a prudent and effective political leader, detached from the existing ruling mechanism, to initiate bold reforms.

Thus, as with its initiation, graduation from authoritarian developmentalism is not a natural tendency but a very important policy problem. Unless the government gracefully leaves the stage at the critical moment, further economic development will be thwarted.

Replicability?

Is authoritarian developmentalism valid for developing and transition countries outside East Asia? Can we transplant the political systems of Japan, Korea, Taiwan, and Singapore, in whole or in part, to Sub-Saharan Africa or the former Soviet republics? Unfortunately, we do not yet have a clear answer to this important question. Certainly, this is a major research topic for the twenty-first century.

Many Sub-Saharan African countries which have not established an effective nation or state as a governing unit appear incapable of directly benefiting from the East Asian authoritarian model. Similarly, the present Russian society with its volatile politics and ethnic tension does not seem to have the social basis for consistent economic strategies. We feel that these countries lack certain fundamental conditions for emulating East Asian political economy.

The only thing we can say, at this point, is that authoritarian developmentalism has been instrumental to the remarkable economic performance of East Asia. Even if it is not a universally applicable system, it has provided a very effective *regional* model for rapidly catching up with the West, which East Asian countries have achieved – or are on the verge of achieving. What other regions can learn from this is the question that still lies ahead of us.

VI Japanese intellectual ODA in Viet Nam

In 1995, the Joint Japan–Viet Nam Research Project was launched by the two governments to study Viet Nam's economic development and systemic transition. Although Japan has previously extended small-scale intellectual assistance to many countries through training and visiting programs, dispatching economic advisors, and sponsoring lectures and conferences, this is Japan's first full-scale intellectual ODA program on the overall strategy for marketization. We would like to take up this project to illustrate the kind of policy issues the Japanese government typically discusses with its important aid recipients.[22]

The project was initially proposed by Vietnamese Prime Minister Vo Van Kiet to his Japanese counterpart, Prime Minister Murayama, in Hanoi in October 1994 and was officially agreed upon when Communist Party General Secretary Do Muoi visited Tokyo in April 1995. The Japan International Cooperation Agency (JICA) and the Vietnamese Ministry of Planning and Investment (MPI) are the implementing bodies. The project mobilizes a large number of officials, academic researchers, and aid consultants in both countries in joint research on various aspects of the Vietnamese economy. It was expected to last two years with a possible extension. During phase I (ending in June 1996) and phase II (ending in summer 1997), many research missions were exchanged and several large two-day joint workshops were held in Hanoi and Tokyo.

For the Japanese government, this is an important learning experience for the execution of intellectual ODA. It has provided Japan with an excellent opportunity to implement what it has been preaching. For the Vietnamese side, the project offers not only Japanese expertise and improved analytical skills for Vietnamese officials and researchers, but also a chance to compare the Japanese view with the views of international financial institutions before arriving at its own decisions. It may also be noted that the project is further reinforced by the personal friendship between General Secretary Do Muoi and Professor Shigeru Ishikawa, academic director on the Japanese side.

A few things must be said about this ongoing project. First, its organization and design remain fluid as this is the first major intellectual aid effort for Japan and the administrative procedure is yet to be firmly established. Second, the project focuses on long-term development strategy rather than macroeconomic stabilization or "structural adjustment" which have been already properly handled by the IMF and the World Bank (see below). Third, instead of recommending one ideal policy package, whenever possible, the preference was to present a range of policy options among which the Vietnamese government can choose. This reflects in part the diversity of opinion even among Japanese economists, as well as an unwillingness to arrive at premature conclusions when information is incomplete.

JICA report of March 1995

Prior to the inauguration of the project, JICA produced a country report on Viet Nam as part of its routine research work (JICA 1995; see also Chapter 14 of this volume). Drafted and edited by Shigeru Ishikawa, the report caught the attention of the highest authorities in Viet Nam and subsequently led to the current joint project, also directed by Ishikawa.

The report is noteworthy because it lays out Japan's current thinking for assisting very poor countries like Viet Nam. It classifies the tasks of the Vietnamese government into three types:

1. *macroeconomic stabilization* which, fortunately, has been largely achieved, thanks to restrictive monetary and fiscal policies since 1989. Good performance should be maintained. (Interestingly, the report warns against over-ambitious macroeconomic stabilization which may damage long-term growth potential.);
2. *"structural adjustment,"* that is, the effort to shift production from state-owned and regulated units to the free private-sector economy, should be continued;
3. *long-term development strategy* should be designed and implemented by the government to lift the economy from poverty and achieve industrialization.

Of these three policies, the first two are already supported by the IMF and the World Bank. The main emphasis of the report rests on the third task which has been largely neglected by the international financial institutions. Ishikawa argues that the problems faced by China and Viet Nam are fundamentally different from those for Russia. In Russia, industrialization was already achieved under the previous communist government and the current task is to undo and restructure existing capacity. In China and Viet Nam, by contrast, the economy remains seriously underdeveloped. Their main task is not systemic transition but economic development (Figure 1.1 and Ishikawa 1996a).

The main part of the report is devoted to discussion of specific ingredients of the long-term development strategy:

- Agriculture and rural development
- Infrastructure
- Selective industrial policy
- Regional development strategy
- Poverty alleviation
- Environment protection
- Human resources and education
- Health and medical care
- Women in development

At a glance, this list may resemble a typical World Bank report, but its sense of prioritization is greater than any Bank publication. It is also notable that selective industrial policy, rejected as ineffective by *The East Asian Miracle* report (World Bank 1993), is deemed "essential."

Creating a market economy in Viet Nam

During the course of two years, the Japanese side has identified the following aspects of the Vietnamese economy which make up its unique state of under-development. Some of these have been studied intensely with the Vietnamese team and incorporated in joint research documents, while others remain to be investigated in the future. In either case, the primary concern of the Japanese economists is to propose appropriate policy options for overcoming unique difficulties in creating a market economy in Viet Nam.

1 First and foremost, the Vietnamese government should formulate a comprehensive and concrete blueprint for achieving the national goal of "industrialization and modernization." No such blueprint, with sufficient detail and consistency, currently exists. All policies should be designed and implemented as mutually dependent components of the blueprint, rather than as *ad hoc* reaction to domestic and external political pressures. Given limited human and financial resources, prioritization and proper sequencing of these policies is essential.

2 The top priority for Viet Nam, where 80 percent of the population live in rural areas, is raising agricultural productivity. This will also lead to the emergence of rural industries. Unlike China, Vietnamese towns and villages have not been significantly industrialized. Laissez-faire policy is unlikely to invigorate Vietnamese family farming characterized by low technology, tiny plots, and vulnerability to flooding. Public investment in rural infrastructure (irrigation, drainage, roads, etc.) is imperative, and financial services must be extended to each village.

3 While the Vietnamese economy is growing briskly in the 8–10 percent range, the low domestic saving rate (16 percent of GDP in 1996) is a big problem. This figure perhaps covers only capital depreciation, and net saving may be

close to zero. In order to sustain high growth, it is essential to mobilize domestic savings into productive investment. Unfortunately, the Vietnamese banking and fiscal systems are currently incapable of performing this task.

4 Unless and until the saving rate is significantly increased, the target for real GDP growth should not be set too high. A further acceleration of growth is likely to cause inflation, balance-of-payments crises, and external debt accumulation. Viet Nam should not try to catch up with the rest of East Asia too quickly.

5 Selective industrial policy is necessary to lift the economy to the next stage of development. While some light and food processing industries may grow without protection, other industries with large setup costs are less likely to emerge without proper official guidance. In order to avoid protecting too many industries or capture by vested interests, candidate industries should be chosen carefully. The clear "flying geese" pattern and product cycles in East Asia should help Viet Nam to identify such industries. By studying technical requirements and market trends of the industry in question, coupled with in-depth analysis of conditions prevailing in the home country, a relatively short list of infant industries can be drawn up.

6 The potential dilemma between free trade and industrial promotion must be resolved. Viet Nam joined the ASEAN Free Trade Area (AFTA) in 1996, accepting the obligation to reduce virtually all intra-regional tariffs to 5 percent or less by 2006. It has also applied for membership of APEC and WTO. The merit of early commitment to free trade – "early" from the viewpoint of the stage of development – is the discipline it imposes on the government and domestic enterprises toward better performance. On the other hand, Vietnamese enterprises are no match for ASEAN's more advanced rivals. Hasty removal of protection may lead to bankruptcies, unemployment, and social discontent. Furthermore, promotion of some (if not all) infant industries will become difficult if even temporary protection is prohibited. Then, Viet Nam will be condemned to export crude oil, rice, coffee, and marine products forever.

7 Vietnamese state-owned enterprises are apparently doing well, growing faster than even the private sector, without any significant transfer of ownership (Chapter 15). At the same time, however, they remain uncompetitive with outdated technology and shortage of investment funds. It is necessary to separate SOEs which are to be restructured with temporary official assistance from those which are destined to fail. For the second type, minimization of transition costs should be the policy goal. Industrial policy, participation in AFTA, and SOE reform must be integrated into a consistent whole under a blueprint for industrialization. While the international institutions urge rapid privatization of Vietnamese SOEs, we believe that mere legal changes unaccompanied by improvements in the real sphere (technology, management skills, investment, etc.) are ineffective and even counterproductive.

VII Summary and guide to this book

The Japanese approach to economic development and systemic transition discussed in this chapter can be summarized in two key propositions.

First, Japanese aid officials and researchers take seriously the idea that the nature of underdevelopment of the market economy is unique to each society and cannot be removed by liberalization policy alone. This underdevelopment is an inevitable aspect of non-Western latecomer countries that deliberately adopt the market mechanism, which is foreign to them, in order to achieve economic growth. As the base society may not contain the many necessary conditions for proper operation of the market mechanism, it is of utmost importance to identify and overcome the unique impediments to marketization in each society. The marketization process must be understood as the interaction of two potentially incompatible systems – the existing society and the newly introduced market system – where government action to create and enhance the market economy becomes crucial. Since marketization is not automatic in latecomer developing countries, *laissez-faire* policy may not achieve the desired economic catch-up with the West.

Second, authoritarian developmentalism has been a temporary but very effective political regime to develop the market economy and realize rapid industrialization in East Asia. This is a particular type of dictatorship not seen frequently in other parts of the world, where strong leadership holds up economic development as the supreme national goal and legitimizes its rule by actually delivering on the goal. An elite economic bureaucracy and restrictions on democratic principles are inherent characteristics of this regime. Over time, the very success of economic growth generates internal and external changes that undermine the system, but the final dissolution of authoritarian developmentalism must be accomplished by the government's own decision to step down from heavy economic management at the appropriate moment. Whether East Asian authoritarian developmentalism can be a useful model for the rest of the world, in whole or in part, is an important question for future research.

In Japan, with high income and developed industries, the concept of underdeveloped markets is no longer practical and the remnants of authoritarian developmentalism are now obstacles for further social development. However, this does not by any means imply that these ideas are also obsolete for latecomers in the developing world. Since the validity of any economic policy critically depends on the stage of development of a particular economy, there is no inconsistency in advising for others what Japan itself is trying to discard.

The following chapters present recent writings by Japanese authors reflecting this approach.

Part I

Part I, "How our views differ" (Chapters 2–5), presents overall Japanese views in four relatively short chapters. There is much overlapping and many cross-references among them. The reader will see how the Japanese aid community established its identity as an anti-neoclassical force by reacting to the structural adjustment policy and key documents of the World Bank.

Hirohisa Kohama's "Review of systemic transition" (Chapter 2) is a non-technical serial essay that appeared in the popular press in 1994. This light-hearted discourse covers various topics on economic development and systemic transition and issues discussed here – aversion to neoclassical economic liberalism, the importance of self-help, a call for industrial policy, long-term orientation, and people's trust in the government – are all authentic Japanese features.

The paper "Issues related to the World Bank's approach to structural adjustment: a proposal from a major partner" (Chapter 3) is an official document by the Overseas Economic Cooperation Fund (OECF), implementing body of Japan's ODA loans. The paper was drafted in 1991 by Yasutami Shimomura, then director of the Economics Department, as the report of a study group organized by the OECF. It was subsequently published in both Japanese and English in the OECF's *Research Quarterly*. This is the first Japanese *official* critique of the World Bank's structural adjustment policy and has been widely quoted at home and abroad. The paper urges reconsideration of the existing Bank policies in four areas: (1) growth strategy; (2) trade liberalization; (3) financial liberalization; and (4) privatization. Among these, financial policies occupy the largest space, as the main purpose of this document was to counter the World Bank's criticism of the OECF's subsidized "two-step" development loans (on this point, also see Shiratori, Chapter 5 of this volume, and below). Because the 1992 English translation, which was done in great haste, is awkward and contains many grammatical errors, we have edited this version somewhat more heavily than would ordinarily be advisable for an already published work. In so doing, we have softened the tone – but not the argument – of the paper, and brought its texture closer to the Japanese original.

Toru Yanagihara's "Development and dynamic efficiency: 'framework approach' versus 'ingredients approach'" (Chapter 4) is a previously unpublished manuscript written and circulated in 1992. We included this piece because it discusses two alternative philosophical perspectives in development thinking – framework versus ingredients – that are now well known among Japanese scholars. The framework approach, highlighting the 'level playing field' and government as an impartial judge, characterizes neoclassical development economics. By contrast, the ingredients approach, minding the ability of individual players and the quality of teamplay and where government is a trusted coach, corresponds to Japanese development strategy. From this perspective, Yanagihara compares the World Bank's *World Development Report 1991* with the OECF's critique (Chapter 2).

Masaki Shiratori's "Afterword to the Japanese translation of the World Bank Report *The East Asian Miracle*" (Chapter 5) reveals how Japanese aid organizations evaluate this famous World Bank document. As the Japanese Executive

Director to the World Bank and with the financial backing of the Ministry of Finance, Mr. Shiratori pushed the Bank to launch a research project on East Asian economic development, which led to publication of the Miracle report in 1993. His motive for sponsoring this research is explained at the outset. After reviewing the main conclusions of the report and recognizing its novelty, Shiratori, who edited the Japanese translation of the report, criticizes the Bank's persistent refusal to acknowledge the role of selective industrial policy in the process of economic catch-up.

Part II

Part II, "Society does not jump" (Chapters 6–9), presents theoretical arguments that the creation of a market economy is a long-term endeavor and requires appropriate official intervention. Four views are offered. Despite the diversity of perspectives, all authors question the validity of the neoclassical paradigm when applied to economic development.

Shigeru Ishikawa's *Basic Issues in Development Economics*, published in 1990, is a very influential book among Japanese development economists. We include a chapter entitled, "Underdevelopment of the market economy and the limits of economic liberalization" in this volume (Chapter 6). In this chapter, the key ideas in Japanese development economics are laid out. Ishikawa first defines the market economy and the three basic conditions that support it. He then argues that if an economy is not adequately equipped with these conditions, liberalization policy alone will not generate a viable market mechanism. The remainder of the chapter is devoted to detailed discussion of actual incidents of stunted markets in the Chinese reform process since 1978. This is a scholarly work based on extensive Chinese data and literature.

Chapter 7 presents extracts from Yonosuke Hara's 1992 book, *A Blueprint for Asian Economics*. The work is, in essence, a discussion by an Asian economist dissatisfied with the neoclassical approach and making a journey through the theoretical landscape in quest of a new paradigm. Hara's concern is mainly methodological. He rejects neoclassical development economics as relying too heavily on formalization and deduction. He believes that describing the dynamic process of market creation requires attention to many ideas and characteristics ignored by neoclassical economics. These include each country's institutions, market segmentation, information asymmetries, degree of social diversity, and historical pattern of labor and capital market evolution. On policy implications, he arrives at the same conclusion as Ishikawa: economic liberalization alone will not necessarily induce a strong response from the private sector.

Masahiko Aoki's "Controlling insider control: issues of corporate governance in transition economies" (Chapter 8) was originally published in a volume by the World Bank Economic Development Institute. Aoki, a Stanford University professor, is one of the key founders of comparative institutional analysis, on which this chapter is based. In this essay, he poses a theoretical question: is the Anglo-American model of stockholder sovereignty the only option for disciplining corporate behavior in transition economies? He argues that since insider control (dominance of managers and employees in privatized state enterprises) in those economies is an evolutionary outcome of the communist past, an entirely foreign model of corporate monitoring through outside stockholders and competitive capital markets cannot be easily introduced. He argues that an alternative model of contingent governance by an outside bank ("lead bank") should also be considered along with the stock-market-based model. In transition economies where both capital markets and banks are severely underdeveloped, he recommends an eclectic approach where both are promoted simultaneously. In a state of institutional uncertainty, exclusive reliance on one model may unnecessarily constrain the transition path.

Economic anthropologist Keiji Maegawa examines the cultural context of marketization in the "The continuity of cultures and civilization: an introduction to the concept of translative adaptation" (Chapter 9). The chapter provides the methodological framework for his main occupation, which is field research on an aboriginal society on the islands of the Torres Strait between Australia and Papua New Guinea. Maegawa argues that the power relationship between the West, which supplies international norms, and the non-West, which adapts to them, is ever present in the process of "modernization." Neither cultural relativism nor revived universalism can analyze this situation adequately. He proposes an alternative method: rather than observing the marketization of a non-Western society from outside, view it from within. Marketization is not a replacement of the old system by the new, but rather a genuine merger of the two. In transformation, the indigenous society is modified but its basic structure survives. New values and institutions are not passively adopted, but actively adapted in the context of the unique traditional culture. This perspective is presented as a better guide for studying non-Western societies than Huntington's clash-of-civilizations theory or Fukuyama's end of Hegelian history.

Part III

Part III, "Authoritarian developmentalism" (Chapters 10–11), discusses the remarkable political regime under which East Asian economies achieved rapid industrialization.

Yasusuke Murakami's "Theory of developmentalism" (Chapter 10) is translated from his unfinished posthumous book, *Outline of Anti-Classical Political Economy*, published in 1994. His earlier two-volume work[23] presented developmentalism as an alternative regime to economic liberalism. The chapter translated in this volume is his last word on the issue. As in the previous work, he defines developmentalism as a deliberate effort to take advantage of dynamic increasing returns in production by individual firms (micro level) or the state (macro level). However, the state's developmentalism must deal with additional issues which do not concern individual entrepreneurs. When production cost declines with capacity, unmitigated investment competition often leads to unstable markets or monopoly. The purpose of "industrial policy" is to deter this undesirable trend through official intervention while preserving the benefit of ever-lower cost. In less developed countries, industrial policy must always be supplemented by a broader array of policies, including financial control, promotion of small- and medium-sized enterprises, and especially income redistribution that also sustains production incentives. Without these measures, economic growth will be subverted by social instability.

Chapter 11 is from Toshio Watanabe's book, *Designing Asia for the New Century*. In the excerpted section (prologue and first chapter), Watanabe presents authoritarian developmentalism as the key to the rapid economic development of Japan and the East Asian NIEs (except Hong Kong). Authoritarian developmentalism gains legitimacy from the very economic growth it brings. Economic policies are designed and implemented by the elite bureaucracy. The regime is sustained by external threat and a strong popular desire for a better material life. Watanabe reviews the emergence of authoritarian states in Korea, Taiwan, and Singapore during the postwar period in some detail. He also argues that well-executed developmentalism tends to dissolve itself over time, as in Korea and Taiwan.

Part IV

Part IV, "Policy advice and country studies" (Chapters 12–15), presents four examples of Japanese analyses of specific problems in the context of individual countries.

Chapter 12, "Kyrgyzstan's road to economic recovery: an effort in intellectual assistance," is written by Tatsuo Kaneda, who served as an official advisor to President Akaev of the Kyrgyz Republic during 1992–95. In the first two sections of the original paper, Kaneda analyzes the current political and economic situation in Kyrgyzstan and lists key factors in Japanese – and Asian – economic success in the past. We include the third section, "Some proposals for development strategy of the Kyrgyz economy (excerpts)" in our volume. Here, Kaneda takes the role of government in building market infrastructure and national consensus for granted. Selective industrial policy is strongly urged, and agriculture and light industry are suggested as the two industries worthy of official support. Despite limited information, concrete measures to promote these industries are explored. We should bear in mind that Kaneda's proposals were written in 1992, the very first year of Kyrgyzstan's radical reforms. The Kyrgyz economy continued to decline for three more years until mid-1995, when output finally stabilized at roughly half the 1990 level.

Yoshiaki Nishimura's technical essay, "Russian privatization: progress report no. 1" (Chapter 13) evaluates Russia's privatization drive as of end-1993, complementing Aoki's argument (Chapter 8) on the evolution of former socialist economies. Based exclusively on Russian materials, Nishimura provides detailed factual information on the early stage of Russian privatization. He clearly sees overwhelming evidence of insider control and gross irregularities due to the very immature nature of Russian capitalism. Rapid privatization transferred wealth and enterprise control to managers and employees on a massive scale. Nishimura's pessimism about the prospects for Russian privatization is now widely shared in Japan and abroad. It is interesting to compare this essay with the surprisingly sanguine survey study by two World Bank economists (Webster and Charap 1993) who argue that capitalist entrepreneurship is thriving in privatized Russia.[24] The contrast with the Nishimura paper could not be greater.

The Japan International Cooperation Agency (JICA) report, "Country study for Japan's official development assistance to the Socialist Republic of Viet Nam" (Chapter 14) was drafted by Shigeru Ishikawa, who chaired the JICA study group which prepared this document. JICA, the implementing agency for Japanese grant aid and technical assistance, selectively publishes country studies for its most important aid recipients. In this report (an excerpt from the executive summary), which sets the basic ODA policy stance toward Viet Nam, the idea of an under-developed market economy permeates, and the long-term real sector orientation is unmistakable. Agriculture and rural development are accorded top priority. Active industrial policy is strongly recommended. Comparisons with Chinese and Russian reforms are made, and appropriate development models for Viet Nam are explored. The important distinction between "innate" and "artificial" distortions preventing the emergence of a market economy is introduced. The circulation of this report in Vietnamese translation among Vietnamese officials led to the Japan–Viet Nam official joint research project discussed in Section 6 of the current chapter.

Finally, Chapter 15 presents an OECF paper drafted by Izumi Ohno entitled "Ownership, performance, and managerial autonomy: a survey of manufacturing enterprises in Viet Nam." Vietnamese state-owned enterprises are performing relatively well under gradual reform and without any change in ownership. Viet Nam's impressive economic growth, in the range 8–10 percent, has been supported mainly by SOEs, not by the weak private sector. This is in stark contrast with the dismal performance of privatized SOEs in Russia (Chapters 8 and 13). The Ohno paper introduces results of a microeconomic survey of 199 Vietnamese enterprises conducted jointly by OECF and Viet Nam's State Planning Committee (now the Ministry of Planning and Investment) in late 1994. The survey reveals that SOEs are indeed doing better than private firms on average, though with a wide range of performance variation. Most SOEs now enjoy a high degree of management autonomy, and large SOEs tend to perform better than small ones. No serious labor redundancy is reported. Clearly, the common-sense view of weak SOEs versus strong private firms does not apply to Viet Nam. The main purpose of this study, however, was not to praise gradualism but to uncover problems unique to Vietnamese SOEs for future policy formulation. Recently, two follow-up enterprise surveys were conducted by OECF and JICA to probe issues raised by this survey.

Notes

1 This chapter was newly written for this volume.

2 See, for example, Stallings and Sakurai (1993: 9); Fishlow and Gwin (1994: 3); and George and Sabelli (1994: 60).

3 In Japanese official documents, the name of this country is spelled in two words, Viet Nam. While this is unusual in English, it is closer to the Vietnamese original; therefore, we follow this convention throughout the book.

4 For details of the Foreign Ministry Report and the anti-inflation debate, see Arisawa and Nakamura (1990). In reality, the decisive stabilization measures were designed by American advisor Joseph Dodge and implemented by the Japanese government in early 1949 ("Dodge Line"). The content of the Dodge Line was similar to the IMF conditionality menu of today, including tight budget and money, elimination of subsidies, unification of exchange rates, etc. However, this was implemented not immediately after the war but in 1949, when output had recovered to more than half the prewar level. In this sense, the actual outcome was close to Conditional Quick Stabilization recommended by Professor Arisawa.

5 Lest readers confuse these with "plans" in socialist planned economies of the past, it must be noted that Japanese planning is very different from socialist planning. In Japan, the private sector plays the primary role in production while the government provides guidance and coordination – unlike the planned economy where the state owns all land and productive capital and state-owned enterprises dominate production.

6 Four years after coming to power, the Meiji government dispatched several key state ministers – including Tomomi Iwakura, Toshimichi Okubo, Takayoshi Kido, and Hirobumi Ito – to the United States and European countries during 1871–73 for the purposes of (1) negotiating the revision of bilateral commercial treaties with those countries which were considered highly unfavorable to Japan, and (2) inspecting the technology and social organization of advanced countries. While the treaty negotiation was unsuccessful, the knowledge gained by this tour significantly influenced Japan's subsequent diplomatic and economic policies.

7 This report was proposed by Masaki Shiratori, then the Bank's Japanese Executive Director, and funded by the Japanese government (see Chapter 5). Despite the large Japanese role in getting the study off the ground, the Bank's conclusions remained intellectually independent, without being influenced by the Japanese government.

8 The perspective explained below is not the universally accepted paradigm in economic anthropology. In fact, it is perhaps the minority view. The emerging concept of "translative adaptation," on which this section relies heavily, is proposed by Keiji Maegawa (see Chapter 9).

9 This framework is an extension of the classical Lewis model where only two sectors – traditional and modern (i.e., market) sectors – are represented. The Sachs–Woo model for comparing Russia and China can also be neatly interpreted using this framework (Sachs and Woo 1994; World Bank 1996). As a further extension of the model, a fourth sector of foreign trade and investment could be added for analyzing the marketization process of China and Viet Nam.

10 Here, our intention, of course, is not to denounce the modern remnants of capitalistic imperialism; value judgment is not the purpose of this book. We are simply asserting the usefulness of viewing the marketization process of a latecomer country in political, cultural and international context.

11 During the Meiji period, the most pressing intellectual questions facing Japan were (1) how to reconcile imported Western value systems – individualism, capitalism, parliamentary government, etc. – with the inherited universe of Japanese culture, and (2) how to position Japan between the West and the East. Leading thinkers like Yukichi Fukuzawa, Soho Tokutomi, Chomin Nakae, Shusui Kotoku, and Soseki

Natsume (see Chapter 9 for discussion on Soseki), each came to different conclusions on these matters. Subsequently, Japan embraced mainly the materialistic aspects of the West and veered to military expansionism over other Asian peoples. Even today, Japan has not satisfactorily resolved the questions raised by these Meiji thinkers.

12 The reader may contend that recent theoretical developments in economics – asymmetric information and transaction costs, moral hazard and adverse selection, endogenous growth, comparative institutional analysis, trade theory under imperfect competition and increasing returns, economics of geography, etc. – have largely overcome the weakness of the original neoclassical doctrine. However, development economics as practiced in the lending operations of the World Bank and especially the IMF has not caught up with these new theories. To date, apart from certain research activities, there is little evidence that basic policy in international financial institutions has been significantly transformed by these theoretical developments (except the World Bank's efforts at institution-building – see the Afterword).

13 Among eminent non-Japanese economists, Joseph E. Stiglitz (1994, 1996) advances theoretical and policy-related arguments highly consistent with many aspects of the Japanese approach. From the perspective of new information economics, which he himself founded, Stiglitz is critical of the neoclassical approach and shows much understanding of East Asian growth strategy. His new position as the World Bank's chief economist since 1997 may further alter the Bank's traditional thinking.

14 To repeat, we are not categorically denying the validity of neoclassical economics. We object only to its indiscriminate application to economic development and systemic transition. Neoclassical economics may prove effective in studying other issues, including consumer behavior, industrial organization, the banking sector, public finance, etc. It may even be useful for analyzing some middle-income developing countries that are already industrialized. However, it does not seem to be an appropriate paradigm for low-income countries and countries embarking on systemic transition.

15 "Underdevelopment of the market economy" should not be confused with "market failure," which is commonly analyzed within the neoclassical framework. The two are completely different concepts. Market failure presupposes an economy which is already dominated by market-sector production but with some dysfunctions due to public goods, uncertainty, externalities, etc. By contrast, underdevelopment of the market economy refers to a situation where the economy is basically made up of traditional agriculture and/or state production, and institutions that can support a market economy do not yet exist. More graphically, the difference is analogous to that of mechanical trouble with a car versus the days when the automobile was yet to be invented.

16 In my Japanese book (Ohno 1996a), I briefly summarize the views of Marx, Weber, Pareto, and Schumpeter on this matter. A fuller historical survey on the theory of relationship between economy and non-economy, including the views of political scientists, sociologists, and anthropologists, would be useful.

17 Recently, Ishikawa (1996b) proposed to study state-owned enterprise reform in China and Viet Nam from the development stages perspective. He argues that SOEs typically evolve in five stages: (1) patrimonialism; (2) central planning; (3) delegation of management autonomy; (4) corporatization; and (5) privatization. Introduction of a new management structure or ownership may not achieve the desired outcome if institutional remnants from the previous stage(s) have not been eradicated. If this is the case, we must identify and confront such legacies of the past in addition to making legal changes.

18 Yanagihara previously proposed the distinction between the neoclassical "framework" approach, where the market is a level playing field and the role of the government is to

establish rules and act as an impartial judge; and the Japanese "ingredients" approach, whose main concerns are a winning strategy, teamwork, and the ability of each player, and where the government is a coach (see also Chapter 4 of this volume). In his more recent "economic system approach," this distinction is extended and further developed – also see Yanagihara and Sambommatu (1997).

19 In addition to the uniqueness of the path to democracy, another key issue is the type of democracy that non-Western countries should eventually establish. As a market economy functions differently from one mature industrial country to another, so too democracy may well evolve into different types reflecting the uniqueness of each base society.

20 Of the two, I prefer the management consultant analogy because his problem (financial distress) is solved by the very success of his profession. This is just as the government wins legitimacy and enhances its capacity to implement policies by the very success of economic development.

21 The nation-state is a marriage of the "nation" as a natural group of people based on shared race, language, religion, value, customs, etc., and the "state" which is a political unit for the execution of sovereign power. The fiction that the two are identical is a relatively new invention of the European age of royal states.

22 At the request of the Vietnamese government, documents prepared for this project are kept confidential at this time. Our discussion on policy issues must therefore remain general, except for the 1995 JICA report which is a public document of the Japanese government.

23 For an English translation of Murakami's 1992 work, see Kozo Yamamura, *Anti-Classical Political Economy*, Stanford University Press, 1996.

24 While noting many irregularities, the authors nonetheless conclude that the "vitality of Russian entrepreneurship was evident in St. Petersburg. . . . This first wave of private manufacturers tended to be highly educated, technically skilled and adept at survival and growth in the turbulent Russian business environment. If the rate of market entry remains high and the privatization program continues at a fast pace, the private manufacturing sector should grow rapidly" (p. 60); and "Russian entre-preneurs showed themselves able to respond rapidly and effectively to opportunities. There appeared to be no shortage of entrepreneurs in St. Petersburg. Indeed, many of those interviewed were able to use resources efficiently and build substantial businesses, despite the difficulties presented by the environment" (p. 61).

References

Abe, Nozomu (1993) *Crisis and Collapse of the Yugoslav Economic System*, Tokyo: Nihon Hyoronsha (in Japanese).

Anderson, Benedict (1983) *Imagined Communities: Reflections on the Origin and Spread of Nationalism*, London: Verso.

Aoki, Masahiko (1995a) *Evolution and Multiplicity of Economic Systems: Introduction to Comparative Institutional Analysis*, Tokyo: Toyo Keizai Shimposha (in Japanese).

—— (1995b) "Controlling Insider Control: Issues of Corporate Governance in Transition Economies," in M. Aoki and H.K. Kim, (eds) *Corporate Governance in Transition Economies*, Washington, DC: World Bank Economic Development Institute (see also Chapter 8 of this volume).

Aoki, Masahiko, and Masahiro Okuno (1996) *Comparative Institutional Analysis of Economic Systems*, Tokyo: Tokyo University Press (in Japanese).

Aoki, Masahiko, Kevin Murdock, and Masahiro Okuno-Fujiwara (1995) "Beyond *The*

East Asian Miracle: Introducing the Market Enhancing View," CEPR Publication no. 442, Stanford University.

Arisawa, Hiromi, and Takahide Nakamura (eds) (1990) *Data: Design of Postwar Economic Policies*, vol. 1, Tokyo: Tokyo University Press (in Japanese).

Fishlow, Albert, and Catherine Gwin (1994) "Lessons from the East Asian Experience," in Overseas Development Council, *Miracle or Design?: Lessons from the East Asian Experience*, Policy Essay no. 11, Washington, DC: Overseas Development Council.

George, Susan, and Fabrizio Sabelli (1994) *Faith and Credit: The World Bank's Secular Empire*, Boulder, CO: Westview Press. (Japanese translation by Ryoichi Mohri, published by Asahi Shimbunsha, Tokyo, 1996.)

Hara, Yonosuke (1985) *Economics of Clifford Geertz: Between Asian Studies and Economic Theory*, Tokyo: Libroport (in Japanese).

—— (1992) *A Blueprint for Asian Economics: Beyond Neoclassical Development Economics*, Tokyo: Libroport (in Japanese) (see also Chapter 7 of this volume).

—— (1994) "Area Study and Economics: Toward the Understanding of Regional Characteristics of Economic Development," research report, Institute of Oriental Cultures, Tokyo University (in Japanese).

Hara, Yonosuke (1996a) *Development Economics*, Tokyo: Iwanami Shoten (in Japanese).

—— (1996b) *Asia Dynamism: Capitalist Networks and Regional Characteristics of Development*, Tokyo: NTT Press (in Japanese).

Huntington, Samuel P. (1993) "The Clash of Civilizations?" *Foreign Affairs*, Summer: 22–49.

International Monetary Fund (1993) "Russia's Hyperinflation Must Be Prevented, Says Camdessus," *IMF Survey*, February 22.

Ishikawa, Shigeru (1990) *Basic Issues of Development Economics*, Tokyo: Iwanami Shoten (in Japanese) (see also Chapter 6 of this volume).

—— (1994) "Economic Reform and the Fostering of the Market Economy," draft, Aoyama Gakuin University, January (in Japanese).

—— (1996a) "From Development Economics to Development Aid Policy," in S. Ishikawa, (ed.) *Theoretical Studies on Development Aid Policy*, Tokyo: Institute of Development Economics (in Japanese).

—— (1996b) "A Memorandum on Stages of Market Economic Development and Coordination Mechanisms," presented at the Joint OECF–World Bank Workshop for 1997 *World Development Report*, Tokyo, October 8, 1996.

Itoh, Motoshige, Kazuharu Kiyono, Masahiro Okuno, and Kotaro Suzumura (1988) *Economic Analysis of Industrial Policy*, Tokyo: Tokyo University Press (in Japanese).

Japan Research Institute (1996) "Study on the Appropriate Development Policy in Less Developed Countries: A Report," March (in Japanese).

JICA (Japan International Cooperation Agency) (1995) *Country Study for Japan's Official Development Assistance to the Social Republic of Viet Nam*, Tokyo: JICA (see also Chapter 14 of this volume).

Kaneda, Tatsuo (1995) *Regime and People: Revival of A Small Country in Central Asia*, Tokyo: Japan Institute of International Affairs (in Japanese).

Komiya, Ryutaro, Masahiro Okuno, and Kotaro Suzumura, (eds) (1988) *Industrial Policy of Japan*, Tokyo and San Diego, CA: Academic Press.

Krugman, Paul (1994) "The Myth of Asia's Miracle," *Foreign Affairs*, November/December: 62–78.

Maegawa, Keiji (1994a) "An Anthropological Perspective on Social Change in the Modern World-System," *Rekishi Jinrui* [History and Anthropology], (Tsukuba University), vol. 22 March.

—— (1994b) "The Continuity of Cultures and Civilization: An Introduction to the Concept of Translative Adaptation," *Hikaku Bunmei* [Comparative Culture], vol. 10, November: 100–13 (in Japanese) (see also Chapter 9 of this volume).

Minami, Ryoshin (1992) *Economic Development of Japan*, 2nd edn, Tokyo: Toyo Keizai Shimposha (in Japanese).

Ministry of Foreign Affairs (1946) *Basic Issues of Japanese Economic Reconstruction* (in Japanese), Tokyo: Ministry of Foreign Affairs.

Murakami, Yasusuke (1992) *Anti-Classical Political Economy*, vol. 2, Tokyo: Chuo Koronsha (in Japanese). (English translation by Kozo Yamamura, Stanford, CA, Stanford University Press, 1996.)

—— (1994) *Outline of Anti-Classical Political Economy: A Memorandum for the Next Century*, Tokyo: Chuo Koronsha (in Japanese) (see also Chapter 10 of this volume).

Nihon Keizai Shimbunsha (ed.) (1993) *My Capitalism* Tokyo: Nihon Kaizai Shimbunsha, (in Japanese).

Nishimura, Yoshiaki (1994) "Russian Privatization: Progress Report No. 1," *Economic Research*, (Hitotsubashi University) vol. 45, no. 3, July (in Japanese). (see also Chapter 13 of this volume).

Ohno, Kenichi (1996a) *Strategy for Transition to Market Economies*, Tokyo: Yuhikaku (in Japanese).

—— (1996b) "The Formation Process of the Market Economy and the Paradigm of Economics: In Search of a New Perspective in Development Economics," in S. Ishikawa, (ed.) *Theoretical Studies on Development Aid Policy*, Tokyo: Institute of Development Economics (in Japanese).

Okubo, Toshimichi (1874) *Kangyo Kempaku Sho* [Report on Industrial Promotion].

Overseas Economic Cooperation Fund (1992) "Issues Related to the World Bank's Approach to Structural Adjustment: Proposal from a Major Partner," OECF Occasional Paper no. 1, October 1991; reprinted in OECF's *Research Quarterly*, no. 73 (2) (see also Chapter 3 of this volume).

Sachs, Jeffrey, and Wing Thye Woo (1994) "Structural Factors in the Economic Reforms of China, Eastern Europe, and the Former Soviet Union," *Economic Policy*, Spring.

Sakamoto, Takao (1994) *Can Japan Describe Its Own Past?*, Tokyo: Chikuma Shobo (in Japanese).

Stallings, Barbara, and Makoto Sakurai (1993) "Development in the 1990s: U.S. and Japanese Paradigms," in Barbara Stallings *et al.* (eds) *Common Vision, Different Paths: The United States and Japan in the Developing World*, Washington, DC: Overseas Development Council.

Stiglitz, Joseph E. (1994) *Whither Socialism?*, Cambridge, MA, MIT Press.

—— (1996) "Some Lessons from the East Asian Miracle," *World Bank Research Observer*, vol. 11, no. 2, August: 151–77.

Teranishi, Juro, and Yutaka Kosai (eds) (1993) *The Japanese Experience of Economic Reforms*, London: Macmillan.

Watanabe, Toshio (1995) *Designing Asia for the New Century*, Tokyo: Chikuma Shinsho (in Japanese) (see also Chapter 11 of this volume).

Webster, Leila M., and Joshua Charap (1993) *The Emergence of Private Sector*

Manufacturing in St. Petersburg: A Survey of Firms, World Bank Technical Paper no. 228.

World Bank (1991) *World Development Report 1991: The Challenge of Development*, New York: Oxford University Press.

—— (1993) *The East Asian Miracle: Economic Growth and Public Policy*, Oxford University Press.

—— (1995) *Bureaucrats in Business: The Economics and Politics of Government Ownership*, New York: Oxford University Press.

World Bank (1996) *World Development Report 1996: From Plan to Market*, New York: Oxford University Press.

World Bank (1997) *World Development Report 1997: The State in a Changing World*, New York: Oxford University Press.

Yanagihara, Toru, and Susumu Sambommatu (eds) (1997) *East Asian Development Experience: Economic System Approach and Its Applicability*, Tokyo: Institute of Development Economics.

Part I

HOW OUR VIEWS DIFFER

2

A REVIEW OF SYSTEMIC TRANSITION[1]

Hirohisa Kohama

Diversity in transitional economies

Only four and half years have passed since the collapse of the Berlin Wall on November 9, 1989 but the event seems like the distant past. Now German unification is a reality and despite short-term problems, a strong Germany is likely to emerge in Europe in the medium- to long-term.

Since the disintegration of the Soviet Union and COMECON (Council of Mutual Economic Cooperation) in 1991, Russia and Eastern European economies have been moving full speed ahead with the historic experiment of transition to a market economy. China and Viet Nam have also adopted open liberal economic policies. Stimulated by neighboring states as well as internal factors, other socialist economies have joined the wave of systemic transition. Headlines about reforms in countries from Laos to Cuba are no longer unusual.

Despite high media interest, there is no consensus among economists on approaches to the transition of former socialist economies, just as there is no agreement on approaches to structural adjustment in developing countries. The purpose of this article is to discuss these issues. In what follows, the terms "former socialist economies" and "transitional economies" are used interchangeably.

Is it possible to analyze transitional economies collectively, using a common framework? Table 2.1 shows key economic indicators of selected transitional economies. First, these economies differ in population size. Viet Nam, with 70 million people, is a medium-sized country by Asian standards but is larger than all European transitional economies except Russia. Second, there are significant gaps in income level and macroeconomic performance among transitional economies. Asian transitional economies are typical low-income developing countries, whereas their European counterparts have much higher per capita income levels. The income gap between Asian and European economies in transition narrows if income is measured by purchasing power parity, but the change is only a matter of degree. In contrast, if compared in terms of growth and inflation rates, China and Viet Nam have been performing far better than

Table 2.1 Economic indicators of selected transitional economies

	Population (million) 1991	Per capita GNP (US$) 1991	Growth rates (%)	
			1992	1993
Russia	148.7	3,220	−19	−13
Czech Republic	10.3	2,460	−7	−1
Hungary	10.3	2,720	−5	−2
Poland	38.2	1,790	1	4
Slovakia	5.3	1,930	−6	−5
Bulgaria	9.0	1,840	−8	−5
Romania	23.2	1,390	−15	0
China	1,155.8	370	13	13
Viet Nam	69.2	150	8	8

European transitional economies, most of which posted zero or negative growth rates in 1992 and 1993. Initial conditions in Asian transitional economies are also different from those in European transitional economies.

What about Russia and Central and Eastern Europe? Are the conditions similar among them? The answer is no. The most notable difference is that for Russia, the transition meant the collapse of the Soviet empire, while for Central and Eastern Europe, it meant liberation from subordination under the Soviet empire. The length of each country's experience under socialism is also different.

In addition, one perceives a significant difference in the vitality of the people when comparing China and Viet Nam with Central and Eastern Europe. The Vietnamese people seem to be full of energy regardless of age or gender. Having experienced thousands of years of foreign invasions, the Vietnamese seem to regard fifty years of socialism as no big deal.

In this way, transitional economies vary greatly in their initial economic, social, and historic conditions. Bearing these differences in mind, however, the following sections will primarily focus on issues transitional economies have in common.

Transition is structural adjustment

The transition of former socialist economies can be broadly interpreted as structural adjustment. Undoubtedly, the adjustment taking place in Russia and Central and Eastern Europe is the most radical form of structural adjustment.

There is wide consensus among economists and policy makers that balance of payments crises – such as those faced by developing countries struggling through the debt crisis of the early 1980s – cannot be resolved only through traditional short-term macroeconomic measures focusing on the demand side. Structural adjustment is a complementary way to address the balance of payments problem over the medium-term by enhancing the supply-side response.

Balance of payments problems in many developing countries resulted from the government-led economic development policies adopted in the 1970s. Policies that relied heavily on government intervention distorted the market, made the economy inefficient, and resulted in huge fiscal deficits. Based on lessons from such economic mismanagement, many developing countries have adopted a general policy framework that emphasizes greater reliance on the market and private-sector-led economic management. Another common element of the adjustment framework has been expanding manufactured goods exports through improved economic efficiency.

The purpose of structural adjustment is to put an economy on a sustainable growth path. For this, macroeconomic balance and improved investment efficiency are key. Achievement of macroeconomic balance requires more than just traditional short-term demand management; it must be supplemented by rising savings and exports generated by medium- and long-term structural changes, including institutional reforms for enhancing supply-side response. Short-term stabilization measures are absolutely necessary but not sufficient for attaining this goal.

Should short-term stabilization and medium and long-term structural adjustment measures be implemented simultaneously? Or should these reform measures be sequenced and carried out more gradually? This is a very important policy question.

Japan's postwar experience provides insight for the analysis of approaches to structural adjustment. Although one must take account of differences in initial conditions and stages of development between postwar Japan and current transitional economies, the problems faced by Japan in those days – especially the need to overcome hyperinflation and attain rapid transformation from a military to a democratic state – are similar to those facing Russia and Central and Eastern Europe. According to studies by Yutaka Kosai, president of the Japan Center for Economic Research, and Juro Teranishi, professor of economics at Hitotsubashi University, there are three key features of how the postwar stabilization and economic reform were carried out in Japan: (i) establishment of such basic goals as democratization and de-militarization; (ii) gradualism; and (iii) emphasis on microeconomic, supply-side measures. These three points provide useful lessons for the analysis of structural adjustment.

Here, we should not dwell on the often cited dichotomy between shock therapy and gradualism. The important issue is not to pursue which approach is absolutely correct, but rather to clarify under which political and economic conditions shock therapy is more appropriate than gradualism or vice versa.

Economic development and self-help effort

The driving force behind economic development is the willingness of a government and people to help themselves. The presence of such "self-help effort" critically affects the success of systemic transformation as well. Emphasis on self-help does not necessarily deny a valuable role to foreign aid or other forms of external capital or to advice from foreign experts. In fact, structural adjustment lending and financial support from G7 countries are intended to complement self-help efforts. Some countries have succeeded in economic development by relying on foreign capital; others have failed.

Regardless of the role of foreign capital and advice, no country has ever achieved economic development without introducing advanced technology from more developed countries. It is vitally important for a country to import foreign technology, adapt it to local conditions, and use it for the sake of economic development.

Self-help effort can be defined as the willingness and determination of local politicians and technocrats to draw up a medium- and long-term blueprint of development for their own country, formulate and carry out development plans on their own initiative, and persevere until the effort bears fruit. Toshio Watanabe, professor of economics at the Tokyo Institute of Technology states that for latecomers (implying all but the United Kingdom) to succeed in economic development, it is crucial to have religious fervor, a "passion and dedication to development." This is exactly right. The existence of this passion will determine the success or failure of systemic transition.

In the Meiji era, the Japanese government hired foreign advisers, paying them higher salaries than even the prime minister out of scarce foreign exchange earnings. The government then made efforts to master advanced foreign technology in the shortest possible time period, promoting economic development through adaptation of these technologies. This is a typical example of self-help. Another example is the enthusiasm of officials of the Ministry of Agriculture and Commerce, then responsible for formulating economic plans. So anxious were officials to do their part to move the economy forward that they used to line up before dawn with lanterns waiting for the office to open. These anecdotes strongly demonstrate the existence of a spirit of self-help during Meiji Japan.

Indonesia in the latter half of the 1980s also provides a good example of self-help. Indonesia, like other developing countries, depends on foreign capital. However, Indonesia does not receive financial support from the IMF and the World Bank in exchange for typical conditionalities attached to stabilization and structural adjustment programs. The Indonesian government has implemented structural adjustment and reform measures on its own initiative since the mid-1980s. The government itself has designed and implemented a program of structural adjustment with an eye toward long-term economic development. Indonesia benefits from a cadre of technocrats capable of implementing the economic program and backed by political support.

The Indonesian case offers a powerful lesson for former socialist countries facing economic transition. Although in 1965 per capita GNP in Indonesia was lower than that of Nigeria, now it is more than three times as high as that of Nigeria. Both are oil producing developing countries; however, right policy, political will, and a strong spirit of self-help have made a pivotal difference in their economic performance.

IMF approach

The IMF plays a lead role in systemic transformation in former socialist countries, particularly in Russia. Nevertheless, the appropriateness of the IMF approach remains a controversial issue. For example, from November 1993 to March/April 1994, a series of debates over the correct approach to reform in Russia (including the feasibility of gradualism) appeared in the *Financial Times* between IMF economists and academic economists, including Jeffrey Sachs.

The primary role of the IMF is to secure macroeconomic stabilization and promote economic liberalization. Controlling inflation is an important policy objective and the most fundamental condition for sustainable growth. The IMF believes that liberalization and tight financial policies should be introduced from the very beginning of the reform process.

According to Professor Kenichi Ohno of Tsukuba University, the main task of the IMF is to "provide financing to deficit-ridden countries and arrange debt relief in exchange for the implementation of policy reform (conditionality)." The primary features of the IMF approach can be summarized in the following three points. First, the IMF focuses almost exclusively on economic policies: social problems, political conditions and ethnic problems are treated as separate from the process of economic reform. Second, the IMF adopts a short-term orientation. The typical IMF reform sets goals for only a one–two year time horizon. Although these reforms require decades or even generations of effort to take root, typical IMF missions are interested in monthly inflation and quarterly fiscal deficits. Economic ministers who negotiate with the IMF also become infected with similar short-termism. This unfortunate situation makes the Japanese approach to economic development, discussed below, all the more important. Third, the IMF is known for its strong reliance on the market-mechanism and skepticism about government intervention. The idea of a policy of supporting individual industries is out of the question for the IMF.

There is a serious problem inherent in the IMF approach. As Ohno states, "what is true from an economic viewpoint is not necessarily valid for the society as a whole. While the IMF approach can be effective in countries where political processes have been institutionalized and the market economy has matured, it is too narrow for countries that face the enormous challenge of building the institutions and framework of the society from nothing."

The theoretical underpinnings of the IMF approach lie in neoclassical economics. Under neoclassical economic theory, efficient resource allocation is achieved through free competition, provided there are no market failures. This may hold from a short-term, static perspective; however, what we are trying to analyze is the systemic transition of former socialist economies. The problems facing these countries are not short-term but medium- to long-term, and they require substantial structural adjustment.

IMF economists do not envision an economic system five or ten years down the line. In their view, an economic system will improve automatically once market distortions are removed through liberalization; therefore, there is no need to worry about the final image of an economic system.

Japanese approach

As many economists point out, the main features of the Japanese approach are that

1 the highest priority of reform is placed on the supply side of the economy, including production, employment, and economic structure;
2 reform is designed with a long-term orientation. Long-term economic development goals are formulated, then specific policy measures are designed to realize those goals; and
3 there is a widely shared view that in latecomers, the market does not grow spontaneously without the help of the government.

These points are quite different from views prevailing among IMF economists.

Comparing IMF and Japanese philosophies, Toru Yanagihara of Hosei University refers to the former as a "framework approach" while he calls the latter an "ingredients approach" [see Chapter 4 of this volume]. The framework approach is built on the view that government interventions distort the market, preventing the achievement of efficient resource allocation. Following the logic of this argument, rapid liberalization is essential to eliminate distortions brought on by protectionism and regulation. Under the framework approach, which industries have growth potential or which should be promoted is not even a policy issue. To use a sports analogy, the framework approach aims to strengthen a soccer team by leveling a rough playing field.

In contrast, the Japanese "ingredients approach" is results-oriented. Policy makers create a reform program by first imagining a desirable economic system for their country then designing policy measures to make that image a reality. In this approach, government interventions are justified on the basis of dynamic efficiency. The ingredient approach aims to strengthen a soccer team by nurturing the ability of individual players, rather than by smoothing out bumps in the play ground.

For systemic transition to succeed, an environment where investors can make a profit if they invest properly and work hard is needed. Such an environment cannot be realized simply through liberalization.

According to Daito Bunka University Professor Tadashi Mio, the Doi Moi reform in Viet Nam differs from the reform approach adopted by Russia and Eastern Europe in the sense that: (i) economic liberalization has preceded political liberalization; and (ii) the authorities have been taking an experimental approach, testing policies in selected areas for a certain period, evaluating their appropriateness, and then nurturing a consensus among various sectors on the larger-scale implementation of the policies. Mio observes that amid the transition process in Viet Nam, the logic of political ideology is being replaced by the logic of capitalism. Based on the belief that political stability is indispensable to the continuation of economic opening, he suggests that Western donors should not request rapid democratization as conditions for economic assistance. We should be reminded of the famous remarks by former Prime Minister Lee Kuan-yew of Singapore that the meaning of democracy and human rights differ from country to country.

For a country to succeed in systemic transition, it must analyze whether and where private sector dynamism exists. Ownership transfer is only the first step in privatization. True privatization lies in the accumulation of entrepreneurial spirit and the creation of an environment conducive to private sector dynamism. The government can play an important role in this respect.

Confidence of people in the government

Transition from a centrally planned to a market economy is achieved through structural adjustment of the most radical sort. Confidence of the people in their government is an essential factor in the difficult adjustment process. Government must work hard to win the confidence of the population; it should not lie or present unrealistic goals to the people.

Let's take the example of Slovakia. Although that country's original economic plan envisaged a balanced budget in 1993, the actual performance has been far below expectations, with the level of fiscal deficit corresponding to 28 percent of revenues during January–April 1993 and 15 percent up to the third quarter of 1993. Although balancing the budget is important in stabilizing the macro-economy, it is more important for the government to develop a realistic deficit reduction plan; otherwise, it will lose credibility, which will hinder its ability to plan and implement future reform.

To implement structural adjustment and economic reform in a successful and sustained manner, it is not sufficient for the government to design policies that are correct from an economic viewpoint. Popular support is indispensable. How can a government build political support? As the experience of Russian economic reforms indicates, reform is likely to impose social costs and force the people to sacrifice, at least in the short- and medium-term. The issue is how to persuade the people to accept the costs of the reform. The government must explain to the people, actively and sincerely, why such painful measures are necessary and why they should be implemented in a certain sequence.

Moreover, the government needs to present a future vision of the kind of economic system the country is working to develop and ask for popular cooperation and support. It is important to present these concrete goals to the population to generate public confidence. Strong political leadership and rational economic policy are indispensable. Recent improvements in the Argentine economy owe much to public trust in the Menem administration.

It appears that in Russia and Eastern Europe, the population had the illusion that their living standards would improve quickly under reform, say, within three years or so, allowing everybody to enjoy a luxurious life as the result of systemic transition. Unless such unrealistic expectations are destroyed, serious efforts at reform will be stymied.

The most important thing is the existence of: (1) public confidence in the government, and (2) the government's vision of the economic development over the medium- to long-term, widely shared with the population. What are the urgent policy issues? How does the government plan to set targets for production and exports in the medium-term? Presentation of these goals to the general public will generate popular confidence.

We economists tend to think that because people were repressed under socialism, they will happily accept a liberal economic regime and immediately respond to free competition. But, as Nanami Shiono urges, we must question such simplistic thinking; otherwise, we will offer little meaningful help to countries facing systemic transformation.

Note

1 This article appeared in serialized form in the column *Yasashii Keizaigaku* [Economics Made Easy] in the *Japan Economic Journal*, May 12–19, 1994 [Editors].

3

ISSUES RELATED TO THE WORLD BANK'S APPROACH TO STRUCTURAL ADJUSTMENT: A PROPOSAL FROM A MAJOR PARTNER[1]

Overseas Economic Cooperation Fund

I Introduction[2]

During the late 1970s and early 1980s, many developing countries faced serious fiscal deficits, balance-of-payments difficulties, and accelerating inflation. These problems traced their roots to both domestic and external factors, including oil price increases, the falling prices of other primary commodities, a rise in international interest rates, and macroeconomic mismanagement which led to inefficient resource allocation. These events unfolded in the following manner.

In the 1970s, when access to external finance was fairly easy, developing countries accumulated external debt by aggressive borrowing for the purpose of economic development. As the 1980s dawned, however, the supply of funds available to less developed countries was reduced and, compounded by rising global interest rates, their balance-of-payments positions deteriorated. Furthermore, the overvalued currencies of many less developed countries undermined their export competitiveness, while sluggish global demand retarded their exports. Imports rose, however, worsening developing country trade balances. Domestically, fiscal deficits ballooned and inefficient resource allocation spread as a result of ever-rising subsidies and public-sector activities.

In response to this economic crisis caused by domestic mismanagement and an adverse external environment, the World Bank initiated structural adjustment lending (SAL) for developing countries at the end of the 1970s. SALs are rapidly disbursing policy-based lending operations for dealing with these changed circumstances at home and abroad. The provision of SALs averts balance-of-payments difficulties (i.e. a shortage of foreign exchange) and permits the implementation of macroeconomic stabilization measures – fiscal deficit reduction, aggregate demand restraint, correction of the exchange rate, etc. – and structural adjustment measures (which are required conditions for loan disbursement) for improving policies, institutions, and procedures. Together, these measures are expected to downsize the public sector and strengthen the incentives for the private sector, leading to private sector-led sustainable growth.

The Overseas Economic Cooperation Fund (OECF) has co-financed SAL programs with the World Bank and other international organizations since the mid-1980s, with an outstanding balance of 450 billion yen at end-September 1991 on a commitment basis. SALs have produced some positive results in many countries, but much room for improvement also remains. At various levels, efforts are being made to effect these improvements. Among the many questions that can be raised about SAL design and implementation, this report presents OECF's views on those issues that have, in our opinion, been neglected by the World Bank itself. The report was first presented as a reference paper at a regular consultation meeting with the World Bank on November 5–7, 1991.

In preparation, a Study Group on the Structural Adjustment Approach, comprised of academic experts and OECF officials, was formed in June 1991. The present report was drafted by the OECF based on the discussions of this group. All responsibility for the content of this report remains with the OECF.

Membership in the Study Group on the Structural Adjustment Approach was as follows: from the academic community, Shujiro Urata of Waseda University, Hidenobu Okuda of Hitotsubashi University, Akiyoshi Horiuchi of Tokyo University, and Toru Yanagihara of Hosei University; and from OECF, Yasutami Shimomura, (then) director of the Economics Department, Keiichi Tango, (then) Coordination Department, and other officials in related departments.

II Objectives

This paper discusses problems related to the World Bank's approach to structural adjustment and proposes ways to address these problems based on the experience of the Overseas Economic Cooperation Fund as a major Bank partner in structural adjustment lending.

Since the mid-1980s, the OECF has collaborated with the Bank in structural adjustment lending. The cumulative total of OECF's SAL co-financing on a commitment basis reached over 450 billion yen as of the end of September 1991.

III Basic argument on structural adjustment

Structural adjustment is a medium-term microeconomic policy that supplements stabilization, itself a short-term macroeconomic policy. Structural adjustment aims at improving the efficiency of resource allocation by reforming institutions and procedures, thereby allowing recovery of economic growth on a sustainable basis.

Structural adjustment lending is defined as quick-disbursing lending designed to improve the international balance of payments position and support the adjustment policies of a developing country in order to help that country achieve sustainable growth.

In many developing countries, economic activities are excessively restricted. In addition, they often face the heavy burden of foreign debt and balance of payments difficulties. Under such circumstances, structural adjustment lending, which supports the balance of payments and the execution of programs for economic vitalization and efficiency, including deregulation, is a promising option for assisting developing countries and has produced positive results in many.

At the same time, there is still much room for improvement in the content and implementation of structural adjustment lending. The World Bank is aware of many of these points, as discussed in the 1990 report "Adjustment lending policies for sustainable growth." However, there are many other important issues which are not taken up in the 1990 report. This paper takes up four of these issues.

A common thread runs through all four points. It is fully recognized that efficient resource allocation through the market mechanism is important in economic policy. However, in designing an economic reform program in the context of actual economies, factors other than efficiency must also be taken into account. If efficiency of resource allocation is stressed too strongly without giving sufficient consideration to other factors, the reform program will not be balanced and may inadvertently hinder efforts to strengthen the market mechanism. A well-balanced reform program must pursue more than just economic efficiency; furthermore, efficiency must always be considered from a long-term perspective as well as in the short run.

IV Issues discussed in this paper

This paper does not intend to discuss all the problems of the World Bank's approach to structural adjustment. Instead it concentrates on four specific points that seem to have been often overlooked by the Bank. The four points are as follows:

1   What steps are necessary to attain sustainable growth after the completion of structural adjustment? Can the impetus for sustained growth be created by structural adjustment alone? If not, isn't it necessary to introduce additional measures for investment promotion?

2   If imports are liberalized too quickly, is it still possible to develop industries which will play a leading role in the next stage of economic development? If not, isn't it necessary to protect domestic industry for a certain period of time in order to allow a viable export sector to develop?

3   Doesn't the Bank place too much stress on the market mechanism in its

financial sector policy? Isn't it indispensable to have development finance institutions lending at subsidized interest rates to maximize social welfare?

4   Is privatization being carried out only when adequate conditions are found? Is the privatization program giving sufficient consideration to factors other than economic efficiency?

V Policies for attaining sustainable growth

The World Bank's approach to structural adjustment is based on the assumption that introducing the market mechanism and eliminating restrictions on the private sector will produce an improved investment climate and will stimulate economic activity, creating the necessary conditions for sustainable growth.

Structural adjustment measures, including deregulation, no doubt have a favorable impact on economic activity. But will these adjustments by themselves be sufficient to generate sustainable growth? Perhaps in an economy with strong investment demand the answer is yes, but in many developing countries improvement in the investment climate through deregulation is not sufficient to attract a large wave of investment. For instance, in the countries of Sub-Saharan Africa, it is hard to find entrepreneurs to generate the anticipated wave of investment. Many other developing countries face a similar predicament of low investment, even under structural adjustment.

If the World Bank's strategy of moving "from structural adjustment to sustainable growth" is not workable, what additional measures are required? We believe measures aimed *directly* at promoting investment are important. In this respect, Japanese postwar fiscal and monetary policies, which were centered on preferential tax treatment and lending by official development finance institutions, are worthy of consideration. We must, however, be cautious because the experience of one country cannot be easily applied to other countries. Modifications, taking into consideration the unique conditions of each country, will be necessary. It is also important that such investment promotion policies be implemented only for a limited period of time. However, in the absence of alternative policy options, these investment promotion measures based on postwar Japanese experience should be considered seriously for adoption.

VI Balance between trade liberalization and industrial development

Trade liberalization is an important component of World Bank structural adjustment programs. We fully recognize the importance of trade liberalization as international trade in many developing countries is over-regulated, causing serious inefficiency. However, excessive reliance on trade liberalization is also risky. If trade is deregulated too hastily, it may impose heavy costs.

When economists argue that trade liberalization leads to the optimum allocation of resources, they refer to optimum allocation under a country's existing industrial structure and technological level. In this case, the comparative advantage of each country is static. The comparative advantage of developing countries tends to be found mainly in primary products and light industry, which both have low value-added. However, most developing countries naturally and earnestly wish to transform their industrial structures toward industries of higher value-added, higher technology and higher growth potential. From the standpoint of developing countries, pursuing dynamic comparative advantage to create this shift is indispensable in the long-term improvement of living standards. Sticking to simple trade liberalization based on static comparative advantage may have a negative impact on economic development potential.

When we consider trade liberalization, we must always focus on how best to develop industries that can support long-term economic development. To expect that the next generation of industries will pop up automatically through the activities of the private sector is overly optimistic. Governments must adopt measures to foster industry. As frequently pointed out, industrial policy, which played a central role in the economic development strategies of East Asia, could offer valuable lessons for other developing countries. While the World Bank is aware of the importance of export industries and supporting outward-oriented developing strategies, its structural adjustment approach lacks a long-term vision of how to develop the industries of tomorrow. The Bank seems to assume that the activities of the private sector alone are sufficient to attain this goal. This thinking is regrettable.

Industrial development takes time and involves social set-up costs; therefore, following the infant industries argument, protection for a certain period of time is indispensable. At the same time, protection is often accompanied by harmful effects and measures must be taken to minimize such effects. The measures include: (1) identification of industries which will have a leading role in the future, (2) a minimum level of necessary protection, (3) specific actions and the required period for promotion must be carefully determined, including in terms of GATT consistency.

In this respect, we wish to propose a policy dialogue on industrial development between donors and individual developing countries. Such a dialogue would identify promising products and international marketing strategies for each developing country. The opinions of private sector actors in developed countries would be particularly beneficial in this respect.

VII Significance of development finance institutions and subsidized interest rates

The financial sector is expected to play a central role in spreading the market mechanism in developing countries. Understandably, therefore, the financial sector plays an important role in the World Bank's approach toward structural adjustment. Placing too much emphasis on the market mechanism in financial sector reform, however, can be problematic and may cause some of the many roles of the financial sector in developing economies to be overlooked. A typical example is the discussion of interest rates. The importance of market interest rates is well recognized, but their exclusive application is a different matter. The World Bank has criticized OECF's "two-step loans" from time to time.[3] In so doing, the Bank has overlooked the benefits to be gained under certain circumstances from lending at subsidized interest rates by development finance institutions.

Among various financial sector issues, we would like to focus our attention on subsidized interest rates. The following three points are raised for discussion.

1   In developing countries, financial sectors frequently are under-developed and financial institutions lack experience and capability; therefore, the market mechanism cannot fully function.

2   The market mechanism itself has inherent limitations and cannot handle all issues properly. Government intervention is indispensable in areas where the market alone is insufficient.

3   Official development assistance (ODA) has market distorting aspects; therefore, it is not appropriate to criticize only "two-step loans" for their market distorting effects.

Financial-sector imperfections in developing countries

Needless to say, it is inappropriate to assume that conditions in the financial sectors of developing countries are similar to those in developed countries. Especially in the case of the Least Less Developed Countries (LLDCs), financial sectors are still in the preliminary stages of development and interest rates do not produce the desired results. In such cases, it is not proper to discuss the difference between market interest rates and subsidized interest rates. Even in more-advanced developing countries, the financial sector often does not function as expected, as the capability and experience of financial institutions are limited. As a result, the role of market interest rates in promoting efficient resource allocation is much more limited than in developed countries. Under these circumstances, it is indispensable for government to intervene to overcome the limits of market interest rates. Hasty introduction of market-determined interest rates is unrealistic and should be avoided.

Limits of the market mechanism

It is impossible to achieve optimum allocation of resources solely through market principles, regardless of the level of development. There are many areas which cannot be handled by the market mechanism and government intervention is necessary to cope with these market failures.

Some problems that cannot be handled by market interest rates can be addressed effectively through the introduction of subsidized interest rates. For instance, when socially beneficial activities are not initiated due to insufficient incentive for private sector actors in the financial market, it becomes necessary for government to provide additional incentives through interest rate subsidies. Introduction of subsidized interest rates can induce the desired activity, thus improving social welfare. Consider these examples:

1 When the investment risk of certain socially beneficial activities is too high, subsidized interest rate will lessen the cost – for example, cases of scale merits, long gestation periods, and new technology and immature markets.
2 When there is a significant discrepancy between private and social returns on investment ("externalities"), interest rate subsidies can increase private benefits and spur investment.
    Examples:

    (a) the case of rural industry, which offers the social benefits of increasing job opportunities and preventing excessive outward migration to urban regions;
    (b) the case of supporting or parts industries, which increase value-added and thus strengthen a country's balance of payments;
    (c) the case of investment for pollution control and environmental protection.

3 When, due to imperfect information, some enterprises are disadvantaged in the market-driven financial market. Subsidized loans can partly ameliorate this problem for small- and medium-sized enterprises, venture businesses, and so forth.
4 When infant industries face significant start-up costs, subsidized loans can cover part of this cost.

The World Bank accepts direct subsidies for such market failures. Direct subsidies are permitted, but subsidized interest rates are not. Is there any theoretical rationale for this seeming contradiction? From both a theoretical and a practical viewpoint, we believe subsidies and subsidized interest rates are equally useful tools. Subsidies sometimes have certain advantages; in other cases subsidized interest rates may best achieve the desired goals. Therefore, the flexibility to fully utilize the two options is important. Accepting the one and rejecting the other, as the World Bank does, is highly questionable.

ODA and distortion of the market mechanism

ODA is supposed to deal with cases of market failure. While concessional aid tends to distort the market, this aspect of ODA is usually not discussed. Strangely, it is taken up only in the case of on-lending operations (so-called "two-step loans") of the OECF. But if one is to criticize OECF's "two-step loans" then one should review other types of ODA for market distorting effects.

In both "two-step loans" and ordinary project loans, the developing country enjoys the benefit of receiving funds on soft terms. This merit can trickle down through the recipient country. In the case of OECF "two-step loans," the benefits of concessionality are passed on to the end-users (farmers, for instance). In the case of OECF project financing – a fertilizer plant, for example – fertilizer prices for farmers are lower than they would have been in the absence of ODA due to the low interest on aid funds. Why should we criticize one form of loan but not the other?

The World Bank often points out that subsidized interest rates cause corruption. It is true that corruption is frequently found in the financial sector of developing countries. But is this unique to subsidized interest rates, and would corruption disappear if interest subsidies were eliminated? A convincing argument is lacking on this point.

What is important, in our opinion, is to check at the time of appraisal whether there is the possibility of excessive inefficiency and unfairness due to interest rate subsidies. Assistance should be granted only if it is expected that such problems will not be too serious. When the discipline of the financial sector is in doubt, neither market-determined nor subsidized interest rates are likely to do any good.

We recommend policy loans with subsidized interest as a viable policy option, provided that the necessary conditions for their proper operation are satisfied.

VIII Issues in privatization

Promotion of the private sector is one of the most important elements of World Bank structural adjustment. This is appropriate, as the essence of economic development is unleashing the creativity of entrepreneurs and promoting investment. Privatization is important since many developing countries have large, inefficient public firms.

However, privatization is not always the solution for improving public sector efficiency. It is necessary to consider factors unique to each country when designing a privatization program. The specific conditions of each individual country must be taken into account. Unfortunately, the World Bank's approach seems to be too similar in every country. For instance, in Sub-Saharan Africa the indigenous private sector is very much underdeveloped and private capital is insufficient to operate privatized enterprises, but the World Bank has promoted privatization in many countries in this region. This is not a realistic approach.

Another problem is the requirement that all private sector actors should be treated equally, whether indigenous or foreign. This may be ideal from an efficiency standpoint, but political and social realities in developing countries frequently do not allow it.

Most developing countries have had a long and bitter experience with colonialism. The idea of transferring basic industries to foreign capital entails a serious political risk which may upset long-term social stability. Moreover, even from an economic standpoint, we must be aware that a monopoly of foreign capital will lead to repatriation of rents. The same argument can be made regarding non-indigenous capital, such as Indian capital in East Africa and Chinese capital in Malaysia and Indonesia. The dominance of non-indigenous capital in key industries is not always a feasible option in a broad social context. As in other cases, the efficiency criterion should not rule exclusively in the process of privatization.

IX Beyond the "Decade of Efficiency"

Although efficiency and equity are the major objectives of economic policy, there is sometimes a trade-off between the two. In the 1980s, economic theory and policy were heavily oriented toward the pursuit of efficiency. In this sense, it was a unique period; however, this period has come to an end. What is now needed is a policy that seeks to balance efficiency and equity in order to improve the welfare of the entire society. The World Bank's approach to structural adjustment may have to be adjusted to reflect these changing needs.

Notes

1 This is an edited version of the English translation of "*Sekai ginko no kozo chosei approach no mondaiten ni tsuite – shuyona partner no tachiba kara no teigen*," which was presented at the OECF–World Bank regular consultation in October 1991. It was published, together with an English translation, in *Kikin Chosa Kiho* (the OECF *Research Quarterly*), February 1992 (no. 73), pp. 4–18 [Editors].
2 These introductory remarks were omitted in the 1992 English translation. While some overlapping exists with the main text, we include this section because it discusses the circumstances under which the paper was written [Editors].
3 For example, the World Bank raised objections to an OECF loan to the Philippines under the ASEAN–Japan Development Fund (AJDF) in September 1990. The World Bank's basic concerns were as follows: (1) AJDF provides long-term credit with interest rates below prevailing market rates; and (2) this will have a negative impact on the development of the financial market and will hamper the objectives of a Financial Sector Adjustment Loan (FSAL) which was being co-financed by the World Bank and the OECF. As a result of discussions between the World Bank and the OECF, it was agreed that the interest rate for small-to-medium scale industries under AJDF would be set at a level 2 percent below the six-month time deposit interest rate.

4

DEVELOPMENT AND DYNAMIC EFFICIENCY: "FRAMEWORK APPROACH" VERSUS "INGREDIENTS APPROACH"[1]

Toru Yanagihara

This note identifies two philosophical perspectives on economic development that inform debates about development and structural adjustment policies: the "framework approach" typical of Western aid donors, particularly multilateral development finance institutions such as the World Bank, and the "ingredients approach" adopted by the government of Japan in its development assistance policies. Discussion focuses on general conceptual clarification of issues differentiating these two approaches, with only occasional reference to specific experiences. Discourse at this level of generality will help clarify the nature and extent of philosophical differences between Japan and multilateral institutions on specific development policy issues.

"Framework" and "ingredients"

There are two contrasting ways of understanding and analyzing economic development and structural adjustment. One focuses on the "framework" of an economic system and its management; the other focuses on an economy as the sum total of its "ingredients" or component parts.

The "framework" represents rules of the game according to which economic agents make decisions and take action in a given economy. In the framework approach, which dominates thinking in Anglo-American university economics departments and multilateral development institutions like the World Bank, an economy is conceived in terms of the functions of institutions and mechanisms (the invisible hand), and its performance is evaluated in light of the extent to which the rules of the game are established and enforced among key economic agents.

In contrast, the "ingredients" refer to tangible organizational units such as enterprises, official bureaus, and industrial projects and their aggregations such as industries, sectors and regions. They may, however, also relate to factors of production – land, labor, capital and technology – at different levels of aggregation and specificity. The ingredients approach conceives the economy as a collection of these components. It envisions economic development as the quantitative expansion and qualitative upgrading of the components, accompanied by shifts in composition.

These approaches see development and structural adjustment policies in distinctly different ways. In the "framework approach" the central task of policy and institutional reforms is correcting distortions in the incentive scheme, defined by the policy environment and institutional arrangements. By contrast, in the "ingredients approach" policies and institutions are viewed as tangible inputs, like conventional factors of production, that shape the process of economic change. They are the means to achieve a future vision of the economy, typically depicted in terms of a collection of industrial or regional economies.

In essence, the "framework approach" is principle-oriented while the "ingredients approach" is results-oriented. In the former, setting the framework right is considered a necessary, if not always sufficient, condition for successful development which will be manifested in improved macroeconomic indicators. By the very essence of this approach, little consideration is given to what sort of real-sector economy will result once the framework is in place: that is left to the market to determine.

Conversely, in the ingredients approach the economic outcome in terms of concrete sectoral composition or industrial organization occupies center stage, while the mode of economic management remains flexible and uncommitted. Certain economic orientations, such as what sectors or activities ought to be given priority, come into play but they are derived from, and therefore subordinate to, the ultimate goal – or premeditated result – of economic development.

The World Bank approach

The *World Development Report 1991* presents the concept of "market-friendly" government intervention as its key conceptual innovation. The report advises governments to intervene reluctantly, thus placing the burden of proof squarely on those who advocate activist government: "Let markets work unless it is demonstrably better to step in" (p. 5). Public goods not adequately provided by the private sector – basic education, infrastructure, poverty alleviation programs, population control and environmental protection – pass this test. Other actions usually fail: " . . . it is usually a mistake for the state to carry out physical production, or to protect the domestic production of a good that can be imported more cheaply and whose local production offers few spillover benefits" (p. 5).

In cases where governments do attempt intervention, the "market-friendly" approach offers three pieces of advice. First, interventions should be designed to maintain domestic and international competition. Second, they should be moderate in the sense of minimizing price distortions. Third, they must be subjected to market discipline and should be withdrawn if they fail to produce competitive industries.

From this perspective, the Bank argues that the success of East Asian economies – Japan and Korea in particular – confirms the rules of market-friendly intervention. "First, these governments disciplined their interventions with international and domestic competition. . . . Second, these governments, on the whole, were careful to ensure that intervention did not end up distorting relative prices unduly. . . . Third, their intervention was more moderate than in most developing countries." In sum, "these economies refute the case for thoroughgoing dirigisme as convincingly as they refute the case for *laissez-faire*" (p. 5).

This is a fair statement; however, the question remains whether strict application of the market-friendly approach is advisable. The central issue here is how one understands the process of economic development and the nature of dynamic efficiency. In *World Development Report 1991* and other documents, the World Bank bases its case for the market-friendly approach on observed regularities between degree of intervention and price distortion on the one hand and output growth and productivity gain on the other. These statistical associations are cited as evidence for a theoretical position that argues that investment, innovation and production decisions are made in response to market signals and assumes that critical market failures are absent. This view sees development as essentially the result of investment and innovation decisions by individual economic agents responding to evolving conditions in goods and factor markets. Dynamic efficiency is realized, so it is claimed, because undistorted markets send the right signals for these private decisions.

Japanese critique

The Japanese government has engaged in co-financing with the World Bank on structural adjustment lendings (SALs) since the mid-1980s through the Overseas Economic Cooperation Fund (OECF) and the Export-Import Bank of Japan (Ex-Im). All along, many Japanese have felt uncomfortable with the Bank's thinking on structural adjustment though their concerns were not voiced until recently. Of late, the Japanese government and its agencies have adopted a more activist stance, advocating alternative perspectives based on Japanese and East Asian experiences. The most systematic manifestation of this activism to date is found in the OECF document, "Issues Related to the World Bank's Approach to Structural Adjustment: A Proposal from a Major Partner" (OECF Occasional Paper No. 1, October 1991). [See also Chapter 3 of this volume]

The OECF document is a Japanese manifesto that adopts the ingredients approach in interpreting Japanese and East Asian development experiences. It implicitly criticizes the framework approach that informs Bank structural adjustment as only half the truth and proposes its own set of policy prescriptions as the missing half. The document criticizes the lopsided emphasis on "efficient resource allocation through the market mechanism" in Bank-led structural adjustment. The OECF raises four issues:

1 the need for "measures aimed 'directly' at promoting investment" in order to achieve sustainable growth;
2 the need for a long-term approach to development, including a conscious industrial policy to promote potential leading industries;
3 the value of subsidized policy-directed credit for the promotion of investment and infant industries;
4 the need to consider a developing country's economic, political and social conditions in making privatization decisions.

On the first point, the paper advocates a results-oriented approach: the use of direct policy measures to realize desirable investments ("ingredients"). Fiscal and financial policies utilized for the promotion of strategic growth industries in postwar Japan are suggested as potentially valuable in today's developing and transitional economies. Such measures are presented as a necessary complement to the Bank's principle-oriented approach that focuses on correcting distortions in the incentive structure ("framework") through policy and institutional reforms.

On point 2, the Bank's advocacy of indiscriminate trade liberalization ("framework approach") is criticized for relying exclusively on the notion of static comparative advantage, in contrast to Japan's proactive, promotional approach to creating desirable industries ("ingredients approach"): "To expect that the next generation of industries will pop up automatically through the activities of the private sector is overly optimistic." [See also Chapter 3 of this volume]

Point 3 makes a frontal attack on World Bank thinking on financial sector reform. While the Bank criticizes policy-directed, subsidized credits as causing distortions in the market framework of the financial sector, the Japanese alternative argues that the financial sector of many developing countries is underdeveloped and suffers widespread market failure. As a result, the market mechanism does not function as expected – and thereby fails to provide a meaningful "framework" for capital allocation. Under such circumstances, directed and subsidized credits can play a critical role in encouraging desired economic development activities ("ingredients").

Point 4 criticizes the World Bank's emphasis on the leading role of the private sector and its advocacy of privatization of state-owned enterprises as often infeasible or undesirable. The Bank is viewed as simple-mindedly and unduly concerned with efficiency criteria ("framework") in total neglect of socio-political conditions and national sentiments with regard to ownership structure within developing economies ("ingredients").

Allocative efficiency and unit efficiency

The two conceptual approaches derive to a large extent from different definitions of efficiency. The approach that dominates Anglo-American university economics departments and most multilateral development banks defines efficiency in allocative terms: efficiency is achieved by shifting resources from less to more productive sectors or firms. In Japan, efficiency is primarily conceptualized in relation to individual economic units: make as efficient use as possible of resources where they are now in order to increase the efficiency of all units and make everyone better off.

More efficient use of economic resources involves changes in "allocative efficiency" and in "unit efficiency." Allocative efficiency relates to the operation of economic institutions and mechanisms that impinge upon the mobilization and allocation of resources. Unit efficiency on the other hand refers to the capacity of specific organizational units such as enterprises, official bureaus, and industrial projects. These two determinants of the overall economic efficiency interact with each other. In other words, institutions and mechanisms define the incentive and selection environment for economic units; and conversely, efficiency at the level of economic units may affect the operation of institutions and mechanisms.

The two determinants of efficiency in an economy correspond to the contrast between the framework and ingredients approaches. Roughly speaking, the framework approach is concerned with efficiency of resource allocation or allocative efficiency while the ingredients approach focuses on efficiency of resource utilization or unit efficiency.

A number of supplementary remarks are necessary here. First, the framework approach may encompass factors relating to unit efficiency insofar as the policy and institutional framework determines the incentive environment for economic units, thus affecting their X-inefficiency.

Secondly, the ingredients approach has its own way of discussing allocative efficiency, which is mostly, if not exclusively, in terms of resource shift over time rather than at a given point in time. "Ingredients" advocates conceptualize allocative efficiency in terms of a vision of industrial composition at a future date. The notion of opportunity cost, central to the framework approach, is only implicitly reflected in the ingredients approach in the guise of the choice of industry for the future.

Final remarks

The Japanese are not comfortable with the notion that a universally applicable "framework" for development exists. Instead, they find a different approach based on the recognition of different stages of development more satisfying. In the clearest official statement of this view to date, the May 1988 report *Sekai to tomo ni ikiru nihon* [Japan Living with the World], put out by the Economic Council under the sponsorship of the Economic Planning Agency, calls for country-specific aid programs based on development stages and types. Japanese development finance agencies are urged to approach structural adjustment with a clear understanding of real sector differences across economies.

Japanese understanding of their own economic development process is not based on the Anglo-American framework but rather on ingredients – for example, production and trade targets set for industry. Targets have usually been announced in so-called "visions", most notably MITI industry visions. Once targets are set, policy debate focuses on the means ("ingredients") to achieve them. The approach is quintessentially results-oriented, conceptualized in tangible rather than functional terms (building new factories versus enhancing the market mechanism in general). Development strategy aims to achieve economic expansion via accumulation of appropriate ingredients to increase productive capacity at the firm or project level.

A fundamental disagreement exists over the role of government in a developing economy. On the one hand, the framework approach emphasizes liberalization – trade liberalization and overall domestic deregulation; on the other hand, the Japanese believe this is not always appropriate, particularly in economies at an early stage of development.

A corollary to the important role for government is that industrial policy matters in development. In Japan, industrial policy is conceptualized in the form of visions, a series of concrete medium- and long-term goals.

Credit policy is a second concrete area where views diverge. Drawing on their own development experience plus that of Korea, Japanese believe that directed credit policy is more effective in promoting economic development than freely market-determined credit allocation. This, of course, presupposes the existence of an industrial policy.

Another area of disagreement with the Anglo-American framework approach is in attention to history. This is half an academic point and half common sense. Heavily influenced, consciously or unconsciously, by the German historical school, Japanese analysts and decision-makers tend to view economic problems in a historical time-series perspective as opposed to a functional cross-sectional approach that characterizes Anglo-American economics. The latter concentrates on the allocation of resources across an economy at a specific point in time. The Japanese approach instead views an economy by taking each unit and examining its historical evolution. In this sense the Japanese approach is essentially developmental; it is integrally aware of the evolution of an economy's component parts – "ingredients" – over time. This point captures an underlying attitude that crystallizes in more specific debates over issues such as industrial policy or credit policy.

Where does this leave the Japanese as far as formulating policy analysis goes? Again, the issue can be meaningfully addressed in comparison with the standard framework approach.

In the tradition of Anglo-American economics, the economy is treated as a functional cross-sectional model with policy inputs and performance outputs.

Cause–effect relationships between inputs and outputs are then turned around and viewed as ends–means relationships. The model itself is often not well understood: the economy is typically treated as a black box. Much policy analysis that is attributed to deductive reasoning is really inductive: economists compare several existing economies and attribute divergence in performance to differences in policy.

The Japanese approach begins with the initial conditions of an economy. These initial conditions undergo various historical processes en route to producing economic performance. Rather than being inputs into an economic black box, policies intervene at certain junctures in certain types of historical processes to affect performance. Economic development is viewed as a process in which economic agents and the market mechanism emerge and become increasingly more efficient with time, while at the same time productive and technical capabilities are accumulated and upgraded. Policy analysis must be rooted in the understanding of the mechanism of development and the nature of economic institutions at different stages and in varied types of economic development.

This is a tall order, but I believe that this type of alternative methodology needs to be explored if Japanese views are to be presented as an alternative framework for policy making.

Note

1 This manuscript, dated November 12, 1992, has not been published previously [Editors].

5

AFTERWORD TO THE JAPANESE TRANSLATION OF THE WORLD BANK REPORT *THE EAST ASIAN MIRACLE*

Masaki Shiratori[1]

It was September 1989 – soon after I was dispatched by the Ministry of Finance to assume the post of Executive Director of the World Bank on behalf of the Japanese Government. I received a copy of a puzzling letter, addressed to the Japanese Government from the management of the World Bank. To be exact, the letter was from a Senior Vice President of the World Bank to the president of Japan's Overseas Economic Cooperation Fund (OECF). The letter asked that OECF reconsider its subsidized policy-directed loans to developing countries. The letter stated that such loans would militate against market determination of interest rates, "could have an adverse impact on the development of the financial sector," and hence "would create unnecessary distortions and set back financial reforms" which had been supported by the Bank and the IMF. This argument was hardly acceptable to us, both for practical reasons and in light of Japan's postwar experience of economic development.

OECF provides so-called "two-step loans" at concessional interest rates with long maturities to governments or public financial institutions in developing countries. Loan funds are on-lent by borrower governments at below-market interest rates to target groups, including small- and medium-sized businesses. Because "two-step loans" are one of the main vehicles for Japan's ODA loans (yen loans), denying their usefulness would have had a serious negative impact on implementation of Japan's ODA. Moreover, it is a well-known fact that the Japan Development Bank made a great contribution to industrialization in Japan's postwar economic reconstruction and high growth eras by channeling long-term financing (often backed by World Bank loans) to key strategic industries at subsidized interest rates. Other financial intermediaries – for example, the Export-Import Bank of Japan, the People's Finance Corporation, the Small Business Finance Corporation, the Agriculture and Forestry Finance Corporation, and Housing Loans Corporation – also played significant roles in their respective fields by providing long-term loans, often at lower-than-market rates. This experience can be replicated in developing countries today, but the World Bank is quite negative toward such subsidized directed credits.[2]

During the course of my discussions with World Bank staff, I came to realize that Bank also opposed supporting specific industries through industrial policy and it, through structural adjustment lending,[3] imposed on developing countries conditionalities that relied too heavily on the market mechanism without giving due consideration to actual conditions in borrowing countries. For these reasons, at the Bank board meetings and on other occasions, I frequently insisted on the need to assess more positively the role of government in development and to learn from the experience of Asian economies, including Japan.

In October 1991, OECF also presented a paper, "Issues Related to the World Bank's Approach to Structural Adjustment" (Occasional Paper No. 1)[4] raising questions about the development philosophy of the World Bank. Furthermore, at the Annual Meetings of the Board of Governors of the IMF and the World Bank the same month, Mr. Yasushi Mieno, then Governor of the Bank of Japan, made the following statement on behalf of the Minister of Finance: "Experience in Asia has shown that although development strategies require a healthy respect for the market mechanism, the role of government cannot be forgotten. I would like to see the World Bank and the IMF take the lead in a wide-ranging study that would define the theoretical underpinnings of this approach and clarify the areas in which it can be successfully applied to other parts of the globe." The Ministry of Finance offered to finance such a study.

With this strong urging and financial support from the Japanese Government, in early 1992 the World Bank undertook a study on the East Asian experience of economic development under the leadership of Lawrence Summers, then Chief Economist of the World Bank.[5] Scholars and practitioners from around the world conducted various research projects, and the results were presented in September 1993 at the occasion of the IMF–World Bank Annual Meetings, as a report entitled *The East Asian Miracle: Economic Growth and Public Policy*.

As the subtitle indicates, the central theme of this report is economic growth and public policy. Indeed, the question of the appropriate role of the government in development has occupied policy makers and scholars for a long time. In the 1950s and 1960s, economic development was regarded as the government's responsibility. The government was supposed to not only maintain macro-economic stability and supply public goods and services, but also to direct scarce resources to productive investment. According to this view, the engine of economic development was capital formation. If the market mechanism functions sufficiently, resources will be transferred to investment, and hence the economy will grow, through the optimum allocation of resources. However, in developing countries the market mechanism does not function as predicted, nor do such efficient markets exist. Leaving key decisions to the market runs the risk of wasting scarce resources on unproductive activities. The government should intervene to correct such "market failure." Based on this "structuralist" view, the

World Bank vigorously supported infrastructure development, strengthening of state-owned enterprises, and the promotion of import-substitution policies.

As it gradually became clear that these measures were not producing the expected results, the dominant thinking shifted to emphasizing the market mechanism. The promotion of import-substitution industrialization had resulted in inefficient state-owned enterprises; extensive government interventions generated massive rent-seeking and corruption. With increasing "government failure," it was argued that governments could not be relied upon because of weak civil service capacity. Thus, the market mechanism was seen as a better alternative; accordingly, the Bank recommended that various regulations should be abolished, transactions liberalized, and state-owned enterprises privatized.

This "neoclassical" view became more influential from the second half of the 1960s to the early 1970s and dominant after the World Bank adopted the structural adjustment approach in 1980. This school argues that the engine of economic development is not capital formation but efficient resource allocation; capital formation will be achieved automatically provided that resources are allocated optimally through market mechanisms. Since the late 1980s, however, there has been a move to revise the excessive reliance on markets and recognize the positive role of the government in development – given the fact that the active intervention policies of East Asian governments have achieved rapid growth with equity, while the "shock therapy" the IMF and World Bank have applied to former socialist economies has shown disappointing results. *The East Asian Miracle* refers to this as "revisionism" (Chapter 2).

The present mainstream thinking of the World Bank is called the "market-friendly approach." According to the *World Development Report 1991*:

1   governments should not intervene in the areas where markets do or can function properly, i.e., the production sector;
2   on the other hand, governments should take an active role in the areas where the market mechanism generally fails to work, e.g., education, health and nutrition, family planning, and investments aimed at poverty alleviation; development of social, economic, administrative and legal infrastructure; protection of the environment; as well as maintenance of a stable macro-economy.

The report introduces a new concept of a "functional approach" to growth. It acknowledges that East Asian economies, by properly combining two sets of policy choices – sound fundamentals and "selective interventions," maintained macroeconomic stability and accomplished the three functions of growth: accumulation, allocation, and productivity (Overview and Chapter 2). This functional approach differs from *laissez-faire* thinking, positively assessing some forms of interventions to enhance the market mechanism; for instance, establishing efficient and secure financial systems, limiting price distortions, promoting basic education, and maintaining openness to foreign technology.

Moreover, it recognizes that some East Asian interventions went beyond helping markets perform better to guiding and, in some cases even bypassing, markets. In perfect markets, all individuals have complete information and pursuing individual interests maximizes welfare for both individuals and society. In reality, market failure caused by imperfect information and insufficient functioning of markets make government intervention necessary. Some East Asian economies, including Japan and South Korea, corrected market failures by establishing coordination mechanisms (e.g., deliberation councils) where the government and private sector exchange information and coordinate investment decisions. However, public–private coordination also involves risks, such as price collusion, limited competition, and rent-seeking. East Asian economies avoided these risks by creating contest-based competition.

From the perspective of replicability, the conclusion of *The East Asian Miracle* can be summarized in the following four points:

1   getting the fundamentals right is essential to achieve economic growth with equity;
2   mild financial repression and directed credit worked in Japan and South Korea;
3   government intervention in export promotion (export-push strategy) worked under the certain conditions;
4   other government interventions, including industrial policy, were generally not successful even in East Asia; hence, it cannot be recommended to other developing countries.

Given that macroeconomic instability and inflation are the primary causes of economic stagnation and poverty in many developing countries, there is no doubt that priority should be placed on "keeping the basics right," as the report concludes. Moreover, the report recommends that the government play an active role in getting the fundamentals right to enhance the market mechanism, not leaving it to the market. While not exactly *laissez-faire*, this line of thinking is based on the neoclassical view and is consistent with current World Bank policy. In this sense, there is nothing radically new here. The report also admits that if implemented with sound fundamentals and an export-push strategy, government interventions to guide and bypass markets under the functional approach can work under certain conditions and thus can be applied to developing countries today. The potentially useful interventions include setting well-defined economic performance criteria with exports as a yardstick, rewarding winners of contest-based competition, and having competent bureaucrats insulated from political pressures monitor performance (Chapter 4).

This is a departure from the traditional neoclassical view which regards all government intervention as harmful to economic growth. I welcome this development because it widens the World Bank's policy menu for possible replication in other developing countries. *The East Asian Miracle* asserts that official interventions (other than export promotion), especially those aimed at selected industries have not been effective (except in Japan), and therefore cannot be transferred to other developing countries (Chapter 6). This negative conclusion regarding industrial policy is reached because the report is still influenced by the neoclassical view. The neoclassicals are particularly opposed to industrial policy. They argue that each country's industrial development must be guided by competitive advantage based on factor endowments and should be realized through the market mechanism, which allocates resources efficiently. They contend that the government is technically incapable of choosing and fostering specific industries. However, competitive advantage should be understood in a dynamic context, not a static one as used in the neoclassical approach. It is theoretically justifiable to select a currently uncompetitive industry that is judged important for an economy's future and accelerate its development using policy instruments.

Many developing countries which produce currently competitive primary commodities (coffee, cocoa, copper, tin, etc.) are suffering from excess global supply and domestic stagnation. To escape from monoculture, industrial promotion is essential. The East Asian experience shows that picking winners is not impossible. For example, Japan succeeded in elevating once-infant industries (e.g., steel, shipbuilding, automobile, electrical machinery, electronics) to the status of internationally competitive industries using import restrictions, policy loans, and preferential tax treatment. These "winners" were not difficult to choose, because Europe and America showed us examples.

In East Asia, each country faced unique conditions and adopted different policies in accordance with its stage of development. In this sense, *The East Asian Miracle*'s conclusion that "there is no East Asian model of rapid growth with equity" (Overview and Chapter 7) is valid. Other developing countries that wish to learn from the East Asian experience also face quite different conditions. Nevertheless, some of the East Asian experiences discussed in the report are applicable, and more useful lessons can be drawn after further studies. Since the report broadens the range of policy choices, the World Bank should make efforts to prescribe policies that take into account country-specific situations instead of applying universally market-oriented policies based on the neoclassical view. Pragmatic and flexible policy response, a key factor in East Asian success, is needed in the World Bank.

Immediately after its publication, *The East Asian Miracle* attracted wide interest and was taken up by various international conferences. The report was mentioned in the communique of the IMF–World Bank Development Committee in September 1993, and the replicability of the Asian experience to Africa was discussed at the African Development Conference. Seminars and symposiums were held all over the world, including a symposium jointly organized by the OECF and the World Bank in Tokyo in December 1993. The Ministry of Finance also co-sponsored a seminar with the IMF and the World Bank in March 1994 titled "Development Strategy for Africa – Can the East Asian Miracle Be

Replicated in Africa?" Furthermore, based on various background papers for this report, the World Bank published *The Lessons of East Asia: Overview of Country Experience* and related country studies in December 1993. In the near future, the quarterly journal *World Development* is to publish "Symposium on the World Bank's *East Asian Miracle Report*," and the Overseas Development Council, a prominent private U.S. think tank, is to produce a brief report that analyzes the report's background and issues. *Institutional Investor* published an interesting inside story titled "The State Strikes Back" in its September 1993 issue. In Japan, Isao Kubota, Deputy-Director General of the International Finance Bureau of the Ministry of Finance, published "The East Asian Miracle – Issues on Recent Development Policy" in MOF's journal *Finance* (December 1992 and January 1994, in Japanese); similarly, I wrote "How to Read the World Bank's *East Asian Miracle*" in the journal of the Economic Planning Agency, *EPS* (February and March 1994, in Japanese).

The East Asian Miracle is a voluminous work, running to 389 pages, including some sophisticated econometric analyses. Furthermore, because the report, like any other World Bank document, went through a series of internal reviews and incorporated numerous comments, consistency has been sacrificed. Despite these problems, in translation we adhered to the original text as closely as possible.

The OECF Study Group on Development Issues, comprised of young officials of OECF and MOF's International Finance Bureau, undertook the translation under my overall supervision. I would like to express my deep thanks to them for undertaking the challenge of this difficult translation and for their daily commitment to their work. Any remaining errors are my responsibility.[6]

Notes

1 Mr. Shiratori edited the Japanese translation of *The East Asian Miracle* [Editors].
2 The conflict over the above-mentioned directed credits was settled when the OECF and the World Bank agreed to set the on-lending rate at the lowest market interest rate in the country in question.
3 Structural adjustment lending operations provide quick-disbursing loans at dealing with short-term balance of payment difficulties, to be disbursed in tranches in accordance with the fulfillment of a set of policy goals, e.g., controlling inflation and liberalizing the trade and financial sectors (so called "conditionality").
4 See Chapter 3 in this volume [Editors].
5 Mr. Summers is currently Undersecretary of International Affairs at the U.S. Department of the Treasury. [In January 1997, he became Deputy Secretary of the Treasury: Editors.]
6 After this, the afterword continues with the member list of the translating team and the indication that certain charts and tables have been omitted from the translation due to space considerations. After consulting Mr. Shiratori, we have decided not to include these passages which are not directly related to the main subject [Editors].

References

Institutional Investor (1993) "The State Strikes Back", September.

Kubota, Isao (1993, 1994) "The East Asian Miracle – Issues on Recent Development Policy," *The Finance*, vol. 29, nos. 9–10, December 1993 and January 1994.

—— (1994)

Overseas Development Council (1994) *Miracle or Design?: Lessons from the East Asian Experiences*, Washington.

Overseas Economic Cooperation Fund (1991) "Issues Related to the World Bank's Approach to Structural Adjustment," Occasional Paper No. 1.

Shiratori, Masaki (1994) "How to Read the World Bank's *East Asian Miracle*," *EPS*, February and March.

World Bank (1991) *World Development Report 1991: The Challenge of Development*, New York: Oxford University Press.

—— (1993a) *The East Asian Miracle: Economic Growth and Public Policy*, New York: Oxford University Press.

—— (1993b) *The Lessons of East Asia: Overview of Country Experience*.

Part II

SOCIETY DOES NOT JUMP

6

UNDERDEVELOPMENT OF THE MARKET ECONOMY AND THE LIMITS OF ECONOMIC LIBERALIZATION[1]

Shigeru Ishikawa

I The issue

In the previous chapter [of *Basic Issues in Development Economics*], we studied the underdevelopment of one type of resource allocation mechanism, the market economy, and its development process, from the viewpoint of the changes in the customary economy.[2] We examined the functions and ultimate disappearance of the customary economy, which complements the weak allocative capacity of underdeveloped markets. However, research on underdeveloped market economies should also include analysis of the underdeveloped state of the market economy itself, independent from the customary economy. The reason for this is as follows. The strength of the customary economy differs from one less developed country (LDC) to another. In some cases, the customary economy was uprooted prematurely by external forces even though the market economy remained severely underdeveloped. An extreme example was the destruction of village communities in the floodplains of Northern China by foreign intruders. Similar devastation visited many LDCs in the colonization process, beginning in the sixteenth century. Even in countries where the customary economy is firmly established, the development of the market economy itself must be explained, whether the customary economy subsequently thrives or weakens.

In sum, our studies should demonstrate that the issue of underdeveloped markets is not a trivial, but a significant factor in describing the development process. As [we have previously shown], however, a fairly large number of studies exist to demonstrate this non-triviality for economies where the customary economy is dominant.

Overall, our study of the underdevelopment of the market economy has produced some conceptual results toward that aspect involving the existence of the customary economy, but still suffers from a lack of progress toward another

87

aspect of proving the empirical relevance of underdeveloped markets from the logic of the market economy itself. Thus, the main purpose of the present chapter is to advance discussion of the underdevelopment of the market economy in the second aspect, by presenting actual significant incidents which I have come across. I intend to do this by describing concrete cases of failed liberalization in China's market-oriented systemic reform (i.e., economic liberalization) since 1978. The failures were caused by the unwarranted optimism of Chinese authorities who expected, quite naively, that highly developed markets would spontaneously emerge once the existing centralized planning system was removed. In other words, they resulted from the remarkable gap between the low actual level of market development in the Chinese economy and the level required for successful implementation of the Chinese government's reform policies.

Before we get to the main theme (section III), a few preliminary considerations will be presented in section II. First, key conceptual findings of my research on underdeveloped markets and their development will be summarized. Additionally, a few important facts related to Chinese liberalization, from which we will later extract actual incidents of failed policies, will be discussed. Of particular importance is the fact that a large number of LDCs initiated similar reforms at about the same time China began its economic liberalization. In section IV, some proposals for future research will be offered on the basis of findings in section III. The appendix to this chapter [not included here – see note 1] is a reproduction of my review article on Professor Chakravarty's new book. In this appendix, I evaluate the evolving roles of planning and liberalization in Indian economic development in comparison to those of China and other East Asian countries. This complements the main argument of the chapter by examining the relevance of factual evidence from China to liberalization problems of India and other dirigiste countries. The appendix also touches on the well-known debate over "plan versus market." While this issue may seem quite distinct from our main objective, we cannot avoid discussing it in our research on underdeveloped markets.

II Preliminary considerations: market and liberalization

1 Concepts of market and the market economy [3]

A few definitions are in order at the outset. In our study, the market economy is defined as an economic system in which mobilization and allocation of all economic resources occur with terms of exchange established through market competition – typically prices – as the principal regulator. Borrowing the terminology of economic systems theory, the market economy is composed of two major spheres, real process and control process.[4] The real process is the mobilization and allocation of resources itself, that is, the process of physical production, while the control process is the act of economic agents directing the real process (including the preliminary task of collecting and processing information). Some control processes are subject to constant institutionalization. The market is one of the key processes which is thus institutionalized in the market economic system. The market is defined as an institutionalized process by which certain products or factors of production are bought and sold among trading participants according to the "market" rule. The market rule in turn is social consent to observe the terms of exchange stipulated in contracts.

The definition of the customary economy as an alternative resource allocation system was given in Chapter 6 [of the original]. The customary economy is an economy where families residing in a certain small areas depend mutually and directly on each other through customary rules to improve their collective welfare. In comparison, the market system can be described as an economy where families residing in a larger area depend on each other only indirectly through markets to further individual motives. This depiction adds another element to the definition of the market economy given above.

The degree of development or underdevelopment of the market economy can be measured comprehensively by indicators spanning both the real and the control spheres, including the number and size of resources mobilized and allocated by prices; the geographic reach of such resource mobilization and allocation; and the uniformity of prices within that geographic area.

As a process of change, the development of the market economy can be analyzed as interaction among its three key components: (1) social division of labor in production; (2) infrastructure for merchandise distribution; and (3) institutions of market exchange.

1 *Social division of labor in production*: development of this aspect can be evaluated by the degree of specialization and cooperation in objects of market transaction (ε), market participants (α), industrial organization for market transactions (ν), and type and scope of markets (μ).

    ε The number of products and factors of production that appear in markets increases as the economy develops. At the same time, many of these products become standardized in quality and specification. Input–output relations among them deepen. Higher levels of technology and knowledge and larger amounts of fixed investments will be required for their production.

    α Individuals and families, as market participants, evolve gradually from a state of self-sufficiency to differentiation of occupation and industrial sectors. Individuals and families specializing in managing enterprises will begin to purchase factors of production from outside the family and evolve into increasingly complex organizations – from proprietorship and cooperatives to unlimited partnership, limited partnership, and joint stock companies.

    ν Interdependent relations among economic agents in product markets will be institutionalized in a way that depends on the particular characteristics of each product – for example, franchise networks, wholesalers, subcontractors, enterprise groups such as *keiretsu*, and oligopoly. Furthermore, markets for factors of production also develop into complex organizations – for example, financial markets organized under a central bank and a labor market that also encompasses the school system.

μ As an economy develops, market types increase from product and credit markets to land and labor markets, each with further divisions and specialization. Moreover, as the market penetrates the economies of local communities, segmented markets with divergent prices will be integrated into national markets with a uniform price for each good.

2 *Physical[5] infrastructure for merchandise distribution*: the means and organizations of merchandise distribution including transportation, communications, commerce, finance, and insurance. Primary market networks in rural areas are one example of such organizations.

3 *Institutions of market exchange*: the minimum requirement under this heading are rules stipulating the protection of property rights and compliance with contracts. As markets develop, the content of property rights and contracts to be protected grows more complex, and restrictive measures to enforce order on competition emerge. As the aspects of ε, α, v, and μ above deepen, new market rules will be created to cover new market activities and internal organizations; for example, joint stock company law, more specialized laws such as banking law and insurance company law, securities exchange law, and labor union law. Market rules first appear as voluntary and autonomous agreements among merchants and subsequently increase their compulsive power by developing into laws and ordinances sanctioned by governmental authority. (Thus, the continuous evolution of the market system offsets transaction costs which tend to rise with the expansion of the scope of economy.)

It should be underscored that the developed markets which we consider here are totally different from the neoclassical conception of a "market under perfect competition." While the neoclassical concept presupposes developed markets, it further assumes a state where competition is played out until Pareto optimality is achieved. Perfect information, homogeneity of goods, price-taking behavior, and free entry and exit are the four conditions characterizing this state. By contrast, as Hayek emphasizes,[6] fierce competition among producers (and merchants) persists in the markets we envision. Competition proceeds through price cuts, quality improvements (i.e., product differentiation), advanced marketing, better information gathering, etc., under intrinsic uncertainty as to the cost curves of rival firms and the preferences of consumers. To prevail over competitors, expansion of organizations to the optimal size becomes imperative.

Another neoclassical concept, "market under imperfect competition," is often mixed up with our concept of an underdeveloped market. However, the two are completely unrelated. Imperfect competition is simply a state of a market that is highly developed yet lacks one of the four conditions of perfect competition mentioned above.

Welfare benefits to the national economy from development of the market economy can be illustrated by a comparison with the previous underdeveloped stage. The greatest benefit comes from the emergence of competitive pressure in Hayek's sense. Benefits will also arise from an increasingly complex social division of labor enabled by the development of market rules. There are many benefits under this category, but most can be explained by gains from integrating previously segmented markets. These gains, in turn, can be approximated by familiar "gains from trade" in the theory of international trade.[7] As to gains from the establishment and development of financial markets, an analogy to gains from capital transfer from a low-productivity, high-saving country to high-productivity, low-saving country can be useful.[8] Economies of scale which arise from vertical division of labor in production are treated by Stigler's famous argument.[9]

2 Economic liberalization and underdeveloped markets

Before we demonstrate the empirical relevance of the underdevelopment of the market economy in Chinese liberalization, the following points should be noted.

First, the economic system to be liberalized in this case is neither a market nor a customary economy. It is a third category of economy which might be called a "socialist economy under centralized planning" – or a "centrally planned economy" in the United Nations terminology. However, it should be duly recognized that the Chinese economic system was, unlike that of the Soviet Union and Eastern Europe in the past, a mixed socialism characterized by extensive remnants of an underdeveloped market economy and a customary economy. Similar systemic mixtures are also detected in many LDCs where the market economy is officially espoused, yet the existing market economy is seriously underdeveloped and subject to vigorous state intervention. I shall call the Chinese system, which shares these features with other LDCs, a "less developed economy under dirigisme."

Second, certain common characteristics are visible in the way governments of dirigiste less developed economies, including China, intervene in the economy. While implementation may differ from one country to another, state intervention in market-based economies is conducted basically in two forms: (1) control of principal industries or enterprises through nationalization; and (2) regulation of private enterprises through a maze of permissions and authorizations for economic activities (entry, capacity expansion, procurement of key inputs and capital goods, distribution of important consumer goods, international trade, foreign exchange trading, etc.). These two forms of control are mainly directed at modern industrial sectors which are considered of paramount importance to economic development. In China, virtually all units of production and management in targeted sectors had been nationalized. Physical production and management of these units were controlled through central and local government directives. Additionally, landed and tenant farmers, who usually remain autonomous units of production and management in most market-based LDCs, were transformed to collective ownership and management in China through land reform and the establishment of cooperatives and people's communes. Chinese agricultural products were also subjected to the fetters of compulsory delivery to the state. (The situation was similar in other socialist LDCs such as Viet Nam and North Korea.) However, these differences should be interpreted as variations in a continuum of economic systems rather than an irreconcilable gap between market and socialism. Indeed, economic control in countries like India and Egypt is intense and pervasive. Apart from their political regime, the Indian and Egyptian systems are not very different from Chinese dirigisme.

Third, since the mid-1970s, efforts toward economic liberalization have been gathering strength in the less developed world under dirigisme, including China, with varying scope and depth, replacing state economic intervention with autonomous management by private firms (and individual farmers) under the market mechanism. The circumstances under which this policy switch was made differ from country to country. China was special in initiating the shift on its own. In most other market-based LDCs, the change was brought about more passively, by accepting the policy advice of the International Monetary Fund (IMF) and the World Bank. Economic liberalization was presented as the key component of "conditionality" attached to balance-of-payments support lending from these international organizations, along with a call for short-term macroeconomic stabilization to reduce inflation and the current-account deficit. These loans were used to cover the external deficits which emerged in these countries in the mid 1970s as a result of exogenous shocks such as oil price hikes, rising interest rates, and recession in developed countries. Liberalization policy, or "structural adjustment," was supposed to be medium-term, and contained a variety of measures – from liberalization of intermediate imports to export promotion, removal of foreign exchange controls, budget reform to cut public expenditure and boost tax revenues, financial reform centered on deregulation of interest rates, and restructuring and privatization of state-owned enterprises. The main message of the IMF and the World Bank, consistent with their original purposes, was the importance of removing dirigisme and promoting the market mechanism and private-sector activities. While Chinese liberalization was initiated internally, it is possible that the decision was partly influenced by the international trend toward liberalization and the resulting access to information on the design of such reforms. (In China, the balance-of-payments crisis and inflation arose as a consequence of economic reform. Thus, "stabilization" came after "liberalization.")

Fourth – we now come to the most crucial point in this subsection – a possible conflict between the central aim of economic liberalization and the reality of underdeveloped markets, discussed earlier, must be considered. Three facts commonly observed behind the liberalization problem of China and other dirigiste LDCs are as follows.

1   The backwardness of economic structure at the time of independence, which these countries tried to remedy through dirigiste economic development, has been relieved to a large extent in recent years. In particular, a large number of modern enterprises have been established and a new industrial sector has emerged.

2   While this purpose of dirigisme is being partly achieved, in parallel, waste and inefficiency associated with dirigisme have worsened, accompanied by surging rent-seeking and directly unproductive profit-seeking activities (which might have emerged through the weakening of the original national resolve toward economic independence), lack of competitive pressure, and declining productivity and profits of enterprises. In some cases, this waste and inefficiency has grown to such an extent that it can repress the fiscal and external balance as well as national consumption.

3   Despite progress toward a more complex economic structure, the market economy still remains seriously underdeveloped. In market-based LDCs, the underdevelopment of markets can be measured relatively easily by the criteria proposed in the previous subsection. In contrast, such measurement is more difficult for socialist LDCs where underdeveloped markets are often concealed. The state of infrastructure for merchandise distribution may be evaluated objectively across different types of LDCs, but the criteria for assessing the social division of labor and institutions of market exchange must be modified for socialist LDCs in order to preserve international comparability. If such adjustment is made, it is suspected that the hidden markets of socialist LDCs would show very low levels of development.

When these three facts are put together, we come to the following conclusion. While liberalization is the correct policy prescription for removing the inefficiencies of dirigisme (we leave open the question of whether complete liberalization should be the ultimate goal), there is always a potential gap between the development of the market economy required for the successful implementation of a particular liberalization measure on the one hand, and the development of the market economy which has actually been achieved on the other. The potential gap varies in size, but can be quite large if the market economy targeted by liberalization policy is close to an ideal *laissez-faire* type.

General arguments aside, what determines the actual size of this gap? First, from a purely economic viewpoint, the ability of economic policy officials to anticipate the size and nature of the potential gap and design a consistent, realistic liberalization program and a medium-term scenario for implementing it in appropriate stages, is crucial. Second, the extent to which the most economically desirable program must be altered to maintain the domestic power balance is also important. Third, when liberalization is prompted by policy advice from the IMF and the World Bank, the nature and quality of the advice on the first two points are critical – how hasty or patient the international organizations are in pursuing their objective of promoting the market mechanism, how their negotiations with national authorities proceed, etc.

Since Chinese liberalization was started on domestic initiative, we can safely ignore the third aspect. On the first point, we must say that Chinese economic policy authorities were naive in their judgment; comprehensive reforms were often launched without carefully designed programs or scenarios. As to the second point, it should be noted that the Chinese political regime permits top-down decision making by the central authority on systemic reforms, partly due to the eradication at the time of Revolution of traditional classes that might have opposed liberalization. However, Chinese dirigisme has spawned a large number of bureaucrats, managers, and workers who benefit from the administrative control and uncompetitive management of state-owned enterprises. They now constitute a major force in resisting radical restructuring of those enterprises. These two points have contributed to the emergence of gaps between policy and reality in many areas of the Chinese economy, some of which will be analyzed in the rest of this chapter.

III Difficulties of economic liberalization: cases from China

1 Reactivated markets and traditional organizations in rural areas

1-A

Beginning in 1978, compulsory state procurement of principal agricultural products was phased out. With reform of the people's communes, family farming reappeared. However, the market structure – distributional infrastructure and rules of market exchange in particular – which re-emerged in Chinese villages as a result of these reforms was, apart from the existing distribution channels of state commercial companies and supply cooperatives, not much different from the traditional marketing system. This system was composed of commercial networks based on *shiji* (weekly market towns) and *shizhen* (daily market towns), and long-distance trade routes for a number of famed local specialties. Nevertheless, in some regions where farm products were increasingly commercialized and local "township and village enterprises" (TVEs) thrived, the market structure of *shiji* and *shizhen* has seen some internal development.

Between 1980 and 1984, China's agricultural and food output increased briskly, at the rate of 3.4–5.4 percent per year. As a consequence, real income per farmer also rose 2.7 times between 1978 and 1986. During the same period, the ratio of agricultural products shipped to non-agricultural sectors, which had been on a long decline, rose from 14.0 percent to 25.6 percent. Per capita consumption of urban workers' households increased 1.8 fold.

In early 1985, some even considered that China was no longer at the stage where development of food and agriculture had to be planned on the basis of people's consumption of coarse grains and poor clothes. Also, the stage was considered overcome in China in which stagnant food and agricultural production acted as constraints on industrialization.[10] Introduction of new crop varieties (particularly of hybrid rice), increased use of chemical fertilizers, and provision of basic agricultural infrastructure such as irrigation and drainage greatly contributed to the increased agricultural output. In addition, it is widely agreed that the good performance of agriculture was also the result of renewed private incentives which came with the resumption of individual farming and increases in state procurement prices for main crops, which had long been suppressed below production costs. (Individual farming was restored by the implementation of the management contract and responsibility system during this period.)

Shiji and *shizhen* are market towns located at the center of traditional primary marketing areas in rural China. As a survey conducted by W. Skinner shows,[11] the primary marketing area covers the range of *xiang* (an administrative village) comprising nearly twenty natural villages, and is in recent years equivalent to the range of a people's commune. *Shiji* is a type of the primary market in which the market opens regularly, once or twice every ten days; *shizhen* is another type of regular market, one which opens every day. The difference between the two depends on the productivity and income of each primary marketing area. These market towns once provided the most important site for exchanging commercial crops and handicrafts produced by largely self-sufficient farmers and manu-factured products from cities. In the late 1950s, however, *shiji* and *shizhen* lost their functions when state commercial companies and supply cooperatives assumed monopoly control of agricultural and food distribution, eliminating private commerce. Only those market towns located in prefectural capitals and headquarters of people's communes survived as administrative centers or advance posts of these state and cooperative commercial operations. With the liberalization of agriculture beginning in 1978, *shiji* and *shizhen* re-emerged.

Private commerce was not the only type of transactions in these revived market towns. According to studies of market towns in southern Jiangsu Province organized by the renowned sociologist Fei Xiaotong,[12] renewed market towns handled several types of trading, including private commerce, state commerce companies and supply cooperatives, collectively owned private commerce, retail departments of TVEs, various service agencies, and family management units. Since state and collective units continued to suffer from organizational rigidity left over from the planning era, they were unable to respond adequately to rising commercial needs. As a result, other channels of trading and transportation, such as market towns and related private agents, expanded rapidly.

Fei's other studies on northern Jiangsu are equally informative. Historically, northern Jiangsu prospered for its prime location on the Great Canal between the economic centers of the Lower Yangtze River Region and Beijing. However, the region reverted to destitute agriculture near the turn of the nineteenth century with the re-routing of commerce partly to the sea lanes and further, at the start of the twentieth century, when newly-opened railroads diminished the canal's significance. In Xuzhou, one such impoverished district, only one *shizhen* (daily market town) existed in every prefectural capital; all other market towns were *shiji* which did not open daily. Only a few districts in northern Jiangsu with a significant transport or economic base (such as Lianyungang, Yancheng, and Yangzhou) boasted more than one *shizhen*, although this was common in southern Jiangsu. The fact that only a small number of prefectures in this region had more than one *shizhen* was reconfirmed in Fei's 1984 study.

Generally speaking, the revival of *shiji* was prompted by an increased marketing of agricultural commodities, while *shizhen*'s re-emergence was supported additionally by the growth of TVEs. (Initially, TVEs meant only those enterprises established and managed by the organizations attached to people's communes. After the endorsement of private entrepreneurship in rural areas in 1984, newly created or converted private units were also counted as TVEs.) In this way, rural markets were revived within the framework of pre-existing traditional systems.

Traditional product markets were linked to the outside world by the layered structure of markets consisting, in ascending order, of primary markets, intermediate markets, and the central market. By contrast, certain local specialties were circulated through unique channels independent of this market structure. Sales and transportation of local specialties were based on personal trust between local merchants and travelling traders (*keshang*), who resided in major markets. The interest of travelling traders was protected by trade associations and associations of neighbouring provinces, both of which were well-known for guild-like solidarity. Cotton cloth of Gaoyang, silk fabrics of Suzhou and Hangzhou, and ceramics of Jingdezhen are examples of such local specialties.[13] It is probable that long-distance trading of these special products was also revived at the time of agricultural liberalization.

Another case of revitalized local industry is rural handicraft producing dress accessories and metal products in Wenzhou, Zhejiang Province, the case which was cited as the Wenzhou model of TVE development in a recent survey by the Economic Research Institute of the Chinese Academy of Social Sciences. Historically, Wenzhou was a densely populated region where farmers traditionally engaged in handicrafts and commerce to supplement their meager agricultural income. Today, population pressure remains high (perhaps higher than in the past), with 89 percent of the local population engaged in agriculture and arable land of a mere 300 square meters per farmer. When agriculture was liberalized, Wenzhou farmers naturally resumed their supplementary business, the success of which critically depended on the re-emergence of long-distance commercial networks. Currently, the city of Wenzhou has 417 markets (of which

10 are specialized markets), and approximately 100,000 farmer-salesmen are dispatched from Wenzhou to all corners of the country.[14]

In this connection, the conclusion of a 1986 study on rural areas by the Agricultural Development Research Center of the State Council should be recalled.[15] This study reports the inability of local governments to satisfy farmers' demand for greater opportunities for merchandise trade which emerged after rural liberalization. Moreover, in the aftermath of price liberalization, local governments often closed down markets, issued directives, and raised prices at the first sign of disorder. Consequently, farmers were forced to take up distribution themselves. However, for farmers, trading proved profitable only within the confines of traditional primary marketing. Beyond this, transaction costs rose sharply as the risk of conducting long-distance business without proper protection of laws and trade associations was enormous. Thus, farmers' entry to inter-regional trade was virtually impossible unless the expected returns were exceptionally high. By contrast, more traditional long-distance merchants could significantly reduce such transaction costs thanks to the existence of personal trust as well as provincial and trade associations.

In the suburbs of large industrial cities such as Jiading Prefecture of Shanghai and Xindu Prefecture of Chengdu, or within a cluster of large and medium-size cities such as Wuxi region of southern Jiangsu, TVEs proliferated by becoming subcontractors of large urban industries. Accordingly, the traditional rural market structure has largely disappeared in these areas.[16] This is the typical process through which primary market-based *shizhen* establish new commercial links with larger cities. It is also consistent with Skinner's idea of "modern change." However, subcontracting relationships do not emerge spontaneously. As Fei Xiaotong's survey of 28 TVE factories in southern Jiangsu indicates, subcontracting is almost always based on a pre-existing personal relationship. It is often established through personal intermediation by retired workers and managers at urban industrial enterprises who return to their native villages.[17]

1-B

However, if the speed of liberalization greatly exceeds the capacity of the market structure which has re-emerged, an increased burden of product distribution and supply–demand adjustment will strain the structure and generate disorder in resource allocation. Two such incidents were reported during the privatization of agricultural services and market deregulation since 1978.

The first such incident was the disruption of state procurement of grain, cotton, and edible oil which began in 1982 and peaked in 1984. This was partly because farmers delivered increased crops, in excess of urban consumption demand. More importantly, supply also greatly exceeded existing transportation and storage capacity. Due to a lack of warehousing, the government had to stockpile as much as 30 million tons of foodstuffs in the open at end-1984. This amounted to one-fifth of total state procurement that year.

The second crisis was created in the aftermath of the first. In 1985, in response to the above confusion, the government rushed to abolish compulsory food delivery to the state, which had continued since the 1950s. Instead, a contract procurement system was introduced where farmers were permitted to sell products to the market after contracted amounts were delivered to the state at official prices. This changed the situation drastically. In cities, and later also in rural areas, "food crises" arose because people were uncertain whether the availability of food was guaranteed under the new system.[18] The immediate cause of the crisis was farmers' refusal to deliver food to the state at prices lower than those prevailing in the market, as the contract required. (In 1985, total state procurement of foodstuffs declined by 26 million tons, or 18 percent, from the previous year.)

Since 1985, food production has stagnated. Output in 1988 failed to reach 1984 levels. The ratio of agricultural products shipped to non-agricultural sectors stopped rising and fluctuated erratically. The reasons for the recent agricultural stagnation are many, and one of them is examined in the next subsection; nonetheless, the disruption of product distribution was certainly the most direct cause.

2 Village government or village community: a prerequisite for a market economy

2-A

In market-oriented reforms, deregulation allows each individual to exert his or her economic creativity and talent to the fullest extent in the domain of *individual action*. At the same time, such individual action must be supported by a mechanism of *collective action* to make possible appropriate investment in social overhead capital and undertaking of joint activities for conducting and servicing current production (e.g., replanting and harvesting, crop protection, purchase of fertilizers, and marketing of rice). As for Chinese agricultural society before Revolution, a survey of rural society in the Northern Plains conducted during World War II by the South Manchurian Railway Company's Northern China Economic Research Institute showed that the authority of local governments and village communities was too weak to support organization of collective action. However, this observation based on dry farming of the Northern Plains cannot be generalized to agriculture dependent on irrigation in the rest of the country. Even so, if we can tentatively conclude that Chinese villages tend to operate with relatively low levels of collective action, one explanation lies in history. During the Ming Dynasty (1368–1644), irrigation works in the rice paddy regions of Southern China were constructed with compulsory labor mobilized under the *lijia* system[19] administered by local governments and under the supervision of resident landlords who cultivated land. Toward the end of the Ming Dynasty, resident landlords were replaced by absentee landlords who lived in remote cities.[20] With this the *lijia* system itself disintegrated, and irrigation and flood control facilities fell into ruins. The dilapidation of rural infrastructure was not reversed by the Qing Dynasty [1644–1912] or the Republic of China. (Rice output per acre in the 1930s did not exceed the highs achieved during the Song and Ming Dynasties.) From this perspective, it can be argued that one of the historical functions of the people's communes established in the 1950s was to fundamentally restore those dilapidated irrigation and flood control facilities in order to achieve a break-through in land productivity, which had stagnated for so long.

The concept of *collective action*, its inconsistency with *individual action*, and its relationship with community and government were all examined in Chapter 1 [not included] and thus shall not be repeated here.

We will be highly selective in reviewing historical evidence. First, the above-mentioned survey of the rural Northern Plains by the South Manchurian Railway Company[21] was conducted in Hebei and Shandong Provinces during 1939–41 and later published as *Survey on Chinese Rural Practices* (six volumes, Iwanami Shoten, 1952–58). Using these data, Yuji Muramatsu investigated the social and economic structure of Chinese rural villages in his *Social Structure of the Chinese Economy* (Toyo Keizai Shimposha, 1949). Muramatsu concluded that (1) pre-fectural governments were interested only in extracting taxes, which were partly used to support the "patrimonial" officials who doubled as private retainers of the prefectural governor; (2) the most important functions of village governments were to hire guards against crop theft and levy charges; they played no further function in communal activities; (3) the basic social unit was the family and communal restrictions were virtually non-existent; farmers behaved freely and competitively. However, another prewar study by Motonosuke Amano, *Regional Development of Chinese Agriculture* (Tokyo, Ryukei Shoten, 1979, and especially appendix to Part IV, "Irrigation practices in China"), covering regions with flood control and irrigation, found strong rural communities and collective practices in the construction, maintenance, and utilization of water-use facilities. Moreover, governments in these regions supervised these activities and coordinated water use among localities. As to water control and use during the Ming and Qing Dynasties, Akira Morita's *Study on Irrigation in the Qing Period* analyzes water projects and implementing organizations in relation to the village and the state. His book also offers concrete evidence on the transformation of the *lijia* system in different regions.[22]

2-B

After the Revolution, the decision-making unit for agricultural production and management rapidly expanded in scale. No sooner had land reform aimed at creating landed farmers been completed in 1952, than Chinese agricultural units were reorganized into "mutual aid teams" (consisting of neighbors), "primary agricultural production cooperatives" (collectivization of a natural village), "advanced agricultural production cooperatives" (collection of roughly ten primary cooperatives), and finally, by 1958, into the huge "people's communes" of the early years, which also served as the lowest level of state administration. Enlargement of agricultural production units was supposed to facilitate the planning and mobilization of labor and materials for flood control and irrigation projects, leading to an increase in agricultural output and subsequent delivery to the state. The thinking was that the smaller the number of organizations the government had to deal with, the more efficient its policy would be.[23] However, excessive expansion and forced collectivization erased farmers' incentive to work. In response, the government resorted to compulsory delivery of food during the Great Leap Forward of 1958–59, which led to massive starvation.

2-C

The dismal failure of the Great Leap Forward led the government in 1961 to modify the system of people's communes by introducing the "three-level owner-ship system" under which management authority was delegated, as the name suggests to three levels: "people's communes," that is, management committees which were scaled back to the size of former administrative villages; "production brigades" the size of former advanced agricultural production cooperatives; and "production teams" the size of former primary agricultural production cooperatives. At least in theory, this arrangement should have been effective in promoting Chinese agricultural policy – if the production team functioned as a united village community organizing collective action for mutual welfare, production, and investment; and if production brigades and people's communes performed similar services at higher levels under a favorable political environment (in particular, if officials of higher units had the trust of production teams they supervised).

It is conceivable that there are cases in which the system fails to function as supposed. First, the output of production teams might be so low that the incentive for collective production and investment hardly emerged. Second, due to political antagonism, collective action at the levels of production brigades and people's communes might not materialize. The performance of this system was in practice mixed, in light of actual agricultural output during the 1970s. Successes and failures were observed in different proportions across different regions. However, even in unsuccessful cases, the role of people's communes in administering at least the minimum level of economic management – including the provision of services related to agricultural production – should be duly recognized.

Subsection 2-A suggested a clear regional difference in the strength of rural communal practices between the Northern Plains and southern rice-growing regions of China. In this connection, I would like to advance my "pseudo-community" hypothesis, that even a loosely associated natural village will turn into a more united organization when confronted with a common external enemy or internal pressure.[24] Within a natural village, the "free rider" problem often associated with collective action rarely emerges. The most fundamental function of a village community is mutual assistance and sharing of income and work. This function is partly duplicated in the labor remuneration system (*gongfenzhi*) adopted by production teams. On the other hand, it is not so easy to produce clear evidence of collective action which was expanded to the levels of production brigades and people's communes under a favorable political climate. Nonetheless, a recent World Bank study on TVEs is highly suggestive.[25] The study reports that, in regions where industrial enterprises attached to people's communes and production brigades saw early development, TVEs (which were created from such enterprises) took the alleviation of income disparity into consideration in allocating jobs and duties; furthermore, township governments also paid attention to regional gaps in family income when deciding the location of new enterprises. More recently, production teams and related *gongfenzhi* were abolished as the agricultural management and contract system was introduced. One can interpret this to mean that the income equalization function of the former system is now performed through a different mechanism under the new system.

Regional differences in the effectiveness of the "three-level ownership system" can be inferred also by the process by which the agricultural management and contract system was adopted. This new system was officially and nationally recognized in the draft constitution announced in early 1982 and applied to the entire country in 1983. Prior to this, the initial reform program on agricultural production and management units, which was a part of a comprehensive agricultural reform, aimed at strengthening production teams as the base unit of the existing three-level ownership system. The agricultural management and contract system (then called *baochan daohu* or *baogan daohu*) and similar arrangements for reviving family farming were presented as exceptional measures to invigorate agriculture in mountainous or remote areas with extremely low productivity, or in politically troubled areas.[26] These "exceptional" arrangements started to spread nationwide, partly because of a green light from the party secretaries of Sichuan, Anhui, and other provinces beginning in 1977. But a more significant reason was the rise in mid-1981 of a local mass movement demanding those arrangements in provinces with relatively low productivity. By contrast, regions (such as southern Jiangsu) which had already succeeded in capital accumulation at each level of the three-level ownership system and achieved significant improvement in agricultural productivity balked at what was, in effect, a dismantling of production teams. The agricultural management and contract system was introduced to these regions only after the official proclamation of 1982 and through "guidance from a higher authority."[27] Incidentally, "politically troubled areas" mentioned above seems to imply those areas where mutual trust between high officials and the masses had been lost.

2-D

The reform of the people's commune system consisted of two main pillars: replacement of collective production by the agricultural management and contract system, effectively restoring family farming; and returning the administrative functions of the people's communes to township (*xiang*) governments. This reform was part of a comprehensive program for the market-oriented development of agriculture and farming families. Generally speaking, the Chinese government was overly confident about the effectiveness of this policy shift. The government supposed that the admission of farm households as independent parties under agricultural management contracts and liberating them from the onerous production and delivery requirements of people's communes would automatically stimulate their growth as independent management units. It was further expected that collective action hitherto organized by communes, brigades, and teams, as well as communes' economic management functions in supplying production services, would soon be replaced by specialized and commercially operated proprietorships or partnerships formed by independent farmers.

However, such optimism was not borne out by reality. For example, while the *de facto* dismantling of production teams was a correct measure to reinstall private incentives for productivity improvement, it also had the negative effect of suppressing scale economies in regions such as southern Jiangsu where high accumulation and productivity had already been achieved under the previous system. Moreover, in many regions, the new system greatly aggravated income disparities among production team members and destroyed the previous social welfare mechanism.

Even more serious problems arose from the separation of administrative functions from people's communes. In certain areas, several functions required for the normal operation of farm economies simply evaporated. Many aspects of collective action in production, distribution, and finance previously undertaken by the top-down economic management mechanism of people's communes were left unattended. For instance, since no one controlled the use and storage of chemical fertilizers, cases of chemical poisoning and even deaths were frequently reported. Another difficulty arose in the shipment of agricultural products, as discussed above. Delay or stoppage in the organized maintenance and construction of irrigation systems, confusion in the management and use of these systems, discontinuation of joint purchases of materials and inputs, and termination of collective welfare services, were all caused by the transition to the new system. Total area under irrigation (including irrigation by electric pumping) has stagnated and even declined since its peak year 1979.

The Chinese government's blueprint for market-oriented reform of agriculture and farm economies consisted of the following points: (1) all activities originally performed by individual farmers should be returned to individual farmers; (2) productive services with scale economies which cannot be supplied by individual farmers should be provided by private entrepreneurs; (3) construction, maintenance, and management of basic infrastructure such as large- and medium-scale flood control and irrigation projects, and public works which cannot be handled by the private sector, should be implemented by the state with adequate provision of capital and current expenditures from the state budget; and (4) beyond that, the state's role should be confined to macroeconomic management, administrative coordination, and monitoring activities (1) and (2) above. This blueprint reminds us of a model of agricultural society in highly developed industrial countries.[28] The government may have contemplated a transitional period and phased implementation of this blueprint. In reality, however, the blueprint was often put into practice abruptly without proper preparation, which inevitably caused confusion.

As the problems created by hasty reform were recognized, re-evaluation of the multiple functions previously performed by people's communes began, as can be seen in the writings of Chen Yizi and others at the Institute for Restructuring the Economic System and You Mingquan of the Agricultural Development Research Center. Liu Zhenwei's paper published in the Chinese Communist Party organ *Hongqi* should also be counted as one such contribution.[29] The paper by Chen Yizi and others classifies rural economic activities into "economic functions that should be performed directly by a large number of decentralized producers and production units" such as allocation of labor, choice of technology suitable for each tract of land, and division of income into consumption and saving; and "economic and social functions not directly performed by these units."

The former functions have already been transferred from people's communes to individual farmers by the introduction of the "agricultural contract production responsibility system." (Collectively held assets of production teams were redistributed among team members. Farmland was leased to farmers.)

The latter functions were more difficult to reassign. It must first be noted that these functions were originally composed of collective production-related activities by communes and brigades on the one hand, and the economic management functions of people's communes (management committees) as an administrative authority on the other. On this last point, people's communes were the lowest administrative unit in the centralized chain of economic command which extended from the center to provinces, prefectures, and communes. Three types of administration under this chain of command existed: (1) production-related administration such as veterinary stations, technical extension stations, crop protection stations, business management stations, tractor stations, and irrigation control agencies; (2) distributional administration such as supply cooperatives, food procurement agencies, and production data companies; and (3) financial administration such as agricultural banks and credit cooperatives.

Under the new system, collectively managed production units and collectively owned assets of communes and brigades were supposed to be transferred to new economic cooperative units or companies at the township (*zhen*) level. Some of the economic management functions of communes, at the lowest level of centralized administration, were also expected to be taken up by newly organized and independent management units. For example, crop protection companies, special crop protection teams emerged as well as farmers taking on the spraying, etc. for a locality. The remaining functions were to be performed by newly created *xiang* governments, at least for a time.

In reality, the transition did not go smoothly. Few communes succeeded in' transferring authority separately to *xiang* governments and business organizations created at the *xiang* level. In most cases, separation was incomplete, as business organizations were absorbed by new *xiang* governments and stopped functioning as commercial units. Commune administrative functions were simply terminated rather than transferred to new management systems. Most stations were abandoned and personnel were dispersed. Stations not disbanded were swamped with a greatly increased work load as the nature of their clientele shifted from production teams to individual farmers. The accidents and anomalies cited above were caused by these circumstances.

3 Creating product markets for large urban industries: a new challenge

3-A

"Large urban industries" include approximately 9,900 enterprises, of which about 2,900 are large-scale industrial enterprises by Chinese definition, with the rest being roughly speaking, medium-size industrial enterprises. While large urban industries are small in number relative to the total of 747,000 industrial enterprises, they were built as a technological springboard for the economic modernization of the People's Republic of China. The government put its heart and soul into their creation and development. Because of this, large urban industries were born and nurtured under the system of centralized material planning and have never known any markets. The question we ask here is: what kind of markets emerged for their products in response to market-oriented reform and liberalization?

A large number of large urban industries were enterprises requisitioned from the Nationalist government; in turn, many of these had been established by Japanese foreign direct investment. However, Japanese enterprises in the Northeastern Region cannot be regarded as the origin of large urban industries due to the postwar removal of production facilities to the Soviet Union, personnel changes, and subsequent reorganization and expansion. Private enterprises of considerable size had existed in modern industries such as textiles, chemicals, and machinery since the 1930s, but they were absorbed into the state sector in the "movement toward joint public–private enterprises" in the mid-1950s and the Great Leap Forward of 1958.[30]

The Chinese machinery industry dates back to the mid-nineteenth century treaties that opened Shanghai, Tianjin, and other ports to foreign commerce. Growth in the machinery industry, which mostly consisted of small- and medium-sized enterprises, was based on intra-industry division of labor and supported by traditional trade and craft guilds. Dailong Machine Factory, a large advanced enterprise producing a full range of modern spinning and weaving machines by the end of the 1930s, was an exceptional case. This factory was merged with neighboring state-owned enterprises during the movement toward joint public–private enterprises and was converted to manufacturing oil rigs – then urgently needed – with an increasing infusion of state money.[31]

3-B

Prior to economic liberalization, large urban industries operated as state-owned enterprises under centralized planning as in the Soviet Union. Management authority, which would be exercised by individual enterprises under the market economy, was concentrated in the government's hand. Allocation, production, sales, and investment (especially so-called "basic construction investment") of key production goods – raw materials and energy in particular – were determined by physical indicators issued by the State Planning Commission on the basis of national economic plans, and administered through central government's departments and local governments. (Allocation and sales of these inputs were directed by the State Bureau of Supplies, while consumer goods were sold through state commercial companies.) The design of collective plans was essentially the same in China as in the Soviet Union: once the output target for high growth was set, attention was mainly focused on the supply-and-demand balance of production goods for achieving that target. (A methodology known as the "material balance method" existed for the execution of this planning but had not been fully adopted in China.) Neither the rationality of the price system nor equivalence of supply and demand under that price system was a concern. Under material planning, prices were needed only for computational purposes. (In China, the price system of the early 1950s continued to be used with little adjustment. Consequently, shifts in economic structure significantly distorted the price and cost relations.) Moreover, organizations for planning and administration were separated vertically ("*tiaotiao*") and horizontally ("*kuaikuai*"), which further impeded the required flows of materials and capital.[32]

3-C

Liberalization measures which granted freer product markets to large urban industries were introduced during the 1981–82 Economic Adjustment Period, with the aim of curbing an overheated investment boom which began in 1978. Directive plans specified output levels far below production capacity for machinery and other industries, forcing the enterprises to plan and market the remaining output on their own. We do not have sufficient data on the supply-and-demand balance after this policy change. At any rate, after market-oriented reform of the modern industrial sector began in 1984, large urban industries were governed by two separate principles: the command economy subject to directive plans and the market mechanism which allowed autonomous decision-making by individual enterprises in response to market conditions. The government controlled the former through traditional means of directive allocation, production, and sales, while the latter was, at least officially, controlled indirectly through macroeconomic management. From the viewpoint of price policy, "adjustment by command" was based on existing official prices and "adjustment by market" was effected via actual market prices. This hybrid system was called *shuangguizhi*, meaning duality. Relative weights of the two mechanisms differed depending on phases (i.e., allocation, production, or sales) and from one industry or product to another. The adoption of *shuangguizhi* and its uneven application can be explained by the difficulty in replacing the confused price system by a more rational one. Under the existing price system, market conditions (i.e., excess supply or demand) differed significantly from product to product. It is therefore necessary to consider the response of enterprises to this partial liberalization by different product groups.

Only little evidence is available on the extent to which the existing price system has been distorted. Nonetheless, the following 1978 statistics should be sufficiently accurate indicators of the degree of price distortion today, since only minor revisions have been made in the official price list since that year. Table 6.1 presents the profit-to-wage, profit-to-cost, and profit-to-capital ratios (before-tax profit divided by wage payments, production cost, and fixed plus liquid assets, respectively) of state-owned enterprises by industry. These ratios are expressed in a standardized index with the national average equal to 100.[33] The consistency of the price system would be best approximated by the equalization of profit-to-capital ratios across industries. (However, if one accepts the production cost theory of Marxian economics and insists on the labor theory of value, either the profit-to-wage or profit-to-cost ratio would be a better approximation.) By this criterion, raw materials and energy are generally underpriced, and manufactured goods, especially consumer durables, are highly overpriced.

In China, as in other socialist countries, given that plans are not in practice expected to achieve consistency, directive plan targets are determined through bargaining between enterprises and their supervising authorities. Such bargaining often leads to different types of subordination to supervising authorities. In China, room for bargaining seems greater than in other socialist countries since the material balance method is applied much less strictly. Bargaining (*taojia huanjia*) as well as the vertical and horizontal separation of organizations for planning and administration tend to introduce behavioral patterns typical of the customary economy into the collective system. These practices give rise to interest groups which benefit from the existing system. If these groups are not eliminated when the socialist system is transformed into the market economic system, they will become rent-seekers and directly unproductive profit-seekers in the new economic regime.

Table 6.1 China: indices of profitability by industry

	Profit-to-wage ratio	Profit-to-cost ratio	Profit-to-capital ratio
Average of all state-owned enterprises	100.0	100.0	100.0
Coke	5.9	18.5	11.5
Crude oil	588.4	577.0	310.8
Refined oil	1,242.4	166.3	416.3
Electricity (for use by key industries)	455.7	280.5	98.4
Steel (for use by key industries)	148.1	123.8	84.5
Rolling mills	504.2	130.7	573.0
Iron ore	69.2	144.7	43.6
Aluminum	242.8	203.4	118.8
Tin	13.1	39.2	16.7
Cement	83.7	82.9	47.5
Synthetic fiber	664.5	177.2	169.6
Cotton cloth	137.6	58.0	493.2
Bicycles (by large enterprises)	373.3	139.7	606.4
Watches	803.1	813.4	654.1
Sewing machines (by large enterprises)	249.3	135.4	513.7
Sewing machine parts	28.7	75.8	52.7
Matches	24.0	48.6	80.8
Flashlights	232.3	192.4	646.0
Heavy machinery	34.2	51.0	15.9
Electrical appliances	160.2	166.3	131.9

Source: H Jianzhang *et al.* "Economic System Reform Requires the Use of Production Cost as the Basis of Industrial Pricing," *Chinese Social Sciences*, 1981, no. 1 (in Chinese).

3-D

Raw materials (steel, nonferrous metals, wood, etc.), coal, oil, and electricity form one group of commodities which are underpriced relative to their production costs. Manufacturers who use these raw materials and energy constantly face shortage. Liberalization measures permitted producers of these inputs to sell output in excess of the level stipulated by the plan. Gains from these sales were supposed to cover losses incurred through state procurement, stimulating production. However, operational departments at various levels of government are reluctant to relinquish the supply procurement system based on directive plans. As a result, the system of vertically and horizontally separated administration of supply networks, headed by departments of the central government and extending to provincial and municipal governments, functions as before with little substantial change. This can be seen in the continued dominance of resources under directive control.

So what did liberalization achieve? While policy makers hoped for an increase in voluntary sales of output over and above plan requirements, what really happened was the remarkable reversion of "voluntary" sales into the hands of local governments and related departments of the central government.

These authorities use such extra inputs to obtain energy and raw materials needed by production units under their jurisdiction in barter trade with other departments or provincial governments. Although part of the output assigned to the market is actually sold at market prices which are many times higher than the official prices, such transactions remain only a small portion of total turnover.

This raises the question of whether manufacturing firms are prepared to develop an efficient marketing system for their products when an ever larger part of them begin to be subjected to true market discipline, and what kind of assistance can be expected from the nationwide distribution network of the State Bureau of Supplies which used to handle the planned allocation of production goods. Furthermore, illegal sales of goods in short supply by government organizations and officials (*guandao*) are rapidly rising.[34] Often, these sales are made through various "companies" established by official organizations. While these illegal sales are caused undoubtedly by the enormous gap between official and market prices, their wide popularity is further explained by serious deficiency in market networks which are totally incapable of handling surging demand.

Official statements of the Chinese government stress the rapid reduction of state management over key production inputs. The number of key inputs under state control ("materials under the state's central allocation") declined sharply from 256 in 1980 to a mere 20 in 1987. As a result, the proportion of state allocation in total domestic production also declined for each individual input. Between 1980 and 1987, the above ratio fell from 74.3 to 47.1 percent for steel, from 57.9 to 47.2 percent for coal, and from 80.9 to 27.6 percent for wood. However, besides state allocation by the State Planning Commission, these goods are also subject to official control by central departments and local governments ("materials under local management"). Thus, the reduction of state allocation in the former sense does not automatically produce market-based transactions. The removal of steel (or any other key inputs) from the state allocation list should not therefore be taken at face value due to the existence of other non-market based distribution channels.

According to the 1984 national survey of 429 large state-owned enterprises by the Institute for Restructuring the Economic System, 86 percent of total amount marketed in basic raw materials was subject to planned allocation by various levels of government, 4 percent was purchased from commercial and materials departments on a selective purchase basis, and the remaining 10 percent was sold by producers themselves. No comprehensive data exist on the further division of planned allocation into allocation by the state, departments of the central government, and local governments. Among the sampled enterprises, the first two allocation mechanisms covered 54 percent of output of basic raw materials, and the rest was controlled by provincial and municipal governments.[35] It is suspected that similar ratios have continued to prevail since 1984, because central government's departments and local governments have been eager to seize inputs released from state control and even resources earmarked for market-based distribution. They are desperate to secure raw materials for the normal operation of enterprises under their control. When a curtailment of planned allocation to them is announced, they raise no objection officially. Nonetheless, they bargain very hard with the State Planning Commission to avert any such reduction by stressing the strategic importance of the enterprises under their jurisdiction.[36] Recapture of commodities liberalized from state planning occurs from the same motive.

Difficulty in releasing key production inputs to market-based distribution is encountered even by the remaining output which is supposed to be at enterprises' disposal. The following numbers are informative. In 1986, total "own-account sales" by the four largest Chinese steel makers – Anshan, Benxihu, Shoudu, and Taiyuan – amounted to 1.41 million tons. Of this, 0.52 million tons were retained by local governments, 0.21 million went to compensation trade, 0.153 million were used in barter exchange for materials and capital equipment, 0.340 million were used in barter exchange for necessities of life, 0.005 million were earmarked to repay advance loans for inputs, and only 0.137 million were sold in retail markets of steel products. Thus, true retail sales were less than 10 percent of the reported "own-account" sales. The rest was mostly used by enterprises themselves and local governments to secure necessary inputs and capital equipment, which were in short supply.[37] From this, Zhao Renwei concludes that market-oriented reforms are inadvertently encouraging the barter economy.[38]

3-E

In comparison with goods in short supply, some products are at the opposite end of the commodity spectrum, with supply sufficiently large or even excessive relative to demand. Many goods in machinery, and light and textile industries belong to this group. For example, clothing and a number of consumer durables, including bicycles, sewing machines, wrist watches, electric fans, and washing machines, are clearly in oversupply. In particular, among all enterprises, those under the Department of Machinery Industry suffered the largest reduction in targeted output during the adjustment period of 1981–83 and faced an acute need to develop new markets. Since 1984, targeted output of intermediate products such as investment goods (including machinery and equipment), machine parts, sundry processed materials, and cotton cloth has remained small relative to market-oriented output.[39] For these products, vertical and horizontal separation of administrative control has already disappeared, and nationally integrated markets are beginning to emerge.

How do existing large enterprises develop new markets, how do entries occur, and how are prices determined in these emerging markets? At first, individual enterprises explore new markets by renewing contacts with previous suppliers and establishing retail divisions in consumption centers. This proved ineffective and led to the accumulation of unsold stock and slow turnover of liquid capital.

The mounting pressure of commercial expenses severely constrained enterprise finances. Thus, individual efforts were soon replaced by a new method of marketing called "industrial and commercial association," which relied on the existing state wholesale distribution network. According to the 1985 survey of 400 industrial enterprises by the Institute for Restructuring the Economic System, autonomous sales at these enterprises accounted for 48 percent of total sales, while 38 percent was dependent on the state wholesale distribution network.[40] Under the new market environment, even state commercial companies and enterprises held by the State Bureau of Supplies must struggle for survival, and they are naturally eager to tie up with industrial enterprises. However, reports to date suggest that such associations often fail to be competitive in the national market. A few exceptions do exist, but those are confined to inter-provincial "enterprise groups"[41] of related enterprises led by large manufacturers with well recognized brand names – such as *Jiefang* trucks, *Dongfeng* jeeps, and *Fenghuang* bicycles. It will be quite some time before we will see a vibrant Chinese market economy in which large- and medium-sized industrial enterprises compete with each other based on marketing activities of their own or with the help of commercial companies.

Examples of concrete marketing activities are reported in the 1986 survey of the machinery industry in Shandong Province by the Institute for Restructuring the Economic System.[42] The total sales of the machinery industry under the jurisdiction of Shandong provincial government were 3.94 billion yuan in 1985 (of which 10 percent was attributed to directive plans). Of this amount, 57.4 percent was sold by enterprises themselves, 39.3 percent through the state supplies network, and 3.2 percent by provinces and municipalities. Geographically, 75 percent was sold within Shandong Province while the remaining 25 percent was shipped outside. One of the products sold outside the province was the 25-horse-power tractor, which monopolized the local market and won a 50 percent market share in Hubei Province. Small 12-horse-power four-wheel tractors were also successfully marketed in eleven provinces, raising production from 20,000 to 113,000 units in five years. On the other hand, the local market for 50-horse-power tractors was completely dominated by Shanghai producers. Of the two 50-horse-power tractor producers in Shandong, established in the late 1970s with capacity of 5,000 units each, one went bankrupt and the other switched to another line of business. Shandong Province's success in creating nationally integrated markets for the first two products was largely due to the formation of intra- and inter-provincial economic associations. Intra-provincial economic associations were formed only for those goods in which Shandong had a comparative advantage and by featuring new products made by well-known and high-quality producers. In the case of small four-wheel tractors, thirteen principal enterprises were organized into an association at the behest of the machinery division of the provincial government. Externally, inter-provincial associations were sought to link up with the providers of superior technology in order to boost competitiveness.

"Industrial and commercial associations" (or "economic associations") were created to bypass existing vertical and horizontal administrative barriers, encourage industrial linkage across sectors and regions, and deepen cooperation in production through specialization. Adoption of this policy was compelled by the tremendous appetite for business expansion by large growth-oriented enterprises, including No. 1 Automobile Company, producer of *Jiefang* trucks; No. 2 Automobile Company, producer of *Dongfeng* jeeps; Shanghai Bicycle Factory, producer of *Yongjiu* and *Fenghuang* bicycles; and Bicycle No. 3 Factory of Shanghai. These enterprises formed "enterprise groups," which are an advanced type of industrial and commercial association. Unlike Japanese enterprise groups, they remained purely industrial associations without any guidance from financial institutions. Industrial groups now number 2,000, a great majority of which belong to the machinery, electronics, spinning, and light industries.[43] However, the creation of product markets for these industries needs to be supported by similar joint activities of smaller industrial and commercial associations. Moreover, the importance of marketing and investment in human resources must also be recognized.[44] As marketing activities expand to a large number of sectors and regions, effective implementation of civil, enterprise, bankruptcy, and contract laws, as well as a social agreement on the importance of strictly observing these laws, will become crucial.[45]

4 Reform for revitalizing enterprises and the labor market

4-A

The labor market faced by large urban industries remains even more primitive than the product market. Despite this, radical decentralization and liberalization measures to convert existing enterprises into autonomous management units were rapidly introduced. This haste is creating a horde of unanticipated problems that impede the overall progress of economic reform, such as an explosion of wage funds and acceleration of inflation. We will examine this issue below.

In addition to the liberalization of allocation, production, and sales discussed above, policies aimed at revitalizing enterprises also included a series of enterprise finance reform in which enterprises with good performance, measured by profits, are given the right to retain and freely use a certain proportion of profits. This was intended to give enterprise managers and workers incentives to work harder and produce more. However, since prices were still distorted, evaluation of enterprise performance remained arbitrary and subject to negotiation. In the period prior to World War II, the Chinese labor market was characterized by a traditional labor system featuring a master, workmen, and apprentices at handicraft factories organized by a wholesaler. Even at modern factories, workers were recruited as private worker groups organized by job mediators called *gongtou*.[46] Given the technological progress achieved since then, it is unthinkable that the Chinese labor market and organizations will revert to such an outmoded state, even with full liberalization. Instead, since the 1980s, the Chinese labor market has been more strongly influenced by the employment and wage practices established during the preceding era of centralized planning. Namely, they have been driven by full-employment policy consisting of two components: first, a system of low but egalitarian wages undifferentiated by occupation or skill and supplemented by social welfare benefits; and second, the system of lifetime employment at a specific enterprise. These practices were supported institutionally by the fact that local labor authorities, and not enterprises themselves, had the right to hire and fire workers and determine their wages. Despite various economic changes, these institutions survived until the late 1970s. As a result, Chinese enterprises retained the characteristics of welfare communities, and worker expectations of equal treatment across different enterprises were firmly established.

Enterprise finance reform was aimed at eliminating the situation of total dependency where all expenses were covered by the state budget and all profits were surrendered to the state coffer. In 1979, enterprises were allowed to retain a portion of profits. Subsequently, in 1983, a system of *ligaishui* was introduced in which previous profit surrender to the state were converted to income tax and the remaining profit was divided between the enterprise and the state.[47] Thus, the new tax system created retained profits which depended on enterprise performance and could be used to supplement production development funds, collective welfare funds, or employee bonuses, in the proportions chosen by the enterprises. As enterprise finance reform progressed, the enterprise tax burden was reduced and a large amount of profits began to be retained by enterprises. Retained profits of state-owned enterprises steadily rose from 9.6 billion yuan in 1979 to 46.2 billion yuan in 1985. During the same period, the ratio of retained profits to total realized profits also jumped from 12.3 percent to 39.0 percent.[48] In parallel to the new tax system, an enterprise management contract system similar to the agricultural management and contract system was introduced on a trial basis in 1982 and nationally adopted in 1987. This further stimulated the profit motive of enterprises.

The wage and employment policy of state-owned enterprises[49] dates back to the 1956 wage reform which imposed a "rationally low wage policy" (or "five people sharing food prepared for three people") in order to employ the large pool of surplus labor in the public sector at the minimum subsistence level. The low wage policy was effectively maintained until 1977. Full employment policy was also sustained, partly through strict control on rural–urban migration. During the Cultural Revolution, the organized migration of 17 million high school students from cities to rural villages also helped to ease unemployment pressure in urban areas. When the Cultural Revolution ended and these young people returned to the cities in droves, the government ordered employers to absorb the young family members or relatives of their workers. This increased labor redundancy within the enterprises but kept unemployment in society to a minimum. Wage restraint was also pursued with resolve. The cumulative increase in the average wage between 1956 and 1977 did not even amount a one-level increase in the original eight-level standard wage schedule. As to wage differentials among individuals, workers hired before the 1956 schedule went into effect, continued to run the gamut of all eight levels, but among later recruits there was virtually no wage disparity while the system lasted.[50]

In studying Chinese wages, we must track the movement of total wage payments, of which standard wage is but one component. Until 1977, total wage payments consisted of "wage funds" paid directly to workers (the standard wage plus various incentive bonuses and allowances) and "wage supplements" (fringe benefits) paid by enterprises (contribution to welfare funds, workers' insurance payments, etc.). "Wage funds," including bonuses which were eliminated during the Cultural Revolution, were strictly controlled as one of the key indicators of directive control. "Wage supplements" were also kept to a certain percentage of total wages – about 20 percent during the first five-year plan and 14.3 percent in 1978. "Wage supplements" were particularly important in enhancing the communal characteristics of enterprises. Part of the welfare fund was used for purchasing apartments, to which all workers were entitled. In addition, severance payments at retirement and old-age pensions bolstered enterprises as a place of lifetime employment.[51]

Under the revised wage policy of 1978, some upward revisions in the standard wage schedule were seen during 1978–80, but fundamentally the situation remained the same. A more significant reform was introduced in 1985, making salaries dependent on duties performed at each administrative and production unit. For workers, this meant that faster increases than the standard wage schedule were officially permitted in incentive bonuses, various payments, workers' insurance, and welfare funds. Between 1978 and 1986, the standard wage of all collectively held units increased by 9.6 percent annually; in contrast, incentive bonuses increased by 40.6 percent, various payments by 29.5 percent, and contributions to workers' insurance and welfare funds by 22.5 percent.[52] In 1986, the standard wage made up 65.0 percent of "wage funds," while incentive bonuses, various payments, and other items occupied 12.8 percent, 18.8 percent, and 3.4 percent, respectively. The ratio of contributions to workers' insurance and welfare funds to total wages was 26.4 percent.[53]

4-B

When the policy for revitalizing enterprises was adopted in the 1980s in the absence of price reform, Chinese enterprises with these unique labor practices responded by demanding that preferential financial treatment and wage and benefit increases, which were intended only for "high-performing enterprises," be available indiscriminately for all enterprises. This resulted from the *panbi* mechanism by which benefits enjoyed by one enterprise are to be equally shared by all other enterprises. The outcome defeated the very purpose of the discriminatory incentive scheme as a key policy instrument. Thus, the egalitarianism ingrained in Chinese society prevented the revitalization of enterprises through an incentive scheme based on profits, wages, and bonuses. Macroeconomically, the *panbi* mechanism has also led to uncontrollable expansion of consumption demand and persistent inflation.

The *panbi* mechanism works as follows. When a high-performing firm is granted an additional profit retention, which can boost real compensation for its employees, employees of other enterprises in the same sector and district put pressures on their managers to do the same. Managers, in turn, negotiate with supervising authorities to obtain similar profit retention. Employees argue that the good performance of the one firm was due to favorable external conditions, such as low input costs and high product prices under a distorted price system and prioritized allocation of investment funds by the state's industrial policy. Thus, good performance cannot be attributed to the enterprise's efforts. Moreover, employees at other enterprises have been assigned to work there by the state, not by their own choice. The protestation of disgruntled employees often wins the sympathy of managers as well as the understanding and tacit approval of local governments, banks, tax offices, and auditing authorities.[54] As this clearly indicates, the *panbi* mechanism was activated by market-oriented enterprise reform executed in the absence of price reform. Once activated, egalitarianism and the sense of community which were initially confined to each enterprise were expanded to include other enterprises. It is also possible to interpret this result as a natural outcome of the long period of "rationally low wage policy" under which all enterprises hired workers at a common low wage, fostering compassion among workers in different enterprises.

Behind these labor practices is the acute problem of surplus labor in China. Surplus labor exists not only in rural villages but also in state-owned enterprises in the modern sector. The latter is reflected in the surprisingly short actual working hours at those enterprises. This is a result of forced absorption in those enterprises of what would have been open unemployment under the market mechanism, which we may call "hired unemployment." The Ministry of Labor and Personnel of the central government estimates the total number of hired unemployed to be no less than 20 million.[55] Introduction of the market principle based on competition and labor mobility would mean reducing the level of employment to the point where the marginal productivity of labor is equal to the wage rate. If such a policy is implemented forcefully and immediately, massive open unemployment would surely emerge.[56] The jobless could not all be rescued by the social security system, given the limited capacity of the state budget and enterprises. Under these circumstances, the current labor practices may be evaluated as one valid option; however, they conflict with the aim of enterprise revitalization. In Eastern European socialist countries, labor is far more mobile and fierce competition exists among enterprises as well as among workers over job placement and the choice of profession. But, unlike in China, their labor markets are already at or above full employment.

4-C

It is not that the Chinese government did nothing to change these peculiar labor practices. Gradually, as a part of overall economic reform, the government tried to correct inefficient labor allocation (especially mismatches between skills and jobs at the time of recruitment) and the lack of work incentives arising from the communal characteristics of enterprises. A series of policies were introduced, of which the "contract labor system" of July 1986 was most important.[57] The key features of this system included the following: (1) beginning in 1986, new recruits would be hired as long-term (usually five-year) "contract workers" rather than lifetime "permanent workers" (this had already been started on a trial basis in 1981); (2) hiring would be through open recruitment under the guidance of local labor authorities, abolishing the practice of hiring family members and relatives of existing workers; (3) all contract workers would receive equal compensation, including benefits, social security, and newly created unemployment payments; and (4) enterprises may fire certain workers depending on their work performance. In parallel to the revised recruitment system, new "labor markets" were created by local governments in order to coordinate labor needs.

At the beginning of March 1989, contract workers numbered 9.9 million, or about 10 percent of all employees at collectively held units. However, these statistics may overstate the achievement of the new labor policy. First, many unsettled issues surrounding contract workers remain, including their relationship with existing surplus labor or permanent workers at the enterprises. At this moment, the contract labor system cannot be regarded as a well-established institution. Second, it is reported that contract workers have been converted in reality to permanent workers because both managers and workers prefer the existing system to the contract labor system.[58] While "labor markets" have been established in many locations, their active participants are confined to workers from rural areas, collectively-held units, and proprietorships. Inter-regional exchange of professionals, technical information, and workers remains disappointingly small.[59] It will be quite some time before the new labor policy takes root and true labor markets develop.

According to the survey (approximately 50,000 respondents, all currently hired workers) conducted by the *Workers Daily*, a national labor union organ, a surprisingly large number of workers approve of the new labor policy.[60] Furthermore, the majority are dissatisfied with the current level of wages (60.6 percent), and expect the reform to provide them with increased income opportunities (52.6 percent) as well as a greater chance to use their skills more effectively (89.6 percent). At the same time, few of these workers are prepared to quit their current jobs in search of better opportunities. Most would accept labor mobility, but they also value highly the stability enjoyed by permanent workers. From these results, an analyst at the *Workers Daily* concludes that the masses are ardent supporters of reform but lack the pragmatic capacity to adapt to inevitable changes – and this constitutes a major obstacle to reform. One way to improve adaptability to reform may be a rise in per capita disposable income.

In Shenyang, the largest industrial city in the Northeastern Region, the municipal labor authority tried in 1987–88 to reduce surplus labor among permanent workers by reassigning such workers to jobs outside state-owned enterprises. In retrospect, the authority concluded that the success of this policy was dependent on how much progress had already been made in enterprise management reform. At enterprises where the management responsibility system was yet to be established, the policy was ineffective. By contrast, the policy was accepted with enthusiasm by enterprises which were already run through management contracts.[61] However, enterprise management reform in turn often requires labor reform as a precondition. The solution of these interdependent problems is likely to take time. We have argued above that labor reform is necessary for enterprise reform and that labor reform also depends on institutional changes at the enterprise level.

IV Summary and tentative conclusions

The present chapter has demonstrated that the underdevelopment of the market economy is a non-trivial issue in the development process. We have questioned the validity of *laissez-faire* economic liberalization in dirigiste LDCs with under-developed markets, citing four aspects of Chinese reform since 1978 as case studies. Failures of liberalization were caused by the gap between the level of market development which was anticipated and that which actually prevailed. Table 6.2 summarizes these gaps by showing which particular conditions for the creation of the market economy were lacking.

Besides the four aspects discussed above, China also suffers from under-developed financial markets (including inadequate financial reform) which also impedes enterprise revitalization. This interesting topic still remains to be investigated. Implications of these problems on open door policy should also be examined. Equally important, macroeconomic imbalances such as inflation and current-account deficits which emerged in the process of liberalization are also fundamentally connected to the underdevelopment of the market economy. Nonetheless, the four aspects taken up above should be sufficient to make the main argument of this chapter.[62]

I offer two tentative conclusions: first, the fact of underdeveloped market economies is important not only analytically, as a key theoretical question in development economics, but also empirically, in the actual process of economic development. I believe this latter point has convincingly been demonstrated by the limits of Chinese liberalization policies examined in this chapter. Even so, the scope of our analysis should be enlarged to include the experiences of liberalization in market-oriented [non-socialist] dirigiste economies. The appendix to this chapter [not included here] attempts such an analysis.[63] More-over, it is worth studying whether policies other than liberalization can similarly be impeded by underdeveloped markets.[64]

Second, once the point above is accepted, a clear policy implication emerges.

Liberalization of a dirigiste economy cannot be achieved solely by issuing new directives on institutional changes and reforms; it also requires additional policies and measures to create the market economy itself. These policies and measures must be designed and implemented to replace weak links in the process of market development, as indicated in Table 6.2. This is a major task in policy analysis which calls for an entirely new research effort. Formulation of such a policy package is the most urgent challenge in the study of the market economy.

Notes

1 This is the entire main text of Chapter 7 of Professor Ishikawa's *Kaihatsu Keizaigaku no Kihon Mondai* [Basic Issues in Development Economics], (Tokyo, Iwanami Shoten, 1990). The sixteen-page appendix to this chapter, entitled, "Development Planning and the Indian Experience: An Article Reviewing Professor Chakravarty's New Book," is not included here. For interested readers, this appendix was originally published in English. See Shigeru Ishikawa, "Review Article: Sukhamoy Chakravarty, *Development Planning: The Indian Experience*, Delhi: Oxford University Press, 1987," in *Structural Change and Economic Dynamics*, Applied Economics Department, Cambridge University, no. 2, 1990 [Editors].

2 The customary economy is defined by Ishikawa below. It is an economic system where a family and a natural village are basic units and economic activities are performed in order to promote collective welfare through mutual dependence and assistance. It is characterized by low productivity, vulnerability to the natural environment, limited areas of exchange, and the prominence of cultural factors such as race, language, religion, and social values and customs [Editors].

3 This subsection is based on my paper, "The Underdevelopment of the Market Economy and the Role of Government," *Keizai Kenkyu* [Economic Review], vol. 26, no. 4, October 1975 [in Japanese].

4 Janos Kornai, *Anti-Equilibrium: On Economic Systems Theory and the Task of Research*, Amsterdam: North-Holland, 1971.

5 Here, Ishikawa uses the adjective *butteki* (physical or material) in a broad sense, including both tangible and intangible infrastructure (such as distribution networks and systems of finance and insurance), and not just roads and trucks – as his subsequent explanation makes clear. This interpretation is also confirmed by his other writings and speeches [Editors].

6 F.A. Hayek, *Individualism and Economic Order*, London, Routledge and Kegan Paul, 1949, chapter V, "The Meaning of Competition."

7 Srinivasan presents an interesting comparison of gains to an economy newly opened to foreign trade and gains from removing commercial barriers across different regions within a country. See T.N. Srinivasan, "Economic Liberalization in China and India: Issues and an Analytical Framework," *Journal of Comparative Economics*, vol. 11, no. 3, September 1987.

8 This gain can be easily explained by the Fisherian two-period model of saving, investment, and consumption. McKinnon's often-cited gains associated with moving from self-finance to finance through capital markets is a special case of this, where gains are amplified by the adoption of indivisible new technology. See R.I. McKinnon, *Money and Capital in Economic Development*, Washington, DC, Brookings Institution, 1973, pp. 19–21.

9 G.J. Stigler, "The Division of Labor is Limited by the Extent of the Market," *Journal of Political Economy*, June 1951.

Table 6.2 Economic liberalization measures and weak responses of an underdeveloped market economy in dirigiste LDCs: the case of China

| | Agriculture | | Large urban industries | |
	(1) Liberalization of production and distribution	(2) Abolition of people's communes	(1) Liberalization of product markets	(2) Granting management autonomy
A Liberalization measures	• Abolishing production teams • Restoring family farming • Phase-out of forced delivery • Increase in procurement prices	Phase-out of management committees of people's communes – productive and collective services to be transferred to village government, cooperatives, or new firms	Increased autonomy of SOEs; Shifting production, procurement, and sales authority from state to enterprises; a large part of previous planning moved to the market mechanism	To vitalize SOEs and encourage competition, introduce price reform; profit-based SOE performance evaluation; large profit retention to high-performing SOEs, enabling higher bonuses and benefits for workers
B Market economy response Social division of labor				
ε products	• Increased supply of marketable grain and crops		• Only shortage products (some machinery) can benefit from competition; no gain for others	
α participants	• Family farming in food production expands; some specialize in commercial crops and specialties	• No suitable cooperatives or firms emerge to undertake irrigation, public works, and other collective activities	• No managers with market adaptability emerge	• With no price reform, no competitive firms emerge in product markets; enterprise finance is still dependent on state protection
ν organizations	• State commercial companies unable to handle increased transaction	• Village government unable to supply productive services	• Vertical division of labor, product markets, marketing organization do not emerge (except for industrial and commercial associations)	
μ market types	• Revival of traditional market towns, private carriers, private lenders		• Strict restrictions on inter-industry and inter-provincial commerce persist	• No labor market; state allocates jobs; enterprise is a community of lifetime employment; special

Table 6.2 (cont.)

Infrastructure for distribution	Limited capacity of state commercial networks, railroads, etc., unable to handle increased cargo; traditional primary product markets revive with active farmers and merchants – but their capacity also limited		Inter-industry and inter-provincial commercial networks do not emerge	financial treatment of one SOE invites similar demand from other SOEs
Market rules	No protection for small farmers and merchants outside native village; very high transaction costs		No rules for long-distance commerce; administrative authority is the only framework	Performance-based increases in wage, payments, benefits are permitted; however, differentiation does not actually occur in egalitarian society
C Outcome	Market cannot absorb increased supply; government also unable to buy it due to high fiscal cost; farmers upset; some quit farming	Construction, maintenance of rural collective infrastructure such as irrigation cease; reduced supply of productive services	Market mechanism does not function; plan continues; inter-governmental barter; widespread rent-seeking; social discontent	Enterprises continue to be protected by state in uncompetitive environment; low profit and productivity, high cost and no competitiveness; reform leads to rising consumption and inflation

10 See the paper by the Study Team on Chinese Food Production Problems, *Economic Research*, 1985, no. 7 [in Chinese].

11 G. William Skinner, "Marketing and Social Structure in Rural China," *Journal of Asian Studies*, November 1964, February 1965, and May 1965.

12 These studies were part of ongoing research by the Study Team on Townships led by Fei and supported by the provincial government of Jiangsu. The studies cover northern, southern, and "middle" regions (Nanjing, Yangzhou, and Zhenjiang, according to Fei's definition) of Jiangsu, each with distinct local characteristics. See "Great Problems of Townships" and "Research on Townships" for southern Jiangsu, and "Townships in Northern Jiangsu" and "New Developments in Townships" for northern Jiangsu. All of these papers are contained in the *Collected Papers in Sociology by Fei Xiaotong: Townships and Other Issues*, Tianjin, Tianjin People's Press, 1985 [in Chinese].

13 Tadashi Negishi, *Chinese Guild*, Tokyo, Nihon Hyoron Shinsha, 1953. See Part 2, Chapter 1, Section 3 (*Keshang* and Trade Name Guild) [in Japanese].

14 Study Team on Rural Wenzhou at the Economic Research Institute of the Chinese Academy of Social Sciences, "Consideration of the Commodity Economy of Rural Wenzhou and the Road to Modernization of Rural China," *Economic Research*, 1986, no. 6 [in Chinese].

15 General Research Team at the Agricultural Development Research Center of the State Council, *Reform Faces Institutional Innovation*, Sanlian Publisher, Shanghai Branch, 1988, pp. 21–22 and Chapter 5 (by Zhou Qiren) [in Chinese].

16 Zhang Yulin, "The City-Zhen-Xiang Network and the Entire Structure of Small Townships," Research Team on Small Cities of Jiangsu Province (eds) *New Development of Small Cities*, Nanjing, Jiangsu People's Press, 1986, p. 91; Academy of Social Sciences of Hubei Province (eds) *Reform and Development of China's Prefectural Economies*, Beijing, Economic Management Press, 1987, pp. 6, 9.

17 *Collected Papers in Sociology by Fei Xiaotong*, op. cit., pp. 71–74.

18 General Research Team at the Agricultural Development Research Center of the State Council, op. cit., p. 17.

19 *Lijia* is a system of rural government created by the Ming dynasty. One *li* consisted of 110 families where the ten richest families assumed the *li* head in turn. The remaining 100 families were divided into ten *jia*. The purposes of the *lijia* system were tax administration, mobilization of compulsory labor, and maintenance of security [Editors].

20 In Japan, a system similar to the *lijia* system with resident landlords existed during the Meiji period until around the time of the Russo-Japanese War [1904–05] and World War I [1914–18]. Unlike China, the replacement of Japanese resident landlords by absentees was accompanied by the rise of medium-sized farmers as village leaders.

21 The motive, statistical data, and evaluation of this survey are presented and analyzed in Ramon H. Myers, *The Chinese Peasant Economy: Agricultural Development in Hopei and Shantung 1890–1949*, Harvard University Press, Cambridge, MA, 1970. The survey's data are critically reviewed by Seiji Imabori, *Looking into the Essence of China*, Tokyo, Keiso Shobo, 1985, Part II [in Japanese].

22 Another informative study on the same subject is given by Peter Perdue, "Water Control in the Dongting Lake Region during the Ming and Qing Period," *Journal of Asian Studies*, August 1982. In essence, it describes the government's interest in large-scale water projects on Dongting Lake during this period, project management systems at various levels of government, and the bargaining process of local noblemen and landlords over the assignment of finance and labor for the works.

23 [A point made in] Anthony Tang's paper, "China's Economic Reform: Background and Analysis," presented at the First Meeting of the East Asia Economic Association, October 29, 1988, and my comment on his paper.

24 Shigeru Ishikawa, "Agricultural and Agrarian Problems in Economic Development in China and Japan: A Comparison," 31st International Congress of Human Sciences in Asia and North Africa, Tokyo, September 1983; Shigeru Ishikawa, "China's Personal Income Disparity and Its Causes, Part 1," *Asian Economies*, vol. 17, no. 6, May 1976 [the latter is in Japanese]. Parish and Whyte's book cited earlier [W.L. Parish and M.K. Whyte, *Village and Family in Contemporary China*, Chicago, Chicago University Press, 1977, Chapter 15] empirically vindicates my hypothesis.

25 World Bank, "China: Rural Industry: Overview, Issues and Prospects," mimeo, Washington, 1988.

26 Among key decisions, the most important was "Make Another Step Forward by Strengthening and Perfecting the Agricultural Production Responsibility System," Central Party Committee, document no. 75, September 27, 1980 [in Chinese]. Transformation of agricultural policy in this period is analyzed by Yasuo Kondo and Kusuhiko Sakamoto, (eds) *Revival of Family Management under Socialism*, Tokyo, Association of Agricultural, Forestry, and Fishing Villages, 1983 [in Japanese].

27 Du Jin, "Theory and Practice of Collective Agriculture: A Case Study from China," mimeo, Hitotsubashi University, January 1988 [in Japanese]. This study attempts statistical analysis on the two-step diffusion of the agricultural management and contract system as described in the text. The actual processes of introducing the management and contract system in Fengyang Prefecture of Anhui Province are reported in Toshio Tajima, "Chinese Agriculture under Agricultural Policy Reform: Current Status of De-collectivization," in Naraomi Imamura and Toshiaki Matsuura (eds) *Transformation of Socialist Agriculture*, Tokyo, Association of Agricultural, Forestry, and Fishing Villages, 1988 [in Japanese].

28 Concerning the third point in the blueprint, the traditional method of mobilizing local compulsory labor for water projects was replaced around 1980 by contracts between construction brigades of local people's communes and the state which placed orders. For other items in the blueprint, actual developments can easily be traced from the citations in the text.

29 General Research Team at the Agricultural Development Research Center, *Reform Faces Institutional Innovation*, op. cit., chapter 6, drafted by You Mingquan; Chen Yizi and Wang Xiaoqiang, "Several Perspectives on the Systemic Reform of Rural People's Communes," in *Rural Villages, Economy, and Society*, vol. 2, Beijing, Zhishi Press, 1985; Liu Zhenwei, "Several Issues on the Construction and Reform of Township and Village Organizations," *Hongqi*, 1988, no. 11; also see Academy of Social Sciences of Hubei Province (eds) *Reform and Development of Chinese Prefectural Economies*, Beijing, Economic Management Press, 1987, pp. 275–79 [all the above are in Chinese].

30 Economic Research Institute of Shanghai Academy of Social Sciences, *Socialist Transformation of Capitalist Industry and Commerce in Shanghai*, Shanghai, Shanghai People's Press, 1980, p. 299 [in Chinese].

31 For the machinery industry in Shanghai, see the excellent documentation and analysis in Economic Research Institute of Shanghai Academy of Social Sciences, *Shanghai's Indigenous Machinery Industry*, two volumes, Shanghai, Shanghai Zhonghua Book Agency, 1979 [in Chinese]. Also see my study based on this work, "The Development of Capital-Goods Sector: Experiences of Pre-PRC China," ILO World Employment Programme Research Working Paper no. 139, Geneva, January 1985. For Dailong Machine Factory, see *The Birth, Development, and Transformation of Dailong Machine Factory*, also by the Economic Research Institute of Shanghai Academy of Social Sciences, Shanghai, Shanghai People's Press, 1980 [in Chinese].

32 For the explanation and analysis of how the production and management of state-owned enterprises under collective planning are subordinated to the plan, see

my *Capital Accumulation Mechanism in China*, Tokyo, Iwanami Shoten, 1960, pp. 66–100. Also see David Granick, "The Industrial Environment in China and the SMEA Countries," G. Tidrick and Chen Jiyuan (eds) *China's Industrial Reform*, New York: Oxford University Press, 1987. This paper compares industrial organization and government management in China, the Soviet Union, and Eastern Europe.

33 He Jianzhang and others, "Economic Systemic Reform Requires the Use of Production Cost as the Basis of Industrial Pricing," *Chinese Social Sciences*, 1981, no. 1 [in Chinese].

34 The most important decision against these official crimes was "Decision on the Restoration of Order at Enterprises by the Communist Party Central Committee and the State Council," October 3, 1988 [in Chinese]. Also see Premier Li Peng's address to the National People's Congress on March 2, 1989, "Firmly Hold the Policy of Restoration of Order and Deepening of Reform," reprinted in *Pekin Shuho* [*Beijing Review*], April 11, 1989 [in Japanese].

35 General Research Team at the Institute for Restructuring the Economic System, *Reform: Challenges and Options We Face*, Beijing: Chinese Economic Press, 1986, pp. 66–67 [in Chinese].

36 Zhang Xiaoming and Song Yaohua, "Dilemmas and Direction of Reform of the Production Materials Distribution System," *Economic Research*, 1987, no. 10 [in Chinese].

37 Zhang Xiaoming and Song Yaohua, op. cit.

38 Zhao Renwei, Chen Dongqi, and Wang Zhongmin, "A Trend toward Barter in the Process of Market-Oriented Reforms," *Economic Research*, 1989, no. 4 [in Chinese].

39 Zhang Xiaoming and Song Yaohua, op. cit.

40 Microeconomic Research Group at the Institute for Restructuring the Economic System, *The Market Mechanism and Enterprise System under Reform*, Chengdu, Sichuan People's Press, 1988, chapter 4 [in Chinese]. This chapter is one of the rare studies on the marketing activities of Chinese industrial enterprises, using empirical data supplied by a 1985 survey of 400 industrial enterprises.

41 Traditionally, Chinese enterprises were tightly controlled by vertically separated lines of command of administrative departments and localities. Since 1980, a movement aimed at breaking such vertical segmentation to revitalize enterprises led to the creation of horizontal associations encompassing different sectors and regions, promoting mutual cooperation in production and distribution. "Enterprise groups" were introduced in 1986 to further strengthen the functions of those enterprise associations. Principal documents governing enterprise groups include "Draft Instructions on the Advancement of Economic Associations by the State Council," dated July 1, 1980; and "Instructions on a Few Issues Concerning a Further Step to Advance Horizontal Economic Associations by the State Council," dated March 23, 1986 [both in Chinese].

42 Institute for Restructuring the Economic System, ed., *Reform: Problems and Paths We Face*, Beijing: Economic Management Press, 1987, pp. 78–81 [in Chinese].

43 He Ting and Xiao Xue, "General Outlook of Enterprise Groups," in *China's Economic Systems Reform*, July 1988 [in Chinese]. Chief enterprise groups include: the Automobile Industrial Group consisting of No. 1, No. 2, and Heavy Automobile Companies; an enterprise group made up of four electrical equipment companies of Shanghai, Harbin, Dongfang, and Xi'an; China Mining Machinery Production Company; Jialing Industrial Company; No. 1 Rolling Mill Machinery Association Company; Luoyang Ball Bearing Industrial Association Company; Dairen Refrigeration Equipment Association Company; North Eastern Heavy Machinery Group Company; and Wuhan Engine Group Company.

44 Microeconomic Research Group at the Institute for Restructuring the Economic System, op. cit., pp. 110–15.

45 See China Department of the World Bank, "China: State Enterprise Management and Organization, Reform Issues and Options," mimeo, September 1987, chapter II-C (The Legal Framework). Also, Li Maoguan, "Why Laws Are Not Obeyed," *Pekin Shuho* [*Beijing Review*], March 28, 1989 [in Japanese].

46 For an excellent summary of prewar Chinese industrial and labor organizations, see Yuji Muramatsu, *Social Structure of the Chinese Economy*, Tokyo: Toyo Keizai Shimposha, 1949, chapter 4, section 3 [in Japanese].

47 An Tifu (ed.) *Socialist Budget and Credit*, Beijing, Chinese People's University Press, 1987, pp. 136–9 [in Chinese].

48 Dai Yuanchen and Li Hanming, "Wages Encroach Profits," *Economic Research*, 1988, no. 6 [in Chinese].

49 For employment and wage policy and systems of modern industries in the early years of the People's Republic of China, see my *Capital Accumulation Mechanism in China*, Tokyo, Iwanami Shoten, 1960, chapters 3–4 [in Japanese].

50 Dai and Li, op. cit.

51 See *Reform: Challenges and Options We Face*, op. cit., p. 36.

52 *China Statistical Yearbook*, 1987, p. 690.

53 Cao Erjie, "A Preliminary Study on the Low-wage Supply Allocation System and Expansion of Aggregate Demand," *Economic Research*, 1988, no. 10 [in Chinese].

54 *Reform: Challenges and Options We Face*, op. cit., p. 23; Ning Xiaoxiong, "The *Panbi* Mechanism and the Egalitarian Standard," *Guangming Daily*, February 11, 1988 [both in Chinese].

55 *People's Daily*, June 13, 1988 [in Chinese].

56 Chen Xiaomei, "Options for Enterprise Wage Reform," *Economic Research*, 1987, no. 4 [in Chinese].

57 *Xinhua Monthly*, September 1986 [in Chinese].

58 Yang Guansan, "Labor System Reform and Social Psychology," Institute for Restructuring the Economic System (eds) *China: Development and Reform*, vol. 2, 1986; Lu Zhongyuan, "The Market Allocation Mechanism of Labor," *Economic Research*, 1988, no. 4 [both in Chinese].

59 Gan Faming, "Remarkable Success of Our Labor Market," *Chinese Economic Systemic Reform*, 1988, no. 4 [in Chinese].

60 Yang Guansan, op. cit.

61 Municipal Labor Authority of Shenyang, "Successful Execution of Rationalization and Reallocation of Surplus Workers at Enterprises," *Chinese Economic Systemic Reform*, 1988, no. 9 [in Chinese].

62 For broader background materials on the case studies presented here, including issues not covered, see my "China's Economic Development: From the Perspective of Economic Development Theory," Kazuo Yamanouchi (ed.) *Transformation of the Chinese Economy*, Tokyo, Iwanami Shoten, 1989. For inflation and balance-of-payments problems, see Ryutaro Komiya, *Today's Chinese Economy: A Comparative Study of Japan and China*, chapter 4, "Economic Overheating of 1984–87: Issues in the Improvement of Macroeconomic Management," Tokyo, Tokyo University Press, 1989 [both in Japanese].

63 In many dirigiste LDCs, including India, it is more difficult to find discussions of the limits of liberalization in the published literature. There seem to be two reasons for this. First, domestic vested interests often strongly oppose liberalization, over-powering the government and the ruling party who are forced to resist the policy advice of the IMF and the World Bank. As a consequence, liberalization measures drastic enough to reveal their limits are rarely implemented. Second, even when liberalization is actually impeded by underdeveloped markets, such instances are not systematically analyzed or publicized.

64 The monetarist–structuralist debate between the IMF and Latin American governments over the inflation and balance-of-payments stabilization program may well
provide one such example. Stabilization is a short-term problem, unlike economic
development which is a medium- to long-term task. Despite this, structuralists argue
that stabilization measures stipulated in IMF conditionality (fiscal austerity, credit
restraint, high interest rates, exchange-rate devaluation, etc.) fail to achieve the
expected results due to "structural bottlenecks" which can be removed only through
long-term development efforts. Expected results must mean the restoration of current-
account sustainability and price stability without seriously inhibiting growth capacity.
Critics of the IMF assert that actual stabilization measures in Latin America too often
result in shrinking output and persistent inflation even though the current-account
balance is restored. See Lance Taylor, *Structuralist Macroeconomics: Applicable
Models for the Third World*, New York: Basic Books, 1983, chapter 1; also his "IMF
Conditionality: Incomplete Theory, Policy Malpractice," in R.J. Myers (ed.) *The
Political Morality of the International Monetary Fund*, New York, Transaction Press,
1987. The concept of "structural bottlenecks" is not clearly defined, but it is likely
that they result from the underdevelopment of the market economy. In addition, Latin
American economic policy cannot be explained without taking into account aggressive labor unions which exert a strong social influence in populist regimes. The
relationship between macroeconomic stabilization and underdeveloped markets is an
important area for future research, to which the Latin American experience can give
us a clue.

7

A BLUEPRINT FOR ASIAN ECONOMICS[1]

Yonosuke Hara

I How to proceed with Asian economics

Since the early 1970s, I have made many research trips to different Asian countries, including Korea and Hong Kong, which lie at the center of Asia-Pacific economic dynamism, ASEAN countries which are catching up with the center, and India, Burma, and Laos which at present remain on the border or outside of this regional dynamism. Through these research excursions, I have come to believe very strongly that active contacts with foreign economies through trade and investment and guarantee of freedom in domestic economic activity are the prerequisites for economic development. At the same time, however, I began to question with equally strong conviction the validity of the view that a country can advance along a long-term development path *only if* government policies are appropriate. This simple optimism is what neoclassical development economics, as the predominant development doctrine of our time, seems to imply.

On the contrary, I gradually came to the belief that development depends more crucially on whether or not the indigenous society is equipped with the ability to respond positively to such appropriate government policies. The positive response in this case essentially means the formation of an efficient market-economic system within the existing domestic economy and society. This is a dynamic process which requires a long period of time to complete. I believe that understanding this process in the context of each society should be the central theme of development economics. Unfortunately, economic theory at present seems unable to handle this problem properly. Given that today's economics provides us with few theoretical insights into the process of formation of a market economy, those who wish to analyze the process should begin by asking the "right questions," questions which can incorporate both reality and theory. Raising the right questions is itself an important intellectual challenge. This is where I have arrived after these research excursions.

This thought has been prompted by my dissatisfaction with the way the study of Asian economies is divided into two main approaches. The division is further reinforced by the emergence of a professional group in support of each approach.

At the risk of overstatement, the problem can be presented roughly as the conspicuous coexistence of exceedingly formal neoclassical economics and excessively historical area studies. At the one extreme of Asian economic studies lies development economics, which presupposes the rationality of all economic units – including even farmers – and the existence of all goods and factor markets in the absence of government control[2] as indisputable facts. It explains the differences in economic performance solely on the basis of the type of economic policies adopted by each government. At the other extreme, we have area studies which emphasize the uniqueness of each economy. Through extensive fieldwork, area specialists seek to reveal the functioning of various economic systems embedded in each society. Due perhaps to the sharp methodological incompatibility between the two approaches, little constructive interaction has occurred between them. This is a very unfortunate situation as we seek a theory of economic development that can closely track Asian reality.

We do not deny the weight of remarkable empirical evidence produced by the statistical works of neoclassical development economics on the factors of economic growth and the effects of different economic policies on the growth path. Notwithstanding these achievements, neoclassical research in development economics leaves us unhappy and dissatisfied. We fear that growth theory which relies too heavily on growth accounting (i.e., a statistical procedure to decompose growth into the contribution of each growth factor) tends to overlook the most important causes of economic growth. As neoclassical economic historian North (1981) aptly puts it, the so-called growth factors in growth accounting analysis – such as capital accumulation, improvement in the quality of labor, scale economy, and technical progress – are not really the *factors* but the *process* of growth itself. It is far more important to know the type of economic behavior of individuals and firms and the kind of economic system which enabled such capital accumulation, improvement in the quality of labor, technical progress, and so on.

Another serious problem with neoclassical development economics is that it assumes the efficiency of market competition too readily and formally even when the highly dynamic process of economic development is at issue. Incomplete and underdeveloped market mechanisms impose constraints on the rational behavior of individuals and other economic units, but the neoclassical approach almost completely ignores such constraints. In discussions of economic development, neoclassical economists often dwell on such price variables as wages and interest rates. But their analyses are meaningful only if relevant markets are well formed, permitting these prices to work normally. We cannot focus on price variables alone when the crucial question is whether markets are sufficiently developed or not. Instead of theorizing over non-existent prices, we need to adopt the institutional approach in order to understand how and where these variables emerge.

We also highly appreciate the rich information gathered by area specialists on the transformation of domestic social structure en route to economic growth and industrialization. These studies are backed by extensive fieldwork and careful interpretation of historical data. However, most area specialists too easily envision a formal, self-regulating market economy (which is regarded as the exact opposite to other non-market economies embedded in society), instead of critically examining its inner mechanism. Perhaps because of this, rational economic behavior is often assumed to be relevant only in a market economy. This presumption effectively blocks the pursuit of how different types of economic activity emerge in response to different circumstances that individuals face under non-market economies.

Thus, the two main approaches in the study of Asian economies each suffer methodological weaknesses. It is important to clearly recognize these weaknesses before we attempt to build a new theory of economic development based on Asian experience. This recognition is also the minimum requirement for initiating a fruitful dialogue between the two approaches.

Economic development or growth is commonly defined as measurable increases in wealth and income. We do not take this statistical approach. Rather, following Lewis (1955), this book defines economic development to be the process by which options available to various people in their daily life and work are expanded within each society. Undoubtedly, Korea, Thailand, and other high-growth achievers in Asia are registering steady increases in per capita income. More important than these statistics, however, is the fact that a large number of people in these countries are enhancing their ability to seize ever-larger job opportunities in the labor market through education and other efforts. In various ways, these people have also begun to participate in direct and indirect financial markets as well as in non-market civil activities. Economic growth is important not so much for the wealth and income it brings as because it expands people's opportunities in their ordinary life, which makes them freer. This explains why the phenomenon of economic growth is inseparable from broader social changes, including political liberalization.

These are the thoughts that grew on me as a result of my research excursions to many Asian countries during the last ten years and more. My current view on how to proceed with Asian economics in a way that captures the vivid reality of the region is as follows. Careful empirical observation of each society on the one hand and logical reasoning based on economic theory on the other are each incomplete on their own. These two approaches must be adopted simultaneously and interactively, with inevitable strain arising from the two different method-ologies, to generate meaningful hypotheses and visions that can begin to uncover the secrets of Asian economies. This is the most urgent task required of Asian economics. I cannot be widely off the mark when I say that inexact sciences like Asian economics would be greatly invigorated by the competitive presentation of such hypotheses and visions.

The main purpose of this book [A Blueprint for Asian Economics] is to critically examine neoclassical development economics. Before we begin, let me make one additional remark on alternative directions that thinking on economic theory might take. Theoretic studies in economics contain two dissimilar research programs. The first is an empirical search for "what is likely to happen" in general under the conditions satisfied by most cases, and this supposition is checked against statistical observations. The second is pure logical thinking of "what can happen" under a certain specialized condition, regardless of whether that condition holds generally or not.

Since neoclassical development economics aims mainly at discovering a common policy framework conducive to economic growth, its research interest is focused on the first question of "what is likely to happen" in the largest number of cases. Without doubt, this approach is necessary for the proper analysis of Asian economies. We should not, however, forget the premise of neoclassical development economics which validates its logical investigation, namely, that all markets exist or would exist in the absence of government control.[3] If a case arises where this premise cannot be justified as self-evident, then we must certainly turn to the second question of "what can happen" in that specialized circumstance.

II The neoclassical resurgence in development economics

The fact that Asian economies are divided into two separate groups – the one achieving high growth and the other not – provides a clue to understanding an important aspect of international relations. Many Asian countries outside the high-performing region are now attempting to join the elite group by reforming their economic systems and policies. One prominent example is India, a giant country in Asia. During the 1950s and 1960s, development economists regarded India's state-plan-based development strategy as a useful model for the rest of the developing world. During the 1970s and 1980s, however, India revised its strategy and sought to join the Asia–Pacific high growth region through domestic economic liberalization. China, another large country, has also adopted the policy of reform and the open-door even under socialism.

The most popular theory of development economics asserts that the contents of economic strategy adopted independently by each country hold the key to participation in the high growth region. Specifically, it is argued that a strategy of outward-looking export promotion is the gateway to Asia-Pacific economic dynamism, whereas a strategy of inward-looking import substitution will only bring economic stagnation. This belief in development economics seems to be winning an increasing number of followers among Asian policy makers. During the 1980s, many Asian countries turned to economic liberalization with outward-looking export promotion as its core policy, in order to achieve high growth. As Linder (1986) puts it, the success of Asian high-performers is beginning to have a strong international demonstration effect.

Nonetheless, economic liberalization in countries outside the Asian high growth region does not seem to be producing the desired results. Some economists contend that the lack of results is due to the incomplete implementation of economic liberalization policies. True, liberalization processes in these countries are often slowed by the resistance of domestic interest groups, but this fact alone cannot fully explain the recent economic difficulties in India and China. I believe that these difficulties stem mainly from constraints that remain in these countries, impeding the government's effort to join the high growth region despite economic liberalization and outward-looking policies. Among such domestic constraints, the most crucial is the fact that the market mechanism does not function as effectively as the proponents of economic liberalization policies presume. The actual market is not an "impersonal *deux ex machina* operating with clock-like precision" as the neoclassical textbook supposes, but a "complex institution run by human beings and requires . . . much time to become an efficient institution" (Oshima 1987: 349). It is only natural that hasty liberalization which neglected this fact did not yield the intended results.

Neoclassical school in economic development

Since the mid-1970s, with the success of export-led high economic growth in East Asia, neoclassical economics has rapidly emerged as the dominant theory in the formulation of development strategy in less developed countries. It remains the most popular theory in development economics to date. Neoclassical economists recommend, first and foremost, a full application of the market mechanism to both domestic and external activities through economic and trade liberalization. Neoclassical development theory arose as a strong antithesis to import substitution strategy, which was the mainstream theory of the 1950s and 1960s that called for government's direct interventions and protectionism. This movement came to be called the "resurgence of the neoclassical paradigm." Needless to say, this trend was part of a broader change in economics toward conservatism, as witnessed in the decline of Keynesian economics and the concurrent rise of monetarists and the rational expectations school. From the 1980s to the present, a revived neoclassical theory has exerted an increasing influence on India, China, and other countries in Asia (including socialist ones) located at the border or outside of the Asian high growth region.

The revived neoclassical paradigm must be examined from the perspectives of economic theory and policy advice. In economic theory, this paradigm asserts that orthodox economic theory, and especially price theory, is highly effective in analyzing developing economies. In policy advice, it underscores the importance of the market mechanism which bestows economic freedom on the private sector, and abhors official intervention based on state planning.

Theoretically, the neoclassical resurgence was launched by Schultz (1964) who asserted that even farmers apparently immersed in the premodern traditional customs of a developing country could respond rationally to economic incentives such as profit. If farmers behave rationally and consistently with the market principle, the argument went, then the economic behavior of anyone in the developing world should be no different from that in the advanced market economies. This leads to the conclusion that the market mechanism should work efficiently as an economic institution for coordinating the behavior of many rational economic actors in a developing country. In short, neoclassical theorists argue that the same price theory is equally useful for analyzing developing and developed economies.

Until the 1960s, the dominant thinking had it that people in developing countries did not act rationally by the standards of the market economy, and that this situation called for an alternative economic theory different from the one used to analyze advanced market economies. Revived neoclassical theorists reject such an idea, and apply one economics to all economies regardless of the level of development. Deepak Lal's (1985) book, *The Poverty of Development Economics*, whose title reminds us of Popper's famous treatise, is a typical example. As Hirschman (1987) correctly points out, the denial of the need for special economics which accounts for the unique economic and social characteristics of developing countries was tantamount to the acceptance of *mono-economics* which fits developed and developing economies equally well.

In the aspect of policy advice, neoclassical economists criticize import substitution policy which relies on state intervention and heavy protection, and recommend trade liberalization which allows a country to actively participate in the global market. This is, as noted, a reaction to the idea that justified industrialization through import substitution, which ruled until the early 1970s. In particular, neoclassical economists argue that free trade promotes labor-intensive manufactured exports of labor-abundant developing countries where such industries naturally have comparative advantage.

This further leads to an observation that the existence of capital-intensive industries in developing economies which are failing to export is due to wage control, repressed interest rates, and other unnecessary policy interventions. Therefore, elimination of these interventions in factor markets is recommended to unleash the free market mechanism which is supposed to achieve the most efficient resource allocation and selection of industries. Even subsidized food production programs in countries with food shortages are condemned as an excuse for import substitution policy.

The slogan "getting prices right" neatly sums up this neoclassical policy advice (Timmer 1986). When this policy is advocated, the correct prices to which other prices should be adjusted are those prevailing in international markets, as the neoclassical assertion of trade liberalization makes clear.

As noted earlier, the major shift in economic development strategy was accompanied by the changing perception of how efficiently markets work in developing countries. Around the early 1970s, the previous view that pervasive "market failure" in developing countries prevented an efficient working of the market mechanism, which led to import substitution through state allocation of investment funds, was superseded by market-oriented policy advice based on a diametrically opposed conviction of the efficiency of these markets.

In addition, the two schools also differed in the evaluation of the institutional capacity of developing countries. The old view presumed that governments in the developing world had the ability to effectively correct "market failure," an idea that John Maynard Keynes held with respect to the governments in more advanced economies (the Presumption of Harvey Road). In contrast, revived neoclassical development economics, in defense of the efficiency of potentially ubiquitous markets, emphasized "government failure," or the failure of state intervention to achieve its intended results. Thus, the resurgence of neoclassical development economics completely reversed the roles of the market and the state.

One factor which contributed to the shifting focus in development economics during the 1970s was undoubtedly the high growth of East Asian economies such as Korea and Taiwan based on the expansion of labor-intensive manufactured exports since the 1960s. In the 1970s, export-led industrialization in East Asia caught the eye of many economists and spurred them to analyze this experience. The main objective of their research was to explain the different economic performance of South Asia and East Asia: the former, typically India, stagnated under a state-led import substitution strategy while the latter prospered under outward-looking policies. Let us review some of these studies.

East Asian economics from the perspective of economic policy

Why is it that East Asian countries alone are firmly on the path of economic growth, while the vast majority of the rest of developing countries are languishing? The orthodox neoclassical answer to this question is that the economic development strategy adopted by the governments of East Asian countries have been appropriate. While other developing countries continued to heavily protect domestic industries to achieve industrialization through import substitution, East Asian countries removed such policy distortions at an early stage and introduced an export-oriented development strategy. This, it is asserted, is the main reason why they prospered.

Among neoclassical economists, Balassa (1982) argues that the export-oriented strategy of East Asia was not simply the provision of export subsidies but, more importantly, a policy regime that assured neutrality of economic incentives between export and import-substitution industries. Under an import substitution strategy, protection at the border and an overvalued exchange rate distort price incentives to the advantage of import-substitution industries while the growth of export industries remains suppressed. In East Asia, the regime shift from import substitution policy to the neutrality of incentives occurred in the mid-1960s. Adjustment of the exchange rate to an appropriate level was especially highly regarded by neoclassical economists for establishing neutral incentives between the two types of industries which subsequently generated export-led high growth.

Similarly, Linder (1986) argues that economic growth is not a miracle, but can be achieved by any country which adopts correct policies. Although Korea's success cannot be attributed to *laissez-faire* economic policy, and the country did have policy distortions in the double sense, through protecting import-substitution industries and subsidizing export industries, he nonetheless contends that the overall effect of these distortions was far less damaging than import substitution policies implemented in other regions.

Thus, neoclassical economists are not arguing that, as a matter of fact, Korea implemented a *laissez-faire* economic strategy. Nevertheless, as the phrase "getting prices right" shows, they essentially believe that providing correct price incentives to all domestic industries is the key to economic growth since private-sector agents are assumed to respond positively to such incentives and achieve an efficient allocation of resources in the country.

When orthodox neoclassical economists argue this way on East Asian economic growth, a dualistic thinking on state and market is clearly in their minds. While they highly evaluate the role of market, as an efficient device for allocating resources, they equally stress the inevitable failure of state intervention such as protection for the purpose of fostering import-substitution industries. They in effect contend that the private sector would strongly respond to price incentives, and the market mechanism works nearly perfectly in *any* developing countries, and not just East Asia. This leads them to conclude that allocative efficiency and economic growth will be achieved through the proper functions of the market mechanism *only if* government intervention is removed.

East Asian economics from the perspective of political economy

Among neoclassical economists who attribute East Asian success to the type of economic policies adopted by these countries, some go a step further and ask a related and very interesting question: what enabled East Asia to adopt incentive-neutral policies, unlike other developing countries which are still caught in a generally inefficient import substitution strategy? This query, which investigates the circumstances in which the policies advanced by economists as correct are actually adopted, can be called East Asian economics from the perspective of political economy.

One such theory of political economy is presented by Ranis (1988) who compares the experiences of East Asia and Latin America. Ranis points out that, in Latin America, the strategy for industrialization alternated between protectionism and openness, while in East Asia the strategy gradually shifted over time from import substitution under protection to export promotion. He attributes the different patterns of policy evolution in these regions to the difference in resource endowments. Because of its rich natural resources, Latin America gave birth to a vocal landowning class which controlled the region's primary commodity exports. As a result, national economic policies are dictated largely by the economic interest of this class. Since landowners prefer cheap manufactured imports, effort to industrialize the domestic economy by substituting imports does not get much support in the first place. Furthermore, even if economic nationalism and other reasons favored import substitution of certain manufactured products, the need to export such goods would not be felt strongly as long as primary commodity exports remain robust. This argument is similar to what international economists now call Dutch disease, a situation where a country's industrialization is impeded by a rich endowment of natural resources. Thus, the cyclical pattern of economic policy in Latin America is generated by the relative strength of economic nationalism which favor protection *vis-à-vis* the landowning class.

In contrast to Latin America, resource-poor East Asia did not have a land-owning class which could dominate primary commodity production. Thus governments in East Asia formulated economic policies without strong pressure from the landowning class. Instead of natural resources, East Asia had an ample supply of well-educated labor, which could be efficiently employed in labor-intensive manufacturing industries – provided that appropriate economic policies were implemented to promote such a growth pattern. For this reason, East Asian economic strategy shifted smoothly from a short period of import substitution under protection to export promotion under liberalized trade. In essence, Ranis characterizes the political economy of East Asian countries by the conspicuous absence of a rent-seeking landowning class which could dominate primary commodity production.

With the publication of these and other studies of East Asia by neoclassical economists, the view that East Asian experience confirmed the validity of neo-classical propositions in development economics came to be widely accepted. In the 1980s, moreover, regenerated neoclassical development economics also began to significantly influence the economic policies of Asian countries through the policy advice of international development organizations such as the IMF and World Bank. These organizations now demand the implementation of neoclassical economic policies – fiscal prudence, exchange-rate devaluation, reduction of import protection, etc. – in exchange for structural adjustment lending and other loans. This policy conditionality increasingly constrains the formulation of economic policies in developing countries.

III Beyond neoclassical theory

The lack of Keynesian perspective in neoclassical development economics

To us, the neoclassical explanation of rapidly growing East Asian NIEs based solely on the quality of economic policies is hardly acceptable. First of all, it is evident that free markets were not the only factor that propelled East Asian exports. The role of very powerful and persistent export promotion policies such as low-interest finance and preferential tax treatment should be equally emphasized. Most textbooks of neoclassical development economics are curiously silent on this point. Despite their neglect, East Asia's aggressive export promotion may furnish an empirical basis of a new theory of *infant exports*, in which the experience of external commerce is accumulated through protected exports.

Although neoclassical economists highlight the appropriateness of domestic economic policy in East Asian countries, the fact that their export drive during the 1960s and 1970s was supported significantly by a vigorous expansion of global trade should not be forgotten. Focusing on the speed of global trade expansion provides an angle similar to that of Keynes who worried about the level of effective demand in the macroeconomy. It is very odd that revived neoclassical development economics overlooks this important Keynesian perspective.

A related problem that should be mentioned is that revived neoclassical development economics too easily assumes the formal efficiency of market competition on a global scale. The risk that simultaneous industrialization of many developing economies might generate an oversupply of manufactured goods relative to effective world demand is underestimated. Neoclassical economists are wrong to believe that global market equilibrium is automatically attained by flexible price adjustment. In projecting the world economy over the long run, price adjustment may not always close the gap between demand and supply. Here, the Keynesian perspective of insufficient effective demand relative to supply capacity becomes indispensable.

Price distortions or underdeveloped markets?

There are several other problems with the neoclassical description of export-led economic growth of the East Asian NIEs. They will be examined closely in chapter 4.[4] For the purpose of this section, the most important difficulty with the neoclassical theory is this: apart from East Asian NIEs which are poised to join the Organization for Economic Cooperation and Development (OECD) in the near future, the validity of neoclassical economic theory seems severely limited when applied to the currently stagnant economies in Southeast and South Asia. How realistic is the idea that all markets, including factor markets, of any developing country would start functioning properly as soon as distortions imposed by state intervention are removed? As Hicks argues very convincingly in *A Theory of Economic History* (1969), factor markets are "relatively refractory territory" [p. 101] for the market economy. Southeast and South Asia are economically less developed than East Asian NIEs. Unattended, there is a great possibility that factor markets, such as labor and capital markets, of these underdeveloped countries may not allocate resources properly.

I would like to cite Myint's paper entitled, "The Neoclassical Resurgence of Development Economics" (1987), to make my point. Myint raises an important objection to neoclassical economics by saying that any theory of the market which reduces all economic difficulties to policy distortions alone is virtually useless in analyzing the economic development process of less developed countries.

According to Myint, the crucial problem of economic development facing these countries is not policy distortions, but dualistic economic structure which segments domestic factor markets. In many countries in Southeast and South Asia, capital markets are divided into modern banking and traditional money lenders, and labor markets into modern organized workers and traditional unorganized workers. Segmentation of these factor markets is not caused by government intervention alone; rather, it is an inevitable phenomenon in the dynamic process of marketization occurring in a non-market economy, that is, economic development itself. In this case, eliminating policy distortions will not automatically integrate segmented factor markets.

Because of this, the neoclassical advice to get rid of policy distortions is unlikely to immediately vitalize the market economies of Southeast and South Asia, permitting them to operate on, rather than inside, the production possibility frontier defined by available resources and technology.

Development economics that Myint presents is not the "conventional perfect competition model, which postulates the existence of a fully developed domestic system working in a frictionless manner," that is, neoclassical market theory; rather, it is the one that focuses attention on the "process by which a developing economy is enabled to make more flexible economic adjustments through the development of a domestic organizational framework" [Myint 1987: 130].

Through my own observation of Southeast and South Asian economies over the years, I myself have come to believe that the key question surrounding the economic development of those countries is how their labor, capital, and land markets, which are currently severely segmented, will become integrated and develop into functioning factor markets. So I basically agree with Myint's critique of neoclassical market theory.

Research on Asian economic development must therefore feature historical processes by which underdeveloped markets become more developed, rather than how policy distorts the economy. We may even say that neoclassical economists who stress harmful policy distortions too much fail to see the most fundamental issues in economic development. This leads us to conclude that two kinds of economics are necessary after all: one for the economies of developing countries and another for those of advanced countries.

The concept of market competition in information economics

The model of market economy envisaged by neoclassical development economics is that of market equilibrium under what is normally called perfect competition. Competition in this model is assumed to take place among a large number of sellers who are searching for buyers, and vice versa, under the condition that all market participants share the common price information determined by either an auctioneer or the market. There are two key assumptions in neoclassical market theory: first, all information required for the decision making of each individual firm and consumer is contained in prices; and second, all market participants are perfectly aware of this price information. Under these assumptions, each economic unit needs to know only the price announced by the auctioneer or market before arriving at a decision. All other information, such as on endowment, preference, and behavioral patterns of others, becomes irrelevant. In this sense, the market mechanism under perfect competition is said to be an "informationally economical or efficient" economic system (Arrow 1974).

However, the following point must be made in anticipation of my later argument. An auctioneer, whose existence is presupposed by the self-regulating market model of neoclassical economics, is not a *homo economicus* driven by selfish economic interest alone. When the assumption of rational individuals is applied consistently to every aspect of the market economic model, logic requires that the auctioneer be banished. But once we withdraw the service of the auctioneer who coordinates the economic behavior of numerous price takers from the center, individuals will no longer be able to act passively on self-interest in response to price information alone. This surely leads to a breakdown of the self-regulating market mechanism (Iwai 1987). This logical possibility is a serious defect in neoclassical market economic theory.

Proponents of revived neoclassical economics claim that this perfect-competition-based market model is more or less directly applicable to all markets, even to factor markets, in Asian countries. I believe they are seriously mistaken. The study of Asia's economic development must consist at the core of an effort to understand the dynamic process of evolving domestic markets. What neoclassical economists imagine is the ideal state of fully developed markets when they assume that prices contain all relevant information and that all market participants share common price information. It is obvious that such a model is incapable of analyzing the dynamism of developing market economies. This is where I disagree most with the revived neoclassical paradigm. As Ishikawa [1990, see also Chapter 6 of this volume] emphasizes, what is required for our intellectual pursuit is an approach or vision that can describe the dynamic process of how various markets, and factor markets such as labor and capital markets in particular, emerge. This should be the central issue in economic development.

Which theories can provide us with a clue to constructing such an approach? Let us start with Hayek (1948) who regards market competition as an apparatus for discovering efficient production methods in a world where information is distributed unevenly among economic agents. The skills and knowledge necessary for economic activity and resource allocation are scattered among a large number of individuals and therefore cannot be assembled in a neat way by a central planning authority or any other single organization. Hayek pays attention to this wide diffusion of useful information in the form of "local knowledge." If socially useful skills and knowledge are held unevenly by individuals as "private information," efficient production methods and technology must be found through natural selection in which inefficient individuals and firms are eliminated as a result of competition among a large number of economically free individuals.

According to Hayek, a market economy develops and functions as a spontaneous order among individuals holding private knowledge and participating in free competition.

Hayek's market competition is not the one described in neoclassical textbooks where information is perfect and everyone is a price taker. His argument shows us how to begin the study of market competition as a process of forming a network of relations evolving gradually from spontaneous exchange among individuals. Whether such a market satisfies Pareto efficiency or not should not concern us too much. Although Hayek's theory comes from the same Western tradition of individualism as does the neoclassical paradigm, it provides us with an important clue to realistically understand the dynamic process of developing markets.

However, Hayek's view of the market economy is still unsatisfactory because it does not clarify the crucial relationship between incentives and individual behavior – that is, the question of when individuals correctly reveal useful local skills and knowledge remains unanswered. On this key question, Stiglitz (1988) provides a very useful argument for us from the perspective of an information theoretic approach to the market economy.

As with neoclassical economists, Stiglitz assumes that all individuals and households – including farmers – behave rationally. However, unlike neoclassical economists, he contends that these rational economic beings face incomplete markets and must operate within them. As the reader will recall, the completeness [existence] of all markets in neoclassical theory is guaranteed by the crucial assumption of the existence of an auctioneer. But his existence cannot be logically derived from individual rationality. Once the auctioneer leaves the stage, economic transactions would require much more information than just prices, which is dispersed among a large number of people as private information – as Hayek asserts. Collecting such information would require enormous cost. Stiglitz therefore concludes that rationality of individuals is not sufficient to deduce the completeness of all markets. In other words, the implicit neoclassical assertion that "rationality implies efficiency" is not a self-evident truth (Roumasset 1976).

There are two types of private information that must be accumulated by those who intend to engage in economic transactions. The first is what may be called "hidden knowledge," or information about consumer preference, the quality of a commodity, the ability of a worker, and the like. The other is what we may call "hidden action," or information regarding economic behavior such as the diligence of a worker. Unavailability of the first type of information leads to an inefficient "adverse selection" and the lack of access to the second type is likely to cause an equally inefficient "moral hazard" (Okuno and Suzumura, 1988). The critical question for the smooth operation of economic transactions is whether or not the mode of transaction provides proper incentives so that individuals are willing to reveal their private information correctly.

In a situation where individuals are rational but the markets they face are incomplete, the logical pursuit of the consequence of free economic exchange among individuals – the type of economic theoretic thinking I have called the question of "what can happen" – leads us to the following important conclusion. When gathering information is costly and individuals, therefore, can obtain only part of the information needed for transaction, free transactions will not achieve Pareto efficiency, namely, a state where no one can improve his welfare without harming others. This means that government intervention through tax, subsidy, and other policy instruments may be desirable from the point of view of enhancing welfare. Thus, any actual market transaction potentially requires government intervention. The neoclassical assertion that free market transactions will attain Pareto efficiency *only if* government does not intervene – assuming no public goods – is rejected. In this way, an apparently minor modification to neoclassical theory of recognizing the incompleteness of markets because information is costly leads us to a drastically different conclusion.

Of course, the potential benefit of government intervention does not guarantee that such intervention will actually be efficient. Government faces the cost of collecting information just as private traders do. Neoclassical economists' preference for free market transaction based on the undeniable experience of failed government intervention is understandable. All the same, the potential benefit of government intervention cannot be ruled out theoretically.

Given limited space, I refrain from a fuller discussion of information theories which analyze economic management under imperfect information – except to say that Bardhan's paper entitled "Alternative Approaches to Development Economics" (1988) provides an interesting review on this matter. What should be stressed here is that this line of research yields important implications.

The first implication is the inadequacy of the neoclassical dichotomy of state versus market in the analysis of actual economies. This dichotomy reflects another neoclassical dichotomy of the state as a collective body versus individuals who pursue self-interest. Neoclassical orthodoxy is founded on the basis of this separation, where individual market participants are normally assumed to be equipped with all necessary information. In an actual economy, however, both government and private citizens confront similar difficulty in gathering useful information dispersed unevenly all over society. Economics which clearly separates state and individuals, or state and market, is not an appropriate tool. As Bardhan states, economic analysis under imperfect information should recognize the existence and importance of social and economic organizations which lie between the two extremes of state and individual, or state and market.

In this regard, neoclassical concepts of the individual as an atomistic participant and the firm as a volumeless mass in the market are highly deficient. Unable, *ex ante* as well as *ex post*, to gather private information held by each worker as to his own ability and diligence, a firm needs to invent an institutional mechanism to provide workers with incentives to train themselves, work hard, and stay with the firm for a reasonable period of time. When technical requirements call for an expansion of a firm to employ a sufficiently large number of workers, its internal organization gradually develops to satisfy these institutional needs to provide incentives. A firm with developed internal organization is no longer a volumeless mass in the market. Moreover, when firms lack perfect information on consumer preference toward their products, they tend to operate in an oligopolistic market structure. These firms are not atomistic participants in perfectly competitive markets under perfect information, either.

Akerlof (1984) is another economist who studies economic transaction under imperfect information. He stresses that factors such as mutual trust, sympathy, and shared values and customs, which lie outside the purview of standard economics based on individual rationality, may well improve spontaneous economic transactions in a world where information is imperfect. For instance, an employer's inability to detect the hidden action of his workers is said to cause the problem of moral hazard where the workers do not expend their maximum effort under the prescribed labor contract. But even in this case, the existence of mutual trust between the employer and workers could well prevent such an inefficient outcome. In a world with imperfect information, this and other social factors which are not derived from individual rationality can definitely improve economic efficiency. We need to recognize the importance of social organizations operating in the middle ground between the state and individuals, such as communities bound by blood relationship and alumni associations, which contribute significantly to the efficient working of the economy.

The second important implication of new information economics is that non-price information and the incentive to report it correctly become the key determinants of economic efficiency in a world of imperfect information. This invalidates the separability of the asset endowment problem and the problem of efficient resource allocation under market competition, as supported by the fundamental theorems of neoclassical welfare economics. These theorems assert that the market mechanism under perfect competition would achieve an efficient resource allocation in the sense of Pareto against any state of initial asset endowment. However, the assumption of a perfectly competitive market includes the possession of all information relevant to economic activity by every market participant.

By contrast, if information is imperfect, as Stiglitz stresses, incentive schemes to avoid moral hazard and other similar inefficiencies become necessary, and the idea that asset distribution and resource allocation are two separable issues is no longer tenable. On certain occasions, initial asset distribution may strongly affect the economic incentives of various groups. For example, share-cropping may be an efficient system if the extreme inequality in land ownership is taken as given. But there is also an undeniable possibility that agricultural productivity may improve even further when land is redistributed among villagers and former tenants who now are small landowners begin to work harder than ever.

More generally, when overall economic efficiency requires the provision of incentives to work hard to every participant in the system, the perception that everyone is treated equally in terms of the opportunity and qualification to enter competition is absolutely crucial. Such a sense of equality is an significant source of work incentive for every participant. Simply put, societies with hereditary discrimination and those without it will produce very different efficiency results because the former do not give work incentive to every group in the society, as the latter do, even when market competition is introduced to both. Thus, the economics of imperfect information permits us to examine the relationship between social organization and the performance of a market economy.

Economic development and market development: Japanese experience

The question raised by Stiglitz and Akerlof of how to design incentives so that individuals will reveal information correctly is critically important in understanding the formation and performance of labor and capital markets in rapidly developing Asian countries. Division of labor in production and the development of factor markets, both of which contribute to economic growth, are dynamic processes where an increasingly large number of participants enter an increasingly diverse markets. This undoubtedly imposes the need to assemble a greater amount of information on traders. According to North (1981), the promotion of division of labor and factor markets can reduce direct production costs, but it also increases transaction costs of various kinds. To minimize such transaction costs, some device to correctly reveal private information must be invented. In other words, market participants themselves are forced to contrive an institution in order to reduce the cost of gathering information held by diverse trading partners.

Using this theoretical approach, many aspects of the formation and performance of factor markets can be adequately analyzed. In the labor market, for instance, the situation where wages and unemployment remain high in farming villages even though many potential workers are vying for jobs can be explained. Similarly, dualism in an urban employment structure which exhibits distinct wage differentials can also be nicely interpreted. In capital markets, the linking of credit and land and labor markets observed in rural areas, the existence of credit rationing in urban capital markets with no interest regulation, and the like, can also be studied. In this way, the information-theoretic approach is an extremely useful tool for analyzing the dynamic process of how labor and capital markets are formed.

To prove the validity of this theoretical approach with more concrete examples, let us examine institutional changes which occurred in Japanese labor-service and capital transactions during the early twentieth century. In the process of modern economic growth following the Meiji Restoration [1868], the Japanese faced the need to devise new institutions to minimize transaction costs. These devices normally take the form of intermediary organizations which specialize in the collection of information on the behavior and ability of various economic groups and the quality of different products.

Let us first look at changes in the labor market in response to the industrialization process with imported technology. Introduction of the twentieth-century-style mass production system during World War I caused enormous structural shifts in the Japanese labor market. A so-called internal labor market began to emerge in manufacturing industries which adopted this modern system – see, for example, Odaka (1984). Mass production technology is normally embodied in large-scale fixed capital equipment, and its efficient operation requires a large number of workers who have incentives to improve their skills through on-the-job training and to work hard. The seniority wage system was an institution adopted at that time to elicit such behavior from workers.

I would like to emphasize that the traditional hierarchical structure of Japanese society was a positive factor that allowed smooth transition to new labor institutions in response to a changing technological environment. The technical need to use large-scale production equipment efficiently, called for an incentive scheme that could induce workers to refrain from opportunistic behavior and remain with an enterprise for a sufficiently long period of time. Japanese society already had a tradition highly consistent with these requirements for shaping an internal organization of firms, which facilitated a transition to the new institutional arrangement. The important point is that Japan happened to have a traditional social structure that promoted – rather than impeded – the introduction of new institutions required by the market economy.

As internal labor markets developed within large manufacturing enterprises which adopted mass production technology, the Japanese labor market began to exhibit a dual structure. People with higher education were recruited into large enterprises whereas the less educated worked for small- and medium-size enterprises using traditional technology. Since the two sectors paid wages according to different wage-determination principles, a significant wage gap emerged between them.

In the process of labor market segmentation, I believe that the Japanese education system, which was also being established during this period, played an instrumental role as an intermediary to furnish necessary information to entrepreneurs regarding the potential skills of a large number of workers. For entrepreneurs and managers, it was difficult to know which workers possessed the skills demanded by their enterprises. The problem was especially acute for modern large-scale manufacturers that needed workers with long-time commitment to the workplace. Under such imperfect information, education records served as an effective signal for the potential of each individual. The school system as an informational intermediary was not created spontaneously by merchants or through the operation of the market. Nevertheless, it was a very important institutional device for reducing uncertainty in labor contracts between employers and workers.

Let us now turn to institutional changes in the capital market. As is well known, banks were the main financial intermediaries in the process of Japanese economic development, connecting savers with investors. It should be noted that, in the early stages of development of the banking sector, indigenous social relations formed in and inherited from the Edo period [1603–1867] greatly expedited the establishment of modern financial intermediation. The experience of the postal saving system shows that, when most households were unfamiliar with modern banking and information about individual financial institutions was lacking, people would not deposit a part of their income with a bank unless the banker was someone whom they trusted personally. On the loan side also, indigenous financial institutions had an informational advantage because they knew the behavioral patterns of borrowers well through the social relations in which they operated (Teranishi 1991). These cases suggest that traditional social relations in Japanese society were conducive to the development of modern financial intermediaries. The importance of this fact cannot be overstated.

As an increasingly large number of households became wage earners, the modern banking sector began to assume an even more important role. The development of the banking sector in turn diminished the need for depositors to gather information on ultimate borrowers and their investment projects. Depositors now needed to know only the interest rates that the banks offered to them and the current inflation rate before they made a decision on saving. They did not have to know which firms ultimately borrowed their funds, because banks evaluated the borrowers' business plans and investment projects for them. By lessening the information cost for depositors, banks were able to accumulate a large volume of funds from numerous small savers, securing a stable source of saving deposits. With the development of banks as financial intermediaries, potential savings were mobilized en masse to the needs of productive investment.

I have described how Japan after the Meiji Restoration and especially in the early twentieth century devised new institutions in response to the changing menu of available technology and the expanding scope of market transactions. The process entailed the creation of intermediaries which bridged transactions in production factors such as labor and capital. While labor and capital carry different characteristics as factors, the school system [in the case of labor] and the banking system [in the case of capital] both specialized in collecting information on the factor in question and reduced the associated transaction cost. It should also be recalled that traditional social customs of Japanese society played a positive role in establishing these intermediaries.

Notes

1 This is a translation of *Asia Keizairon no Kozu* (A Blueprint for Asian Economics), Libroport, Tokyo, 1992. The first section of the present chapter, "How to Proceed with Asian Economics," reproduces section 2 of the prologue in the original. The remaining sections cover the entire original chapter 1. The included sections have been renumbered for consistency. In the original work, the prologue and chapter 1 are entitled, respectively, "Dualism of Asian Economies" (dualism here refers to the co-existence of high performers and stagnant economies) and "The Neoclassical Resurgence and Its Problems" [Editors].

2 Literally, the Japanese original says "the potential completeness of all goods and factor markets." "Complete markets" is a technical term implying that all markets exist. The

word *potential* seems to indicate, in this case, that all markets exist or would exist if government did not intervene unnecessarily. Hence our translation in the text [Editors].
3 Literally, "the potential completeness of all markets" – see note 2 above [Editors].
4 Not included in this volume [Editors].

References

Akerlof, G. (1984) *An Economic Theorist's Book of Tales*, Cambridge: Cambridge University Press.

Arrow, K.J. (1974) "Limited Knowledge and Economic Analysis," *American Economic Review*, March: 1–10.

Balassa, Bela, with associates (1982) *Development Strategies in Semi-industrialized Countries*, Baltimore, MD: Johns Hopkins University Press.

Bardhan, P.K. (1988) "Alternative Approaches to Development Economics," in H. Chenery and T.N. Srinivasan (eds) *Handbook of Development Economics*, vol. 1, Amsterdam: North-Holland.

Hayek, Friedrich A. von (1948) *Individualism and Economic Order*, Chicago: University of Chicago Press.

Hicks, John Richard (1969) *A Theory of Economic History*, Oxford: Clarendon Press.

Hirschman, A. (1987) "The Rise and Decline of Development Economics," in *Essays in Trespassing: Economics to Politics and Beyond*, Cambridge: Cambridge University Press.

Ishikawa, Shigeru (1990) *Basic Issues of Development Economics*, Tokyo: Iwanami Shoten (in Japanese) (see also Chapter 6 of this volume).

Iwai, Katsuhito (1987) *Theory of Disequilibrium Dynamics*, Tokyo: Iwanami Shoten (in Japanese).

Lal, Deepak (1985) *The Poverty of Development Economics*, Cambridge, MA: Harvard University Press.

Lewis, W. Arthur (1955) *The Theory of Economic Growth*, London: George Allen and Unwin.

Linder, S.B. (1986) *The Pacific Century: Economic and Political Consequences of Asia-Pacific Dynamism*, Stanford, CA: Stanford University Press.

Myint, Hla (1987) "The Neoclassical Resurgence of Development Economics: Its Strength and Limitations," G.M. Meier (ed.) *Pioneers in Development: Second Series*, Oxford: Oxford University Press.

North, Douglass C. (1981) *Structure and Change in Economic History*, New York: Norton.

Odaka, Konosuke (1984) *Analysis of Labor Market*, Tokyo: Iwanami Shoten (in Japanese).

Okuno, Masahiro, and Kotaro Suzumura (1988) *Microeconomics II*, Tokyo: Iwanami Shoten (in Japanese).

Oshima, Harry T. (1987) *Economic Growth in Monsoon Asia: A Comparative Survey*, Tokyo: University of Tokyo Press.

Ranis, Gustav, with John Fei (1988) "Development Economics: What Next?" G. Ranis and T. Schultz (eds) *The State of Development Economics: Progress and Perspective*, Oxford: Blackwell.

Roumasset, J.A. (1976) *Rice and Risk*, Amsterdam: North-Holland.

Schultz, Theodore (1964) *Transforming Traditional Agriculture*, New Haven, CT: Yale University Press.

Stiglitz, J.E. (1988) "Economic Organization, Information and Development," H. Chenery and T.N. Srinivasan (eds) *Handbook of Development Economics*, vol. 1, North-Holland.

Teranishi, Juro (1991) *Industrialization and the Financial System*, Tokyo: Toyo Keizai Shimposha (in Japanese).

Timmer, C.P. (1986) *Getting Prices Right: The Scope and Limits of Agricultural Price Policy*, Ithaca, NY: Cornell University Press.

8

CONTROLLING INSIDER CONTROL: ISSUES OF CORPORATE GOVERNANCE IN TRANSITION ECONOMIES[1]

Masahiko Aoki

This chapter identifies and discusses some fundamental issues of corporate governance in the transition economy. In the first part we present an overview of the generic tendency toward insider control in transitional economies. By insider control, we mean the capture of substantial control rights by the management or the workers of a formerly state-owned enterprise (SOE) in the process of its corporatization. There are variations in the degree and scope of insider control across transitional economies, depending on national conditions. The tendency is generic, however, in the sense that it is an evolutionary outcome of communist legacies. We argue that the mechanical application of the neoclassical model of stockholder sovereignty for corporate governance design in the transition is not effective in coping with the insider control problem; worse, it may even prolong the transition process.

The second part of the chapter shows that there can be an alternative model of corporate governance to monitor and control incentive issues unique to the insider-controlled enterprise. The essential idea is to rely on the development of banking institutions that can selectively intervene in the insider-controlled enterprise at the time of financial distress. The model considers the problem of how the bank is motivated to monitor the insider-controlled enterprise, while diversifying lending risk to some extent.

The second part of the chapter is purely theoretical; the preconditions assumed for the workability of the model do not seem to exist in transition economies. The fundamental question of which model is superior – the model of stockholder sovereignty with competitive capital markets or the model of the governance in which control rights shift from the insider to the outsider (the bank), contingent on the financial state of the enterprise – cannot be answered in isolation from other institutional characteristics of the economy, particularly the mode of internal organization of enterprises. We argue that the future course of the transition economy in this respect is too uncertain to predict. Therefore, we advocate an eclectic approach to corporate governance in the transition, including the simultaneous development of capital markets and banking institutions. They are presumably complementary in their roles in the development of sound corporate governance in transitional economies.

It seems certain, however, that sole reliance on the neoclassical model of stockholder sovereignty will be untenable. With this in mind, the last part of the chapter discusses banking reform in transition economies.

I Setting a conceptual framework

In order to discuss issues on corporate governance in transitional economies, let us first make clear what we mean by the transition: transition from which regime to which regime? In orthodox neoclassical economics, the latter should be something close to the neoclassical ideal of a regime of perfectly competitive markets. If all marketable factors of production are valued in competitive markets, the allocative efficiency of the economy would be assured by the maximization of residual after payments to those marketable factors. If the claimant of residual is identified with the shareholders, who do not gain any benefits other than the residual, they would be unanimously interested in maximizing the stock value of enterprises as reflecting the discounted sum of expected future flow of residual. Therefore, what is needed is to value enterprises competitively and effectively correct the management of enterprises if their values become lowered. The corporate governance structure that assures the sovereignty of the shareholders, combined with the competitive stock market, provides the necessary and sufficient institutional framework for that purpose. The task of the transition is to jump as quickly as possible to the regime in which such framework prevails.

This neoclassical paradigm is crystal clear in its logic and useful for some purposes, but in our opinion its mechanical application to transitional policy may not always yield good results because of its incompatibility with historical constraints. We want to propose more practical and inclusive definitions of the transition and the post-transition that allow for more diverse approaches. We believe it important to recognize two central issues in considering corporate governance.

First, the conditions inherited from the communist regime and those extant at the outset of the transition constrain the feasible options for corporate governance design in the transition process both politically and economically. Second, the neoclassical stockholder-sovereignty model of corporate governance may not be the only efficient solution. Any corporate governance structure may be in complementary relationships with other institutional arrangements of the economy – such as the internal work organization of the enterprise, the labor market and financial market institutions, and so forth – and the performance of a governance structure cannot be judged independently of how those other institutions are arranged. More specifically, the stockholder-sovereignty model can be efficient when it is surrounded by a cluster of complementary institutions of a particular kind, such as the hierarchical work organization and competitive labor and capital markets. We cannot preclude the possibility that for another cluster of institutions including the team-oriented work organization, another type of corporate governance could be more efficient. Recent results of comparative institutional analysis indicate that these two systems may not be efficiency-rankable independent of technological parameters of the economy. Accordingly, the transition path could be also diverse. We will elaborate these points gradually.

Anticipating the diversity of institutional arrangements, we begin with a less specific definition of the time-line, composed of the *communist regime*, the *post-transition regime*, and the intermediate *transition process*. Because our immediate concern is about corporate governance, we deal only with ownership and management of enterprises as defining factors. First, we refer to the communist regime as the period when the following conditions prevail:

C1 All enterprises are owned by the state, and their continuity is at the discretion of the state.

C2 The management (directors) of enterprises are appointed by the state organ controlled by the Communist Party.

The transition process is defined as the time period characterized by the following conditions.

T1 All enterprises are transformed into corporations (corporatization or "commercialization"), but their ownership structures are in the process of being defined.

T2 The state has lost the discretionary power to appoint and dismiss the management of enterprises, yet no definite power to do so has emerged.

Finally, the post-transition regime is defined as the one satisfying the following conditions.

P1 The corporate governance structure has been well defined for each enterprise and the share ownership structure has become stable in a statistical sense.

P2 The management of enterprises is chosen through due process, defined by the corporate law. There is a credible mechanism operating to replace poorly performing management.

This time-line construction is purely conceptual and its mechanical application to any economy may entail some classification problems. For instance, Poland introduced the State Enterprise Law in 1981, while the Communist Party still held political control. It enabled the workers to appoint the managing director of enterprises through democratically elected workers' councils. At the same time, the state retained the power to create and liquidate enterprises. In China enterprises are now being corporatized, and varied ownership structures are being tried (see the chapter by Qian in [the original] volume). The selection of the management, however, is still placed under the personnel administration of the Communist Party. According to the above definitions, we cannot say whether or not Poland in 1981 and China today are in the transition process. *Ad hoc* and somewhat inconsistent it may be, but we say that both Poland after 1981 and China today are in the transitional process. We expect that the mass corporatization of enterprises in China will eventually lead to depoliticization of management appointments.

Note that we do not necessarily identify the transition with the privatization of enterprises. The majority stocks of a significant number of corporatized enterprises may remain owned by the state (as in Hungary). Also note that we do not include the market control of corporate governance as a condition for the arrival of the post-transition regime (for example, we do not observe it in Japan). We intend to include in that regime, cases in which the majority or minority blocks of the stock of enterprises are stably owned by the state or insiders (workers, managers, enterprise pension funds, and the like), when there is a credible mechanism to punish poor management, if not through takeover. We deem that the existence of such a mechanism is imperative for an economic system to be viable without discretionary state intervention.

One of the purposes of this chapter is to ask: if insider control is likely to evolve in many enterprises in the transition process because of conditions prevailing at the demise of the communist regime, what public policies would be desirable and politically feasible for transiting to an efficient post-transition regime? This inquiry will inevitably entail another important question: is it possible for a post-transition regime to include a significant number of enterprises efficiently controlled by insiders?

II Emergent insider control in the transition

Insider control (either by the manager or the worker) appears to be a generic potential in the transition process, evolving out of inheritances of the communist regime. When the stagnation of communist regimes deepened in the 1970s and 1980s in Central and Eastern Europe, central planning bureaucrats tried to cope with the problem by relinquishing most of the planning instruments to the management of SOEs. The directors built up an irreversible jurisdictional authority within their own SOEs. The gradual retreat of the central planning authority ended with its sudden dismantling. The managers of the SOEs who had already carved out substantial controlling rights from the planning apparatus further enhanced their rights in the vacuum created by the collapse of the communist state. There seems to be nobody who has obvious legal and/or political power to dismiss the managers of ex-SOEs, while they have the support of their own workers.

The other quality of the communist regime that constrained the worker's freedom of job choice was their *de facto* job security. They were provided with medicare, child care, leisure facilities, housing, pensions, and so forth by the employing SOEs or the state. Workers had strong stakes at the employing enterprise. After the collapse of communism and the end of its "egalitarian" ideology, the workers are threatened by the possibility of losing those vested interests. Their fear may be greater the more uncertain the outcome of corporatization of their enterprises. Their possible opposition to massive privatization may have to be overcome by virtually giving them a substantial portion of enterprise assets.

Needless to say, the actualization of the potential of insider control varies across economies. We define insider control as a majority or substantial block-holding by the insiders in the case of privatization or strong assertion of insiders' interests in strategic decision-making when the enterprises remain owned by the state. Among possible factors conditioning the extent of insider control, the most important ones are the degree of management autonomy and the workers' strength against communist control in the final stage of the communist regime, and the political autonomy of the privatization authority against various interest groups in the transition process.

At one end of this continuum, there is Poland. As already noted, even before the fall of the communist regime, the workers' councils, composed of members elected by the employees, had attained a powerful position analogous to the board of directors in capitalist corporations, including the right to appoint the director and approve the annual plans of the enterprise. Once the transition phase began, the workers quickly moved to capture control of the assets of the enterprises before any market-based privatization plan was to be put into effect. The most common form of state property transformation worked as follows. Rather than corporatizing, the viable SOE was "liquidated" and a new company, in which the majority of the workers of the liquidated SOE became stockholders, leased or bought the assets. The much-publicized massive privatization plan through state-sponsored investment funds, an artifact of the neoclassical dogma of stockholder sovereignty, has thus been virtually defeated by the coalition of workers and managers of the better enterprises.

Russia is a case of strong manager control. The director of the SOE, who had already built the virtually autonomous empire in the communist regime, became almost invincible after the dismantling of the party and its planning apparatus. For any privatization plan to be implementable, it would have had to recognize this *de facto* control power of the director (see the chapter by Litwack in [the original] volume). The State Committee on Property Administration (GKI), which was charged with mass privatization, has become the most politically successful reform authority in Russia through its generous accommodation of insiders' interests.

The details of the scheme is described in the chapter by Akamatsu in [the original] volume. Simply put, according to the scheme the privatization of the

SOE proceeds in three stages. In the first stage, mandated by a decree of President Yeltsin of July 1991, the SOEs were to be corporatized and made legally autonomous entities, although all the shares were held initially by the state (the Federal Property Foundation) and administered by GKI. In the second stage, the insiders (the workers) choose an option for their privatization benefits from three variants specified by GKI, and the local committee of GKI approved an adopted plan. At this stage, the managers and the workers obtained a large share free-of-charge, or a majority share purchased at discounted value, depending on the adopted variant. In the third stage, the remaining shares were auctioned for vouchers that had been given to every citizen of Russia, sold in a package to investment funds by tenders, or kept under state control for the next several years.

The full implications of the scheme have not been worked out yet, but so far the insiders have overwhelmingly selected an option to guarantee them a majority share – that is, the option which gives managers and workers together individual ownerships of 51 percent of the equity at a low purchase price (at 1.7 times the July 1992 book value of assets). The managers can also increase their shares by purchasing vouchers in the market or by buying back shares from their own workers and markets (the workers are now given incentives to sell their shares tax-free). At the same time, investment funds that participate in voucher auctioning are limited initially in their ownership in one privatized SOE to 10 percent (raised to 25 percent after January 1994). The board of directors of the newly privatized SOE, before the first meeting of shareholders (which has to take place within one year after privatization), is composed exclusively of the general manager and worker representatives, except for representatives of the local GKI and the Property Foundation. As a result, the insiders, particularly the managers, have built solid controlling power in their enterprises.[2]

At the other end of the spectrum is the former German Democratic Republic (East Germany), whose privatization process under the centralized privatization authority, the Treuhandanstalt (THA), is described in detail in the chapter by von Thadden in [the original] volume. Even in East Germany, however, asset stripping by the insiders was an imminent danger at the time of demise of the communist regime. The only factor that prevented the subsequent development of insider control was the authority given to the THA. von Thadden shows that the institutional commitment to complete privatization by the end of 1994 prevented the THA from being susceptible to influence by the insiders. The recruitment of professionally capable THA managers from western Germany is also a positive factor unique to East Germany. The privatization of the SOEs was to be completed predominantly through the partial or whole acquisition of assets by West German (former Federal Republic of Germany) corporations. In that sense, the privatization in East Germany may be said to be comparable to a takeover in capital markets, although it was mediated by the centralized privatization agency. Even in this case, however, the end result of the transition would be the absorption of the SOEs into the West German corporate governance structure, which is different from the neoclassical model of stockholder sovereignty. This governance structure is characterized by insider (worker) participation in the supervisory councils through the legal requirement of codetermination.

The Czech Republic and Hungary provide intermediate cases. The insiders were weaker in the era of the communist regime in comparison with Poland or Russia, and the political power of the state (the privatization agency) in the transition process is weaker in comparison with East Germany. As a result, the tendency toward insider control has not been clearly resolved. Privatization in the Czech Republic is widely viewed as an ideal example of an approximation of the neoclassical model of outside stockholders' control through "voucher" privatization. The matter does not seem to be so simple, however. The privatization process is initiated with the decentralized submissions of a "privatization project," which can be done by anybody. The Ministry of Privatization has the centralized power to select a project. The Ministry has a political preference for projects including the competitive bidding of shares for vouchers. Nevertheless, project proposals for direct sales of assets to a new company formed by a group of insiders are also possible. According to data from the Ministry of Privatization, and quoted in Frydman *et al.* (1993: 84), only 53 percent of the total book value of privatized enterprises have gone to vouchers. The first preference of managers who were able to submit the most informative plans is said to be buyout (Frydman *et al.* 1993: 81). The tendency toward insider control surely exists, but has been moderated by the centralization of project selection.

In Hungary, a self-management system similar to the 1981 Polish scheme was introduced in 1984 (Law on Enterprise Councils), although the relative authority of managers in relation of the workers was stronger. The free-market-oriented post-communist government adopted a decentralized privatization scheme that gave the initiative to privatize to the enterprise councils, subject to approval of the State Property Agency (SPA). In contrast to the semicentralized Czech approach, this scheme seems to have provided more room for maneuvering by the managers to retain control and to fend off intervention by "outsiders". Privatized enterprises tend to be cross-owned by other enterprises, banks, and the state (SPA). Unfortunately, because of the unavailability of data, the extent of cross-holding is not precisely known, but something similar to the corporate grouping in Japan may be emerging.

Thus, although there is a variation in its degree, the tendency toward insider control is manifested everywhere in Eastern and Central Europe except for the newly emergent entrepreneurial enterprises and joint ventures with foreign corporations. This is an evolutionary outcome of legacies of the communist regime, which can be moderated only by a strong privatization agency. But an attempt to introduce outside stockholders control does not seem to effectively counteract this tide. Privatization of SOEs is *ex ante* constrained by the legacy of socialism, and in most it is cases *ex post* constrained by the weakness of the privatization agency in relation to the inside interest groups (see the chapter by Roland in [the original] volume).

This lesson may be instructive for China, which has now begun experimenting on various corporate governance structures. Even in China, where the Communist Party has retained solid control over the personnel selection and dismissal of management of the SOEs, the evolutionary tendency toward insider control is not unknown. The chapter by Qian [in the original volume] illustrates this point in detail. One commonly observed method for enhancing insider control is the spin-off of subsidiaries by the management of the SOEs and the leasing or sale of assets to these subsidiaries, created for this purpose. The "non-state-owned" enterprises thus created, together with smaller township and village enterprises, constitute the essential carriers of vital entrepreneurial initiatives in present-day China. This state asset stripping by insiders is often regarded as illegitimate by the population in general and, unless placed under a transparent due process, this "privatization" process may provoke a political backlash. The mechanical application of the neoclassical paradigm, however, such as voucher privatization by investment funds, does not seem to be an alternative solution. We next present theoretical reasons for this.

III Inadequacy of the investment fund scheme for the transition

Many economists have argued that the creation of investment funds (IF) that hold a substantial block of shares of the privatized enterprise may serve as an effective external check on insider control. The hope is that the IF would be interested in capital gains made possible by efficiency-enhancing restructuring, while at the same time being capable of exercising sufficient pressure or control over the management to implement the restructuring (see the chapter [in the original volume] by Akamatsu for a detail description of the IF in Russia and a comparison with those in the Czech Republic).

Nevertheless, it generally seems to be the case that the effectiveness of IFs in external monitoring has been limited. First of all, facing a substantial insider holding of shares, even a block of shares by the IF may not be sufficient for effectively controlling the privatized SOE (as in Russia). To advance the case for the active role of the IF in corporate governance, a well-known proposition by Schleifer-Vishny, which points to the importance of a blockholder, is often mentioned. What the proposition asserts, however, is that the existence of a blockholder is "necessary" for overcoming free-riding by small, passive shareholders in disciplining inefficient management by a takeover. Differing from the presumption of the Schleifer-Vishny model, the Russian situation is characterized by the existence of a large body of inside shareholders. How can the minority IF overcome this imbalance of power at a critical moment when the possible dismissal of the inside managers (and massive labor shedding) should be placed on the agenda?

Secondly, the IFs were formed as privatization intermediaries and funded primarily by vouchers that were entrusted by investors or purchased by the IF.

They are therefore under pressure to realize reasonable dividends for investors. If the markets for shares develop, however, they paradoxically may not be interested in monitoring and restructuring individual enterprises. By investing in the market index, like funds in developed, securities-oriented economies, the IF would be able to perform at least as well as the market (this possibility is also emphasized by Phelps *et al.* 1993). To respond to this concern, it has been proposed that the range of portfolio selection of the IF be restricted. But such a move would be inconsistent with the IF function of expected profit maximization, and it would effectively transform the IF into a holding company. The next issue raises a question about the ability of the IF to function as a holding company.

Third, the privatized SOE may be in desperate need of additional funding for restructuring, but the IF, as a share redistributing intermediary, may not be able to readily mobilize financial resources to meet such needs. Even if the IF could mobilize new financial resources, the insider majority control may imply tremendous agency costs for equity financing. The management and the workers may be interested in consuming on-the-job potential residual before it is distributed as dividends. The IF may be able to mediate bank loans because the IF is often controlled by a holding company that also controls a bank (as in Russia) or is owned by a bank (as in the Czech Republic). In this case, however, the conflict of interests issue needs to be addressed (see the chapter [in the original] by Akamatsu). For example, the assets of the IF may have been heavily invested in a failing enterprise and the holding company/bank may be interested in funnelling funds to salvage it at the depositors' risk.

These discussions are not intended to deny any role of the IF in the governance structure in the transition process. On the contrary, it may be an indispensable institutional component in counteracting the ill-effects of insider control. The point is to argue that the IF *alone* may not effectively resolve the problem of corporate governance design in the transition process posed by the evolutionary tendency toward insider control. To attempt to rely solely on the IF may actually prolong the transitional process by encouraging inefficient influence of insiders to reduce outside intervention. The management may sabotage restructuring by colluding with the workers to fend off the outsider intervention. Further, public policy that may be needed to foster the development of other institutions, such as the banks, may lag behind.

The transition economy has to face the evolutionary tendency toward insider control, and to do so an application of the abstract neoclassical model or the straightforward transplant of the Anglo-American model seems to be of limited value. In the next section, we propose an alternative model of external control of the insider control enterprise based on the idea of "selective intervention." Following the presentation of the theoretical model, we discuss whether it suggests any public policy approach toward the insider control problem in the transition process.

IV Bank syndication and contingent governance

The insider-controlled enterprise may have unique incentive problems, even if it is potentially productive. The management may try to borrow to build an empire (in the case of management control), to spend on non-productive projects to enhance workers' benefits, or to construct plants excessively equipped with machines to increase per capita outputs, while staying away from risky entrepreneurial projects (adverse selection problems). The workers may shirk to free ride on each other's efforts when team work is involved (moral hazard problem). The insiders may have incentives to consume as much revenue of the enterprise as possible on the job or in the form of supracompetitive compensation before repayments to lenders or dividend payments to shareholders are made. Poor management may be tolerated out of collegiate compassion.

To cope with possible inefficiencies of such incentive problems, some external agents must play active roles in monitoring the insider-controlled enterprises. To facilitate the following discussion, it is useful to distinguish conceptually, three phases of investors' monitoring in reference to the timing of investment: *ex ante* monitoring, in which potential new projects and/or new clients are evaluated to cope with the problem of adverse selection; interim (ongoing) monitoring, to uncover moral hazard problems arising from the divergence of interests between outside investors and the insiders, as well as free-riding among the insiders; and, finally *ex post* monitoring, to verify the true financial state of the enterprise, to assure the (re)payments of debts or dividends and to punish the management in the event of a failure to do so.

This section presents a purely theoretical model of corporate governance that resolves incentive problems of insider control by integrating the three stages of monitoring by a single bank, while other investors can diversify risk. The model is derived by a modification of the bankruptcy procedure proposed by Bebchuck (1988) and Aghion, Hart, and Moore (1992), which attempts to strike a balance between the merits of equity and debt contracts as controlling instruments. The novelty of the model presented below is to explicitly consider the incentives of the monitor – in this case, a bank – to monitor the insider-controlled enterprise in an integrative way, while preserving the essential feature of their model.

Suppose that when the viable insider-controlled enterprise is in need of external long-term investment funds, a bank which has had a long-term relationship with the enterprise organizes a loan syndicate with many other banks. This lead bank (LB) may own a minority share of the borrowing enterprise up to a certain limit (say, 5 percent). The LB is assumed to perform the commercial banking function by running the major payment system accounts as well as the deposit accounts of the borrowing enterprise. These two attributes may provide the information advantage necessary for the bank to be an LB. The question is how this advantage can be utilized for the reduction of agency costs of the external financing and monitoring costs, rather than allowing the LB to exploit its private benefits at the cost of other banks and investors.

Suppose that the LB is limited to provide only a minority share, say 20 percent, of the syndicate loans, but the LB must guarantee the repayment of the claims of other member banks (this stringent requirement will be relaxed later). This imposes a heavy responsibility on the LB. In return, however, the LB may charge a syndicate management premium, as well as enjoying the benefits of running the payment settlement and deposit accounts of the borrowing enterprise. Meanwhile, the IF and other types of investors may be active in share markets, evaluating the performance of the enterprise through trading on the basis of their own interim monitoring.

When the enterprise becomes unable to meet repayment obligation, the LB is obliged to buy the defaulted claims of syndicate member banks. The LB then completely writes off these debts and converts them into new equity. The LB either auctions off the new equity rights to reorganization specialists or holds them for a certain specified period of time (for instance, three years). In the latter case, the LB is engaged in restructuring the defaulting enterprise by replacing the managers, laying off workers, liquidating some assets, and so forth. If the insiders refuse to cooperate, the LB could threaten to invoke the liquidation procedure. After restructuring within the said period, the LB may sell the amount of shares beyond the normal limit (5 percent, for example) for possible capital gains from restructuring. In either case, the restructured enterprise would be transformed into an outsider-controlled enterprise, while the insiders are penalized for debt default by the loss of their share values, and possibly the loss of employment continuation values as well. If there is no prospect for capital gains from restructuring, the LB may decide to liquidate the enterprise. In this case the uncovered value of debts would be borne by the LB.

The scheme has merit. First, in contrast to the Aghion–Hart–Moore model, the postbankruptcy procedure is administered by the LB rather than by the court, which may lack expertise in *ex post* management of the bankrupt enterprise. The LB is clearly advantaged in information useful for *ex post* management, but prevented from using it at the expense of other creditors' interests because of its repayment guarantee.

In our scheme the LB is also responsible for *ex ante* monitoring to cope with adverse selection of the borrowing enterprise and for interim monitoring to control its moral hazard. The LB would be motivated to earnestly perform *ex ante* and interim monitoring in order to avoid the heavy costs of liquidation and/or restructuring arising from debt guarantees for other member banks.

Second, generally speaking, from the point of view of the bank, there are trade-offs between the diversification of lending risk and incentives to monitor. An arm's-length relationship between the bank and the borrower may allow the bank to diversify risk, provided that risk is distributed independently of bank action. But risk diversification may dilute the incentives of the bank to monitor the enterprise *ex ante* and interim. At the same time, the exclusive lending relationship will not only expose the bank to idiosyncratic risk, but may also dilute its commitment to *ex post* monitoring because once lending is made, the continuation of the enterprise may become *ex post* desirable even for the bank.

As noted above, in our scheme the LB is certainly motivated to monitor. But what about the risk diversification opportunities of the LB? Does the proposed scheme not amount to the same thing as the LB bearing full risk costs, as in exclusive relational lending? That is, is the LB not exposed to the same degree of idiosyncratic risk as the relational bank? Why then is syndication worth the trouble?

Suppose that a sufficient number of qualified banks that have the required monitoring capability exist to allow for workable competition among them (roughly, the number is not too small nor too large). Suppose that each of them has a mutually exclusive group of customer enterprises for which they function as LBs. These banks become ordinary syndicate members for non-affiliated enterprises for which other banks act as LBs. In other words, there is "reciprocal delegation of monitoring" (Sheard 1994) among those banks. Other minor banks may participate in any syndicate as ordinary members. Responsible monitoring by the LB saves the duplication of monitoring costs, particularly by minor banks.

Now let us modify the described scheme in such a way that the group of qualified banks mutually agree to rebate a fraction of the LB's guaranteed repayment to them in case the revenue of the LB from liquidation of assets or the prerestructuring auction falls short of a certain level. Such reciprocal arrangements may spread the cost of risk-bearing among qualified banks, while somewhat diluting the incentives for the LB to monitor. The modified syndicate arrangement is a device to strike a balance between the conflicting requirements of risk diversification and incentive provision.

The third advantage of the scheme is that the risk of bad performance by the borrowing enterprise is not distributed independently of insider and bank actions. The risk may be reduced by more intensive *ex ante* and interim monitoring of the LB. The requirement of syndication severs qualified banks from exclusive relationships with the borrowing enterprise. This would reduce the hazard of the banks being captured by the interests of the customer enterprises and make them more independent in their judgements at the *ex ante* monitoring stage.

Fourth, after the initial investment is sunk, the continuation of a bad project might become *ex post* profitable, if bad debt were written off. In such a situation, if the relationship between the bank and the enterprise is that of the exclusive relational bank, they would be induced to renegotiate. The enterprise's insiders may have strong motives to negotiate for the survival of the enterprise to save the loss of employment continuation values if the labor market is imperfectly competitive. The bank may be induced to accept an insider's concession, while keeping the insiders control intact. Such a prospect would dilute the *ex ante* and interim incentives of the insiders. In our scheme, the shift of control rights can be automatically triggered by a debt–equity swap when the insider-controlled enterprise defaults. Insider control is maintained contingent only on the financial viability of the enterprise. The corporate governance structure implied by the scheme may thus be called *contingent*.

The LB or the reorganizer (IFs, or another enterprise) that acquires the shares in the restructuring auction has incentives to restructure for capital gains. As opposed to the creditor rescue operation, the restructuring agent can secure future returns to restructuring costs without fearing the emancipation of the rescued enterprise. Thus, premature liquidation (Type I error) may be avoided, while the threat of punishing poorly performing insiders is made credible. This is the essential feature of the Aghion–Hart–Moore model.

The fifth major advantage of the scheme is that the contingent governance structure may have positive incentive effects on the insiders. The contingent governance implies that as long as the insider-controlled enterprise is financially healthy and able to repay its debts without any problem, the insiders remain as residual claimants. If they always remain residual claimants, regardless of the financial state of the enterprise, the moral hazard of free-riding among insiders would become a problem or, sheer bad luck might make the insiders lose large asset values (in financial and human capital) in liquidation. These possibilities may be prevented by the existence of the LB, which may restructure the failed yet viable enterprise, but imposes harsh penalties when the post-bankruptcy situation is hopeless.

If the contingent governance is efficiently designed, the insiders may develop incentives to accumulate internal financial resources to become autonomous from possible external intervention. The relative autonomy of the enterprise from external loans would in turn stimulate insiders' incentives for greater effort, because the fruit of their efforts would accrue to them as residual claimants. Thus, once the contingent governance is put in effect, the virtuous cycle of insider control and enterprise growth may be generated up to a certain threshold point. (The possibility of such dynamics, together with the efficiency property of the contingent governance structure, is analyzed in Aoki 1994a.)

V Eclectic approach – probably the best in the transition

We have shown a theoretical possibility of a governance structure that can cope with the unique incentive problems arising from insider control. But we have assumed that the insider control enterprise is viable and that there is a banking sector comprising a sufficient number of banks capable of assuming the heavy responsibility of lead banks. These last two conditions do not hold in the transition process. The privatized enterprise may need to be restructured, for which outside financing is needed. Nevertheless, incentive problems of insider control may be rampant and any bank may consider it too risky to assume the responsibility of the LB. First of all, no bank may have either the financial resources to bear the responsibility or the capacity to monitor.

The merit of the theoretical exercise in the last section was to show that a corporate governance structure alternative to the neoclassical model of stock-holder sovereignty is conceptually possible in the post-transition regime. The contingent governance structure may not be just a passive reaction to the insider control problem. Rather, it may have an active *raison d'être*: to facilitate the development of a team-oriented production organization characterized by lateral cross-functional coordination, joint task responsibilities, mutual help, and the like in which worker skills and shared knowledge become specific to the organization. According to recent work on comparative institutional analysis, we cannot unequivocally rank the team-oriented work organization and the traditional hierarchical organization according to efficiency criteria. The former may perform better in an industry where coordination among tasks is relatively more important because tasks are complementary, while the latter organization may perform better in the industry where flexible reallocation of scarce corporate assets among tasks is important (Aoki 1994b).

The kind of financial institution that would be desirable to develop would depend on the prevailing type of work organization. If workers' skills and shared knowledge become organization-specific, and thus not individually marketable, stock value maximization may not be consistent with internal and allocative efficiency. This is because the value maximization criteria presupposes that all factors of production other than fixed factors are market valued. If the insiders constitute an immobile factor of production as a team, the enterprise ought to strike a balance between insiders' interests and outsiders' interests. Games between them may no longer be zero-sum, however, and there may be gains from cooperation (Aoki, 1984). Insiders' shared rights of control in corporate governance (as in West Germany) or outsiders' selective intervention through the contingent governance (as in Japan) may facilitate an approximation of the cooperative solution. Thus the bank-oriented financial system may be complementary to the team-oriented organization, while the market-oriented financial system is complementary to the hierarchical organization, as the neoclassical paradigm asserts.

In what direction will the evolution of the transitional economies lead? One scenario may be that the hierarchical aspect of the work organization in the SOE would reform itself so that task assignments in the organization are made more on the basis of individual skills. For this direction, the complementary development of the capital market institutions would be necessary, because the efficiency of such an organization can be best valued by residual after competitive payments for individualized skills. Another scenario may be that the collegial aspect of the work organization in the SOE would develop into an efficient, team-oriented work organization. For this direction, the development of banking institutions might be complementary. Still other scenarios may be feasible. The transition economy may take advantage of the latecomer being able to develop a hybrid by combining the two types of organizations. Or, if the transition economy fails to develop proper governance and financial institutions, it might be locked in permanent stagnation. Nobody seems to be able to predict with certainty which scenario is the most likely.

We may posit that an eclectic approach is an option in the transition process. That is, instead of pursuing solely the possibility of external control of the enterprise through the development of capital markets, or that of banking institutions, it is better to foster their simultaneous development in the transition. Only spontaneous development of organizations through competition would determine the dominant system in the post-transition regime.

VI Other reasons to develop banking institutions in the transition

In the model of syndicate lending presented above, *ex ante*, interim, and *ex post* monitoring of the enterprises are all integrated and delegated to a single LB. In contrast, in a highly advanced securities-oriented financial system, such as the Anglo-American economy, these three phases of monitoring are dispersed among various intermediaries, information-processing agents, and corporate and legal institutions possessed of different specialized expertise. For example, *ex ante* monitoring is performed by investment banks for large enterprises, venture capitalists for entrepreneurial start-ups, and commercial banks for smaller firms; interim monitoring is performed by rating firms, commercial banks, funds of various types, market arbitrageurs, and so forth; *ex post* monitoring is done by accounting firms, the bankruptcy court and reorganization specialists, takeover raiders, LBO [leveraged buy-out] partners, and the like. In general, the transition economy that has evolved from a situation where there is an absence of financial markets initially lacks the accumulation of such diverse monitoring resources. The integrated delegation of the three phases of monitoring to a single bank is a way to economize in the use of scarce monitoring resources.

Further, there is a positive reason for the integration of the three phases of monitoring, rather than their decentralization, to bring about better results. In the transition process, *ex ante* monitoring of the corporatized SOE, if not that of a new, innovative start-up, would be unlikely to require highly sophisticated project analysis. The urgent problem with the corporatized SOE, privatized or not, is to restructure itself rather than to initiate new projects at the technological and commercial frontier. If this is so, the relevant *ex ante* monitoring would be more on the organizational capability of the corporatized SOE to absorb, adapt and improve on the existing organizational, engineering, and commercialization know-how. For that, the bank that would maintain a long-run relationship with the borrowing enterprise may be in an informationally advantageous position because it can feed back information available from interim monitoring to the assessment of relevant organizational capability.

It may also be the case that *ex ante* monitoring and interim monitoring are complementary to *ex post* monitoring. Even if the financial state of the enterprise is critically worsened, the IF may be less adept at finding the problem when the accounting methods are not very informative and disclosure requirements are lax. Even if they are competent enough to find problems at an early stage, they may encounter resistance of the insiders to yielding control power. In contrast, the bank would mediate daily payment settlements for the customer enterprise as well as roll-over short-term loans or discount trade bills necessary for financing working capital. Such operations would give the bank a power similar to that of being able to partially open the books. At the time of automatic transfer of control triggered by debt contracts in the event of repayment default, the bank may utilize knowledge accumulated through interim monitoring to exercise its judgment of whether the enterprise has a chance to survive or would be better served by liquidation.

The merits discussed of the integration of the three phases of monitoring presume that a single bank would credibly commit *ex ante* to interim and *ex post* monitoring. Such a commitment is not credible in the highly developed, market-oriented system where debt instruments are easily marketed. The initial investors may get rid of their claims in the market rather than bear bankruptcy or rescue costs *ex post* if they are in a position to find possible problems with borrowers at an early phase.

As already noted, however, the necessity of developing a sound banking sector should not be taken as precluding the simultaneous functioning of financial markets. On the contrary, competitive and informative financial markets can be complementary to bank monitoring. Instead of the formation of syndicates, the bank may underwrite and guarantee bond issues of the customer enterprise. The price formation of the securities of the enterprise in the market can compete with the interim monitoring of the bank, pointing its mistakes or remedying possible moral hazard. If the IF develops restructuring expertise in the post-transition regime, it can bid for the equity that the LB auctions off after the debt–equity swap operation. The point is, however, that the role of a sound banking sector, composed of a reasonable number of qualified banks, could not be fully substituted for the financial markets when the magnitude of insider control is substantial.

VII Banking reform needed in the transition

Although the case for the development of a sound banking system in the transition process appears to be strong, the current state of banking institutions in transition economies seems to be still far from that needed to perform the kind of tasks suggested above. Is there any hope that they will develop the capacity and incentives to do so? What kind of banking regulations are to be instituted in the transition process to encourage such developments?

In transitional economies, most of the existing banks are either successors or spin-offs of the former state banks or newly established agent banks of corporatized SOEs. Large commercial banks in Central Europe were created in the last few years with the split of the former state mono-bank into a central bank and a number of commercial banks. The loan portfolio was distributed to the new commercial banks along regional (Poland) or sectoral lines (Czech Republic, Hungary). Most of the deposits are with specialized savings institutions, channelled to commercial banks in the form of refinancing credits through central banks. The spin-offs of the former state banks are still owned by the state and their privatization is under preparation (Poland, Hungary), or their majority ownership has now been privatized (Czech Republic). Private commercial banks have been established recently, yet the former state banks are still dominant in assets. In Russia there are now approximately 1,700 independent commercial banks (see the chapter [in the original volume] by Belyanova and Rozinsky for a detailed account of the present-day Russian banking institutions). Among them, about 700 banks, including most of the larger banks, are spin-offs of the former Soviet specialized banks, which are now mostly owned by former SOEs. For these banks the sets of shareholders and borrowers are the same.

The state bank in the centrally planned economy was not an autonomous financial institution, but an administrative instrument of centralized planning to control the SOE. As is well known, one of the most important causes of the failure of centrally planned economies was the soft budget constraint on the SOE because of the lack of commitment by the state bank not to refinance *ex post* inefficient projects. Financing the existing SOE became automatic because of the political necessity of maintaining employment (latent insider control problem), the rising bargaining power of managers, and possibly because refinancing made economic sense once the initial investment was sunk. Insolvency criteria did not exist in the communist regime, and thus soft credits could not be distinguished from outright giveaways. A possible problem with the spin-offs of former state banks is the continuation of soft credits as a form of inertia. Half of all commercial bank loans extended in 1992 in Russia were in the form of directed credits funded by the Central Bank or the budget and channelled through these banks (World Bank 1993: 2).

The newly created agent banks may have their own problems. In Russia more than 1,000 agent banks have been created from nothing since 1990. They were usually created by enterprises or by groups of enterprises to manage their cash flows and to perform payment system transactions on their behalf. These banks also make loans, primarily with funds from enterprise deposits and interbank markets, as well as funds in the process of collection. A possible problem with the agent bank is that, as with the case of most relational banks in developing economies, they are captured by the interests of the parent enterprise and cannot act as independent sources of monitoring. Their credits may be exposed to risks that are too idiosyncratic.

For banks to operate on a sound basis, it is necessary that their assets are sufficiently diversified. When the funding basis of the bank is thin, as is the case with most agent banks, it is difficult to diversify lending while meeting the funds requirements of the parent enterprises. The formation of a loan syndicate may be a possible response. The difficulty is that the sheer number of agent banks and their small size seems to prevent the development of syndicates, because the question of which bank ought to bear the responsibility for syndicate organization (*ex ante* monitoring), interim monitoring, and how to set the priority for claims cannot be settled easily.

In spite of these problems, however, the banking sector in transitional economies appears to be gradually evolving as a viable institution. Peter Dittus (1994) recognized the increasing spread between the deposit and lending rate and the recent noticeable decline of net lending to enterprises in Central European economies. By careful examination, he tentatively concludes that the decline of lending is not a result of a credit crunch from the government deficit, and it can be regarded as a hardening of budget constraints for the enterprises. He cautiously notes: "clearly, the environment in which banks are operating and their behavior have changed much more than seems to be commonly acknowledged. It has also become evident, however, that the difficulties remain to be overcome are substantial" (p. 34). The chapter [in the original volume] by Belyanova and Rozinsky indicates that the difference between better spin-offs of the ex-state banks and newly created banks are beginning to be blurred, and some of them seem to be evolving as viable institutions in spite of the problems.

What difficulties are to be overcome in order for better banks to evolve into active monitors of insider control? Let us try to identify some basic problems to be addressed.

The first is the dilemma between risk diversification and monitoring. In order to be free from soft credits and the excessive exposure to idiosyncratic risks associated with relational lending, it is desirable that the bank diversify its loans. As noted earlier, one method to achieve this is to form syndicates. At the same time, the formation of loan syndicates may dilute incentives for the bank to monitor. How can we resolve this dilemma?

The second problem is related to the social costs of bankruptcy. As we have hinted, one possible advantage of a bank-centered monitoring mechanism is that the default of debt repayment can trigger the automatic shift of control rights from the insider to the creditor bank, even if the latter does not own a block of shares. The mechanical application of bankruptcy procedures would be unproductive given the current state of transitional economies.[3] The newly corporatized SOE seems to need outside financing, and sometimes subsidies, to be viable and perform the necessary restructuring. How can such finance and subsidy be made without perpetuating the soft credit relationship between the bank and the enterprise?

As previously noted, there are today, some 1,700 banks in Russia. This number is simply too large, and the average size of banks is too small to induce risk diversification and delegate responsible monitoring to single banks. Nevertheless, that more than 1,000 banks devoid of traits of the old state bank system have emerged from scratch only in a few years may be considered as a positive sign of the potential for vigorous evolutionary change. It is said that some of those new banks were organized and run by young, competent people (see the chapter by Belyanova and Rozinski in [the original] volume). Such a situation may suggest that, once a prudent and competitive regulatory framework is provided and a stable macroeconomic policy environment is set, some of the existing banks may be given an opportunity to develop as banks accountable for external monitoring.

To emancipate banks from fragmented, exclusive relational banking, there is a need to drastically increase the minimum capital requirements of banks. Such regulation would provide an impetus for acquisition and mergers among banks. Further, it would be desirable to limit the lending of the bank to a single enterprise – for example, to one-quarter of the bank's capital. Such measures would induce banks to restrain the volume of relational lending. Nevertheless, our purpose is not to promote arm's-length banking. If portfolio diversification by banks were merely to accelerate arm's-length relationships, a vacuum would remain for external monitoring of the insider control enterprise. Because many banks are now owned by (a group of) enterprises, the movement toward arms'-length banking following the Anglo-American system may not be likely. Through the process of merger and acquisition, originally close bank–enterprise relationships may be diluted, but maintained with some distance. The enterprise would likely hold major payment system accounts only with a few banks. Those banks would be likely candidates for lead banks if lending diversification should lead to organized syndication.

In the process of past hyperinflation, bad debts of enterprises appear to have been largely wiped out in Central and Eastern European transitional economies, but it has not solved the recapitalization problem of banks. On one hand, enterprises appear to rely upon intricate networks of trade credits rather than bank credits. Default on trade credits by one large enterprise may trigger chain reactions. On the other hand, banks appear to rely on lending based on interbank markets and funds in the collection process, but they have not acquired a solid deposit basis yet, except for deposits by foreign currencies. Spin-offs of state banks also rely upon the central bank's directed credits as lending sources. One solution to cope with all these problems may be to induce the development of an interbank payment settlement system based on trade bills drawable on partner banks by enterprises. The central bank should then gradually limit its capital infusion to the banking sector to "neutral" re-discounting of eligible trade bills at the window rather than directing credits to particular enterprises by discretion. Such a development would not only resolve the problem of supplying money on a sound basis, but also increase the capacity and incentives of the banks to monitor customer enterprises. Nevertheless, necessary state subsidies should be made through the budgetary process separated from the commercial banking sector. Only through such a neutral stance of the central bank and insulation of the commercial banking sector from discretionary subsidization can the soft credits of banks be reduced.

Notes

1 [This is the entire chapter 1 of *Corporate Governance in Transitional Economies: Insider Control and the Role of Banks*, edited by Masahiko Aoki and Hyung-Ki Kim, World Bank Economic Development Institute, 1995. Editors] In writing this chapter, I benefited from comments and discussions by Erik Berglof, John Earle, Hyung-Ki Kim, Gerald Roland, Dimitri Slavnov, Yingyi Qian, and other participants in the project on "Corporate Governance in Transition Economies: Insider Control and the Role of Bank" sponsored by Economic Development Institute of the World Bank and the Center for Economic Policy Research at Stanford University. Bruce Donnell provided research assistance.

2 In a decree issued by President Yeltsin on December 24, 1993 (N2284), some measures were introduced to curb the tendency toward strong insider control. Requirements for worker payment for benefit options were made somewhat stringent (for example, the amount of the first installment for stocks bought with a discount was increased). It was also stipulated that the number of representatives of employee-stockholders may not be more than one third of the board of directors, and that managers or workers may not sit on the board representing the interests of the state. That these provisions were thought necessary may suggest that such practices had been widespread without check.

3 Factors pointed out by many authors as working against the mechanical application of the bankruptcy procedure in the transition: without a sound payment system, many viable enterprises may be forced into bankruptcy by a mere chain reaction; the asset registry does not exist and private ownership in land is not legally well defined; the bankruptcy procedure may involve costs of maintaining a system of commercial courts; and the lack of expertise and discipline in receivership, and the absence of clear rules regarding claim subordination, may also incur additional social costs of bankruptcy.

References

Aghion, Philippe, Oliver Hart, and John Moore (1992) The Economics of Bankruptcy Reform, *Journal of Law, Economics and Organization* 8: 523–46.

Aoki, Masahiko (1984) *The Co-Operative Game Theory of the Firm*, Oxford: Clarendon Press.

Aoki, Masahiko (1994a) "Contingent Governance of Teams: Analysis of Institutional Complementarity," *International Economic Review* 35: 657–76.

Aoki, Masahiko (1994b) "An Evolutionary Parable of the Gains from International Organizational Diversity," Stanford University, mimeo.

Bebchuk, L. (1988) "A New Approach to Corporate Reorganizations," *Harvard Law Review* 101: 775–804.

Berg, Andrew (1994) "The Logistics of Privatization in Poland," in Olivier Jean Blanchard, Kenneth A. Froot, and Jeffrey D. Sachs (eds) *The Transition in Eastern Europe*, Chicago: University of Chicago Press.

Dittus, Peter (1994) "Corporate Governance in Central Europe: The Role of Banks," Bank of International Settlements, Basle, mimeo.

Frydman, Roman, Andrzej Rapaczynski, and John S. Earle (1993) *The Privatization Process in Europe*, Prague: Central European University Press.

Phelps, E.S., Roman Frydman, A. Rapaczynski and A. Scheifer (1993) "Needed

Mechanisms of Corporate Governance and Finance in Eastern Europe," European Bank for Reconstruction and Development, Working Paper No. 1, London.

Sheard, Paul (1994) "Reciprocal Delegated Monitoring in the Japanese Main Bank System," *Journal of the Japanese and International Economies* 8: 1–21.

World Bank (1993) "The Banking System in the Transition – Russia," Europe and Central Asia Department Report No. 12763, Washington, DC.

THE CONTINUITY OF CULTURES AND CIVILIZATION[1]

An introduction to the concept of translative adaptation

Keiji Maegawa

I Political economy of "cultural" perspectives

The Polanyi school of economic anthropology demonstrated in the 1980s that "modernity," an idea that Japanese people had long thought as self-evident, was in fact a relative concept in the epistemological sense. This also led, inevitably, to the reconsideration of the theories of social evolution. The validity of any historical theory based on stages of development, whether unilinear or multilinear, is now in serious doubt. The Marxist theory of multiple-stage development centered on a single country has lost its appeal. Similarly, in mainstream economics, the historical theory of economic growth is no longer able to explain the diverse reality.

With the dismissal of existing historical theories, views that relativize – or even deny – the concept of modernity became popular during the 1980s. The rejection of these historical theories generated new perspectives which laid more weight on the spatial rather than the temporal axis, encouraging the assertive display of cultural diversity. The 1980s also coincided with the economic prosperity of Japan as it poised to overtake the United States as an economic superpower. This nurtured the theory of cultural specificity which affirmed cultural differences between Japan and the West, and the theory of cultural revisionism which viewed such differences as inherently irreconcilable. It should be recognized that these new arguments were closely related to our evolving perception of what is modern and pre-modern. Until the 1970s, Japanese cultural features were considered "pre-modern," and this judgment filled Japanese intellectuals with a sense of cultural inferiority. During the 1980s, by contrast, the same differences came to be regarded as positive values which merited active promotion.

In anthropology, cultural diversity has long been recognized as an important aspect of reality ever since the establishment of cultural relativism[2] as a valid methodology. Cultural relativism was founded by such American anthropologists as Ruth Benedict and Margaret Mead during the 1920s and 1930s. It was only in the 1970s, however, that new Western social sciences, including anthropology, were widely introduced to Japan. Only then, the concept of cultural relativism gained popularity here and began to be applied in the context of Japan as a non-Western society. Cultural relativism, together with the perceived relativity of modernity discussed above, provided the foundation of Japanese thought during the 1980s. In reality, cultural diversity was also vividly experienced as Japanese firms actively invested and Japanese people travelled extensively abroad, thanks to domestic economic prosperity and the appreciating yen. (I admit that packaged group tourism that many of us prefer may impede close encounters with diverse foreign cultures. At the same time, it must be said that our previous bias toward Western culture has been significantly abated by these tours.)

It is important to realize that the acceptance of cultural relativity at this time in our history was brought about by the prosperity of the Japanese economy. That is to say, a country begins to recognize the diversity of foreign cultures only when it is engulfed in the expanding modern world system. The new perspective comes with the spatial expansion of global political economy.

For instance, the main motive behind Columbus' voyage to the New Continent which ushered in the "modern" period was a search for spices. Acquisition of spices was expected to boost the economic power and national strength of Spain. Thus, the new perception of the world which the West came to possess as a result of Columbus' discovery of the New Continent was highly charged with political and economic intentions.

Japan's economic success should also be understood in a similar light. Our "modernization" was initiated with the arrival of the Black Ships at the end of the Edo period,[3] and carried out through the Meiji Restoration, World War II, and to the present day. From the global perspective, this process was Japan's adaptation to the expanding modern world system – namely, the reaching-out of the capitalist world economy with the market economy as its key principle.

II Theory of "internationalization" as an adaptive process

Thus the 1980s was a period of relativization – or denial – of modernity, which gave rise to environmental and other theories. Interestingly, the same decade witnessed a rising call for the "internationalization" of Japan. The new ideas of the 1980s – anti-modernism, postmodernism, and views against equating Japan's internationalization with its Westernization – need to be interpreted against the historical background of non-Western countries' *subsumption* to the modern world system expanding from the West. The meaning of the term "international-ization" can be clearly understood only when this point is grasped.

According to the comparative study of the Japanese and English usages of the term *kokusaika* (internationalization) by Kazukimi Ebuchi,[4] the Japanese meaning of this term which became popular in the 1980s is multiplex and highly ambiguous. Nonetheless, it is certain that the word connotes something progressive and fashionable. On the other hand, its English equivalent carries quite a different meaning. On close examination, one may even say that their implications are quite the opposite. This semantic divergence reflects the different experiences of English and Japanese societies in their relationship with other cultures.

In English, internationalization is a word loaded with heavy political implications. It specifically means the governing of a country or territory under international control or protection, by either a single foreign power or a group of such powers. When the term is used this way, the existence of an "Other" (other societies) is always presumed: western powers are the ones to "internationalize" while other nations or societies are those to be "internationalized." Grammatically, this is internationalization as a transitive verb. Epistemologically, the situation can be described as the pre-existence of a self who recognizes others. The self then places the previously unknown and ambiguous others at the periphery of its own world and identifies them as inferior within its cosmological order. In practice, Western powers towered above other societies in this structure and exploited them for the economic prosperity of the center. Let us see some historical examples.

In the West, the so-called "international society" was established with the formation and subsequent development of modern states. The 1648 Treaty of Westphalia is commonly regarded as providing the first international legal basis for the formation of modern states. With this treaty, the system of European states as the "international society" was born with territory as a new essential component. The Church which had dominated feudal Europe as a sacred as well as secular power was replaced by a new system of separate states governed by absolute monarchs under the idea of the natural right of man. The European political space was no longer a unified whole, but a collection of smaller states as basic components. While new Europe continued to share Christianity as a key cultural element, its political order was now founded in the relationship among different states. Global colonization which followed the Age of Great Voyages was the process by which this "international society" of European origin was spatially enlarged to cover the entire globe, along with the development of the capitalist world economy. Territorial partition was the projection of Europe's territory-based "international society" onto colonized regions. At this point in history, actors in internationalization were Western powers; and non-Western countries were merely the objects to be "internationalized." The process of internationalization was proceeding in its most pure form.

The dichotomy between Western states as active players and non-Western regions which remain passive politically and (as a consequence also) culturally, and the requirement of the latter to adapt to Western culture, are the relational aspects that characterize our world even to this date. In reaction to the lack of political autonomy, non-Western regions subsequently achieved independence and began to build their own nation states. However, this process also took the form of participation in the existing international society which was controlled by the West. This inevitably forced the non-West to accept the internal culture of Europe and the rules that are based on it.

Even today, the United Nations as a supra-national body does not escape this duality. The UN is above nations only formally and in spirit. One may think that the world consists of many sovereign states with equal rights and is without any hierarchical order, and large countries serve as permanent members of the UN Security Council only because of their size. But the historical perspective suggests otherwise; Europe-centered international society existed first, and the rest of the world had to be merged into this society. In the Third World, even the concept of "state" – the basic constituent of the UN of which they are a majority – was generated in reaction to the enlargement of Western international society. As the state-based European political system extended its reach, Christian culture as well as the capitalist world economy originating in Europe also went forth and occupied "compatriot" regions. The world economic system in search of natural resources and labor supply covered the entire planet under the leadership of Western powers. This led to the economic exploitation of the non-West by the West.

The parallel process of internationalization and economic exploitation began in earnest with the onset of industrialization and continued during the Pax Britannica. By then, ethnic cultures were no longer subject to eradication as they were in the days of Columbus. Nevertheless, societies with weak national bases in regions deemed to have economic importance for the world system were clearly placed in economically exploited positions.

Yet, even under these circumstances, there were some non-Western nations that, while inevitably accepting Western culture, still broke loose from its colonial influence. The Western concept of "modernization" also influenced non-Western countries, and some of them even achieved it. In relatively economically developed societies with stable politics, conforming to Western international society meant adaptation to the capitalist economic system. Japan was the prime example of this.

After Japan's forced opening to the world, people in the Meiji period [1868–1912] were amazed at the West's high level of technology. The adoption of Western technology was called *bunmei kaika* (civilization and enlightenment). Technology was not the only Western institution eagerly absorbed by Japan. New industries generated by imported technology, as well as various political systems such as the parliamentary and bureaucratic systems, the economic system of industrial capitalism (*fukoku*, or enriching the country), and the modern military system (*kyohei*, or strengthening the military) were introduced. It should be stressed that Japan had no choice but to open the country and adapt to the outside world, that is, Western international society. From the Meiji period onward, Japan's history is actually a process of gradual adaptation to Western society. At the time of Japan's opening to the outside world, Japanese leaders

169

idealized the modern West as a model, directing Japan's process of development in the same way as the West's, and even striving to separate itself from its Asian roots and join Western society (*datsua-nyuou*). At the same time, some Japanese felt a certain loss of identity from this tendency and inclined toward a nationalism centered on the Emperor.

Soseki Natsume [1867–1916] was an intellectual who was torn by these two courses of values. Soseki was certainly aware of the difference between Western modernization and Japanese modernization, as much as any Japanese individual of that time. He was irritated by the Japanese situation, and felt dissatisfied and impatient. He expressed this feeling by referring to Western modernization as an "endogenous civilization" and Japanese modernization as an "exogenous civilization."[5]

What Soseki aptly called "exogenous civilization" differs from the naive "theory of modernization" which later became popular. According to this theory, Japan as an independent state should strive to develop its economy and society just as the United Kingdom, for instance, developed its economy and society as an independent state. But Soseki's "exogenous civilization" clearly recognizes that Japan's modernization is essentially a process of adaptation to the modern civilization of the powerful Western states that appeared before it. From the global viewpoint, adapting to the modern West was tantamount to adapting to the capitalist world system, which was created in, ruled by, and continuously expanding from the West.

As soon as Japan began to participate in the "international society" through successful adaptation, it followed the Western precedent and colonized the neighboring non-Western societies of Korea and China, which had not yet gone through the course of adaptation. From the global point of view, this could be regarded as one chain of events in the expansionary process of the world system. However, Japan, positioned at the border between the international and *un*international societies, was not permitted to become a full member of the international society, equal to Western nations. Japan was the only nation among them with obviously different racial and cultural backgrounds. Under these circumstances, in order to compete as a member of the international society, Japan's principal objective became the creation of an "international society" in the Asian region to confront European society which developed from Christianity on the one hand and the market economic principle based on modern science and technology on the other. The proposed international society in the Asian region was called *daitoa kyoeiken* (Great East Asian Co-Prosperity Sphere), which became, within a section of the intelligentsia, the ideology for reviving Japan's cultural identity. Despite the fact that Japan was included in the modern world system, or because of it, Japan tried to construct a new world system in Asia, spatially and temporally smaller than the West, to stand against the Western world system. By forcing a passive internationalization on other Asian nations, Japan tried to shed its formerly passive stance in the Western international society and establish its position as an active nation that carried out internationalization of its own.

However, Japan's defeat in World War II overturned this attempt from its foundation. After the war, in the Cold War era of ideological confrontation, Japan was again placed in the passive and adaptive course of internationalization in essentially the same modern world system, namely, the capitalist world economy. Over time, Japan has achieved economic success as a "modern" capitalist state of the *adaptive type*. This is where we are today.

III From the negativity of culture to the clash of civilizations

We have described the relationship between the West and the non-West in the modern world system as a history of internationalization. Given this background, we now come back to the current problem of our world. Again, the anthropological concept of "cultural relativism" will be our guide. This concept was originally used to describe the way we recognize others (i.e., epistemology), but now it also determines what we are (i.e., ontology).

Cultural relativism has been taken for granted as an indispensable tool for understanding other societies. It must be pointed out, however, that cultural relativism contains an inherent paradox in the epistemological as well as practical sense.

The first paradox is that the approach stressing cultural diversity tends also to emphasize the differences of cultures as if they were immutable. Inevitably, this approach makes it difficult to find common ground for mutual exchange among cultures. True, understanding others is a crucially important step to facilitate inter-cultural communication. But when cultural relativism as a means to understand others is taken to the extreme, it leads to the paradoxical result that communication among cultures becomes impossible due to irreconcilable differences.

Equally important, believers in cultural relativism often overlook – though not indefinitely – the power gap that exists in the real world among societies that embody different cultures. While cultural values are said to be relative, in reality, all cultures interact and fuse. As a matter of fact, the relationship in which the dominant culture subsumes the weaker ones is already with us. One may hear that, regardless of size, every culture is autonomous and in possession of unique values. Realistically, however, the conditions that ensure the autonomy and uniqueness of every culture hardly exist.

Furthermore, cultural relativism was born out of the West's self-criticism that unilateral application of Western values had been inappropriate when the West, from its dominant position, evaluated the cultures of primitive or otherwise non-Western inferior societies. If Orientalism was "the discourse in which the supreme power of the modern world, the West, perceives the world as an object which should be conquered, prescribes others through representation and by contrasting oneself with the others, establishes oneself as the subject,"[6] then cultural relativism was a movement which corrected the asymmetry in this power relationship and proposed to understand the others not as an object of subordination but as an independent entity. That is to say, it was an effort to detach the observer from the context of historically formed power relations of cultures, and to elevate this attitude to an idealistically and ethically acceptable methodology. In its struggle to be free from history, cultural relativism demonstrates, quite ironically, the undeniable political reality that the hierarchical power gap among cultures has *always* and *already* existed, and that cultural problems cannot be discussed independently of the history of political and economic relations between societies.

This leads further to the following point. Since cultural relativism is concerned with the question of how the West should view the non-West and does not go beyond this attitudinal framework, the espistemological relationship of "subject" and "object" – who understands whom – is preserved. During the second half of the twentieth century, decolonization became reality and the relative power gap between the West and the non-West narrowed. With political independence came an awakening of ethnic identity, and the non-West began to assert their cultural independence which had been denied to them previously. Under these circumstances, cultural relativism which was born in the West is now used to also support the assertions of a non-Western society as a carrier of one of these diverse cultures. The thesis that human behavior and values should be interpreted and evaluated in the context of the culture to which they belong, thus emphasizing the unique value of each culture, provides a cultural foundation for nationalism, when a non-Western society applies this thesis to *its own* culture. We may call this absolute relativism, or alternatively, counter-Orientalism based on relativism. The West has reacted to this new phenomenon in the non-West by reviving universalism. As the relationship between the West and the non-West gradually shifts from "subject versus object" to "subject versus subject," the West now feels the need to re-establish itself through universalism.[7]

Even in the West, despite its original intention, cultural relativism is sometimes evoked as a new type of argument to justify racial discrimination on the ground of *difference* itself – witness the discriminations against foreign workers in Germany and France.[8] It is ironic that emphasis on differences in cultural diversity gives rise to a principle that excludes others. But this is the reality of ethnic conflicts in the post-Cold War era. From this, one should detect two levels of culture: the one that naturally permeates in the people's actual lives, and the other that arises as "invented tradition"[9] through the conscious effort of "nations."[10]

In the early 1990s, with the disappearance of ideological confrontation and the dawn of the post-Cold War era, Francis Fukuyama declared that the Hegelian notion of history had come to an end, signaling the arrival of a liberal democratic society.[11] He also argued that, from a liberal democratic point of view, cultural diversity, or "superficial difference between ethnic groups," was merely a relic of a particular stage in historical development. This is evolutionist universalism.

However, although the structure of ideological polarity and binary hostility has ended, regional ethnic conflicts are frequent in the actual world where "cultural differences" are cited as one important cause. Moreover, the Japan–United States economic friction has widely publicized the differences between Japanese and American social structures, which stem from cultural differences. Today, conflicts are born not out of ideology but out of ethnic or cultural diversity. While mature "modern society" pays due respect to cultural diversity, many people are at the same time beginning to sense the "negativity of culture"[12] in the eruption of these ethnic conflicts.

With "cultural differences" as a basis, Samuel Huntington perceives current international problems as a "clash of civilizations."[13] His approach admits the fact that present international problems can no longer be analyzed as realistic power bargaining and compromising games by nation states. In this respect, Huntington seems to be breaking away from the framework of Western perception, unlike Fukuyama who is still trapped in evolutionist theory. Emphasis on clashing civilizations is also useful in revealing the limits of ethnocentric American diplomacy and presenting a new strategic outlook for American policy makers.

Yet, from a global perspective, publicizing the idea of the "clash of civilizations" only deprives us of the prospect of resolving international problems in the future. Analyzing international conflicts in the framework of "Western civilization versus non-Western civilization," Huntington counts Japan as an exception, leaving unanswered the question of why Japan succeeded in modernization without being assimilated into Western international society. Essentially, this is a political discourse which leads to Japan's isolation. Worse, his implicit suggestion that the United States, aligned with Europe, should stand against the Islamic and Confucianist nations, merely reflects the shifting targets of American foreign policy, which constantly pursues an enemy, after former Cold War adversaries were purged.[14]

IV The continuity of culture: toward a translative theory of culture

In this chapter, I have intentionally refrained from commenting on the issues that Huntington raised in his paper.[15] Bypassing his text, I have instead discussed a broader historical and cultural-epistemological perspective of "internationalization" and "cultural relativism" in order to illustrate my point which overlaps with the problems that Huntington addressed. From this standpoint, let me present a theory that may take us beyond the clash theory of civilizations.

To escape from the traps of the clash theory of civilizations, it is necessary to understand from a historical perspective how cultural systems "articulate" (merge). That is to say, we need to analyze the merger of different cultures as a structural relationship which arises in the course of history. In studying the process of "subsumption" of the non-West into the Western modern world system (i.e., capitalist world economy), we should not take the position of outside observers. Instead, we should build our views from the level of non-Westerners in the midst of this process, in order to comprehend how they have interpreted, accepted, and digested Western culture (i.e., "civilization") while maintaining the continuity of the indigenous cultural system.

The situation is described graphically in Figure 9.1. W stands for the West, and also implies the world system emanating from the West. O and O′ are two of the Others (non-Western cultures). In particular, O′ denotes the base culture of a non-Western society before contact with the West. Among many principles and institutions included in W, the most abstract and universal principle is the market mechanism. The adjective "universal" here does not mean validity across space and time, but a *historical* universality which emerges in the course of irreversible progression of time. It should be also clear to the reader, who has endured my argument up to this point, that historicity in this context has nothing to do with the theory of modernization.

When a non-Western society encounters a powerful representative of Western civilization, it is hardly possible to escape from its influences. Some ethnic groups have been eradicated in short periods after contact with the West. At the same time, many nations and societies have adopted Western institutions and objects from without in order to survive (or by their own choice). However, it is important to recognize that they did not accept Western inventions in their original forms. Any item in one culture will change its meaning when transplanted to another culture, as seen widely in ethnography around the world.[16] Not only cosmology, religious doctrine, rituals, but also the family system, the institution of exchange, and even socio-economic organizations like the firm exhibit the property of adapting to external institutions and principles with the existing cultural system maintaining its *form* of structure. The essence of what has been called "modernization" is the adaptive acceptance of Western civilization under the persistent form of the existing culture. That is, actors in the existing system have adapted to the new system by reinterpreting each element of Western culture

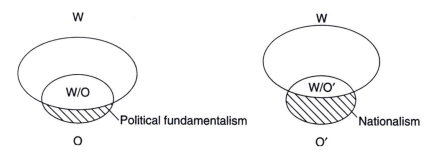

Figure 9.1 The contemporary cultural situation of non-Western society

Note: In these figures the large oval (W) represents the West which embodies the modern world system (of which the market principle is a key component) and the small oval (O and O′) represents other, non-Western systems with their unique base cultures. Society O is more deeply integrated with W than society O′ which has just begun to adapt. In translative adaptation, ideological reaction often arises. Political fundamentalism is more frequently associated with its advanced stage, as with O, while nationalism in general is likely to emerge in an earlier stage, as with O′.

(i.e., "civilization") in their own value structure, modifying yet maintaining the existing institutions. I shall call this "translative adaptation."[17]

The descriptive concept of "modernization" presupposes that non-Western societies will evolve with the passage of time to become like Western society. Actually, however, in societies that have attained "modernization" or are in the process of attaining it, base culture is preserved not only as traces but as the center of social organization and the institution of exchange. A *translative culture*, or a culture that has adapted to Western civilization, is ambiguous. From one angle, it appears as a capitalist society fully equipped with the market economic principle, and from another, it appears as a "pre-modern" society. Viewed from a society like the United States which was created from the particularly "modern" elements of modern Europe, a "translative culture," and above all, a "modernized" one (W/O in Figure 9.1 – for example, Japan), would look very different from the original modern European model (W in Figure 9.1). Of course, there will be variations in translative culture depending on the tenacity of base culture and historical differences in the process of adaptation to the market principle of the modern world system. For example, in Figure 9.1, (W/O') indicates a cultural system in its initial stage of adaptation.

In the adaptation process, nationalism and fundamentalism often emerge as ideological reactions to being "subsumed" into the modern West. Again, their intensity is conditioned on the strength of the base culture and historical differences in the process of adaptation to the modern market system. While these ideological reactions are usually a short- to medium-term phenomenon involving only a limited group of people, the penetration of the market economy is, by contrast, a gradual yet irreversible change encompassing the whole society and requiring substantial and ceaseless adaptation and other actions.[18]

Finally, let me say a few words about Huntington's "clash of civilizations." Clash or not, the most *historically* universal principle invented by Western civilization, namely, the market principle, has already penetrated deeply into other cultures. Yet, a non-Western culture will never become like a Western culture with the passage of time. The reason for this has already been made clear. The West, and until recently, the non-West as well, misunderstood the historical process of adaptation as a process of unilinear "modernization." We may say that the term "modernization" refers to an ideal aspect of change whereas "adaptation" deals with its practical aspect.

Turning to Japan, the significance of the slogan *wakon yosai* (Japanese spirit, Western technique), idiosyncratic corporate culture, and the like can be understood vividly only from the viewpoint of "translative adaptation." Huntington's representation of Japan as the nation that succeeded in modernization without Westernization is half right and half wrong. If we continue to be bound by the dualism which equates modernization with Westernization, the dynamism that we observe in the actual historical scene cannot be comprehended. See Southeast Asia rapidly climbing the path of modernization without losing its traditional cultures, and we know Huntington's argument has already lost its relevance.

Notes

1 This paper was published in Japanese in *Hikaku Bunmei* (Comparative Civilization, Journal of the Japan Society for the Comparative Study of Civilizations), vol. 10, Tokyo, Tosui Shobo, November 1994, pp. 100–13. The volume was dedicated to explore the "Co-existence of Civilizations: Beyond the Clash Theory." Authors assessed, among other things, the clash-of-civilizations theory of Samuel P. Huntington ("The Clash of Civilizations?" *Foreign Affairs*, Summer 1993, pp. 22–49) [Editors].

2 Cultural relativism is the "method whereby social and cultural phenomena are perceived and described in terms of scientific detachment or, ideally, from the perspective of participants in or adherents of a given culture. Further, cultural phenomena are evaluated in terms of their significance in a given cultural and social context." This requires the observer to "transcend, or to eliminate for the moment, his own cultural conditioning and values and to assume the subjective, ethnocentric attitudes and mentality of an adherent of or a participant in the culture" (*International Encyclopedia of the Social Sciences*, vol. 2, New York, Macmillan and Free Press, 1968, p. 543) [Editors].

3 American Commodore Matthew Perry and his "Black Ships" (armed steamboats) sailed to Uraga at the mouth of Edo (Tokyo) Bay in 1853 and demanded the Tokugawa shogunate government to end Japan's isolation policy. With the threat of superior firepower, the American succeeded in the signing of the Japan–United States Friendship Treaty in 1854 which opened Japan to extensive foreign commerce for the first time in 215 years [Editors].

4 Kazukimi Ebuchi, "Kokusaika Shiso no Hikakubunseki" [A Comparative Study of Internationalization Theories], A. Sawada and A. Kadowaki (eds) *Nihonjin no Kokusaika* [Internationalization of the Japanese], Tokyo, Nihon Keizai Shimbunsha, 1990.

5 However, what Soseki felt at that time was not only a dissatisfaction of imported civilization itself. Rather, he was dissatisfied and impatient toward the way Japanese people faced the changes occurring in Japanese society. They thoughtlessly glorified the West; however, it was hardly possible to deny that forced civilization (i.e., modernization) was an unavoidable fate. It is because the Japanese, under these circumstances, could do nothing but pretend that Westernization was civilization itself, that Soseki grieves over the emptiness of Japanese cultural identity.

6 Shunji Ito, *Seinaru Nikutai* [The Sacred Body], Tokyo, Libroport, 1993, pp. 65–6; also see Edward W. Said, *Orientalism*, Tokyo: Heibonsha, 1986.

7 This historical background has its mirror image in anthropology in the academic debate over "relativism versus universalism."

8 This may also be called "absolute relativism." See Alain Finkielkraut, *La Défaite de la pensée*, Paris, Editions Gallimard, 1987.

9 Eric Hobsbawm and Ranger Terence (eds) *The Invention of Tradition*, New York, Cambridge University Press, 1983.

10 Benedict Anderson, *Imagined Communities: Reflections on the Origin and Spread of Nationalism*, London, Verso, 1983.

11 Francis Fukuyama, *The End of History and the Last Man*, New York, International Creative Management, 1992.

12 Tamotsu Aoki, *Bunka no Hiteisei* [The Negativity of Culture], Tokyo, Chuo Koronsha, 1988.

13 Huntington does not distinguish between "culture" and "civilization." In this paper, as a general rule, the term "civilization" is reserved for the ideal culture of the *modern* West, and everything else is referred to as "culture."

14 Fukuyama's and Huntington's arguments are at odds on major issues such as temporal

versus spatial perspective, analysis of current issues, and policy implications. They also argue differently on the interpretation of Japan's historical and cultural circumstances as well as the evaluation of Japan's role in future world situations. However, the two authors share a common base in that they analyze changes in non-Western societies within a Western paradigm. This causes me to think that their apparently contradictory arguments are in fact complementary.

15 See note 1 [Editors].

16 Marshall Sahlins, *Islands of History*, Chicago, University of Chicago Press, 1985.

17 Keiji Maegawa, "An Anthropological Perspective on Social Change in the Modern World-System," *Rekishi Jinrui* [History and Anthropology], vol. 22, Institute of History and Anthropology, Tsukuba University, 1994. My concept of translative adaptation overlaps with similar concepts proposed by other researchers, including Motoko Katakura's "culturalization of civilization" (*Hikaku Bunmei* [Comparative Civilization], vol. 9, Tokyo, Tosui Shobo, 1993) and Masamichi Someya's explanation of the relationship between "modern technological (and moral) aspects" and "traditional moral aspects" (*Hikaku Bunmei*, vol. 8, Tokyo, Tosui Shobo, 1992). Presently, I am examining the historical development of Japanese corporate organizations from the viewpoint of "translative adaptation." I am particularly interested in the way commercial organizations of the Edo era *translated* and *adapted* to the capitalist market system by reforming, yet simultaneously maintaining pre-existing labor relations and other organizational institutions.

18 Other key concepts of the West, such as democracy, freedom, and human rights, do not seem as *historically* universal as the principle of the market economy. Given sufficient time, however, the non-West is likely to also adapt to these Western concepts by *translating* them as it did to the market principle.

Part III

AUTHORITARIAN DEVELOPMENTALISM

10

THEORY OF DEVELOPMENTALISM[1]

Yasusuke Murakami

I Developmentalism at the firm level emerges spontaneously

In prior discussion [in earlier chapters of *Outline of Anti-Classical Political Economy*] we showed that a tendency toward dynamic increasing returns (i.e., decreasing costs)[2] has been the rule rather than the exception in the process of industrialization. When we look back at the long history of industrialization, this tendency is clear *ex post*. Indeed, the concept of dynamic increasing returns is hardly distinguishable from the idea of economic growth, which is commonly defined as rising productivity per head.[3] However, *ex ante*, increasing returns were not always pursued deliberately by decision makers responsible for enterprise management or policy formulation. One important reason for this is that technological breakthroughs were thought to be sporadic and accidental; they were not believed to come with predictable certainty. The further we go back in history, the more this idea appears to accord with reality.

Alfred Marshall, one of the few eminent economists in the nineteenth century who clearly understood the importance of increasing returns, attributed this phenomenon to "economies of skill" and "economies of machines." In the tradition of Adam Smith, Marshall explained economies of machines as "specialization of machines" (a shift from general to more specialized machines) rather than "technical innovation."[4] He classified these "economies" into "external economies," which arise from the general development of an industry and spread to individual firms, and "internal economies," which are generated within each individual firm. According to Marshall, the first type of economies was more important.[5] Thus, he explained the phenomenon of increasing returns by external economies and specialization of machines. His observation reflects the situation at the end of the nineteenth century when tangible and intangible industrial infrastructure (which produces external economies) was built throughout the society, but technical innovation was not yet a common occurrence.

However, at the end of the twentieth century, we now face an entirely different situation: internal economies are exploited through changing internal organization of firms, and a wide range of technical innovation has been generated continuously and institutionalized, far beyond what specialization of machines alone could achieve. (On the other hand, in many aspects of production, economies of skill have been a constant source of productivity growth throughout the centuries.) The future prospects of institutionalized technical innovation and the development of firm internal organization will be discussed in the chapter on information-based society.[6] Here, the important fact is that these tendencies became increasingly apparent after the nineteenth century and now are the central aspects of industrialization. They are also likely to remain important in the foreseeable future.

However, awareness lagged behind reality. For instance, few authors recognized these tendencies during the first half of the twentieth century. Two major wars and the economic depression during the interwar years distracted economists with more short-term problems. John Maynard Keynes and Knut Wicksell, two distinguished economists in the interwar period, paid surprisingly little heed to the questions of technical innovation and shifting internal organization of firms. The only exception among leading economists was Joseph Schumpeter. Outside economics, the change was more clearly realized – for example, gifted social scientist Karl Schmidt was predicting the coming age of technologism as early as the 1920s.[7]

However, the neoclassical school, which came to dominate the economic profession after World War II, continued to neglect the role of institutionalized technical innovation and evolving firm internal organization. The fact that neoclassical economics provided the theoretical basis for the naive (i.e., static) economic liberalism promoted under Pax Americana should be cited as one reason for this neglect. Additionally, the American strategy of pouring a large amount of human and financial resources into technical innovation in the public sector, such as defense and space exploration, also helped to make private sector innovation less spectacular. In reality, however, institutionalization of technical innovation and development of enterprise organization were progressing steadily in the private sectors of advanced countries. As a result, the remarkable tendency toward increasing returns became a central feature of the world economy during the postwar high-growth period.

Despite these striking trends, theories that can explain them have been very slow to emerge – even to this day. (Theoretic endeavors in this direction, including mine, began only around 1980.) But the consequences of these changes are already with us, demanding proper recognition. The most conspicuous demonstration of these changes was the success of the Japanese economy in the postwar period, which came to be recognized globally by the 1970s.[8] Japanese management and industrial policy, which were instrumental to this success, were both highly unconventional by traditional standards. Nonetheless, they were the first conscious attempts to take advantage of dynamic increasing returns. Today,

Japanese-style management and policy are attracting much interest in East Asia, the United States, and elsewhere. (I understand that Russia and China are also showing interest.) At last, dynamic increasing returns have come to be duly recognized.

Once recognized, few can resist exploiting dynamic increasing returns. The immediate reaction of individual firms and governments will be to take advantage of the tendency. In what follows, I define *developmentalism* as a conscious attempt to exploit the tendency toward dynamic increasing returns regardless of who pursues it – whether a firm, a government, or any other organization.

Among these entities, firms embrace developmentalism most naturally. My basic hypothesis, presented in chapter 4 [not included here], is that a firm is a unit which constantly seeks to preserve and expand its own management and technical patterns (what I term "cultural elements") in an uncertain environment. While the pursuit of dynamic increasing returns through technical innovation involves large and continuous risk-taking, the essence of a firm (or the process of evolution in general) is that it welcomes and overcomes such risks. Thus, even when a firm experiences a shift from decreasing to increasing returns, its strategy toward risk should not require a fundamental change.

But some adjustments in management style may be warranted. First, as dynamic increasing returns set in, management time horizon should lengthen. In order to profit from ever-risky R&D investment involving technical innovation, firms must accept risk for a longer period of time compared with business operations under fixed capital stock, or even expansion of production capacity.

Second, investment in human capital becomes essential. Not all technical innovation can be embodied in capital equipment, and the rest must be accumulated and preserved in the form of human capital (from top management down to line workers) through inventing new methods, learning by doing, and reorganizing institutional structures and procedures. Part of such technical knowledge can be encoded in an operations manual, but a complete manual presupposes an established system of knowledge. With on-going technical change, human beings who are equipped with a certain amount of general knowledge and are able to respond flexibly to changes through trial-and-error are more valuable than a manual that has to be rewritten every so often. This implies that the duration of job contracts must be extended (compare this argument with Shimada's humanware theory).[9]

A few words must be said about extending labor contracts. Humans outperform manuals in their ability to adapt to changes flexibly. Investing in such human adaptability can take various forms: on-the-job training (OJT), used most adroitly in Japan; off-the-job training that Europeans prefer; and recruitment of professionals from outside, which is popular in the United States (the high salaries that must be offered and internal adjustment that must be made are considered investments in a broad sense). None of these is absolutely superior to the other two. On the one hand, the first (OJT) is more firm-specific and less general than the other two, so its adaptability to large changes is rather limited.

On the other hand, high general adaptability of skills means that employees are more likely to quit in order to work for another firm. High labor mobility makes the cost recovery of human investment more difficult.

The main goal of personnel management is to strike a balance between these merits and demerits. One factor important in determining the right mix is the magnitude of anticipated changes. The larger the change, the more adaptability is required. The recent call for overhauling Japan's employment system is prompted partly by the perception that future changes are going to be larger than changes in the past.

In sum, developmentalism at the individual firm level requires lengthening the time perspective in labor and other aspects of business management. From this viewpoint, the Japanese practice of lifetime employment can be regarded as a response to new problems that arose in the postwar period. In America, as Doringer and Piore point out, the so-called "seniority rule" had a similar effect in inspiring long-term views.[10] In the latter case, conflict of interest may arise between shareholders who prefer short-term profits and managers who take a long-term perspective, leading to a debate about what a firm really is. Notwithstanding these qualifications, it must be emphasized that no discontinuity exists between developmental and non-developmental firms, and differences between them are a matter of degree. Even American "excellent companies," while not consciously pursuing dynamic increasing returns, often engage in long-term business management and human capital investment.[11]

II Developmentalism at the state level involves unique problems

Developmentalism at the state level involves many awkward problems not encountered by developmental firms. Establishment of a developmental state requires the prevalence of developmentalism at the firm level in the country's major industries. In other words, firm-level developmentalism is a necessary condition for state-level developmentalism.[12] However, the converse is not true: widespread developmentalism at the firm level will not spontaneously lead to developmentalism at the state level.

First, when firms adopt developmental strategies, the result of their collective behavior may be unstable markets rather than harmonious equilibrium. Second, a rapid shift of industrial proportions and social change which results from developmentalism are likely to heighten social tension. Thus, maintaining stability under developmentalism requires institutional devices for alleviating such social tension. The theory of developmentalism squarely deals with these two problems which classical economic theory does not (and will not) recognize. This is where developmentalism is clearly distinguished from classical economic liberalism. The first problem [of market instability] can be rephrased as the problem of *industrial policy* while the second problem [of social tension] can be rephrased as the problem of *distribution policy in a broad sense*. Let us examine each in turn.

184

It must be said at the outset that developmentalism pursued by individual firms does not lead to mutually consistent results. As mentioned previously, the supply behavior of developmental firms under decreasing costs fails to generate stable equilibrium. More precisely, supply behavior (i.e., the supply function) itself cannot be determined uniquely under decreasing costs. It will consist of a large number of possible combinations of output and price strategies.

Consider output strategies first. If the price is assumed as given (for some reason), profit will increase with output under decreasing costs (i.e., under a downward sloping average cost curve). Profit-maximization requires forever-expanding output, which drives each firm to enlarge market share. Thus, under decreasing costs, competition for the largest market share creates a constant pressure of excess supply. In the standard case of increasing marginal cost (i.e., when the supply curve is sloping upward), it is well known that supply stops expanding and profit is maximized at the point where marginal cost equals price. But when the cost decreases with output, no such brake on output is present and market-share competition proceeds without any self-regulating mechanism. Nor are equilibria in the game theoretic sense (e.g., Nash equilibria) conceivable under market-share competition.[13]

Next, consider price strategies. Under decreasing costs, prices can hardly be expected to remain stable (unless fixed by an external authority such as a government or a cartel). At any given price, firms under pressure to expand market share indefinitely have the incentive to underprice rivals and stimulate demand. But even at a reduced price, the impetus for ever larger market share persists and excess supply is not eliminated (as long as average cost slopes downward). The incentive for underpricing still remains, and a fierce price-cutting competition ensues without end. This is how competition is played out under decreasing costs. Under the circumstances, maximization of market share is not unfair business practice (such as dumping) but rational behavior. The standard theory of dumping constructed under the assumption of increasing costs should not be applied to the case of decreasing costs. While the standard theory predicts that the monopolist who wipes out all competitors will eventually raise prices, this rarely happens in reality.

Price-cutting competition may take a complex form. The dynamic cost curve discussed here represents only a unit-cost curve forecast by management and thus is not immediately achievable. Investment in capital equipment and R&D in pursuit of decreasing costs does not yield quick results and may even increase marginal (and average) costs temporarily. Preference for short-term profits (say, by shareholders) may impede the expansion of market share. Because of these short-term hurdles, some bearish firms may drop out of the price-cutting race. It is especially difficult to know how quickly investment in R&D will result in new technology, in comparison with investment in capital equipment. Management psychology alternates between optimism and pessimism. Even so, there will always be some firms which remain bullish and initiate another round of price-cutting. If rapid technical change is the norm, such bullish firms may be numerous. In the long run, it is safe to assume that price-cutting competition will dominate. Thus, the additional considerations above are not likely to affect the fundamental aspect of competition under decreasing costs.

The important question is exactly how such price-cutting competition proceeds over time. Static analyses of decreasing costs exist, but they deal only with the cost-decreasing segment (i.e. the part that exhibits economies of scale) of a fixed production function. Those models inevitably lead to the conclusion that the first firm to expand output will eventually dominate the entire market (in the presence of non-zero sunk costs).[14] But in dynamic analyses with technical innovation, many uncertainties inevitably arise. A firm that introduces new technology may later lose its strength in research and grow slowly, allowing other firms to under-price it by effort or luck. Technical innovation is inherently uncertain, and this causes a large number of firms to endlessly compete for a leading position, without any lasting monopoly. This situation has been largely neglected by the standard static analysis which assumes immutable technology and an unchanging cost function.

I shall use the term *polipoly* to describe the situation where a group of highly innovative firms compete in this way.[15] This term is used to distinguish it from the static concept of *oligopoly* which is normally associated with collusive cartels. Competition among firms under decreasing costs is likely to result in either monopoly or polipoly, and which form ultimately emerges depends largely on accidental factors. We cannot, of course, deny the possibility that oligopoly – characterized by a collusive cartel among a small number of firms which tends to suppress innovation – will appear for some time, even though the ultimate shape of the industry will be either monopoly or polipoly. As I stated previously in an analogy to biological evolution, what is worth studying in competition under decreasing costs is the process of transformation itself – and not the final outcome, which is unpredictable. For example, polipoly was dominant in leading Japanese industries during the postwar period. This industrial structure resulted partly from official administrative guidance, but the more fundamental reason was the continuous competition for innovative application of technology which did not create permanent winners or losers.

Under polipoly, industrial dynamics depend on the technological performance of individual firms and is highly uncertain. Industrial structure is changeable and unpredictable. There is always an inherent risk that a monopolistic firm may emerge. Here, it must be pointed out very clearly that monopoly is undesirable. It is undesirable not only because prices tend be raised to generate excess profit for the monopolist but, more importantly, because technical innovation is nipped in the bud under monopoly. Monopoly works against the freedom of ideas – albeit in the confined area of technology. Thus, when a trend toward decreasing costs is apparent, developmentalism at the state level must include some check against monopolization.

Whether by design or not, Japanese industrial policy in the postwar period had the effect of curbing the tendency toward monopoly. As a result, all leading industries maintained a state of polipoly: as many as six steel makers co-existed; in the car industry, nine manufacturers vied with each other; in the chemical industry, twelve producers of ethylene and ten producers of polyethylene existed. Interestingly, the number of firms in individual industries is distributed around the magic number seven. The important question is to what extent the check against monopoly should be institutionalized. The extent to which institutionalization is appropriate depends on the overall socio-economic environment of each society, including cultural traditions and the availability of new technology. The correct answer will differ from one country to another.

Consider the case of latecomer developing countries. For those countries, a body of technology already tested in advanced countries is available for learning and absorption. Globally, what happens is merely an imitation of existing technology. For individual developing countries, however, it is an introduction of new technology. Uncertainty associated with this "new" technology is much lower for developing countries than for advanced countries where the technology was originally invented. The required cost for R&D is similarly much smaller. The environment in which technology is transferred to developing countries is much more stable, almost to the extent of being static, making the dynamic cost curve easier to predict. This greatly spurs developmentalism at the firm level.

At the same time, however, the unpredictability which gives rise to polipoly is correspondingly low in developing countries. For this reason, monopoly becomes all the more likely. In latecomer countries, the state often adopts a policy of rapidly establishing one (or a very few) large enterprise by providing tangible and intangible assistance and introducing (or permitting an invasion of) foreign capital – as observed widely in South Asia and Latin America. Through these big national projects, latecomers attempt to instantly capture economies of scale. Ironically, this often causes industrial strength to wither in the long run by inhibiting the development of polipoly. Thus, industrial policy to encourage more than one firm to enter an industry and preserve polipoly must be institutionalized all the more forcefully in latecomer countries (industrial policy will be discussed in more detail later). Developmentalism at the state level emerges more naturally and requires more institutionalization in latecomer countries that consciously pursue economic development.

The effectiveness of developmentalism defined above is not confined to latecomers. Developmentalism at the state level is also open to advanced countries if industries which demonstrate increasing returns can be identified. Certain high-tech industries, such as integrated circuits that are mass-produced with common specifications, are obvious candidates. The 1986 Japan–U.S. semiconductor agreement negotiated under the Reagan–Bush administration was a way to reconcile the clash of developmentalism adopted by the two countries in the semiconductor industry, which was clearly showing increasing returns. At present, the Clinton administration seems to be inclining toward similar developmentalist policies, although concrete measures have not been identified.

Whether in developing or developed countries, implementation of developmentalism generates unique problems, especially in international economic relations. This point will be further examined below. The undeniable fact is that the whole world has now come to realize the charm of developmentalism. Even in the United States which has long championed classical economic liberalism, we can see how deeply developmentalist ideas have penetrated the policy initiatives of the Clinton administration. The world over, political leaders are challenged to take a position on developmentalism.

III Developmentalism is a higher-level issue than industrial policy

Unlike developmentalism at the firm level, developmentalism at the state level entails many problems, as discussed above, and cannot be made to work unless proper government intervention is simultaneously initiated. Assuming that developmentalism at the firm level, a necessary condition, is already widespread, developmentalism at the state level can be defined as a system of policies. At the center of this system of policies lies what is now called "industrial policy." Industrial policy, in turn, can be defined in a number of ways. In the past, this term referred (often with negative connotations) to any action by the government to target and intervene in specific industries. Evidently, this definition includes all types of government intervention – from the protection of declining industries to protectionist trade practices aimed at supporting infant industries, to the encouragement of high-tech industries. According to this definition, semi-socialist measures once popular in Europe – nationalization of enterprises in Great Britain, nationalization of investment banks in France, establishment of large investment corporations in Italy – can also be counted as industrial policy. But such a broad definition does not serve any useful analytical purpose. Let us therefore re-define industrial policy.

We define industrial policy as direct policy measures to preserve and promote the growth potential of industries which are supposed to exhibit a tendency toward decreasing costs. Clearly, to execute this policy, it is first necessary to identify industries to be thus targeted. This identification is not always easy. One reason is general uncertainty about the future but for latecomer countries, this uncertainty can be significantly reduced. The real problem is ambiguity surrounding the concept of decreasing costs itself. As the previous chapter [of *Outline of Anti-Classical Political Economy*] showed, it is only easy to know whether costs decrease or increase when we are dealing with standardized products with common specifications – that is, industries producing homogeneous goods. By contrast, cost tendencies of industries making differentiated products cannot be measured so easily. Of course, if the cultural elements of technology are such that they can be easily duplicated, industries will eventually experience decreasing costs. But in general, the tendency toward decreasing costs is not easy to detect, despite the fact that modern economics considers all goods subject to measurement. Take the electronic-device industry, for example, which continues to spawn a bewildering array of new products. With such a rapid shift in product-mix, it is hardly possible to ascertain whether costs are decreasing or increasing for any individual firm. Instead of price-cutting competition, this industry is characterized by non-price competition based on product differentiation. Monopoly in the ordinary sense of the word is unlikely to take root. For such an industry, industrial policy is ineffective.

Be that as it may, let us return to the case where dynamic cost tendencies can be identified. What are the contents of industrial policy in that case? The three factors pointed out earlier that differentiate dynamic from static analyses – i.e., technology, incentive structures, and finance – now take central importance. Since industrial policy is designed essentially with dynamic considerations in mind, policy tools adopted for this purpose will impact on the economy well beyond the variables examined by static analyses, such as price, output, and capital stock. Even in the past, infant industry promotion and protectionism have been permitted, but only in exceptional circumstances. Compared with traditional views, the concept of industrial policy presented here (and its supporting policies) enlarges not only the amount of intervention but also the range of policy measures as well. Specifically, the menu now includes policies to promote R&D, policies to ensure relatively equal distribution of income to enhance the incentive to work, measures to encourage capital markets to serve the needs of the real sector, and the like.

In a sense, our definition of industrial policy is narrower than the traditional one that includes all government intervention targeting specific industries. At the same time, however, the addition of long-term indicative planning, R&D support, and maintenance of polipoly, to the set of available policies is unique to our definition. These measures cannot be neatly classified in the conventional policy framework. Recently, and particularly since the advent of the Clinton administration, the term "industrial policy" has been gaining popularity in the world. However, the term is often used without theoretical consistency. In actual implementation, industrial policy takes various forms employing different policy tools. Differences emerge first, from the different policy tools used and second, from the different development stages of the industries targeted. Too often, however, eye-catching arguments over industrial policy are exchanged without sufficient analysis on these two points. In what follows, let us take up the first point and classify the policy tools of industrial policy.

A *Basic policies*
1 Identification of industries[16] (for example, Japan used income-elasticity and productivity-growth criteria to identify suitable industries);
2 Indicative or educative planning (for example, long-term forecasts of demand and supply);
3 Promotion and diffusion of technical innovation

B *Protection policy in a broad sense*
1 Trade protection (import quotas, import tariffs, export subsidies, etc.)
2 Subsidies (preferential tax and financial treatment, prioritized access to government procurement, tariff reduction on import requirements of specified industries, etc.)
C *Policy for preservation of polipoly*
1 Price regulation (prevention of competitive price-cutting in the case of excess competition, recommendation for cutbacks in operations, approval of recession cartels, etc.)
2 Investment regulation
3 Production regulation
D *Indirect financial controls*
E *Entry and exit policy* (protectionism for the purpose of restricting foreign entry is included here, but not domestic treatment of foreign firms – see below)

Among these, the items listed under basic policies are generally accepted even within the neoclassical policy framework; for example, see J.E. Meade's argument.[17] Identification of industries (A-1) and indicative or educative planning (A-2), aimed at providing relevant information, should be easy to defend. Nor can one find any reason to object to the promotion of technical innovation (A-3). More precisely put, the neoclassical paradigm, which is concerned exclusively with market competition, does not have any criteria for judging policy toward information or technology which logically. precedes market competition. The (tacit) approval of these policies indeed reveals the limited scope of neoclassical theory. At any rate, these basic policies are rarely opposed.

Protection policy in a broad sense, under category B, has been accepted by the neoclassical school in exceptional cases where infant industries are targeted for protection. However, the neoclassical argument for infant industry protection is essentially static and often presumes that the policy is effective only in certain cases with readily identifiable boundaries with respect to duration and project size.

It is critically important to recognize that, under decreasing costs, competition evolves into different forms, and in most cases into one of two typical forms. The first form is monopoly by a dominant firm, and the other is polipoly, where a number of firms continue to compete fiercely with one another and a winner is constantly challenged by its rivals. The actual form of competition under decreasing costs determines the most appropriate choice of policy instruments. If polipoly is the dominant form of competition, policies in categories C, D, and E are unnecessary.

While the situation differs from one industry to another, in general the policy menu of Japanese industrial policy during the postwar period can be summarized as follows. Basic policies under A were used throughout; policies under B were employed up to a certain point in time; a weak form of C-1 was also in place, while policies under C-2 were adopted in a large number of industries; finally, almost all key industries were subjected to entry and exit regulations under E. This policy menu was fundamentally *ad hoc* and cannot be defended as logically consistent. In particular, the value of strict exclusion of foreign firms from domestic markets was highly questionable. (The ban on foreign entry was finally removed in 1975 when regulations on foreign investment in the computer industry were abolished.) Therefore, when other East Asian countries contemplate industrial policy, the menu of Japanese industrial policy should not be replicated. Indeed, Thailand is proceeding with industrialization without any significant restrictions on foreign firm entry.

The foregoing argument examined policy measures to cope with the tendency toward decreasing costs arising from rapid absorption of technology. As mentioned above, there are two additional factors – incentive structures and finance – which affect the shape of industrial policy. The problem of incentives is discussed in the next section. The problem of finance – or more generally, capital markets – will be examined in detail in a separate chapter.[18] Here we just outline the main issues.

Supply and demand functions cannot be articulated as clearly in financial markets as in the real sector of the economy. A large number of financial instruments can be created without end – as witnessed in the United States since the 1970s. As the trend toward *securitization* – such as the securitization of mortgages and the invention of junk bonds – amply demonstrated, the supply function of financial instruments is hardly characterized by increasing costs. Similarly, as many economists point out, demand for financial instruments is determined not structurally but as a sort of beauty contest.[19] As a consequence, all financial markets contain the intrinsic risk of unstable divergence from equilibrium and bubble-like behavior. The most serious danger arises when financial markets begin to follow internal dynamics independent from the real economy. This type of financial disturbance can wreak havoc on late-comer countries trying to catch up and industrialize in the real sectors of the economy.

There are a number of measures to prevent this. Japan's experience offers a very interesting lesson. In postwar Japan, a large part of financial capital was supplied in the form of bank loans based on appraisal of real activities. The central bank and specialized banks also supported this mode of financial intermediation. Consequently, the pattern of capital flows was restricted by the requirements of the real sector, and financial bubbles were avoided (with the exception of the 1966 "securities recession"). Zysman emphasizes the important weight that financial policy carries in the toolbox of industrial policy.[20] Financial policy is crucial not only because it increases the role of government intervention but, more essentially, because it can effectively link financial activities to real activities.

IV Policies supplementing industrial policy

When targeted key industries begin to grow rapidly, people in these and related industries will experience a shift in life style and even in attitude toward life. From the viewpoint of the entire economy, industrial structure will of course change drastically. In addition, especially in latecomer countries, social structure, including the national psychology, will be impacted strongly by the force of "modernization," sowing the seeds of social tension. Such tension typically arises from a widening gap in income and life style between urban and rural populations. Equally notable is the formation of mega-cities and surrounding slums which are often seen in Latin America and Asia. Failure to alleviate social tension under these circumstances can lead to political conflict, which ultimately stymies developmentalism itself. Distribution policy in a broad sense will be required in order to avert these negative aspects of developmentalism. In late-comer countries, in particular, industrial policy must necessarily be accompanied by appropriate distribution policy.

One important form of distribution policy in latecomer countries is income equalization policy for farmers. Typically, in the pre-industrialization stage of development, well over half the population is engaged in agriculture and farm culture (work ethic, life style, group patterns, etc.) is deeply rooted in society. In the early stages of industrialization, an emerging (modern) industrial sector exists side by side with the more dominant agricultural sector which is based on totally different economic and cultural principles. Economists use the term "dual economy" to describe the coexistence of these distinct sectors. Economic modernization is considered complete when such duality finally disappears from the national economy. In essence, neoclassical development economics is a theory of dual economy.

However, the early neoclassical models of dual economy cannot demonstrate the need for income redistribution policy. For instance, consider the model presented by Arthur Lewis, the founder of the dual economy theory. In the agricultural sector (which he called the subsistence sector, implying in effect the rural sector), surplus labor exists in the sense that the marginal productivity of labor is zero. Unlimited supply of labor is available at any wage equal to or above the minimum subsistence level. In the industrial sector (which he called the advanced sector, but can also be termed the urban sector), the prevailing wage is of course equal to the (non-zero) marginal productivity of labor. However, being small, this sector cannot absorb all labor which is supplied virtually without limit. Thus, disguised unemployment remains in rural villages in the form of workers who must accept payments below the industrial wage. The Lewis model correctly reveals the existence of disguised unemployment and explains the income gap between the agricultural and industrial sectors. If interpreted optimistically, this model seems to suggest that increased investment and improved technology will allow the industrial sector to continue to absorb surplus labor and sustain long-term economic development.[21]

Ranis and Fei mathematically improved and extended the Lewis model by explicitly incorporating investment, technical change, and population growth, and tried to show the condition under which industrialization can succeed.[22] This condition turned out to be that "the speed at which the industrial sector absorbs employment should be greater than the growth rate of total population." This may sound self-evident, but it led to two important conclusions: shun capital-intensive industries (in favor of labor-intensive import substitution industries) and hold down population growth. These became the standard neoclassical policy prescriptions which greatly influenced development strategies of the 1960s. This policy package is remarkable for the absence of distribution policy. While the Lewis and the Ranis and Fei models do feature dual economy, they do not directly prove the need for distribution policy.

Naturally, these early theories of dual economy were criticized from various quarters. One reason for mounting criticism was the fact that no country that followed this neoclassical advice ever succeeded in economic development. Some critics were troubled by merely technical points (say, whether the marginal productivity of agricultural labor is zero or not), but the more crucial reviewers were concerned with the fact that neither the Lewis nor the Ranis and Fei model could adequately explain massive unemployment (and semi-unemployment) in the urban sectors of developing countries.[23] The early theories of dual economy, which were highly neoclassical, could not but regard urban unemployment as a temporary and frictional phenomenon. But poverty in the mega-cities of Latin America and Asia was too massive and persistent to be dismissed like that. While labor migration from rural to urban districts was surging, most migrant labor was not being absorbed in the modern industrial sector.

To explain this, assumptions were modified. One hypothesis posited that farmers maximized family income rather than individual income.[24] Another argued that farmers were maximizing expected income which might be obtained in the future instead of current income.[25] These alternative hypotheses could to a certain extent explain the ubiquity of urban poverty. However, as long as one sticks with the neoclassical framework, rural–urban migration must be explained by arguing that the urban poor are better off in some economic sense than rural dwellers. According to neoclassical economists, urban poverty must be relieved by distribution policy aimed at narrowing the gap between modern-sector workers and the unemployed within the urban sector. Furthermore, to implement such distribution policy, a lump sum subsidy is preferred for its neutrality with respect to resource allocation – for example, provision of low-income housing. By contrast, distribution policy which distorts production incentives, such as subsidies linked to agricultural output (Japan's rice-price support system is an infamous case in point), should be avoided at all cost. Let us call distribution policy based on lump sum subsidies *neoclassical distribution policy*.

However, neoclassical distribution policy contains serious problems. When neoclassical economists address the problem of dualism, what they have in mind is primarily a gap in income or wages. However, dualism appears not just in economic aspects such as wage gaps but, more fundamentally, in the discontinuity of culture in a broad sense. After all, the salient feature of capitalism is the fact that it treats labor only from the viewpoint of wages. In all pre-capitalist societies, labor normally carries cultural significance and emotional satisfaction; it is an organic component of overall life style. Migration to cities will separate people from a familiar life style and impose tremendous emotional tension on them. We should not underestimate this psychological aspect.

In Japan during and after the Meiji era, migrant workers from farming villages did not psychologically abandon their rural roots. They routinely returned to native villages for major holidays. They also hoped to return to their birthplace one day, rich and famous, for retirement. These episodes show how strong the emotional ties to the familiar life style are. Therefore, if urban workers feel aggrieved that the emotional strain of their detachment from home is not adequately rewarded by being able to take part in the fruits of industrialization, tension will develop into social discontent. When dissatisfied urban residents gather in a political movement, the effort of industrialization may well be thwarted. Similarly, in rural areas, if villagers think that industrialization only brings poverty and devastated landscapes, support for industrialization will be lost and protest is likely to erupt. Enraged people will become more receptive to calls for social reform through violent means. This perhaps explains why communist guerrillas attract a certain amount of popular support in the Philippines and Latin America. The 2–26 incident[26] in Japan was incited by frustrated military officers from farming villages who were upset by the deteriorating rural life. If such disturbances gather momentum and develop into a powerful political force, the road to industrialization will be effectively closed. Thus, the key to successful industrialization lies in furnishing proper incentives so that farmers willingly adjust to their new life style and participate in industrialization.

It is important to realize that the attraction of a better livelihood is not sufficient incentive under industrialization. People's livelihood can be most efficiently augmented by neoclassical distribution policy based on lump sum subsidies. But this is throwing money at dissent. It is not sufficient incentive for people who are keen to defend their familiar life style. More important, lump sum subsidies with no link to production activities cannot enhance incentives for production. Once the incentive to produce is lost, farmers and workers will become apathetic and their lives will deteriorate. This criticism of income transfers, often evoked by the opponents of the welfare state, holds a certain amount of truth. In some countries, the lack of incentive to search for new jobs while unemployment benefits last, and frequent alternation between work and job search, have become serious problems. While such degradation of the labor force is an inherent weakness of neoclassical distribution policy based on lump sum subsidies, the problem gets even worse when such policy is applied to latecomer countries in the process of rapid industrialization. This is because an additional emotional tension generated by separation from the traditional way of life further strengthens the deprivation felt by workers who are rejected by industrialization.

To avoid such a predicament, distribution policy should be implemented in the form of subsidies linked to production activities, not in the form of neoclassical redistribution through lump sum subsidies. This non-neoclassical policy conditional on production distorts resource allocation – as neoclassical economists correctly point out. On the other hand, subsidies linked to production will induce farmers to produce more and prevent a sudden collapse of rural life style. Instead of languishing, farmers are allowed to engage in a stable occupation and maintain their (tacit) support for industrialization. Migrant workers in cities can also look to their native villages for emotional comfort. For them, such psychological assurance is necessary to overcome the hardships in their quest for the fruits of industrialization.

So we should not be constrained by neoclassical worries over the non-neutrality of redistribution policy. In postwar Japan, for example, income was redistributed *de facto* to farmers through agricultural (and especially rice) price support policy, which enabled a large number of farmers to sustain enthusiasm for tilling the land for a substantial period of time. The sons and daughters of those farmers were recruited into modern industries in urban areas immediately after graduating from high school (i.e., the new-graduate hiring system). An increasing number of them also went on to receive higher education. At present, the Japanese agricultural price support system has become unsustainable under competitive pressure from imported food, and abolition of the price support system, especially of rice, is hotly debated. It is true that Japan, having fully achieved industrialization, no longer needs this kind of agricultural price support policy. But this does not nullify the fact that price-distorting non-neoclassical redistribution policy played an important role during the high growth era when Japan was catching up with the advanced world.

Many countries espousing economic growth try to solve the problem of unemployment by natural selection as a result of free competition or, at best, by introducing neutral income redistribution measures. This is a serious mistake. These policies are influenced by neoclassical economic liberalism which is interested only in a final equilibrium outcome and dismisses intermediate processes as temporary and of secondary importance. However, in order to forestall the widening gap between urban and rural livelihoods, redistribution measures directly linked to production or prices in farming villages and their surroundings are imperative. Developmentalism can succeed only when neoclassical prejudice is jettisoned.

Similar thinking leads to the policy of protecting and supporting small- and medium-sized enterprises, which is almost as important as income equalization policy toward farmers. Giant *zaibatsu* (conglomerates) often emerge to dominate the economies of latecomer countries. These large-scale enterprises in leading industries and their executive officers enjoy advanced technology and lavish life styles which are completely detached from the rest of the society. Children of *zaibatsu* executives in Asia and Latin America often study in the United States and other advanced countries. The life of high officials of such developing country *zaibatsu* is far more luxurious and sophisticated than that of the average Japanese citizen. If industrialization is seen to serve only a small number of large enterprises while small- and medium-sized enterprises are excluded, disgruntled people are likely to react politically. Furthermore, migrant workers from rural villages are usually employed in small- and medium-sized enterprises. Promotion of small- and medium-sized enterprises helps keep these urban workers from becoming disillusioned with industrialization.

Of course, supporting small- and medium-sized enterprises is desirable for other conventional reasons as well. For instance, small firms provide opportunities to individual entrepreneurs full of original business ideas. Their regular entry into existing industries also sustains the state of polipoly. We may also add a lesson that is well recognized in Japan and may apply to other countries: long-term relationship between a large number of small- and medium-sized parts suppliers and parent manufacturers enables the latter to produce high-quality products. What I would like to emphasize here, however, is that small- and medium-sized enterprises should be promoted from the distributional standpoint as well as for these other more conventional reasons. Away from home and under emotional stress, urban workers are nonetheless likely to accept industrialization – albeit tacitly – provided that the road to prosperity and fame is believed to be open to them.

A few words must be said about education[27] in connection with distribution policy. Provision of education is often cited as an effective measure for narrowing the urban–rural gap as well as the gap between the poor and the middle class in urban areas. As neoclassical lump sum subsidies have proved to be a rather ineffective anti-poverty measure in developed countries, education has begun to attract much attention as an alternative cure. It is argued that the urban poor can supply only low quality labor for which there is no demand. This causes the number of poor to increase. It is said that strengthening education can reverse this trend and eliminate the dual economic structure. Since few can seriously object to the provision of education, this argument has gained considerable popularity. Certainly, a minimum level of reading and writing ability is a prerequisite for participating in industrialization. Historical experience suggests that the state normally establishes a system of popular education when the economy is about to begin a climb on the path of industrialization. Our non-neoclassical distributional policy which encourages people to take part in industrialization through job opportunities also strongly supports educational effort. For this reason, the argument that education that teaches the three Rs, diligence, and discipline is important is well understood and absolutely correct.

But it is too optimistic to think that the establishment of a good school system will dissolve the dual economy. In many latecomer countries that exhibit economic duality, the school system is fairly well developed and the population boasts a higher literacy rate than that of European countries in the nineteenth century. Nevertheless, the dual economic structure persists. For example, among Southeast Asian peoples, Filipinos achieved the highest education level during the postwar period. Ironically, the Philippines also developed the largest urban slums in that region. Providing good education is certainly one of the necessary measures to tackle the dual economy, but that is not enough.

The more crucial issue is how to install a mechanism which allows reasonably well-educated farmers who are ready to work in factories proper participation in the process of industrialization, without driving them to political discontent or apathy toward work. In the development processes of Western countries, leading industries grew more slowly than today, and farmers emigrated to cities gradually. (This was especially true in England – see Chapter 6 of my *Anti-Classical Political Economy*.) However, the speed of industrialization is much greater today, and latecomers are required to develop their leading industries at a much accelerated pace. Correspondingly, social changes associated with industrialization are severely compressed, inducing a massive flow of labor and a strikingly evident cultural gap between agriculture (rural villages) and industry (cities). It is for this reason that policies to enhance worker incentives in farming and small- and medium-sized enterprises become all the more necessary.

Finally, it also should be underscored that income redistribution creates domestic demand. The kind of domestic demand which spurs industrialization most is relatively homogeneous mass demand – i.e., popular demand. A chain of products that breeds high growth – from textiles to sundry household goods, home electronics, and popular cars – are all designed for mass demand by families with a similar income level. From the classical British example to the present, mass demand for such products always shows explosive growth as industrialization takes off and accelerates. However, if the society is polarized into a few extremely rich families and the masses in poverty, the only markets that develop are those for specialized goods (high-price art objects and extreme luxuries) for the rich and a limited number of goods for the poor, neither of which can ignite industrialization. In transportation, for example, there will be a market for Rolls-Royces and BMWs along with a market for cheap shoes – but not for bicycles, motor bikes, and popular passenger cars. A distribution policy which can prevent the emergence of an extreme income gap and generate mass demand is very important.

In sum, distribution policy is necessary for developmentalism to succeed, because without it a massive wave of labor migration will result in the destruction of amicable rural communities and rising social tension, which ultimately frustrates industrialization amid political instability. To this, we have added the subsidiary role of redistribution in creating demand. From this perspective neoclassical distribution policy, which tends to weaken the incentive of farmers and workers to produce, will drive them to apathy and is hardly desirable. Our alternative approach is to introduce distribution measures that are linked to production, even though they will cause some inefficiency in resource allocation. This approach will enable rural families to relocate to cities more gradually over a few generations. Even this non-neoclassical distribution policy is not easy to implement properly. A happy balance between the merits and the demerits (allocative inefficiency) of the policy is difficult to strike. Another risk is political capture by interest groups which will perpetuate the support policy long after almost all farmers have gone to cities and industrialization is complete.

In retrospect, however, had Japan failed to adopt a price support distribution policy of the non-neoclassical type during the postwar high growth era, rural deprivation would likely have accelerated, leading to mounting dissatisfaction with industrialization and political agitation of a majority of urban dwellers who retained emotional ties to native villages – and social unrest would have ensued. Even if lump sum subsidies had been provided (in the absence of price supports), farmers who were removed from the land as a basis of their work would have dropped out of the industrialization process despite income compensation. The collapse of the rural life style would have created a large dissatisfied population. In recent years, the *gentan* policy [policy of cutting back on the acreage under cultivation, especially of rice] is accused of deflating the enthusiasm of farmers. The neoclassical distribution policy of providing lump sum subsidies is tantamount to *gentan* policy writ large. In conclusion, a non-neoclassical distribution policy must be accepted as a very desirable – and sometimes even indispensable – supplement for the successful execution of developmentalism, provided that it can be smoothly phased out in the future when the need for such redistribution is no longer present.

Notes

1 This is the entire chapter 6 (last complete chapter) of Murakami Yasusuke's *Hankoten no Seijikeizaigaku Youkou: Raiseiki no tameno Oboegaki* [Outline of Anti-Classical Political Economy: A Memorandum for the Next Century], Tokyo: Chuo Koronsha, 1994. This posthumous and incomplete book was written as a sequel to his earlier and larger work, *Hankoten no Seijikeizaigaku*, in two volumes, Chuo Koronsha, 1992 (in English, *Anti-Classical Political Economy*, translated by Kozo Yamamura, Stanford, CA, Stanford University Press, 1996). We have renumbered subsections to facilitate presentation as a stand-alone essay [Editors].

2 Increasing returns are said to be in operation when output increases more than proportionately when all inputs are increased. The phenomenon is also called economies of scale. It can be rephrased as decreasing costs, that is, reduction of the unit cost of production as output expands. The idea of *dynamic* increasing returns adds a time dimension to this concept: when cumulative output increases *over time*, productivity rises and unit cost declines [Editors].

3 Even without increasing returns, per capita output could increase if capital intensity rises indefinitely. But that cannot be expected to happen under normal circumstances.

4 Alfred Marshall, *The Principles of Economics*, 1890, part 4, chapter 11. In addition, he also cited "economies of raw materials" as a less significant cause.

5 Marshall, *op. cit.*, part 4, chapters 9 and 11. Incidentally, when the term "economy" is used this way, it implies an improvement in productivity.

6 The intended chapter on information problems was not written [Editors].

7 Karl Schmidt, *Das Zeitalter der Neutralisierungen und Endpolitisierungen*, 1929. Included in Ikutaro Shimizu (ed.) *Modern Thought Vol. 1 Karl Schmidt: Political Theory of Crisis*, translated by Ryuichi Nagao and others, Diamond, 1973, pp. 133–48 (in Japanese).

8 The 1972 OECD report, *Industrial Policy of Japan*, was the first systematic evaluation of Japanese industrial policy by non-Japanese. See Ryutaro Komiya, Masahiro Okuno, and Kotaro Suzumura (eds.) *Industrial Policy of Japan*, Academic Press, 1988, p. 20.
9 Haruo Shimada, *Economics of Humanware*, Tokyo: Iwanami Shoten, 1988.
10 P.B. Doringer and M.J. Piore, *Internal Labor Markets and Manpower Analysis*, Heath, Lexington, MA, 1971.
11 For examples of "excellent companies," see T.J. Peters and R.H. Waterman, *In Search of Excellence*, New York, Harper and Row, 1982.
12 In the original text, Murakami uses a subset symbol thus: "state-level developmentalism ⊃ firm-level developmentalism," which, however, contradicts his argument in the rest of the text. In translation we have reversed and stated this relationship without using a mathematical symbol [Editors].
13 It is not clear how best to think of competition based on market-share maximization. At one extreme, if each firm strives to maximize *output*, there will obviously be no stable Cournot–Nash equilibrium. On the other hand, if market-share maximization is interpreted as the maximization of *sales revenue*, outcome will be identical with that of the standard Cournot–Nash model (assuming the marginal cost to be always zero). The spirit of the market-share maximization principle seems to be best represented by a model that encompasses both sales- and output-maximization, with a greater emphasis on the latter. Among existing models, the contestability model is the one that best captures this spirit; see the next note.
14 Some static models show that the possibility of entry may cause too many firms to enter an industry. Even in that case, an existing firm can impose a "credible threat" on potential rivals by expanding capacity sufficiently and thus maintain its monopolistic position. Incidentally, in the contestability model where both price and quantity are strategic variables, monopoly is known to be the only solution under decreasing costs. The concept of contestability is normally understood as free entry and exit without sunk costs, but it also implicitly assumes that price and quantity are both treated as variables. Under such a setting, the hit-and-run strategy is ineffective and no more than one firm can exist under decreasing costs.
15 Yasusuke Murakami, "The Japanese Model of Political Economy," in Kozo Yamamura and Yasukichi Yasuba (eds) *The Political Economy of Japan, Volume 1, The Domestic Transformation*, Stanford, CA, Stanford University Press, 1987, pp. 33–90. Some readers may be interested in how polipoly and perfect competition differ. Perfect competition obtains when a large number of participants exist or they are mere price-takers so that no one can manipulate prices. This definition of perfect competition almost always and *de facto* assumes a fixed production function. By contrast, the concept of polipoly is associated with technical innovation and other dynamic conditions, giving rise to game theoretic price-setting and other strategies. Under polipoly, a strong tendency toward monopolization is sure to emerge, as discussed in the text. According to Michéle and Henrik Schmiegelow, the term polipoly is not new; see M. Schmiegelow and H. Schmiegelow, *Strategic Pragmatism*, New York, Praeger, 1989.
16 In the original, this heading is expressed in a mixture of Japanese and English, thus: "*sangyou no shitei*, targeting policy." However, the English phrase "targeting policy" does not represent what the author wants to say here. Accordingly, we used the literal translation of the Japanese rendition: identification (or specification) of industries [Editors].
17 J.E. Meade, *Indicative Planning*, Manchester, Manchester University Press, 1970.
18 The proposed chapter dealing with financial problems was not written [Editors].
19 In his famous passage, John Maynard Keynes described the instability of long-term expectations in financial markets as follows: "professional investment may be likened

to those newspaper competitions in which the competitors have to pick out the six prettiest faces from a hundred photographs, the prize being awarded to the competitor whose choice most nearly corresponds to the average preferences of the competitors as a whole; so that each competitor has to pick, not those faces which he himself finds prettiest, but those which he thinks likeliest to catch the fancy of the other competitors, all of whom are looking at the problem from the same point of view" (*The General Theory of Employment, Interest and Money*, Chapter 12, 1936) [Editors].

20 John Zysman, *Governments, Markets and Growth*, Ithaca, NY, Cornell University Press, 1983.

21 W.A. Lewis, "Economic Development with Unlimited Supply of Labor," *The Manchester School of Economics and Social Studies*, May 1954, pp. 139–91.

22 G. Ranis and J.C.H. Fei, "A Theory of Economic Development," *American Economic Review*, vol. 51, no. 4, September 1961.

23 The earliest criticism of this type was voiced by Harry Oshima, "The Ranis–Fei Model of Economic Development: Comment," *American Economic Review*, vol. 53, no. 3, June 1963.

24 P.H. Douglas, *The Theory of Wages*, Augustus M. Kelly, 1934; and Hiromi Arisawa, "The Wage Structure and Economic Structure: Significance and Causes of Low Wage," in Ichiro Nakayama (ed.) *Basic Wage Survey*, Tokyo: Toyo Keizai Shimposha, 1955 (in Japanese).

25 M.P. Todaro, "A Model of Labor Migration and Urban Unemployment in Less Developed Countries," *American Economic Review*, vol. 59, no. 1, March 1969, pp. 138–48.

26 Several young radical army officers harboring the idea of emperor-led state socialism staged a military coup in downtown Tokyo in the pre-dawn hours of February 26, 1936. A few key government officials were murdered in the rebellion and the central district of Tokyo was occupied. The coup was suppressed three days later and most of the responsible officers were executed [Editors].

27 The following argument is concerned exclusively with "*gakko kyoiku*" (formal, school-based education), not education in general. Since school-based education is a little awkward, we will use the term education throughout, which should be understood in this narrow sense [Editors].

11

DESIGNING ASIA FOR THE NEXT CENTURY[1]

Toshio Watanabe

I Prologue

It is Alexander Gerschenkron who stated that the industrialization of latecomer developing countries is supported by a sort of religious fever and driven by a catch-up ideology based on this fever.

> To break through the barriers of stagnation in a backward country, to ignite the imaginations of men, and to place their energies in the service of economic development, a stronger medicine is needed than the promise of better allocation of resources or even of the lower price of bread. Under such conditions even the businessman, even the classical daring and innovating entrepreneur, needs a more powerful stimulus than the prospect of high profits. What is needed to remove the mountains of routine and prejudice is faith – faith, in the words of Saint-Simon, that the golden age lies not behind but ahead of mankind.
>
> (Gerschenkron 1966: 24)

The idea underlying these sentences is the "Saint-Simonian doctrine." Gerschenkron draws from this ideology the guiding principles of nationalistic industrialization pursued in France under Napoleon III to compete with England.

Late industrialization was largely promoted by a nationalistic, centripetal ideology. This is related to the fact that in developing countries, banks and states – rather than entrepreneurs – were assigned the role of instruments of economic organization and development, thus launching state-led industrialization. Economic backwardness means that a country is not inherently equipped with either the resource mobilization capacity or the industrial organization required for industrialization.

To initiate the industrialization process the state must assume a principal role in developing institutional vehicles able to mobilize resources, induce and organize industrial development. The Credit Mobilier of France, the world's first investment bank, and German banks that provided long-term financing for the industrial sector were the key institutional instruments of industrialization in the European continent, which initially fell far behind England. In late developer Russia, where the banking system was underdeveloped, the state itself assumed the role of primary agent, propelling industrialization through fiscal policy. Similarly, in Meiji Japan the state played a leading role in promoting industrialization. Thus, "financial capitalism" and "state-led capitalism" were typically adopted in latecomers as vehicles for industrialization.

These discussions give us important perspective in analyzing contemporary development processes in East Asian countries. It is widely known that the ideology that supported nationalistic industrialization in Meiji Japan were "rich country, strong military" (*fukoku kyohei*) and "increase industrial production" (*shokusan kogyo*). Similarly, the ideology of "defeat communism and achieve unification" in South Korea and "retake the mainland" in Taiwan were ideologies of industrialization through rapid strengthening of national security capability, aimed at protecting their countries in life-or-death crises.

Because of the anti-industrialization policy of the Japanese colonial occupation, South Korea and Taiwan had much weaker industrial bases than Japan. The two countries attempted not only to push economic modernization under severe political and military tensions – in the case of South Korea, *vis-à-vis* North Korea, and in the case of Taiwan, *vis-à-vis* mainland China – but also to achieve export-oriented industrialization in very competitive international markets. It is hardly surprising that the two countries, while aiming at capitalist development, pursued state-led development strategies more forcefully than Japan.

A politico-economic system designed to formulate and implement state-led development can be called "authoritarian developmentalism." South Korea under Park Chung Hee and Chun Doo Hwan, Taiwan under Chiang Kai Shek and Chiang Ching Kuo, and Singapore under Lee Kuan Yew are prime examples. Authoritarian developmentalism is defined as a system in which the military or political elite who seize power advance development as the supreme goal, assign the responsibility for designing and implementing economic policies to bureaucratic-technocratic institutions created for the very purpose of development, and derive legitimacy from the success of economic development itself. Under this system, popular participation in decision making is inevitably limited.

Although authoritarian developmentalist states often adopt capitalism as a tool to further economic development, they often pursue strong state intervention in the economy. The most salient features of this system are attaching the highest priority to development and adopting organizational structures, institutions, and policies that allow rapid industrialization. The system does not accept ideological "binding" that hinders development; in this sense, pragmatism or "de-ideologization" is a key feature. If one seeks to name an ideology driving authoritarian developmentalism, development itself is the ideology.

Yasusuke Murakami, in his posthumous work, *Anti-Classical Political Economy*, gave legitimacy to the concept of developmentalism for the first time, stating:

> because liberal economics was born in the context of England, the original industrializer, it cannot be applied to most other countries. What is more realistic and useful to many countries is the political economy of "developmentalism," which aims to catch up with advanced countries.
>
> (Murakami 1992, vol. 1: 180)

> ... from the viewpoint of pure classical liberal economics, developmentalism is a deviation from the basic model of capitalism and is regarded as an exception that is allowed only during a transition period. However, from the viewpoint of the economics of catch-up industrialization, developmentalism can be seen as an alternative regime to the classical economic liberalism designed to achieve industrialization.
>
> (Murakami 1992, vol. 2: 4)

Murakami defined developmentalism as:

> an economic system based on private property and the market economy (i.e., capitalism) whose aim is to achieve industrialization (i.e., sustainable growth in per capita output) and where the government is permitted to intervene in the market from the long-term perspective as long as it is consistent with this aim. Clearly, the state (or a similar political entity) is the founding unit of developmentalism as a political and economic system. This regime often restricts the functioning of parliamentary democracy – as in royalism, one-party dictatorship, and military dictatorship.
>
> (Murakami 1992, vol. 2: 5–6)

The authoritarian developmentalism that I have described here is a political system that institutionalizes developmentalism. Of course, Hong Kong is an exception to this political and economic regime. It has experimented with *laissez-faire* economic policy, and the colonial government pursued "activist non-interventionism." However, the other newly industrializing economies (NIEs) of East Asia, namely South Korea, Taiwan, and Singapore, were (or have been) under authoritarian regimes and achieved remarkable economic success.

China has also made a radical economic policy shift from a centrally planned economic system to a market economic system and is aggressively pursuing a path to marketization. Although the country is under one-party control of the Communist Party, China's national policy is "reform and open door." Here again, authoritarian developmentalism is being established under one-party rule with a post-socialist ideology. As described below, the ASEAN countries have similarly adopted a system closely approaching authoritarian developmentalism, and it is my belief that this is a crucial factor in their present economic success.

This book is a sketch of my theory of East Asian economy. With greater emphasis on the political economy orientation, it attempts to provide a different viewpoint from the other literature in the similar areas. Chapters 1–2 analyze the political and economic system that brought about East Asia's economic prosperity; Chapter 3 discusses the accumulation mechanism of economic development in China; Chapter 4 focuses on the international economic forces, including trade and investment patterns, that triggered dynamic internal forces in East Asia; and lastly Chapter 5 examines Japan's response to East Asian developing countries as well as the direction of future Japanese ODA.

II Causes of prosperity in the NIEs

1 The theory of the developmental state: Japan as a prototype

The economic success of East Asia is largely attributable to the adoption of developmentalism, i.e., the ideology that places highest priority on economic development. Authoritarian developmentalism describes politico-economic regimes that have institutionalized this ideology. As I explained in the prologue [section I], it is the system in which the military or political elite, who derive legitimacy from the efficient promotion of economic development, assign to technocrats the task of designing and implementing economic policies. Under this system, material and human resources required for development are mobilized by a core group of technocrats through a centralized administrative mechanism; broad public participation in decision making on development matters is deferred.

Such a description may remind you of the centrally planned economic system under a socialist regime. There is no doubt that the People's Republic of China, which has achieved rapid growth under the "reform and open door" policy of Deng Xiao Ping, has opted for authoritarian developmentalism. Even though the socialist regime continues, there is an important difference between China today and before. Mainstream socialism, as observed in China under Mao Ze Dong and in the former Soviet Union from Lenin to Stalin, was based on "totalism," i.e., strong dictatorship by individual leaders who possessed dominant power on decisions of how to evaluate and interpret the legitimacy of the regime.

In contrast, under authoritarian developmentalism, the legitimacy of the regime derives from the success of development. To promote rapid and efficient development, technocrats are assigned unusual authority to guide industrial development; in many cases, capitalism has been adopted as a means to achieve development. Of course, the content of capitalism is quite different from that adopted in Western countries.

East Asian NIEs were latecomers to economic development. Driven by nationalism, they launched industrialization upon achieving independence from Western and Japanese colonialism. To industrialize as rapidly as possible, technocrats formulated and implemented economic policies; while capitalism was the basic economic principle in these countries, various regulations and other forms of government protection, that is, state intervention in the economy, were frequently observed.

Why did the NIEs adopt authoritarian developmentalism? In my view, it was primarily because of a sense of political and economic urgency. Fear of foreign encroachment convinced leaders and technocrats of the need to enrich the country through industrial development and thus established catch-up industrialization as a priority national goal. The fears were widely shared by the general public, creating a societal willingness to accept industrialization as a supreme goal. In this way, industrialization was elevated to an ideology of developmentalism and became a central element of the modernization movement. This process is a prototype of industrialization by latecomers, to say nothing of the NIEs.

The Japanese experience offers a good example of this prototype. Japan started industrialization as a response to "the encroachment of western powers in the east" (*seiryoku tozen*). As a latecomer, Japan decided to industrialize on the model of Western capitalism in order to catch up with the advanced countries in the West. In those days, Western capitalism was the only model of economic modernization available to Japan. However, the ideology promoted by Meiji Japan to implement the model was not based on Anglo-American values such as economic individualism and utilitarianism, but rather on values that emphasized spiritualism or even nationalism.

It was natural for Meiji Japan, which lacked the technological and institutional base necessary for industrialization, to adopt spiritualism and appeal to nationalism in the search for a centripetal force. As a latecomer, Japan had no other options but to promote rapid industrialization under authoritarian developmentalism. "Universal" concepts, such as utilitarianism, individualism, free competition, and profit maximization were not driving forces in the industrialization of Japan.

Chalmers Johnson called Japan a capitalistic "developmental state," contrasting it with the "regulatory state" typically found in the United States (Johnson 1982). In the regulatory state, private business is the driving force of economic development, and the government function is limited to setting the rules of economic competition ("market rational" development). The government does not concern itself with such substantive matters as what industries ought to exist and what industries are no longer needed. By contrast, the developmental state has as its dominant feature state-led industrial policy – a strategic or goal-oriented approach to the economy. Here, the government gives precedence to "plan rational" development in close collaboration with private business and is concerned with the structure of domestic industry and with promoting a structure that enhances the nation's international competitiveness.

According to Johnson, Japan has always put emphasis on setting "an overarching, nationally supported goal for its economy" (Johnson 1982: 20–1). Following the Meiji Restoration of 1868, the government set a series of goals, starting with *shokusan kogyo* (increase industrial production) and *fukoku kyohei* (rich country, strong military), and then *seisanryoku kakuju* (expand productive capacity), *yushutsu shinko* (promote exports), *kanzen koyo* (full employment), *kodo seicho* (high-speed growth). To achieve these goals, the government introduced various schemes, such as self-control (*jishu kanri*), meaning that the state licenses private enterprises to achieve developmental goals (a typical example is a state-sponsored cartel, in which the state authorizes cartels in industries it designates as strategic but leaves to enterprises themselves the task of fashioning and operating the cartel); state control (*kokka kanri*), the attempt to separate management from ownership and to put management under state supervision, as occurred in the prewar and wartime electric power generating industry and munitions companies; and public–private cooperation (*kanmin kyocho*), which flourished after World War II based on administrative guidance (*gyosei shido*) (Johnson 1982: 310–12).

Johnson cites four essential features of a developmental state, if the Japanese high-growth system is to be used as an effective model (Johnson 1982: 315–20). The first element of the model is the existence of a small, inexpensive, but elite bureaucracy staffed by the best available managerial talent. In Japan, the talented and prestige-laden economic bureaucracy was assigned the tasks of, first, identifying and choosing the industries to be developed (industrial structure policy); second, identifying and choosing the best means of rapidly developing the chosen industries (industrial rationalization policy); and third, supervising competition in the designated strategic sectors in order to guarantee their economic health and effectiveness.

The second element of the model is a political system in which the bureaucracy is given sufficient scope to take initiative and operate effectively. This means that the legislative and judicial branches of government must be restricted to "safety valve" functions. The third element of the model is the perfection of market-conforming methods of state intervention in the economy, such as administrative guidance (*gyosei shido*). In implementing its industrial policy, the state must take care to preserve competition to as high a degree as is compatible with its priorities. The fourth and final element of the model is a pilot organization like the Ministry of Commerce and Industry and MITI.

In Johnson's view, the concept of an authoritarian, developmental state has derived from nationalism compelled by the "situational imperatives" of latecomers. I attach great importance to this point, because capitalistic development under authoritarian developmentalism, solidly organized to defend itself from external security threat, is a key term to characterize the process of rapid industrialization of Japan and the East Asian NIEs.

The strong urge toward economic modernization in East Asian countries was the product of latecomer nationalism, driven by the prevailing international political and economic climates. Byron K. Marshall analyzed the core of the powerful ideology that prompted the transformation of Japanese society in the late nineteenth century, what he called "reactive nationalism." He stated:

industrialization, in other words, was advocated first and foremost as a means of avoiding humiliation at the hands of the Western powers. The fact that the Meiji Restoration and the far-reaching changes it set in motion took place in and derived their justification from a sense of national crisis colored all subsequent Japanese political, social, and economic thought.

(Marshall 1967: 13)

This expression provides us with insight into the process of economic development in today's NIEs.

2 South Korea: external security threat and development

South Korea and Taiwan were imbued with a sense of political and economic urgency – perhaps deeper than Meiji Japan – that helped reinforce public willingness to accept rule by authoritarian governments that kept order and implemented policies conducive to growth. Leaders in these countries perceived that they had only very limited time to build an industrial base and that unless they moved quickly on industrialization, military intrusion from other parts of their divided countries would be inevitable.

The military coup of May 16, 1961, the so-called "May 16th Revolution," had a decisive impact on the history of economic development in South Korea. Immediately, the Park Chung Hee administration set up the Economic Planning Board, and in 1962, it launched the first Five-Year Economic Development Plan. From that time through the current seventh plan, South Korea has consistently prepared economic development plans and actively promoted development based on the plans, under authoritarian regimes. Korean history offered no precedents for conducting economic management in such an organized way: i.e., setting up clear-cut goals, mobilizing necessary resources and allocating resources to achieve the goals.

In 1961 at the time of the military coup, there was no elite group other than the military that could lead the country toward modernization. The Korean military academy, reorganized in 1951 on the model of the U.S. military academy at West Point, was then the only source in Korea for a cadre of modern elite familiar with the latest knowledge in politics, economics, national development, world strategy, and defense. The Korean War provided an opportunity to test the transformation of the newly created military into a centralized technocratic institution. As Gregory Henderson stated, "[n]o civilian group or institution has come close to it in the development of a definite and comparatively fairly administered career service" (Henderson 1968: 334).

In the Confucian tradition since the Li dynasty, political control by the military itself was unusual. Historically, civilian bureaucrats who mastered Confucian thought and were selected on the basis of merit, assumed the functions of top political officials. It was considered that under their wise guidance, culture, public morals, and order could be elevated and maintained throughout the country. The Confucian bureaucrat had broad responsibility for overall social order, including the moral tone of society, and enjoyed considerable authority and respect from the masses.

Civilian bureaucrats devoted themselves to learning and practicing the original text of the "Four Chinese Classics and Five Canons." Their way of thinking was conservative and ideological, and their behavior pattern was pandering and formal. Progressive attitudes, such as willingness to set goals to change the status quo and to act efficiently to achieve the goals, were almost absent. In fact, in the Confucian tradition, there was deep-rooted prejudice against commerce and the merchant class; merchants were thought to be governed only by self-interest and the pursuit of private profit. In this sense, the 1961 military coup was an epoch-making political change in Korean history because it destroyed the long-standing Confucian tradition of the civilian bureaucratic system, along with its underlying logic.

It should not be overlooked that in the process of consolidating their control, the military elite placed the highest priority on economic modernization and actively fostered bureaucrats charged with economic policy making. This was a very progressive effort, unprecedented in a country where prejudice against commercial activities was deeply rooted.

To prepare the first Five-Year Economic Development Plan, South Korea set up the Economic Planning Board (EPB) and exercised centralized control over critical economic matters. As a powerful bureaucratic organ charged with formulation and implementation of the plan, the EPB was given the authority to supervise and guide economic ministries such as the Ministries of Agriculture and Forestry, Commerce and Industry, Transportation, and Finance. The Deputy Prime Minister was nominated as head of the EPB to undertake development administration in a strongly centralized organizational structure. In the process of creating and reorganizing a modern technocratic bureaucracy such as the EPB, the Park administration eliminated the conservative class of autocratic bureaucrats and widely recruited young, capable officials for development administration.

In South Korea the *chaebôl*, or industrial conglomerates, were an engine of capitalist development. However, their remarkable growth was made possible only with the government's support and protection. The *chaebôl* implemented the blueprint of economic development prepared by technocrats, and the government in turn supported the *chaebôl*; Korean industrialization proceeded smoothly under close partnership between the public and private sectors. South Korea adopted a strategy of export-oriented industrialization in the golden sixties, when the global economy was expanding. To realize this strategy, it introduced massive amounts of foreign loans and technology and utilized them to foster export industries owned by *chaebôl* firms. New *chaebôl* were created one after another, mainly in the textile and electronics sectors.

In the 1970s, South Korea launched its heavy and chemical industrialization drive. The Shipbuilding Promotion Law (1967), the Electronics Promotion Law (1969), and the Steel Industry Promotion Law and Petrochemical Industry Promotion Law (1970) were promulgated, establishing the institutional framework for the drive. *Chaebôl* firms selected those elements of the government's plan suitable to their own firms and submitted business proposals consistent with the plans to the government. Once the proposals were approved, the firms proceeded with construction and expansion of industrial facilities, backed by government financial support.

With government backing, each of the *chaebôl* firms responded quickly and forcefully to opportunities even when they involved expanding into new sectors. Gradually, the *chaebôl* began to diversify into several industrial sectors ("conglomerate"-style management) and through fierce competition, they came to occupy a dominant role in today's Korean economy.

A main instrument in establishing *chaebôl* dominance in the Korean economy was the government directed credit program. Until 1982, the main financial institutions were owned or tightly controlled by the government, and directed credit channeled through banks was the only way for firms to secure preferential financing. In the 1960s and 1970s when South Korea suffered a chronic shortage of financing, the survival of a firm critically depended on access to the government-backed directed credit program. With limited availability of the long-term industrial financing required for industrial growth, firms had no other option than to comply with the directives of the government that controlled the financial system. This gave the economic bureaucracy leverage over big business.

Furthermore, because foreign loans were channeled through the government, only the government was able to mobilize overseas financing and determine its allocation. In this way, in South Korea technocrats played a critical role in guiding the *chaebôl* and promoting economic development.

President Park Chung Hee presided over this hierarchy of authoritarian developmentalism. Amid the military and diplomatic confrontation against North Korea, he was propelled by a strong sense of external threat: if South Korea failed in industrialization, national survival would be endangered. Park was determined to act to this end and concentrated all his energy on rapid industrialization of the country.

His thinking can be summarized as follows: with severe poverty, a high level of illiteracy, and a conservative cultural tradition, it would be premature for South Korea to adopt the Western-style democratic system at this moment. Hasty democratization would only worsen confusion and corruption. To build a true democratic system, South Korea must first establish an industrial base and eliminate poverty. Ideally speaking, such a development effort should be made based on the popular consensus; however, having active pro-North political groups within the country, it is not easy for us to work on a consensual basis. Therefore, the only way left to South Korea is state-led industrialization supported by strong leadership. As long as North Korea has a declared intention to invade the South, South Korea should devote all its national efforts to reinforcing economic power through the heavy and chemical industrialization drive.

Evident in his thinking are: a sense of external security threat, elitism, and above all a strong determination to industrialize. In this sense, Park Chung Hee was a typical politician in East Asia where authoritarian developmentalism prevailed. Nobody questions the remarkable economic success achieved by South Korea under the authoritarian regime. South Korea has demonstrated outstanding performance in industrialization and export growth since the latter half of the 1960s, and has earned a reputation as the "Miracle of the Han River".

In the process of rapid industrialization, a labor class emerged and social strata diversified. A labor movement demanding protection of workers' rights grew rapidly, as did democracy groups calling for citizens' rights. However, Park Chung Hee was reluctant to give in to these demands, and rather attempted to strengthen the authoritarian regime by launching the "Yushin System" in 1972.[2]

The perceived weakening of the U.S. security guarantee also contributed to reinforcing South Korea's determination to pursue authoritarian developmentalism. The reduction of American military presence in the Korean peninsula, which accelerated in the 1970s, and the phased scaling down of U.S. troops from Korea, created a sense of both economic and military urgency. Such a sense of external security threat provided a powerful stimulus for the population to seek an independent industrial base adequate to support its own national defense efforts, and helped reinforce the social acceptance of authoritarian developmentalism. The Carter Administration's January 1977 announcement of the desire to remove U.S. troops from Korea was the biggest political threat to South Korea since the Korean War. It is hardly surprising that the heavy and chemical industrialization drive was accelerated during this period.

In those days, about 400,000 to 500,000 people worked for the military, and military expenditures accounted for 40 percent of the national budget. Although this put a heavy burden on South Korea's economic development, the population endured the burden under Park's strong authority. "Rich country, strong military" was the ideology of industrialization in Meiji Japan. Similarly, "destroy communism and achieve unification" was the ideology that propelled economic modernization in South Korea.

Park Chung Hee was assassinated in a "royal coup" on October 26, 1979. In the succeeding Chun Doo Hwan administration (1980–88), democratic demands grew, and the foundation of the authoritarian regime began to be shaken. Political democratization was finally realized by Roh Tae Woo (1988–93) and Kim Young Sam (1993–). Let us put the detailed analysis of causal relationships aside; in any case, it is evident that the preconditions for South Korea's democratization were laid by authoritarian developmentalism under the Park administration and that because of its very success, the authoritarian regime dissolved itself.

3 Taiwan: renaissance of the Kuomintang leaders

The prototype of the political and economic system of present-day Taiwan was formed in December 1949 when the leaders of the Kuomintang (KMT, or Nationalist Party), defeated by the Communist Party on the mainland, retreated to Taiwan and initiated efforts at nation-building and economic modernization. With the Communist victory in 1949, the People's Republic of China was established. The declared intention of the Communist government on the mainland to 'liberate' Taiwan placed the Taiwan Strait in a very tense, delicate situation. The Korean War, which broke out in June 1950, provided temporary relief to Taiwan. In the military vacuum created by the war, the Taiwanese government, aided by American military and economic assistance, put all its efforts into defending the island it planned to use as a base for reclaiming the mainland.

Taiwan had little time to overcome the crisis, and the military burden in those days was very heavy. When the Kuomintang retreated to Taiwan, about 1.5 million bureaucrats, military officials, and entrepreneurs fled to Taiwan with their families. Simply feeding the suddenly exploding population made economic development an urgent task.

In this way, Taiwan's effort to build its national economy started under a strong external threat and pervasive sense of crisis. It was quite natural for a small country like Taiwan to place top priority on nation-building and strengthening economic power as the basis of national security. To accomplish these urgent tasks in the shortest possible period, Taiwan adopted a state-led development strategy, led by a strong authoritarian developmentalist regime.

Judging from historical precedent, there is no surprise that Taiwan adopted authoritarian developmentalism. Chiang Kai Shek was a brilliant KMT leader who succeeded Dr. Sun Yat Sen in guiding the "unfinished revolution." When Chiang retreated to Taiwan, several leaders who disagreed with his political style did not join him. Those who followed were the KMT elite, primarily the top military leaders who had a strong sense of loyalty to Chiang. The KMT elite, driven by anti-Communism, had dominant power and used its firm authority to unify and control the party, the army, and the government from the beginning of its rule in Taiwan.

Taiwan experienced continuous threat from mainland China. The ongoing tension helped to sustain a high level of unity among KMT leaders and to legitimize tight control over the local population. Party dominance was buttressed by the army and secret police. Although the local Taiwanese felt complex hostility toward the KMT, they were too weak to demonstrate it in explicit actions and remained subservient.

The KMT leaders were forced to adopt a work style different from that common in mainland China. They gradually came to realize that a primary reason for their defeat in the war against the Communist Party was public disaffection. The United States, the Kuomintang's only lifeline, frankly hesitated to support the KMT even after its retreat to Taiwan, citing corruption and political ineptitude. Fortunately, the outbreak of the Korean War forced the U.S. to support the KMT, a critical anti-Communist voice. In any case, the KMT needed a renaissance.

KMT leaders transformed themselves into skilled practitioners of authoritarian developmentalism, assigning top priority to economic development in Taiwan. According to Ezra F. Vogel,

> [i]n their analysis of why they lost the mainland, Kuomintang leaders acknowledged that public support had eroded because of their failure to stop corruption and to provide for the common people's livelihood. Above all, they concluded, they should have done more to control inflation and implement land reform. They were determined to do better on Taiwan. They resolved to be strict with corruption, to expand the role of government enterprise in a way not susceptible to private influence, and to create a greater distance between the government and the private sector.
>
> (Vogel 1991: 18)[3]

The goal of retaking the mainland remained an article of faith for the KMT. However, such slogans faded when the Korean War ended and the Cold War structure in East Asia entered a stalemate. Economic development in Taiwan advanced steadily, backed by the power and prestige of the KMT elite. The "Taiwanization" of the KMT began with the first Four-Year Plan of Economic Construction in 1952.

KMT technocrats devoted their skills and passion to economic development, and in fact, implemented land reform – a difficult hurdle in many developing countries – for the first time in Asia, and succeeded. Many entrepreneurs who assumed management responsibility in the state enterprises that laid the foundation of Taiwan's economic development were former technocrats. This fact itself indicates that they were the ablest, best-educated people in Taiwan. A group of technocrats who had practical bureaucratic experience in mainland China took charge of the urgent task of building a nation in the Republic of China under threat from the mainland giant. Their ability and talent came into full play.

The first Four-Year Economic Construction Plan is one of the earliest state-led economic development plans ever, ranking with India. Strong orientation to strengthening the production base resulted in most important development investments, including electric power and petrochemicals, being carried out by the state. More than half of industrial production assigned under the first Economic Construction Plan was in the hands of state enterprises.

In the late 1960s when development under the authoritarian regime was getting on track, Taiwan was again forced to accept major changes in the international political environment. As the international political trend shifted from the Republic of China to the People's Republic of China, political support for Taiwan weakened. The U.S. security commitment to the Far East also began to decline.

In 1965, the U.S. ended economic assistance to Taiwan. When the U.S. opened up relations with mainland China, Taiwan was forced to withdraw from the United Nations in 1971. With a break of diplomatic relations with Japan in 1972, Taiwan was put in a desperate, politically isolated situation. This crisis was followed by the normalization of Sino-American diplomatic relations in January 1979. It is not difficult to imagine that such severe shifts in the international environment drove Taiwan to redouble efforts to demonstrate its national identity through strengthened economic power.

Convinced that rapid economic development was the only way to survive in international society and strengthen its bargaining power against the mainland (self-reliance and self-reinforcement), Taiwan launched a large-scale nationalist economic construction initiative. In 1973, with bureaucratic guidance, Taiwan launched a heavy and chemical industrialization drive, known as the "Ten Major Development Projects." Under the projects, massive public investments were made in three core industrial sectors – steel, petrochemicals, and shipbuilding – and seven key areas of social and economic infrastructure, such as highways, railways, ports, airports, and nuclear power. In 1977, the government announced twelve new projects, and in 1984, it launched fourteen more to continue modernization of basic industrial sectors.

Needless to say, Taiwan's economic development under authoritarian developmentalism, like the experience of South Korea, was a rare case of success. In the process of industrial breakthrough, the movement toward political democratization quickened at the end of the administration of Chiang Ching Kuo, Chiang Kai Shek's son. The democratization process is purely an "internal revolution" generated by the KMT, brought about by the success of authoritarian developmentalism itself. More attention will be given to this interpretation later.

4 Singapore: administrative state and elitism

Chan Heng Chee of the Singapore University once claimed that in Singapore, politics has disappeared and the country has become an "administrative state" (Chan 1975). This statement perfectly describes the reality of Singapore.

Since winning all political seats in the 1963 national election, the People's Action Party (PAP) has sustained one-party control, despite a slight decline in the PAP's influence recently. Singapore has forcefully and literally promoted authoritarian developmentalism, establishing economic development as the single supreme goal and fostering a close partnership between the PAP and a group of technocrats selected on a strict merit basis.

Up until now, Singapore has succeeded in sustaining a coherent authoritarian regime. The PAP systematically reorganized opposition parties, labor unions, pressure groups, interest groups and others and geared them toward "development administration." Being a typical small country, Singapore was inevitably affected by volatile developments in the international economy, especially in the economic situation of its neighbors. But under authoritarian developmentalism, the country succeeded in achieving a per capita income equal to advanced country levels. The source of power of Singapore's authoritarian developmentalism lies in the PAP, and its symbol is Lee Kuan Yew, its charismatic leader.

Singapore achieved independence from England in June 1959, obtaining autonomy on all but military and diplomatic affairs. In 1961, Malaya's Abdul Raman announced his proposal for a Malaysia Federation, and Singapore joined in 1963 along with Borneo and Sarawak. However, Indonesia opposed the creation of the Malaysia Federation, objecting to the inclusion of northern Borneo. President Sukarno adopted a confrontational policy and criticized the Federation as a conspiracy of the new colonialism. The Singaporean economy, heavily dependent on entrepôt trade at that time, was hit severely.

Other factors also reduced Singapore's entrepôt role. For example, neighboring East Asian countries started to increase direct trading to achieve greater economic independence, decreasing transshipment through Singapore. This convinced Singaporean leaders of the urgent need to upgrade the country's economic structure, reduce reliance on transit trade, and make the economy more autonomous.

Strong population pressure also prompted development of a new economic structure. Unemployment exceeded 14 percent in 1960. Students and workers staged frequent strikes and acts of violence in the late 1950s, and unemployment was a main cause of social unrest. Furthermore, there was concern that the high rate of population growth would lead to excess labor supply in the future, adding pressure to the already serious job shortage.

The PAP assumed power in 1955 with the support of youth and workers who were strongly influenced by the Communist revolution in China. Although the PAP originally had strong inclinations toward socialist ideology, its political style changed drastically in the process of dealing with a series of crises that hit this small country. The PAP transformed itself into a leading example of authoritarian developmentalism, which stresses pragmatism and assigns top priority to the maximization of economic efficiency. Although the exact reason behind Singapore's decision to adopt authoritarian developmentalism differed from that of South Korea and Taiwan, a sense of external threat was again the driving force in the country's transformation.

Singapore's leaders had to decide how to promote industrialization. The Singaporean economy before independence was heavily dependent on entrepôt trade. There was no local industrial development base, except for small, low-productivity establishments that were engaged in the primary processing of rubber and tin, and the food processing industry which was mainly directed at the domestic market. In 1965, Singapore was forced to become independent of the Malaysia Federation, but the loss of the Malay peninsula as a hinterland obliged Singapore to adopt a very particular path of industrialization.

At this time Singapore's power as an administrative state came fully into play. The government implemented a new industrialization policy through the Economic Expansion and Promotion Law in 1968, which provided significant incentives to foreign capital. Singapore launched export-oriented industrialization, relying on foreign investment by firms with worldwide networks (i.e., multinational corporations).

Convinced that local capital was not internationally competitive, Singapore sought from the outset to use multinational corporations as the engine of industrialization, to pursue the expansion of exports and employment, and as collateral to secure Singapore's international status. The Economic Expansion and Promotion Law was amended in 1970, 1975, and 1978 and granted multinationals "pioneer status," which included exemption from corporate taxes for five to ten years and fiscal support.

Prior to the enactment of this law in 1968, the government modified the Employment Law and the Labor Relations Law, revising some labor conditions that had been at high advanced-country levels and strengthening the rights of management in private firms. In the 1950s, left-wing labor unions were powerful, and strikes occurred constantly. For the government, normalization of labor relations was an urgent task in preparing the conditions to attract multinational corporations. The two laws restricted workers' right to strike, and the relation between management and labor shifted rapidly from confrontational to collaborative under PAP guidance.

Singapore is like a strong management unit with a bureaucratic system as its organizational core. One of the biggest bottlenecks facing Singapore immediately after independence was the shortage of capital for economic development. To address this problem, in 1955 the government established the Central Provident Fund with resources generated from wages and salaries. Ten percent of monthly wages and salaries – equal 5 percent contributions from employers and employees – were withheld and placed in a special pension-like fund to finance industry, transportation and communications, infrastructure, parks, and housing. Employees could draw on this fund (with interest) at the age of 55, or when they were otherwise unable to work. Compulsory contributions to the Fund were increased over the years. At its peak in the mid-1980s, contribution to the Central Provident Fund reached 50 percent of all wages and salaries. Workers normally used this fund to secure housing mortgages for the purchase of apartments built by the Housing Authority (created in 1960).

Because Fund interest rates were much lower than those of private financial institutions, the Fund worked like a sort of forced saving mechanism, and the government benefited from easy access to fiscal resources at low cost. Singapore is known as a high-savings country, even in Asia. In 1992, the saving rate – that is, the total of public and private saving as a percentage of GDP – was as high as 47.2 percent. Clearly, the Central Provident Fund is the primary reason for this high saving rate. The government actively used the Central Provident Fund to support public enterprises; however, it also promoted multinationals, and public enterprises have been forced to improve their management efficiency to compete.

With its long tradition as a port city specializing in entrepôt trade, Singapore had no strong basis of local industrial development. To attain rapid development in the late 1960s, the government determined to make maximum effort to attract multinationals and to use their vitality to drive Singapore's industrialization. This principle remains unchanged today. There is no doubt that Singapore succeeded in rapid industrialization and this success is attributable to the effective administrative state built by technocrats under the People's Action Party.

We must pay high regards to the pragmatic and efficient authoritarian developmentalism which was implemented by the economic bureaucracy, such as the technocrats at the Economic Planning Board. The secret to making this small country a prominent economic state lies in the presence of a strong state supported by capable technocrats.

For authoritarian developmentalism to succeed, a state must build a functioning bureaucracy that is entrusted with substantial decision making authority and enjoys high prestige. As Vogel states:

> [t]he bureaucratic system, in its modern form, played a critical role in industrialization. Some of the ablest people in the society were chosen, and they were given broad-gauged training and experience in many different positions before being assigned major responsibilities. On the whole they remained dedicated to overall public goals and, while provided a measure of guaranteed benefits, they exercised restraint in their private pursuit of wealth. The fact that they were selected by meritocratic measures, were reputed to be highly moral, and lived without conspicuous display gave them an unquestioned legitimacy that encouraged public compliance with their decisions and thus helped to provide a stable base of support for their governments.
>
> (Vogel 1991: 95)

I fully concur with this observation and believe that it draws on Singapore's experience.

5 Economic development and political regimes: the dissolution of authoritarian developmentalism

If a latecomer developing country – a country short on the basic preconditions for industrialization – is to achieve rapid development under strong external pressure within a limited time, the adoption of a state-led development strategy is unavoidable. This is an empirical statement strongly supported by history. The state-led development strategy is largely authoritarian developmentalism, if viewed from a governance and political regime perspective. For a latecomer to promote its development strategy efficiently, a political system where a small cadre of elite bureaucrats sets policy goals and mobilizes the masses to achieve the goals is more suitable than a democratic system where policy making is conducted with broad participation of the masses who have a variety of demands.

It is precisely for this reason that authoritarian developmentalism – also called "oligarchy" or "developmental dictatorship" – is often adopted in developing countries. In this sense, it is simplistic to criticize authoritarian developmentalism in developing countries as a political system without popular participation. Such critics give no consideration to the initial pre-industrial conditions in developing countries. To repeat, if a latecomer aims at rapid economic development under difficult external and domestic conditions, the adoption of authoritarian developmentalism is unavoidable.

However, we must take note of the fact that, if development under an authoritarian regime proceeds successfully, the authoritarian regime will sow the seeds of its own dissolution. The recent winds of democracy in South Korea and Taiwan symbolically explain this fact. In other words, South Korea and Taiwan offer prime examples of not only well-executed authoritarian developmentalism, but its successful dissolution as well.

The eight-point democratization proposal known as the June 29th Declaration on Democratization and presented by Roh Tae Woo (Democratic Justice Party) in 1987, was a symbolic event that indicates the South Korean political system has been rapidly transforming from a military-backed authoritarian regime to a democratic system that tries to respond to popular political demands. In South Korea, the military had been the only organized political force since the 1961 military coup. It is natural that the military had excellent capability, given that it had supported the country through severe North–South confrontation. Of course, Park Chung Hee was at the top of the military. Under Park's leadership, capable economic bureaucrats were able to exercise their power and prestige. "Developmentalism" was the ideology they pursued.

Successful economic development resulted in improved living standards and diversification of social strata, and eventually development under an authoritarian regime became unattractive as an ideology of governance. The June 29th Declaration on Democratization filled the gap between economic development and political development in a dramatic way. This declaration triggered a nation-wide movement toward democracy and signaled the end of the Chun Doo Hwan administration (that had been regarded as legitimate successor of the Park Chung Hee administration).

The collapse of the authoritarian regime in South Korea – the product of North–South confrontation – brought important changes in the country's relationship not only with North Korea, but also with the former Soviet Union and China. Immediately after the end of the Cold War, South Korea established diplomatic relations with the former Soviet Union and China. Its relationship with North Korea has softened recently relative to the Park Chung Hee and Chung Doo Hwan eras. The Special Declaration for Self-Respect and Unification Policy, announced one year after the June 29th Declaration on July 7, 1988, was tangible evidence of such changes. These two declarations should be viewed as a pair. The July 7th Declaration advocates a new spirit that would never have flourished under the authoritarian regime. The tension in the Korean peninsula is likely to continue for the time being because of the nuclear threat of North Korea. However, South Korea does not seem to be bracing itself against imminent attack from the North. I am deeply moved by the fact that the South Korean people have attained such a high level of confidence and affluence through successful economic development.

In parallel, Taiwan faced a similar turning point in its long history of authoritarian developmentalism. The present political system in Taiwan was created by the Kuomintang who retreated to the island to build a base for retaking the mainland after losing the military battle with the Communist Party in 1949. Considering the emergency situation of the battle with the Chinese Communist Party on the mainland, it is quite natural that Taiwan established an authoritarian regime based on one-party rule by the Kuomintang. In 1949, the country was placed under martial law, which strengthened the power of the party leader and eviscerated the separation of powers. Martial law remained in effect even after the crisis of the Taiwan Strait eased and functioned to protect the country's authoritarian regime.

However, the Kuomintang lifted martial law in 1987. That year, the Third Plenum of the Twelfth Party Central Committee launched a series of bold political reforms and took drastic action to end completely what were considered the two greatest barriers to democratization in Taiwan: martial law and the prohibition on establishing new political parties. On October 7, 1986, the Kuomintang announced it was lifting the ban on new party formation. Then the KMT ended martial law on October 15 when the National Security Law was promulgated.

In December 1986, Taiwan held the first multiple-party election in its history, and the newly created opposition party, the Democratic Progressive Party made great strides. Furthermore, in 1987, the prohibition on publishing new newspapers was lifted. At ceremonies commemorating Constitution Day in December 1990, party leader Lee Teng Hui announced plans to repeal by May 1991 the emergency article of the Constitution which regards the Communist Party of mainland as a rebel force that must be suppressed. This article was symbolic because it conferred on the party leader strong power to take emergency measures without the approval of the Legislative branch. The article was abolished as announced.

Taiwan's democratization process began with an internal revolution, where authoritarian developmentalism gradually began to dissolve in the hands of the Kuomintang. This is quite similar to the process observed in June 29th Declaration (by Roh Tae Woo) in South Korea. As in South Korea, it was a movement of the middle class emerging from a process of rapid economic development that raised popular consciousness of democratic demands and achieved Kuomintang acceptance of a looser political regime. It is impossible to discuss Taiwan's democratization without giving due regard to the rising power of the middle class as a consequence of urbanization and high educational attainment.

On the other hand, in the case of Singapore, it seems unlikely that authoritarian developmentalism built on the overwhelming dominance of the PAP will give way to a democratic system so easily, although popular support for the PAP has been steadily declining. As a natural consequence of economic development, I believe that Singapore's political system will also gradually soften under the existing authoritarian regime.

Notes

1 This is a translation of *Shinseiki Asia no Koso* [Designing Asia for the New Century], Chikuma Shinsho, Tokyo, 1995. The original book consists of a prologue and five chapters. This volume presents the prologue and Chapter 1 of the book, renumbered here as sections I and II [Editors].
2 Under the "Yushin System" (started in October 1972), the presidential power was further strengthened. Concerned about the need to reinforce national defense and accelerate industrialization, President Park Chung Hee declared an intention to build heavy and chemical industries. The government began the aggressive promotion of domestic production of intermediate and capital goods [Editors].
3 The original book by Ezra Vogel, *The Four Little Dragons*, is also translated by Toshio Watanabe into Japanese (Tokyo: Chuo Koron Sha, 1993) [Editors].

References

Chan, Heng Chee (1975) "Politics in an Administrative State: Where Has the Politics Gone?" in Seah Chee Meow (ed.) *Trends in Singapore*, Singapore: Singapore University Press.

Gerschenkron, Alexander (1966) *Economic Backwardness in Historical Perspective*, Cambridge, MA: Harvard University Press.

Henderson, Gregory (1968) *Korea: The Politics of Vortex*, Cambridge, MA: Harvard University Press.

Johnson, Chalmers (1982) *MITI and Japanese Miracle: The Growth of Industrial Policy 1925–1975*, Stanford, CA: Stanford University Press.

Marshall, Byron K. (1967) *Capitalism and Nationalism in Prewar Japan: The Ideology of the Business Elite, 1868–1941*, Stanford, CA: Stanford University Press.

Murakami, Yasusuke (1992) *Anti-Classical Political Economy*, in two volumes, Tokyo: Chuo Koron Sha (in Japanese).

Vogel, Ezra F. (1991) *The Four Little Dragons: The Spread of Industrialization in East Asia*, Cambridge, MA: Harvard University Press.

Part IV

POLICY ADVICE AND COUNTRY STUDIES

12

KYRGYZSTAN'S ROAD TO ECONOMIC RECOVERY: AN EFFORT IN INTELLECTUAL ASSISTANCE[1]

Tatsuo Kaneda

I The role of the state in the economy

International financial institutions such as the IMF and the World Bank are skeptical about state intervention in the economy. Although price liberalization in January [1992, implemented simultaneously in Russia and Kyrgyzstan] resulted in inflation and contraction of productive activity, the IMF continues to insist that remaining restrictions (such as control on oil prices) be removed as soon as possible. The IMF is convinced that the less the state intervenes in the economy, the more rationally resources are allocated and the more efficiently goods are produced.

IMF and World Bank skepticism over the state's role in the economy is based on lessons learned through many years of advising and working with developing countries. Moreover, it is an instinctive reaction against socialist economic management, which has destroyed an economy by placing all economic activities under state control and subordinating the logic of economics to political demands. Undoubtedly, there is a need to free economies from state control to normalize economic interaction in the post-socialist era.

However, the Kyrgyz economy is in the process of transition to a market economic system. Private economic actors are virtually absent at present; therefore, it is indispensable for the state to play an active role in developing private enterprises and promoting industry, as well as establishing new economic mechanisms. Once the market economic system has been established and private enterprises have developed as principal economic units, there will be ample scope for the country to choose the state–industry relationship best suited to its circumstances; for example, the U.S. model where the state and industry act quite independently, or the Japanese model where the two maintain a close relationship. But, under current reality in Kyrgyzstan, it is inconceivable that a market economic system would flourish automatically, without the guidance and policy support of a wise state.

No actor other than the state can build institutions in support of a market system and implement policies in areas as broad as money, finance, stocks, collateral, companies, commerce, trade, exchange rates, land ownership, public finance, and taxation. The state must also manage the privatization of state-owned enterprises and such problems as social security, labor–management relations, and external economic relationships – both during the transition period and under the market economic system.

There is no major disagreement that the state should play a primary role in macroeconomic management through monetary and fiscal policies. Opinions vary, however, on microeconomic issues, namely, the relationship between the state and individual industries.

The experiences of Japan and Asia suggest that an active state is indispensable for latecomers to develop modern industries (for instance, manufacturing, telecommunication and transport) and modernize traditional sectors (for instance, agriculture and fisheries). At the same time, there are quite a few examples to show that excessive state intervention, inappropriate policies, incompetent and corrupt bureaucracy all do harm to an economy. What determines the success or failure of economic development in each country is *not* whether the state guided the economy or not, *but* what the nature of the government is and what kinds of policies it adopts in specific sectors.

Regarding the nature of the government, the ideals, passions, and knowledge of top policy makers matter, as do their strategic thinking and leadership capabilities. Equally important is the capability of bureaucrats responsible for policy execution at various levels of government. For the government to play a catalytic role in economic development, at minimum the following conditions must be put in place:

1   The public administration apparatus charged with economic management is properly organized and managed with efficiency and agility.
2   Key posts in public institutions are filled with competent professional officials who have received training and accumulated experience in their specialized areas.
3   Impartial institutions are in place to supervise and monitor the activity of public institutions, as is a system of checks and balances to prevent collusion, abuse of public authority, corruption, and the emergence of vested interest groups.
4   Government institutions that have direct contact with firms and the local population are properly organized and managed at the local level as well as in the center.

The greatest challenge facing Kyrgyzstan is to find government officials who satisfy the second qualification above. Although it may be possible to identify a small number of professionals who occupy key central government posts, it is impossible to train tens of thousands of officials working in central and local governments, overnight. Competent and honest technocrats are needed more than ever; however, there is no shortcut to developing such human resources. Therefore, we recommend the following second-best measures:

1　Train a large number of candidates for government office at public institutions in Western advanced countries.
2　Invite a large number of Western and Japanese experts in public administration to provide Kyrgyz officials with on-the-job training and serve as advisers. (Japan's Meiji government employed more than 4,000 foreign experts in the 1870s.)
3　Establish a local training facility for active government officials and re-train senior officials responsible for policy formulation and implementation. It should be relatively easy to secure support from international financial institutions and G7 countries for such a program. In the long run, there is a need to reform the educational system, particularly universities.

Second, regarding the role of the government in specific sectors, we recommend that priority be placed on the following areas in the immediate future:

1　Controlling money supply through fiscal and financial policies. This will help achieve price stability and restore predictability to the economy. (Even if prices continue to rise, people can at least predict costs and balance business and family budgets if inflation is held within a single-digit range.)
2　Establishing stable rules governing external economic relations.
3　Protecting vulnerable groups in the society.
4　Stopping further decline in output.

In parallel, the government must prepare conditions for restoring output levels and getting the economy back on a growth path. On this point, Russian industrial groups claim that first priority should be placed on adopting expansionary fiscal and monetary policies to resolve financial distress in firms. We consider such a choice politically difficult; it is also contrary to IMF policy. Certainly, in Japan, at the time of deep economic recession, the government rescued the hardest hit industries through emergency loans. However, under the existing Kyrgyz situation where all industries face difficulties, it is quite doubtful whether expansionary monetary policy would work without causing a resurgence in inflationary pressure.

It is more appropriate that the government adopt an activist industrial policy and guide output recovery through targeted investments in priority industries, which will also stimulate other industries through input–output linkage, while being mindful of controlling inflation. This is consistent with our views on the economic role of the state over the medium- and long-run:

1   to promote industries selectively;
2   to accumulate savings for industrial promotion and invest in priority sectors;
3   to develop the foundations for industry by, for example, building infrastructure, improving education, and establishing sound labor–management
relations.

More details of industrial promotion and capital accumulation are described in
sections III and IV [Section IV is not included in this volume].

II Efforts toward forming national consensus

The main feature of the economies of Japan and other Asian countries, which
transformed themselves into modern industrial states in a relatively short period,
was the dedication of the population to economic development and industrial
promotion. It was the implicit agreement between the government and people in
Japan that the country should develop its economy to catch up with Western
advanced countries, and in other Asian countries, that they should catch up with
Japan.

Big gaps with the West in military and economic power generated a sense of
national crisis in Japan and united the public and private sectors in pursuit of the
shared goal of "industrial promotion." Asian economies staked their future on
economic growth, motivated by a desire to escape deep poverty on the one hand
and by attraction to advanced-country lifestyles on the other hand. While the
background varies from country to country, each government and population
shared strong aspirations for the future, which drove people to work hard, save
in spite of low income, and embrace advanced technology.

At present, the Kyrgyz economy is in crisis. The majority of the population
suffers from poverty that did not exist even under the repressive Stalin administration. It is not surprising that people complain that their expectations of the
market economy system have been completely deceived. Growing popular
discontent could lead to political instability, which in turn would slow down
economic recovery and discourage external support. Once such a vicious cycle
gets started, any drive to "work hard, save, and learn" would be lost.

Nevertheless, there is no magic potion to turn around the economy quickly. It
is doubtful that the January price liberalization will bring about positive effects
in Russia in a short period, as President Yeltsin pledged.

After World War II, it took Japan and Germany four to five years to restore
production to prewar levels. Similarly, it took a long time before the Asian
Newly Industrializing Economies (NIEs) rose to economic prosperity; it was not
until the latter half of the 1960s that they came to be known as "little dragons."
Another ten years was necessary before the ASEAN countries, including
Thailand and Indonesia, started to experience high-speed growth. The economy
of Poland, which embarked on marketization two years earlier than the Common-
wealth of Independent States (CIS), has not yet shown signs of recovery. Even

Hungary, which began reforming its economic system earlier than its neighbors and was considered to be fairly close to a market economy, faces difficulty in privatization and its GNP continues to decline.

It is said that "nature does not jump." Nor does an economy. Leaders should be aware that it will take a long time before the population enjoys the fruits of marketization. Although campaign promises such as "consumers will experience improvement beginning next year" may serve as a temporary painkiller, they are a double-edged sword that risk further disappointing the population.

However, it is impossible to force people to be patient indefinitely. Without brighter prospects, they lose the incentive to work and save for the future. Moreover, opposition forces may take advantage of public discontent with the government. It is desirable to construct a future vision of the Kyrgyz economy – in parallel with emergency measures aimed at minimizing difficulty during the transition period – and persuade the people that the present sacrifice will be rewarded in the long run.

Regarding the emergency measures, first of all, the government must supply foodstuffs to the population to ease concern about food shortages (see Section VI).

Second, the government must explain to the people in plain words (for example, using TV, newspapers, pamphlets and other means) why the country faces economic difficulty and how the problems can be overcome, what kinds of measures the government is taking, and then ask for their understanding and cooperation. Japan started such an effort in 1947 in the form of the "White Paper on the Japanese Economy."

Some may object that drawing a future vision is simply a reprint of Khrushchev's "The Construction of Communism in the USSR" or Brezhnev's "Food Program"[2] and question why it is necessary to restore directive planning. However, the visions that we discuss here are very different from plans in the command economy. Visions lay out a picture of:

1 how the economy is expected to change after five to ten years;
2 how and to what extent the living conditions of the population are expected to improve;
3 what kinds of policy measures the government should adopt to achieve these objectives;
4 what kinds of actions will be expected from the population, firms, and other organizations.

The purpose of visions is to outline the future orientation of the country for the government itself, Parliament, and the population. In other words, it is a document that gives the Kyrgyz people a perspective on their economy and society five to ten years from now.

The content of the vision document for Kyrgyzstan can be simpler than indicative plans that are produced in Japan, France and other countries, although the purpose should be similar. In Japan, economic planning covers comprehensive topics such as the upgrading of industrial structure, productivity improvement, changes in external economic relations, progress in science and technology, infrastructure development, growth rates of the economy, consumer price indices, trade balance, and unemployment rates in an effort to quantify the overall picture of the Japanese economy at a particular point in time.

In the case of Kyrgyzstan where the economy has de-linked from its past and everything is in flux, it is neither possible nor necessary to predict the future based on past trends. It is sufficient to describe clearly how the country can develop its economy after the transition period, how living standards can be improved, and how the future will be brighter if everyone gives his/her best efforts and the government takes appropriate policy measures.

III Independence and cooperation

Kyrgyzstan is a newly independent state. Like it or not, the country inherited an industrial structure and set of economic linkages built under the Soviet regime. Therefore, in the immediate future, it must build its economic system, organizations and management based on the assumption that diverse economic linkages with the former USSR, particularly Russia, will continue.

Kyrgyzstan cannot afford to put national pride ahead of economic calculations, as Ukraine did by issuing its own currency upon independence. Kyrgyzstan should establish dependable diplomatic relations with all countries (not limited to the CIS) and actively pursue economic relations with them – as long as they contribute to its economic reconstruction and development. In this sense, its current approach of strengthening the CIS and deepening ties with advanced economies, Middle Eastern countries, China, and India, is quite appropriate.

The Kyrgyz government's decision not to possess independent military forces should be highly praised internationally. If the country can maintain "no military" as a national slogan, the absence of a non-productive military burden will generate cumulative economic benefits.

There is a related issue on external trade liberalization. Not only the international financial institutions but also many experts recommend rapid economic liberalization to expose firms to international competition. Kyrgyzstan, which lost international competitiveness through *de facto* isolation in the old Soviet economy, does not need foreign advice to realize the weakness of a closed economy.

There is no doubt that the ultimate goal should be to achieve free mobility of goods, services, capital, and labor. However, it is necessary to consider the process and sequencing of reforms carefully. Outright liberalization runs the risks of destroying industries with growth potential and promoting capital flight. On the other hand, slow liberalization may erode competitiveness and discourage the inflow of foreign investment. The future edge of the Kyrgyz economy critically depends on the optimum mix of openness and protection and the timing of liberalization by product and industry.

Japan became an Article VIII country of the IMF in 1964 by eliminating trade restrictions, and it liberalized its capital accounts in 1967. The Asian NIEs initially developed minimum necessary import-substitution industries and then allocated domestic resources to export-oriented industries, taking into account prevailing international market conditions. In doing so, they opened economic regimes as much as possible and promoted foreign investment and technology transfer.

Japan protected infant industries by banning or restricting imports and allocating foreign exchange. However, after it made commitments to the Bretton Woods system (Japan became a member of the IMF in 1952 and the GATT in 1955), government authorities and private businesses became keenly aware that domestic markets would be entirely liberalized in the near future, and they made strenuous efforts to strengthen international competitiveness during the remaining period of protection.

Product by product, Japanese businessmen understood clearly the relative competitiveness of their manufactured products in the world markets. Because the exchange rate was then fixed at 360 yen to the dollar from 1949, it was easy to make cost comparison between domestic and foreign products and analyze the degree of cost reduction required to ensure survival after liberalization. Businessmen knew very well that protection from foreign competition was temporary and that the only way to survive in highly competitive international markets was to strengthen the attractiveness of their products. By contrast, in the former USSR, all imports were under state control, and nobody ever thought of foreign competition. Moreover, because exchange rates were determined administratively and different rates were applied to different products and trade partners, it was impossible to calculate the competitiveness of domestic products in international markets.

Even if the government wishes to promote infant industries, we do not recommend isolating firms from international markets. It is much better to recognize the existence of rivals and prepare firms for future competition, as was done in Japan.

It is reported that the ruble–dollar exchange rate is to be fixed from July 1992. If Kyrgyzstan follows this route, it will be possible to measure the competitiveness of domestic firms and get objective indicators for identifying products, firms, and industries that have the potential to survive and those that do not. This will also help the government design long-term industrial and trade structures and formulate development policies.

Under such circumstance, Russia will be Kyrgyzstan's most important economic partner and the relationship with Russia should be given first priority. While trade and economic relations with other foreign countries, including the West, are expected to expand gradually, they are unlikely to equal Russia in trade share until the twenty-first century. Kyrgyzstan must depend on Russia for a long period as the leading source of energy, minerals and other major commodities and as the largest market for food and light manufactured exports. For the time being, other CIS republics will be Kyrgyzstan's main rivals for Russian markets. If Kyrgyz firms are exposed to competition in the more liberalized Russian markets, their competitiveness can be strengthened to a level sufficient to survive in international markets.

After Russia, important partners include other CIS republics, Middle Eastern countries, and neighboring Asian countries. While industrial countries in the West are important suppliers of capital, technology, and management skills, they are unlikely to be direct markets in the immediate future.

IV Creation and functions of financial systems [omitted]

V Establishment of fiscal and tax systems [omitted]

VI The direction of industrial policy

1 Identification of key strategic industries

The present Kyrgyz economy cannot afford to invest in all industries simultaneously. The government should identify a limited number of priority industries and concentrate all available financial and physical resources in these areas to restore and increase production as quickly as possible. Once the priority industries have started generating surplus, the government should attempt to gradually strengthen other strategic industries by investing the surplus in them. A good example of this approach is the "priority production system"[3] adopted in postwar Japan.

It is conceivable that the Kyrgyz leaders and population might reject such a system because it reminds them of the Soviet Union's first Five-Year Plan. The early 1930s industrialization imposed unbearable costs on the people. It also created the political and economic regime responsible for the subsequent sixty years of hardships. However, the priority production system can be introduced without the harm done under the Stalinist administration.

Kyrgyzstan must somehow find means to stop further decline in production and turn the economy onto a sustainable growth path. This could be achieved through, for example, immediate reestablishment of economic relations among the CIS, generous Russian financial support, massive aid from the West and Japan, and/or drastic improvements in the external environment. While Kyrgyzstan naturally may wish to normalize economic relations within the CIS, given present circumstances the country should concentrate for the time being on adopting measures implementable within the country. Improving external conditions is important but will be more effective if up-front efforts are made to better domestic economic conditions. Generally, the more progress is made in economic recovery and development through domestic efforts, the greater prospects the country has for international cooperation. Once signs of economic recovery begin to appear, external agents will react quickly and foreign aid donors and private investors will show more interest.

In our view, priority should be placed on agricultural production and the agro-processing industry because:

1   these are the largest industries in Kyrgyzstan both in terms of employment and production shares;
2   foodstuffs and agro-processed products are the goods experiencing the greatest scarcity in Kyrgyzstan and neighboring regions;
3   their industrial potential can be quickly enhanced by introducing household agriculture and reforming traditional state and collective farms;
4   their productivity can be increased at low cost in a short period by improving production technology and equipment;
5   modernization can improve efficiency in agro-processing by cutting losses and increasing value-added;
6   these sectors can build capacity for future manufacturing export industries, such as high-quality textiles and leather products.

As the Japanese and East Asian experiences suggest, it is effective to develop industries that make extensive use of the most abundant factor of production in a country (i.e., industries with comparative advantage) first and then gradually build the capacity to produce other products of higher value-added.

In postwar Japan, the government selected the coal and steel industries for priority production. This is partly because there existed physical capacity in these sectors to boost output in a short period, if financial and material resources were poured into them. It is relatively easy to reconstruct production facilities that were destroyed during wars. If sufficient inputs and raw materials are available, it is not difficult to increase facility utilization rates. Financial incentives for workers are also affordable if only a few industries are targeted.

In the early 1930s, the USSR adopted a development strategy to favor heavy industries such as electricity, steel, and coal. While partly stemming from an obsession with the ideological primacy of large-scale heavy industry, the decision largely results from a belief that heavy industry forms the basis for expanding production in all industries and making the most efficient use of scarce capital.

Compared to the coal, steel, and electricity industries, agriculture is far more labor-intensive, and its production bases are dispersed nationwide; furthermore, its spill-over effects on the entire economy are limited. For these reasons, one might argue that agriculture should not be selected for priority production. I am not thoroughly familiar with the potential of the Kyrgyz economy, so I do not rule out the possibility that industries or products other than agriculture might be more suitable for priority production. Even if this is the case, however, I believe that agriculture should remain a priority sector at the initial stage of development.

2 Measures to promote agriculture

A Goals

Stage I

1   Increase production to the maximum levels achieved in the pre-1991 period.
2   In parallel, make efforts to raise the effective utilization rate of farm products.
3   Through (1) and (2), increase food supply to meet domestic demand, achieving price stability.
4   Bring the real income of farmers into balance with that of urban workers.

Stage II

1   Increase yield per hectare and output per head of livestock to the maximum levels of countries endowed with similar natural conditions.
2   Improve the quality of commercial crops so that they can be used as inputs for high quality, high value-added export-oriented light manufactured goods.
3   Modernize food and foodstuffs production, storage, and transportation facilities to minimize efficiency losses, improve product variety, taste, shape and appearance, and packaging.
4   Expand the export capacity for agro-processing products and foodstuff and become self-sufficient in grains.
5   Maintain the income parity between rural and urban workers and improve the living conditions.

B Producers – who will become the driving force of agriculture production?

From a management system perspective, individual and household agriculture is most suitable to a market economy. Since farmers own their land and production means and operate at their own risk, they can adapt quickly to changes in the production and market environments. Because revenue depends on what they produce and they incur losses if costs are excessive, there is no need to supervise them or urge cost reduction. Incentives for technology upgrading and business rationalization are built into this management system.

In general, the size of individual and household agriculture (i.e., farmland, employees, capital) as well as products, technology, shipping distance, the existence of side business, etc. vary significantly, depending on location and resource endowment. Under Marxism, household agriculture is dogmatically equated with small size. However, as the examples of North American and Australian agriculture show, some household farmers produce 1,000 hectares of grain and breed 1,000 cattle. By contrast, in Japan, vegetable and fruit growers and livestock farmers make full use of labor-intensive production methods and technology and sometimes earn much higher incomes than urban households, despite the fact that the average farm is less than 1 hectare. Similarly, in Kyrgyzstan, individual and household agriculture may develop into a variety of forms, taking advantage of unique endowments of respective regions.

Important questions here are how to develop household agriculture and who should shoulder the burden of production before household farms grow into a leading sector. Another related question is what to do with state and collective farms in the future.

The first alternative is to conclude that household agriculture is the only promising management system in the sector, announce the termination of state and collective farms, end all privileges and protection granted by the state, and give workers a choice of either abandoning farming or moving to family-based farms. In this case, family-based farming is likely to increase because workers have no other options as long as they wish to make a living in agriculture. The second alternative is to regard household agriculture as the principal farming system of the future but avoid the immediate termination of state and collective farms (except for those suffering from chronic deficits) and let the market determine appropriate management systems. There is no need to eliminate state and collective farms if they demonstrate that their productivity is as high as that of household farms. At present, the government appears to be promoting the second option.

While supporting the second alternative as the basic direction to pursue, we propose the following measures to mitigate social tensions that may arise from the lack of future prospects for state and collective farms and their eventual bankruptcy, make full use of all the production forces during the transition period, and facilitate the smooth transition from a large-scale, state-run or collective farming system to a family-based farming system.

1   Divide the state and collective farming system into *de facto* individual and family-based farming and cooperative farming. Cooperative farming envisioned here should be an ideal form of linkage systems known as *zveno* in the Khrushchev era[4] and the collective responsibility system under Gorbachev. It involves organizations (both existing and new) designed to manage activities that, for technical reasons, require collective efforts such as stock raising by using large-scale cattle sheds and farm cultivation by using large tractors. These units may be organized by communal societies comprising of kin and neighborhood group (*Gemeinschaft*).

2   Through the administrative arm of the state and collective farming system, provide common services to each management unit within an organization, particularly in the areas of distribution (to overcome disadvantages faced by small farms in market transaction and offer the benefits of scale economies), product sales and input purchase, collection and dissemination of market and technology information, and fund mobilization. It should also undertake

extension and advisory services on agricultural technology and information until the government establishes a new agency responsible for these tasks. This is an attempt to organize what Mikhail Gorbachev called "cooperatives of cooperatives." Experience from around the world suggests that the most natural and efficient farming systems use a mix of individual and household agriculture (responsible for production) and cooperatives (responsible for distribution). Although it is necessary to recognize that Kyrgyz agriculture has a unique history and traditions that distinguish it from agriculture in developed market economies, we recommend that the country follow world practice, making adjustments to meet its specific situations.

3   Complete the transformation of the state and collective farming system into a cooperative farming system before planting starts next year.

4   Household agriculture is inseparable from private land ownership. However, in Kyrgyzstan, the forms of land ownership are closely related to the life-styles of various racial and ethnic groups. Thus a decision on establishing private land ownership (i.e., completely legalizing land title) should be made not only from an economic efficiency viewpoint but also from non-economic considerations, including popular sentiment. For this reason, we recognize that land title legislation tends to be delayed. Nonetheless, in order to develop household agriculture, it is indispensable for families to secure land and farming rights. Even if public opinion has not matured sufficiently to endorse perfect private property rights, it is necessary to enact laws to define the scope of current land use rights and protect these rights. The establishment of property rights beyond land use (including retaining capital gains from land sale) should be left to future consideration.

C Measures to expand production

Kyrgyzstan has high agriculture productivity compared to neighboring republics. This implies that the gap with more advanced countries is narrow and that the scope for easily expanding production is limited. However, this also means that the natural and human conditions for agriculture production in Kyrgyzstan are more favorable than those of other republics. Freeing farmers from a command system alone may help develop their capability and raise productivity. Any increase in yields this year must come from the positive effects of such spiritual elevation; but this alone is not enough to accomplish the goals. A genuine effort to increase production is needed. We propose the following measures:

1   Carry out technical and managerial diagnostic studies on yield and livestock productivity and prepare recommendations for improvement. This task should be completed within a year with the participation of national and international experts.

2   Train small private farmers and individual producers to improve their technology. Technical experts in reorganized state and collective farming

organizations and/or a new national extension agency should offer extensive guidance in a short period through lectures, visits and other methods. When the introduction of new technology requires increased inputs and materials, preferential measures should be taken to secure their supply. Here, problems emerge regarding how to mobilize financial resources and avoid harmful effects of rationing inputs. One option is to seek international cooperation if domestic resources are severely constrained. It is relatively easy to secure donor support for materials for a temporary period. The harmful effects of rationing should be viewed as a transitory cost of technology improvement.

3   In the longer run, it is necessary to sustain output expansion and establish product composition and production methods. This should be done in line with domestic and export demand, while giving due consideration to climate, soil, topographical conditions, landscape, proximity to markets, technology and management, productivity, and international competitiveness by agricultural region (i.e., Chu Valley, Issyk-Kul Valley, Tian Shan Valley and Fergana Valley). Again, technical and financial support from donors can be sought on this point.

4   In addition to securing steady supply of inputs, it is equally necessary to develop productive and social infrastructure, including farmland improvement, rehabilitation and expansion of irrigation facilities, protection from soil erosion, rehabilitation and construction of rural roads, establishment of agricultural extension centers, and expansion of input production facilities in order to develop agriculture tailored to the particular conditions of each region. Moreover, it is important to recognize that young people may be unwilling to stay in rural areas in the future if attractive living conditions do not exist. Infrastructure development requires enormous financial resources and sophisticated construction technology, which cannot be provided by Kyrgyzstan alone over the short term. This is the area where donor support should be actively sought. To this end, however, it is important to implement measures (1) and (2) first to demonstrate institutional capacity.

5   Improving the use of agricultural inputs yields the most immediate returns. For example, while Kyrgyzstan produces about 1.5 million tons of grain (more than 300 kg per capita), it relies on a significant volume of grain imports every year. This is partly because the feed efficiency for livestock production is extremely low. We do not have data on the feed efficiency of each livestock product. If we assume that it is at the same level as the Soviet average, the efficiency can be improved at maximum by 50 percent by improving compound feed varieties and livestock breeding technology and shifting from extensive to intensive production methods. This would make it possible to cut feed consumption while increasing livestock production. However, despite continuous government efforts, feed efficiency (compared to the European and American standards) did not improve at all during the last twenty years. This indicates that inefficiency is more closely associated with problems in the management system than with inputs and materials.

Now that systemic problems are being addressed, technology improvements should bring remarkable results. The same can be said for the use of chemical fertilizer and the development of various production infrastructure.

6   It is equally important to improve the use of outputs in parallel to increasing production efficiency. The President stated that 60 percent of outputs are wasted. The truth is that even the ministries concerned do not have accurate data on loss, but it is certainly beyond the normally acceptable level. There is no doubt that reducing loss and increasing product use will benefit both producers and consumers. The loss of agricultural products results from multiple factors, such as obsolete facilities for processing, distribution, and storage, the low level of technology, producers accustomed to waste at each stage of production, and government pricing and enterprise policies that encourage inefficient production. The situation is similar to feed consumption; therefore, it is important to take comprehensive measures to improve the rate of product utilization. Above all, priority should be placed on the modernization of production facilities and the improvement of farm employee skills. It is relatively easy to obtain "intellectual support" for the measures recommended in (5) and (6) by inviting foreign experts, training researchers and practitioners at overseas institutions, and providing farmers with knowledge of new facilities and distribution systems. But securing a sizable amount of donor funds to modernize social and production infrastructure is another issue. Therefore, it is advisable to take action in two phases: first to demonstrate the results of self-efforts, even if they are of limited scope, and then to request external resources for further expansion building on the achievements.

7   To expand production and steadily increase labor and capital productivity in the long run, it is necessary to introduce the latest technology and adapt it to the realities of respective regions. It is also necessary to encourage independent technology development. There is a need to absorb and make use of the latest research results, particularly in the area of improving crop and livestock varieties; methods of crop production and livestock breeding; resource-efficient technology for infrastructure development; efficient technology for food processing and distribution networks; and establishing regional agricultural systems. To this end, the government should encourage exchanges between Kyrgyz and foreign researchers, initially by dispatching Kyrgyz researchers to advanced countries and inviting foreign experts to Kyrgyzstan; acquisition of the latest research methods; exchanges of academic information; and improvement of research equipment and facilities. Such programs will help Kyrgyz agriculture specialists catch up with new information and technology and prepare the country for the next stage of development.

8   During the transition period when the market economy is not yet fully developed and new management systems face adverse conditions, it is

inconceivable that individual and household agriculture will develop successfully without government support. The government should support farmers through preferential measures, such as the provision of long-term financing at low or zero-interest rates to encourage the creation of new activities (normally only land can be used as collateral), priority allocation of machinery and materials, reduction and/or exemption from tax obligations, and provision of intensive technical training and advisory services.

3 Other priority industries

We propose selecting light manufacturing as the number two industry for Kyrgyzstan, following agriculture.

Based on the lessons from mistakes made by East European countries, Kyrgyzstan should not aim to manufacture all products domestically. Mass production industries that heavily rely on scale merit, namely heavy industries (e.g., chemicals, cement) and related machinery production are unlikely to be promising in Kyrgyzstan. The domestic market for these industries is small, and the country has no comparative advantage in them over its neighbors. Moreover, it is premature to aim at manufacturing high-technology products and consumer goods.

Certainly, upgrading mineral resource processing from refined and semi-processed goods to final consumer and investment goods is an attractive option for increasing value-added and creating employment opportunities. But we cannot make a judgment on the feasibility of this option due to lack of complete and verifiable data.

The desirability of promoting energy production depends on the government's future energy policy. For example, to what extent can domestic demand be satisfied with electricity generation through coal and hydroelectric power? How should the country cope with a potential energy shortage? Which is more economical to continue imports or increase domestic electricity generation through expansion and new construction of hydroelectric power plants? If the government wishes to aim at increasing domestic electricity generation, the industry must also be added to the list of targeted industries. However, since the development of an energy industry requires a huge initial investment and a long gestation period, it is unlikely to become a candidate for "priority production." Thus, it is impossible to increase domestic energy supply without large-scale aid from international organizations.

Tourism is the quickest way to earn foreign exchange, but it will not become profitable unless a critical mass of tourists visit the country. Besides, it is not really an economical investment. It is first necessary to develop tourist facilities as well as infrastructure to transport massive numbers of tourists, provide accommodation and meals, and arrange sightseeing and shopping.

Compared to the above options, light manufacturing has the following advantages:

1   Kyrgyzstan produces raw materials (e.g., cotton, silk cocoons, raw silk, and leather) and has surplus capacity for increased production;
2   there are big consumer markets in its neighborhood, including Russia. The existing technology level is as high as in other republics;
3   there is an abundant supply of low-cost labor domestically, which favors development of labor-intensive industry;
4   it is possible to spread its brands and acquire market share if Kyrgyzstan initiates production and export of high-quality light manufacturing products ahead of other republics;
5   the investments required to modernize and renovate production facilities are not as costly as those for heavy industry.

4 Conditions for developing manufacturing industry in general

The promotion of agriculture alone is not enough to provide jobs for an expanding workforce and improve income levels on a sustainable basis. There is an obvious need to develop industries – particularly processing and manufacturing industries – that have the capacity to expand output vigorously and increase employment opportunities. A difficult question is how to identify promising products and specific areas of production.

Like other republics under the Soviet system, Kyrgyzstan was not allowed to identify its true comparative advantage based on free competition and to develop internationally competitive industries. Although it produced raw materials for light industries, opportunities to manufacture final consumer goods were limited. Even if final goods were produced, efforts always concentrated on increasing production quantity. There were almost no incentives to improve the quality and design of products because sellers dominated the consumer market in the USSR.

Therefore, there is no reliable information to assess Kyrgyzstan's potential in manufacturing industries. It is always easier to point out constraints than favorable conditions. The main constraints are:

1   The small size of the domestic market in terms of population and purchasing power;
2   the closed nature of the domestic market, which could in turn exclude Kyrgyzstan from potential export markets;
3   lack of well-known brand products – one internationally famed brand will help sales of other products;
4   long distance and difficult access to and from other advanced countries, handicaps aggravated by insufficient transportation and telecommunication networks;
5   lack of investment resources and domestic savings.

By contrast, the favorable conditions include:

1   a highly educated but low-wage work force.
2   access to large consumer markets in the CIS republics, which have roughly
     the same level of technology as Kyrgyzstan;
3   a technology gap with the advanced countries, which provides an opportu-
     nity for catch-up;
4   the availability of local farm products and minerals that can be used as inputs
     for processing industries.

These advantages are not peculiar to Kyrgyzstan; rather they are held commonly by the other states of Central Asia, or more broadly, by many developing countries.

Then, what kinds of products and manufacturing sectors should Kyrgyzstan develop to take advantage of these favorable conditions? And how should it overcome various constraints? Natural conditions do not affect the location of manufacturing industries as critically as agriculture or mining. Land necessary for a factory site can be smaller than that for crop production. Capital and labor needed for manufacturing can move freely across geographical boundaries.

Of course, for some products location does matter. It is more advantageous to establish steel, oil refining and chemical industries (that use heavy materials) close to the areas where inputs are produced. Similarly, it is convenient in terms of production and sales costs to locate food and food processing industries (that manufacture bulky products or products that spoil easily) close to consumption markets. In this sense, Kyrgyzstan is not favorably located for traditional heavy and chemical industries. Even in the case of light manufacturing, it has no comparative advantage in furniture and wood processing industries over other countries producing timber.

However, there is no reason to believe that it has disadvantages compared to other CIS republics in precision machinery, electrical machinery, electronics, or downstream chemical industries. In the late 1970s, a significant number of semiconductor factories were suddenly established in rural areas of Kyushu, Japan, which had no previous exposure to modern industry. The factory location decision was made for the simple reason that the factories could employ local young workers.

Despite its small domestic markets, there is reason to believe that Kyrgyzstan can establish manufacturing plants with the scale to compete internationally – provided that the CIS republics and Middle Eastern countries are considered potential export markets. Japan first established production facilities for domestic markets, and then expanded them for overseas markets. However, now that other CIS republics plan to develop export-oriented industries, there is no time for Kyrgyzstan to repeat the Japanese path. The only feasible way to develop export-oriented industries is to establish factories large enough to export to overseas markets, despite the risks.

At this moment, we do not have enough information to define which manufactured products should be selected as priority industries.

The President stated his intention to begin the manufacturing of semiconductors, building on existing technology to process silicon into semiconductor wafers. It is an attractive idea. But even East Germany which had one of the most advanced technology levels in the former Soviet bloc failed in its effort at mass production of 1 megabyte semiconductors. The technology of semiconductor production is now advanced to 4 megabytes. The only way for Kyrgyzstan to penetrate this market is to introduce technology from Japan or the U.S. and start production at local affiliates of foreign firms. As the example of South Korea shows, it is possible even for latecomers to develop to a level that threatens the advanced country firms in the semiconductor industry.

The problem is how to secure advanced country cooperation to introduce technology and establish facilities. Political and economic stability is absolutely a precondition, but it is not a sufficient condition. The government has to take the initiative to create and present an attractive environment so that firms from other countries are motivated to choose Kyrgyzstan as a partner.

What other manufactured industries are as promising as semiconductors? What incentives can Kyrgyzstan offer to foreign firms? How can it enhance these incentives? We are prepared to think and work together with Kyrgyz authorities on these issues.

Notes

1 This chapter contains excerpts from section III (Some Proposals on Economic Development Strategy of Kyrgyzstan) of Professor Kaneda's paper, "*Kyrgyzstan Keizai Saisei no Michi: Chiteki Shien no Kokoromi*" [Kyrgyzstan's Road to Economic Recovery: An Effort in Intellectual Assistance], Japan Institute of International Affairs (JIIA) paper, Tokyo, 1992, no. 1 [Editors].

2 Brezhnev's "Food Program" (1980) articulated production and other goals through the end of the decade, as well as reforms designed to achieve these goals [Editors].

3 By the end of World War II, Japanese industrial production had collapsed to 30 percent of the prewar (1936) level due to supply shortage and aerial bombing. Under occupation by the Allied forces, the Japanese government planned to resuscitate industrial activity by increasing coal output, the only domestically available energy supply. Available resources were first poured into the steel industry which supplied coal mining equipment, and increased coal output was in turn used to produce more steel. Through this virtuous circle, surplus coal was provided to other industries. This plan, called the "priority production system," was an emergency measure based on the state's directive plan. It was executed successfully in 1947, and industrial production began to recover that year [Editors].

4 Under *zveno*, or the link system, small groups were allowed to organize and were paid by results at the end of the harvest. In other words, the rewards were based on production. This system was quite different from the then prevailing "brigade system" based on much larger units, where the rewards were based on the number of labor days worked [Editors].

13

RUSSIAN PRIVATIZATION: PROGRESS REPORT NO. 1[1]

Yoshiaki Nishimura

Introduction

This paper continues the discussion of my previous paper, "Russian Privatization Policy," (published in *Keizai Kenkyu*, vol. 44, no. 2) where the institutional and policy frameworks of Russian privatization were analyzed. While the previous work mainly covered the period of 1991–92, this one examines the actual implementation of privatization up to 1993. Some minor changes in the institutional and policy frameworks were made in 1993, but they are outside the purview of the present paper. Instead, the purpose here is to evaluate overall achievements and remaining issues, particularly the results of voucher privatization and the small-scale privatization scheme. Privatization of agriculture and residential units will be examined on another occasion.

Events unfold rapidly in Russia but accurate and comprehensive data are difficult to come by in a timely manner. Overall assessment of the current situation is based on available fragmentary information. This paper therefore remains a rough sketch of Russian privatization viewed from afar, which needs updating as more studies are conducted and new information arrives.

I Results of privatization

Two years have passed since the privatization program was launched at the beginning of 1992. Despite a large number of actual and potential problems, progress has been made. Our first task is to ascertain the results of privatization so far.

From January to November 1993, 39,000 enterprises were privatized, bringing the total number of privatized enterprises to 86,000 since the program was initiated (see also Table 13.1). Currently, roughly half of Russian enterprises are in private hands. Of the 39,000 enterprises privatized during 1993, 31 percent were privatized, in whole or part, through corporatization (joint-stock companies) with the remaining 69 percent through direct sales. The sectoral composition of privatized enterprises was as follows: retail and wholesale trade (35 percent),

Table 13.1   Basic statistics on Russian privatization

	1992 Apr 1	1992 Aug 1	1993 Jan 1	1993 Apr 1	1994 Jan 1	
(1) Number of autonomous-balance state enterprises	139,904	221,189	204,998	194,190	180,837	156,635
(2) Number of applications received for privatization	18,366	56,167	102,330	114,725	120,991	125,492
(3) Number of rejected applications	656	2,982	5,390	6,879	9,011	9,985
(4) Number of accepted applications currently being privatized	12,677	31,851	46,628	42,788	35,234	24,992
(5) Number of accepted applications with privatization completed	5,023	12,015	46,815	61,810	77,810	88,577
(6) Privatization receipts transferred to various levels of government, in million rubles	1,893	10,295	157,152	297,230	542,763	n.a.
(7) Asset value of enterprises with completed privatization, in million rubles	1,171	19,208	193,189	405,177	531,219	648,000
(8) a. Number of leasing enterprises	9,451	17,924	22,216	19,435	17,735	20,886
b. Of which: buyout completed	7,581	10,464	13,868	10,850	14,504	14,978

Source: *The Russian Economic Barometer*, 1993, No. 2, p. 42 and No. 4, p. 35, and 1994, No. 4, p. 62.

Notes:

1 Rejected applications (3) include those with incomplete forms and those which were designed not to be privatized by the 1992 Privatization Program.

2 The difference between (2) and (3)+(4)+(5) corresponds to applications currently under consideration.

3 (6) includes received revenues plus receivables in installments.

4 (8a) includes leasing enterprises which are not subject to buyouts.

5 Applications for privatization rose rapidly in 1992 but slowed in 1993. By autumn 1993, most voluntary applications had been processed, and the remaining enterprises are said to be reluctant to be privatized. The number of state enterprises increases with the splitting of existing enterprises and decreases with privatization. While the overall number of state enterprises fell in 1993, the rising trend of (1)+(5) indicates that enterprise breakup continued. Moreover, applications under consideration rose to over 9,000 in August 1992, but declined to 3,497 in January 1993 and to 1,938 in January 1994.

manufacturing (29 percent), consumer services (18 percent), construction (9 percent), restaurants (7 percent), automotive transportation (3 percent), and agriculture (2 percent). As a result, the employment share of the public sector declined from 67 percent in 1992 to 59 percent today, while that of the private and mixed sectors rose from 14 percent to 20 percent and from 18 percent to 20 percent, respectively. In retail trade, the sales share of the private sector (including consumer cooperatives) increased to 71 percent (from 62 percent in

1992) and that of the other non-state sector to 4 percent (from 1 percent in 1992), whereas the state sector's share declined to 25 percent (from 37 percent in 1992). In wholesale trade of producer goods, privatization was not as dramatic, but 90 percent of total turnover is already liberalized.

In terms of previous jurisdiction, the share of privatized units among enterprises previously owned by the federal government rose from 7 percent in 1992 to 16 percent. The ratios for enterprises previously owned by local governments and by municipalities increased from 17 percent to 22 percent and from 16 percent to 62 percent, respectively. Most of the mining and manufacturing enterprises are medium to large in size and were privatized through corporatization. In 1993, enterprises were corporatized at an average pace of 1,000 per month. As of November 1, as many as 11,153 corporatized enterprises existed in all of Russia, of which 4,358 were restructured units of formerly federal operations. Among 14,000 large-scale enterprises to be privatized, 80 percent are already corporatized. Although only 31 percent of all enterprises were privatized through corporatization, the ratio was as high as 75.2 percent if federally-owned enterprises are singled out. After the privatization of January–November 1993, 305 enterprises still remain in state hands (2.7 percent), the majority of them in the mining and manufacturing industry.

In corporatization, the managers and employees of an enterprise scheduled to be privatized were given three preferential options. Over three-quarters of them selected the second option where 51 percent of common stocks with voting rights were reserved for purchase by enterprise managers and employees on a priority basis. One-sixth chose the first option where managers and employees could acquire registered preferred stock without votes up to 25 percent of statutory capital free of charge, and additionally buy common shares up to 10 percent of the remaining statutory capital at a 30 percent discount off face value in three-year installments, and common stocks up to 5 percent of statutory capital are sold to the managers on a priority basis. These two options accounted for 92 percent of total. Only 1 percent selected the third option.[2] In addition, 3.3 percent were leasing enterprises which chose to be corporatized.

Even in the case of the first option, 75 percent of the statutory stocks carry voting rights, which means a minimum holding of 38 percent constitutes a majority. Since 15 percent is purchased by managers and employees on a priority basis, an additional acquisition of 23 percent through auctions will establish worker-dominated ownership. In the case of leasing enterprise buyouts, purchasers are the employees of the enterprises themselves. Thus, not only the second option [which instantly establishes insider control] but the other cases also suggest a strong tendency for insider control. The choices of as many as 99 percent of the privatized enterprises show that the managers and employees, shunning outsiders' buyouts, decided to keep their previous positions in the process of privatization and continue to manage the enterprises. Incidentally, only 13 percent of the corporatized enterprises released all stocks for purchase – the rest were partial corporatizations.

Privatization of small enterprises mostly took the form of direct sales. Roughly 60 percent of commerce, restaurants, and consumer services are already held privately through small-scale privatization. Among them, 9 percent were through auctions, 44 percent through public subscription under certain conditions, and 43 percent through buyouts of leasing enterprises. More than three-quarters of the enterprises which were sold succeeded in receiving the full price from the purchasers.

The total asset value of enterprises privatized during January–October 1993 amounted to over 753 billion rubles (at book value prior to the 1992 reassessment of fixed-asset values). The sales receipts from privatization during January–November 1993 totaled 340 billion rubles, including payments received during this period for privatization that took place in 1992. During these eleven months, however, only 40 million privatization vouchers (each with a face value of 10,000 rubles), or 27 percent of the 148 million vouchers previously issued,[3] were redeemed. In light of this situation, the Russian government issued a presidential decree "on the extension of the term of validity of privatization vouchers" on October 6, 1993, to extend the deadline for redemption by six months to July 1, 1994.

The average asset value of a privatized enterprise was 54 million rubles for the previously federally-owned, 16 million rubles for the previously locally-owned, and 12 million rubles for those previously owned by local municipalities. Federally-owned enterprises were the largest and their thousands of employees could easily acquire over 51 percent of stocks through privatization vouchers and other means. The fact that the average asset value of an enterprise slated for privatization for each privatization voucher was a mere 7,500 rubles (national average, at pre-reassessment price) also backs this supposition. As a consequence of the privatization program described above, a total of 55 million new stockholders emerged (Goskomstat 1993; Kotel'nikova 1994; Bolkin 1993: 17; Volkov 1993).

This is a rough sketch of the results of Russian privatization up to now. In what follows, detailed analysis is given on individual points.

II Privatization vouchers

As mentioned above, approximately 40 million privatization vouchers were redeemed during January–November 1993 – only 27 percent of total.[4] At end-1993, about 60 million were lodged in privatization voucher investment funds (which invest in enterprise stocks with vouchers collected from the public in exchange for their own stocks) and over 40 million remained with private citizens – without being redeemed in state assets. Investment funds have parted with roughly 30 million vouchers for stock purchases. Among 110 million Russian citizens who exercised voucher rights, 55 million became stockholders.[5] Voucher auctions were held frequently – 105 in January 1993 alone, 600 in April, and 800 or more in some later months (Goskomstat 1993b: 95; Kotel'nikova 1994a, 1994b).

This was an unanticipated outcome in two respects. First, the Russian government had incorrectly expected that the impoverished population would rush to cash in vouchers. However, more than 100 million vouchers remained in the hands of citizens or in the form of investment fund stocks. In his statement to representatives of the Supreme Soviet on December 24, 1992, A. Chubais, chairman of the State Property Management Committee predicted that a majority of Russian citizens would soon exchange vouchers for food and necessities. Also, V. Rutgaizer cited the risk of capital dispersion as one of the objections to registered privatization accounts, and argued for transferability on an at-sight basis to promote capital concentration (Gel'vanovskii 1993: 68; V. Rutgaizer 1993b: 118; Rutgaizer, and Shoiko 1992: 10). However, voucher privatization has not functioned properly as a means to create new asset owners as opposed to non-asset owners in the short term.

Second, these actual results indicate that the completion of privatization through voucher auctions would have to be significantly delayed relative to the initial schedule.

A closer examination reveals the following facts. Of the 24 million vouchers redeemed by end-August 1993, only 5 million came from citizens and private companies. Another 10 million were from privatization voucher investment funds. In addition, over 9 million were redeemed in the process of closed advance purchase of enterprise stocks by their managers and employees (Boiko 1993: 107). At this point, 10 million vouchers were expected to be used to buyout their own enterprises by end-1993.

Overall, these facts highlight a few key aspects of voucher redemption. First, it is likely that as many as half of the 40 million vouchers redeemed were used by managers and employees to purchase their own enterprises. Second, stock purchases by individual Russian citizens remained minuscule. In addition, some vouchers were cashed, but that also was only a small portion of the total number of vouchers issued. Third, voucher investment funds are hoarding a large part of the accumulated vouchers without investing in stocks.

On the first point, managers and employees were highly active investors using privatization vouchers. Their motive was to fend off outside purchasers and preserve enterprise control among current insiders. As S. Mikhailov of the Federal Property Fund reports, the redemption rate of vouchers reached an average of 85 percent in the case of the second preferential option.[6] Such behavior was well anticipated from the outset. In fact, some managers and employees were so eager to secure enterprise ownership (amounting to 51 percent of statutory capital) that they acquired additional stocks until they depleted their meager resources. This puts a severe financial constraint on enterprise restructuring in the future (*Ekonomika i zhizn'* 1992c: 21). Articles 5–12 of the 1992 Privatization Program stipulate that managers and employees are entitled to advances from the Economic Stimulation Fund for the purchase of their enterprises. Furthermore, amid this economic disorder, the internal funds of enterprises could well be diverted to this purpose by accounting tricks. Already in late December 1992, the buying-up of vouchers for the purpose of insider privatization in the security market was reported (*Izvestia* December 22, 1992: 2. December 23: 2). In stock auctions which began in earnest in January 1993, early tradings were dominated by employee groups buying stocks with a large number of vouchers. In the *oblast'* of Vladimir, as much as 50–90 percent of the stocks was reported to have gone into the hands of employee groups alone (A. Iakovlev 1993: 2).

On the second point, individual citizens were reluctant to purchase enterprise stocks with vouchers and more often used them to buy investment fund stocks. In an underdeveloped market economy, one of the purposes of privatization voucher investment funds was to help people who were unfamiliar with stock purchases through reducing risks and assistance in stock selection.[7] Mass advertisement by some investment funds promising a ten-fold dividend return in a year also contributed to the popularity of investment funds.

On the other hand, the encashment of vouchers (with a face value of 10,000 rubles) would be affected by the price of the voucher in the securities market. The price fell from about 5,000 rubles in late December 1992 to a little over 4,000 rubles in early 1993, then rose to 10,000 rubles in mid-1993 and to 24,000 rubles by the year's end. Despite the impressive five-fold increase in nominal value, its real purchasing power fell by half when consumer price inflation of 940 percent and wholesale price inflation of 995 percent are taken into account. Given the average wage of 16,000 rubles in December 1992 and 141,000 rubles in December 1993, the price of the voucher fell from a third of monthly wage to a sixth (Federal Property Fund in *Ekonomika i zhizn'* 1994: 14; Goskomstat 1993a: 45, 1993b: 286–7, 1994: 7).

Though depreciated, the voucher still retained a value equivalent to a third to a sixth of the average monthly wage. It is curious that Russian citizens, with undiminished inflation expectation after the price increase of 2,600 percent in 1992, did not rush to cash their vouchers. It is highly unlikely that people chose vouchers as an inflation hedge after the 1992 inflation and the problem of inter-enterprise arrears in the mining and manufacturing sector emerged in mid 1992. One may argue that Russians were overly optimistic about becoming stockholders and fooled into believing the return of 1,000 percent per year that some investment funds advertised with such fanfare. Another explanation is that, in a country where state-sector workers account for 60 percent of the population, most people are holding vouchers in preparation for the future buyout of their own enterprises. In that case, competition among investment funds to lure away the vouchers remaining in public hands is unlikely to be successful.

On the third point of the behavior of privatization voucher investment funds, there seems to be little rational basis for the promise of a certain return of up to 1,000 percent per year for people who exchanged vouchers for the stocks of these investment funds (Kotel nikova 1994b). Dividends cannot be predetermined but should reflect the actual return on the best available investment opportunities. This irregularity can be traced to the environment in which these investment funds operated. In this regard, the following facts are noteworthy.

First, as A. Chubais, chairman of the Federal State Property Management Committee, admits, over 30 percent of regions comprising the Russian Federation are blocking voucher auctions. As a result, only 20 percent of the assets slated for privatization have actually been put on sale. Many local authorities who supervise the local offices of the Property Management Committee and the Property Fund, including those in Moscow, are boycotting the implementation of auctions. The structure of local politics remains basically unchanged after the collapse of the regional Soviet authorities. Not only elected officials but also those appointed by President Yeltsin are resisting auctions for privatization (*Izvestia* 1994: 5). One cause of the resistance is the fiscal distress of local governments. Governments would like to receive cash (which would increase revenues) in exchange for state assets, rather than vouchers (which do not). Not surprisingly, these governments in severe fiscal crisis are waiting for cash auctions to begin in July 1994 when voucher auctions will be terminated.

A related problem in certain regions is that insufficient assets are on sale relative to the value of vouchers distributed. For example, the *oblast'* of Cheliabinsk terminated voucher auctions on the grounds that they did not have enough assets to exchange for vouchers.[8] Of the 88 regional governments making up the Russian Federation, excluding 10 for which data are not available, only 16 (18 percent) have a value of assets scheduled for privatization exceeding 10,000 rubles per voucher, which is the face value. The remaining 82 percent have too few assets for sale. In 16 of them, the total assets do not cover even half the voucher value. In these regions with insufficient assets relative to vouchers in local circulation, authorities often block the use of vouchers originating in other areas even when auctions are held. Such regionalism reduces the effective supply of assets to be privatized (Bolkin 1993: 17, Federal Property Fund in *Ekonomika i zhizn'* 1992b: 8–9).

Second, there is antagonism between the Property Management Committee and the Property Fund. The former promotes rapid privatization while the latter emphasizes stability in production. The Committee is opposed to the Fund's proposal of a new preferential option for managers and employees. The Fund tends to dampen the supply of assets for sale, and at times even seeks enterprise ownership by acquiring stocks. The Fund also suffers from the unreliability of funds transferred from the Finance Ministry which are necessary for conducting voucher auctions. For instance, the advertisement cost for privatization auctions for the first half of 1993, estimated at 2 million rubles per enterprise, was transferred from the Finance Ministry only in June 1993 (Boiko 1993: 107–10, Bulantsev 1993: 44–7, Iakovlev 1993: 2).

Third, by August 1993, only 2,000 of the approximately 5,000 large enterprises which were required to be privatized were actually registered as joint-stock companies. Such delays in corporatization limit the supply of available stocks. Sixty percent of these large enterprises need the approval of line ministries before privatization. Delays are caused as these line ministries try to retain their grip on the enterprises by restricting stock sales and arguing their special status with the government. Procedural complexity also contributes to the slow pace. The small size of the Federal State Property Management Committee, with 450 staff members, also militates against speed in privatization (Boiko 1993).

Fourth, the hesitation and resistance of the enterprises scheduled for privatization must be cited. There are several reasons for this. Enterprise insiders are fearful of the intrusion of outside control and try to buy up their enterprises. Another discouragement is the absence of cash income when enterprises are sold against vouchers. Moreover, enterprises lacking even working capital are naturally reluctant to commit themselves to dividend payments to outsiders. An enterprise may even avoid the sales of its stocks for the moment by transferring the stocks held by the Property Fund to a trust (Boiko 1993; Bulantsev 1993; Berezhnaia 1993). These factors decrease the supply of stocks for voucher privatization, impeding the purchase of stocks by investment funds and individual citizens.[9]

In this regard, consider the demand and supply relationship between stocks and vouchers. Privatization vouchers were issued over a short period of time, 148 million in number, and generated a potential demand for stocks amounting to 1.48 trillion rubles. The term of validity was extended by a half-year from end-1993 to July 1, 1994. On the other hand, the state asset to be sold amounted to 1.12 trillion rubles, which meant that the value of state assets per voucher was only 7,500 rubles. Furthermore, stock available to the general population after the preferential purchases by managers and employees would be much less than the above figure, and could be as low as 1,890 rubles per voucher, according to one estimate. So the supply of assets falls far short of the demand created by vouchers. As privatization vouchers were immediately redeemable and had a limited term of validity, they tended to materialize as demand in auctions. The supply of stocks however was slow to emerge and highly restricted for reasons discussed above (Bolkin 1993: 17, Federal Property Fund in *Ekonomika i zhizn'* 1992b: 9).

In the auctions of state assets against privatization vouchers, the exchange ratio between the two was four stocks (measured in stocks with the face value of 1,000 rubles) per voucher in January 1993 (national average). It gradually slipped to below two shares of stock per voucher by April where it stayed for several months, before regaining the two shares per voucher level. This weakness in voucher value reflects the demand and supply conditions described above. However, there were also regional variations in the stock-price of the voucher: 1.63 in St. Petersburg, 1.18 in Moscow, 0.53 in the republic of Buriat – against 12.55 in the *oblast'* of Kirov and 8.6 in the *oblast'* of Samarsk (Federal Property Fund in *Ekonomika i zhizn'* 1994: 14, V. Volkov 1993: 9).

What is the implication of the average of two 1,000-ruble stocks per voucher? When vouchers issued in 1992 are used, stocks are evaluated by the remaining value of an enterprise's fixed assets on January 1, 1992. For 1993, there was a dispute over the applicability of the July 1, 1992 asset reassessment based on government decision No. 595 on the "reassessment of fixed assets in the

Russian Federation" (August 14, 1992), which delayed the passage of the 1993 Privatization Program. However, actual evaluations continued to be made at pre-reassessment values. In the 1994 Privatization Program, the statutory capital of a new company with publicly held stocks was to be calculated by the asset value on July 1, 1992, and not by the reassessed value based on government decision No. 595. Inflation-adjusted, the real value of enterprise assets were unlikely to change much. This means that the nominal value of enterprise assets (and of a stock with a face value of 1,000 rubles) increased 20- to 30-fold with the inflation of 1992–93.

But this evaluation, based on the remaining value in January or July 1992, is not the actual value of enterprise assets. The "balance" or repurchase value is estimated to be 1.6 times the remaining value (Federal Property Fund in *Ekonomika i zhizn'* 1992b: 9). However, the more serious problem is the lack of capital assessment at the market value.

Some fragmentary examples of how enterprises were evaluated are given below. According to A. Kolan'kov, the stock of Moscow's Tekhnostroiprom Company was exchanged at three shares per voucher, with each share valued at 3,950 rubles in cash auction. This implies that each voucher was traded for assets worth 11,850 rubles. Similarly, Shikom's stocks exchanged at nine shares per voucher, with each share valued at 1,600 in cash auction, implying each voucher was worth 14,400 rubles. In the case of Presnenskii Kolbasnyi Zavod, one voucher bought seven shares worth 2,500 rubles in cash auction, i.e., assets worth 17,500 rubles. Meanwhile, the price of privatization voucher was 4,050 rubles when Shikom's auction was held, and 4,200 rubles for the other cases (Kolan'kov and Grabarnik 1993: 3).

Assuming that enterprises were evaluated correctly, these numbers imply that an asset buyer could legally pocket the difference between the price of a privatization voucher and the value of assets purchased against it. This transfers wealth from the poor who parted with their vouchers to the rich who collected and used them. In this way, transferrable privatization vouchers promote wealth concentration while pretending to distribute state assets equally among the population (Gel'vanovskii 1993: 67).

Another important aspect of privatization is the priority given to getting managers and employees to purchase the shares of their enterprises. According to the "Regulations on Closed Advanced Stock Purchase in State Enterprise Privatization" by the Federal State Property Management Committee (July 27, 1992), the purchase price was determined to be 70 percent of the face value for the first option and 170 percent for the second option. Thus, one voucher is guaranteed to buy fourteen (first option) or six (second option) 1,000-ruble shares. Since the average exchange ratio at auctions were two shares per voucher, the difference (adjusted for incidental cost) would cause a large transfer of wealth from ordinary citizens to the managers and workers of these enterprises. If the latter acquire additional vouchers, a further wealth transfer would occur through the mechanism described immediately above. Among them, the managers and employees of high-performing enterprises are in an extremely advantageous position. The whole process is a sort of "enclosure" of state assets by a small number of citizens, in contradiction to the philosophy that privatized state assets should be distributed equally among all residents. However, it is a different matter to determine whether the concentration of assets through such capital enclosure means much in the economic sense. This issue will be further discussed in the concluding section.

Let us examine the cases of eight enterprises at the Vladimir Auction Center to see how shares are traded in actual voucher auctions. As seen in Table 13.2, there is little correlation between the financial performance of the enterprise and its stock price. Enterprises 1 and 7, which are performing well, are priced as low as or less than 0.190 (one voucher buys about five shares) whereas the price of enterprise 3, with no profits and relatively large arrears, is 0.588 (one voucher buys about 1.7 stocks). On the other hand, the supply of vouchers and the share price are clearly inversely related. It is pointed out that only 10–15 percent of individual purchasers are interested in the financial performance – as opposed to the name – of the enterprise in making investment decisions. Among large buyers, employee groups who buy up 50–90 percent of their own enterprises dominate. A. Kolan'kov reports that, in Moscow auctions, small investors are interested in dividends and therefore pay attention to enterprise profile, product lines, images of factories, popularity of products, and financial conditions, while large purchasers are driven by both investment and speculation motives, paying heed also to enterprise location and quality of structures, preferring premises close to the center of the city (Kolan'kov and Grabarnik 1993).

Finally, let us examine privatization voucher investment funds. The funds collected vouchers on the promise of a 1,000 percent dividend return (100 thousand rubles) after one year. At end-1993, 621 investment funds held approximately 60 million vouchers. There are three types of investment funds, classified by the motive of establishment. The first type aimed at amassing funds by acquiring enterprise stocks in exchange for vouchers, which are then resold to enterprises themselves or used for speculation. This was the most common type of investment funds by mid-1993. Some launched grandiose advertisement campaigns to attract vouchers, but are reported to be using part of the proceeds to cover current expenses. The second type was supposed to channel funds to specific industries with prescribed areas for investment. However, exchanging stocks for vouchers does not generate any cash receipt for the enterprises. Thus, the true purpose of this type of investment fund is suspected to be aversion to outsider control. The third type is purported to manage security portfolios for individual investors. In the absence of functioning security markets, however, these investment funds are forced to either engage in foreign exchange speculation or go bankrupt if they adhere to the original purpose of investing in non-existent security markets.

Most investment funds are expected to go bankrupt and be liquidated. Even the largest among them are reported to be (on the verge of) depleting their

Table 13.2 Enterprise stock sales at Vladimir Auction Center in February 1993

	1	2	3	4	5	6	7	8
	Aftopribor	Avtsvet	Sudar'	Pobeda	Мupom Teploboz	Pred. im. Pari. Kom.	Viaznikovskii	Iartsevskaia
Employee	8,719	5,420	603	1,148	6,453	1,534	2,676	1,434
Sales (million rubles)	1,335.7	775.9	44.1[2]	34.2[3]	403.4	464.2	...	389.7
Premises (ha)	24.7	39.7	1.3	1.4	393.9	117.1	21.8	26.1
Option selected[4]	II	I	II	II	II	II	I	II
Financial data (million rubles)								
Statutory capital	203.1	255.8	8.3	16.2	94.4	20.4	49.0	27.3
Balance profit	539.1	357.2	—	27.3	142.5	139.3	1307.6	89.1
Cash	5.8	0.6	0.001	0.006	0.16	0.52	0.003	—
Settlement account	0.1	0.3	1.0	0.03	5.8	0.52	0.007	0.27
Other accounts	—	0.1	—	2.2	—	—	—	—
Accounts payable	442.4	278.4	22.2	32.2	129.3	113.9	1,175.9	135.0
Accounts receivable	377.7	393.0	43.1	37.9	48.6	97.1	1,117.9	194.6
Debt to fiscal authority	92.3	82.7	—	4.8	0.05	64.6	58.5	10.7
Bank loans								
Short-term	12.1	48.0	20.2	22.7	32.8	24.4	36.0	6.0
Long-term	7.8	—	—	0.9	—	—	—	—
Auction								
Number of stocks sold	48,734	76,724	1,711	4,867	27,366	5,913	12,255	7,903
% of statutory capital	24	30	20	30	29	29	25	29
Price of 1,000 ruble stock in number of vouchers	0.190	0.091	0.588	0.333	0.143	0.160	0.182	0.095

Source: A. Iakovlev, "State enterprises are sold below their values," Finansovie Izvestiia, March 13–19, 1993, No. 20, p. 2.

Notes:
1 All data are at July 1, 1992 or for January–June 1992, except for enterprise no. 7 which is at October 1, 1992 or for January–September 1992.
2 First quarter of 1992
3 January–February 1992.
4 For explanations of the privatization options, see text.

statutory capital in order to survive or continue to pay dividends (Skatershchikov 1993: VIII; Gorbatov 1993: II; Rutgaizer 1993a: 122). Presidential decree No. 1304 granted preferential tax treatment to authorized "social security" privatization voucher investment funds where over 50 percent of the stockholders are social security recipients. However, some criticize the plan as ineffective since the resulting dividend of 100 rubles per stockholder would be too small as a social security protection (Shimov 1993: 6).

In fact, the crises of privatization voucher investment funds are continuing into 1994. High dividend payments (900 percent per year) are also reported, but this is an exception rather than the rule (Kornev 1994: 2). E. Kotel'nikova argues that the financial problems of investment funds are caused by the inability to receive dividends from the enterprises in which they have invested, which in turn is the result of financial distress faced by the enterprises themselves. According to D. Vasiliev, vice-chairman of the State Property Management Committee, an enterprise survey revealed that, among 209 enterprises they inspected, 70 percent are unable to pay dividends at all, and the dividends of none of the remaining enterprises exceeded 30 percent of the stock's face value. Among the latter, two-thirds have selected the second option with most of them blocking the payment of dividends to outside investors (Kotel'nikova 1994b).

Chubais contends that the selection process of investment funds through bankruptcy is a natural one under the market mechanism (in *Izvestia* 1994: 5). However, the bankruptcy of investment funds which assembled vouchers in exchange for their own stocks would deprive a vast majority of Russian citizens, most of them without proper knowledge of investment, of the opportunity to participate in the ownership of state assets. Given the large volume of vouchers hoarded by these investment funds, their crisis is also the crisis of the voucher privatization scheme. It implies that the validity of privatization itself, based on the voucher scheme, is seriously in doubt. In today's Russian economy, the tendency of insider control is not only strong but inevitable under the circumstances. Given the severe shortage of investment capital, the reluctance of Russian enterprises to pay dividends to outsiders is also understandable. The difficulties faced by privatization voucher investment funds are deeply rooted in the Russian economy.

III Small-scale privatization

As shown in Table 13.3, privatization of shops, restaurants, and consumer services has proceeded significantly, with roughly 60 percent transferred to private hands by September 1993. Small-scale businesses dominate in privatization, with two-thirds of privatized enterprises belonging to these sectors. However, there are significant regional variations in the progress of small-scale privatization. The share of private operations in retail trade during January–September 1993 recorded 51–75 percent in Moscow, St. Petersburg, the republic of Khakasiia, and *oblasti* of Kemerovsk and Cheliabinsk. In contrast, the same

Table 13.3 Russia: Privatization of small-scale businesses (%)

	1992 Dec	1993 Jan	Feb	Mar	Apr	May	Jun	Aug	Sep
Commerce	36.1	42.7	46.0	52.4	55.4	53.4	57.2	61.2	63.4
Restaurants	32.1	36.1	39.1	47.0	48.6	47.8	52.2	57.4	58.4
Consumer services	40.8	45.8	48.7	52.9	56.7	56.2	59.5	63.1	64.6
Other	36.8	43.0	46.1	52.0	54.8	53.4	57.1	61.2	—

Source: Volkov 1993: 3, which is obtained at the Ministry of Economy on December 24, 1993. Incidentally, privatized retail and wholesale trade reached 36 percent and 34.5 percent as of December 1992 (*Izvestiia*, January 27, 1993: 2).

share remained at 9 percent or below in the republics of Tatarstan, Kalmkiia-Khal'mg-Tangch, and Bashkortostan and *oblasti* of Leningrad, Tul'sk, Voronezh, and Kamchatka. The average in all of Russia was 33 percent. They were sold by auctions (9.4 percent in January–November 1993), public bidding (44.3 percent), or through buyouts of leasing companies (42.6 percent). There are regional differences in these proportions also (Volkov 1993: 2, Goskomstat 1993b: 94).

Anyone can become a legal purchaser of these small-scale companies except those enterprises with 25 percent or more state ownership (Article 9, Russian Privatization Law). The actual buyers included the manager–employee groups of enterprises to be privatized, other corporations, and individuals. The purchases of manager–employee groups were accomplished through newly established companies (often with limited liabilities). No comprehensive data on the new management of small-scale enterprises are available. However, the share of manager–employee groups which exceeded 42 percent in small-scale privatization during 1993 suggests emerging control by the existing insiders of these enterprises as well.

Interviews conducted by S. Barsukova reveal the motives of manager–employee groups who buy their own enterprises. Most important among them is the fear of acquisition by outsiders and the desire to pre-empt such a purchase. They applied for privatization with a vague hope of better wages, managerial autonomy, and democracy when ownership was achieved, coupled with a belief that these conditions would surely worsen if invaded by outside management. In particular, they dreaded the change in enterprise profile, cuts in employment and wages, reduction in social benefits (subsidies for transportation and kindergartens), ignorance of new managers over specialized business matters, and restriction of official authorities, that new managers might bring. These are concrete issues – and not the class antagonism or mental resistance to work for private enterprises that are often cited. In the case of managers, resistance to a reduction in their authority and activities and control by amateurs was especially strong. Employees also doubted if the guarantee on their status at the time of public bidding would be honored when new management took charge (Barsukova 1993b: 77).

However, when managers and employees set up a new company to buy out their enterprise, only part of the employees – say, only half or a third – may be included as full members of the new company, with the rest becoming hired workers without rights.[10] Whether this happens or not, one strong motivation for privatization is undoubtedly the self-preservation of former managers who wish to keep the same positions in the new company.

Separation of employees into full members and hired workers often occurs when a new company is established at the initiative of the former managers and when the enterprise is profitable. By restricting membership, each member can receive greater profits and more capital is available for investment for future development. In such a case, providing capital to a new company is considered to be a profitable investment. It is relatively easy to exclude the bulk of employees from a new company because they lack necessary legal information. S. Barsukova reports the absence of protest from the designated hired workers who naively believe the managers' word that only a third of employees can become members of a new company. For them, it is difficult to detect the deliberate misinterpretation of privatization laws by managers because only the latter have access to pertinent information. Thus, "collective privatization" is often a convenient cover for "manager privatization" and "secret privatization."[11]

In effect, managers are misappropriating state assets through the manipulation of information. It is well to remember that this separation of previous employees into full members and hired workers – into haves and have-nots – proceeds under the disguise of "collective privatization."

On the other hand, when an enterprise makes little or no profit, there is no conflict of interest that leads to such separation. In this case, all employees tend to be included in a newly formed company in order to gather as much capital as possible for its establishment and to maintain good relationship between managers and employees.

When a manager–employee group does not have enough funds to buy out their enterprise, a sponsor often provides the needed additional funding. This arrangement is advantageous for both parties. Managers and employees can retain the ownership of the new company and avoid outside control. The sponsor, itself an incorporated entity, can obtain part of the enterprise's land and buildings in compensation at the preferential terms granted only to managers and employees. This trick can also circumvent the ban on enterprises with 25 percent or more state ownership purchasing properties slated for privatization. Additionally, if the two parties belong to related industries, the sponsor company can take advantage of the capacity of the privatized company as supplier as well as cooperation in production and sales (Barsukova 1993a: 132–4).

When outside individuals and companies purchase enterprises, three motives can be cited. The first is the case where the purchaser is interested in the enterprise's activities and wishes to maintain it as a going concern. For example, it is reported that a worker at a knitting factory prompted by the law on individual labor activity in 1986 quit his job to start his own knitting business. Later, he purchased the factory he had previously worked for to expand his business. Second, some investors are not interested in the current business of the enterprise and intend to use its land and buildings for other purposes. For example, in St. Petersburg, only 13 of the 40 enterprises privatized through public bidding resumed their activities – the rest were converted to offices and video theaters. The third type of investors are also unconcerned about the enterprise business; instead, their purpose is property speculation. However, since speculation in real estate is prohibited by law, enterprise activities are not immediately terminated. The manager of a company who purchased a beauty parlor next to a metro station declared that what was bought was the location and not the beauty parlor. He showed up only once a month and did not bother to discuss business matters, including pricing (Barsukova 1993b: 74–83; Dmitrieva 1992).

The predominance of the second and third types of outsider purchases is also caused by local governments who seek to augment fiscal revenues through asset sales. As 98 percent of commercial distribution had been previously owned by local governments, these asset sales to outsiders may lead to the breakdown of the Russian distribution system. However, the negative aspect should not be over-emphasized. The cost of the collapse of the old and inefficient commercial network inherited from the socialist days must be weighed against the potential benefit of having a new service industry in the future.

IV Manager privatization

The term "manager privatization" does not refer to any officially recognized privatization scheme. Indeed, it was often argued that managers would lose their positions when state enterprises were privatized, and that this possibility would slow the privatization process. For instance, in a business conference of top executives and managers convened by the Moscow Property Fund and the *Economy and Life* newspaper in early 1992, it was stated that, in the case of large-scale enterprises, "laws in effect repeal the rights of enterprise management. After privatization, the top executive and his managers could lose their power. However, if he knows that the change could deprive him of his leadership status, he is hardly expected to cooperate with privatization. Law makers ignore this basic fact" (*Ekonomika i zhizn'* 1992a: 7).

Interestingly, however, the interviews conducted by L. Babaeva and L. Nelson indicate that this was not the case. They interviewed 4,271 managers and employees in Moscow, Ekaterinburg, Smolensk, and Voronezh during June–August 1992. Of the total, 46.5 percent worked for state enterprises, 23.6 percent for private enterprises, 25 percent for newly privatized enterprises, and 4 percent were members of privatization or asset management committees. At the time of the interviews, the details of the 1992 Privatization Program were not known even in Moscow (Babaeva and Nelson 1993: 95).

Tables 13.4a and 13.4b show that 65.8 percent of managers wanted privatization to be accelerated, and as many as 74.1 percent of them were happy with the

Table 13.4 Russian privatization: managers' responses to survey questions

a. What is the right speed of privatization? (%)

	Faster	*Slower*	*Current speed*	*Don't know*
Employees	48.9	7.3	7.0	32.9
Managers	65.8	9.6	8.3	12.7
Committee members	48.8	22.7	19.8	2.9

b. Will privatization improve, worsen, or not affect your life? (%)

	Improve	*Worsen*	*No change*	*Don't know*
Employees	43.5	17.3	11.0	24.3
Managers	59.4	16.0	9.4	13.3
Committee members	48.8	22.8	19.8	2.9

Source: Baebaeva and Nelson 1993: 95

present or even faster speed. These ratios were higher than those for employees. In addition, 59.4 percent of managers expected their lives to improve after privatization, and 68.8 percent expected the same or better quality of life. While managers at private enterprises are more positive about privatization than those at state enterprises, the difference is not large. Based on these findings, L. Babaeva and others object to the idea of radical economists that collective privatization should be promoted as a means to "smash" enterprise managers, because they are more likely to retain and even enhance their positions in the privatization process. The formality of collective privatization is often a smoke screen for "manager privatization" or "secret privatization" (Babaeva and Nelson: 1993: 108).

Let us examine how privatization can proceed on terms favorable to managers. As discussed in section I, the 1992 Privatization Law offers preferential options to managers and employees in establishing a publicly-held corporation. When either the first or second option is selected, top executives and managers are undoubtedly in a better financial position than employees to acquire a majority of stocks with voting rights. Furthermore, the presidential decree on "organizational measures in the transformation of state enterprises and voluntary state enterprise associations into joint-stock companies" (July 1, 1992) stipulates the appointment of former executives to the management of a new company if the Property Fund is its stockholder. This assures managers of their positions as long as this arrangement lasts. Even in the event that the Property Fund subsequently decides to sell the company's stocks, these stocks will likely end up in the hands of the managers if they maintain a good relationship with the Fund. While the same presidential decree permits the Property Fund to entrust the stocks to individuals or corporations recognized by Article 9 of Russian Privatization Law, this requires the consent of the manager–employee group of the enterprise. This effectively blocks the transfer of stocks to outsiders. Moreover, managers may well collude with trustees, as described in the previous section. These are the provisions for protecting the existing management.

S. Barsukova notes two ways to achieve manager privatization. The first is the use of an external organization controlled directly by the managers of the enterprise to be privatized. Four examples are given: (1) the assets of a state enterprise are transferred to a new private company whose directors are also the managers of the state enterprise; (2) certain departments (procurement, sales, etc.) of a state enterprise association are eliminated and their functions are transferred to new private companies founded by the state enterprise managers; (3) a large enterprise under local jurisdiction transfers the right to privatize to a newly created industrial group, thus circumventing the State Property Management Committee; and (4) an association of state enterprises sets up a closed joint-stock company. This company holds the assets of the member enterprises and handles their sales and procurement activities at inflated prices. With accumulated profits, the company finally purchases the original state enterprises.

Alternatively, if a closed joint-stock company is to be established, manager privatization can be accomplished internally: (1) when a member dies or retires, his stocks are transferred to the board of directors as stipulated by company statutes; (2) since the right to acquire additional stock is given in proportion to current holdings, managers with dominant stock holdings continue to be favored. In addition, the purchase price is also determined by the board of directors; (3) although a capital increase must be approved by a general meeting of stock-holders, an increase up to 20 percent per year is excepted from this requirement by the statutes of a closed joint-stock company. This rule is used to distribute stock among directors as compensation, free of charge; (4) since the model statutes of a joint stock company allow capital contribution in the form of intellectual property, managers "contribute" their management skills to the privatized enterprise (Baruskova 1993c: 63–6).

Among these various methods, some are legal and others illegal (see below). Managers can easily use any of them to preserve their positions.

V Criminal acts

In the lawless Russian society, more than 27,000 crimes in connection with privatization were reported in 1993. In the same year, roughly 39,000 enterprises were privatized. While the precise relationship between the two numbers is unknown, they point to the unusually high frequency of such crimes. In addition, many crimes are not detected by the Ministry of Interior Affairs. Lawsuits are also on the increase. Although the presidential decree on the "regulation of public services of the federal government" (December 22, 1992) stipulating the punishment for public servants engaged in privatization-related illegal activities was supposed to counter these activities, the Ministry of Interior Affairs predicts a surge of such crimes as the privatization process deepens. Many of the following cases are reported by A. Bykov (1994: 22), a Ministry of Interior Affairs investigator.

Crimes related to privatization can be classified into five types. The first is the misappropriation of state assets. Using personal ties with state officials or abusing their own authority, many enterprise managers transfer state assets to themselves or to companies under their control. In Moscow, the general manager of an inter-industry enterprise association conspired with the chief accountant to transfer a substantial sum of state money and state assets worth over 50 million rubles to a newly established commercial organization – whereupon they and their relatives became its managers. Sometimes, a company set up initially by a state enterprise or an agricultural soviet is transferred to private ownership at the time of re-registration. In the most "judicious" case, managers evaluated and then contributed their own intellectual properties (management skills) to a newly established closed joint-stock company "Kolo" (with the statutory capital of 1 billion rubles) and became its managers.

Participation of state officials in newly privatized companies is very common. They often use their authority to underestimate assets transferred to the new company. A high official in the federal department of construction materials is reported to have, in cooperation with enterprise managers under his jurisdiction and with tacit approval of local authorities, transferred the funds and fixed capital of related enterprises at undervalued prices to the statutory capital of a new company, Scheklo Russia.[12]

The second type of privatization crime is illegal acquisition of the enterprise or its control by its former managers. Some managers at a chocolate factory in Samarsk secured control of a new company with 0.5–2.5 million rubles borrowed from banks under the guise of automobile loans. They later repaid the debt from the company's account.[13] As A. Bykov notes, this kind of fraud is effectively *excluding the large majority of Russian workers from the privatization process and diminishing their enthusiasm for the transition to a market economy.*

The third is infringement on the rights of workers in an enterprise. For instance, when a form is circulated among employees for their signature, they are not informed of the content and option of privatization or the minutes of manager–employee meetings. They are simply asked to sign, not knowing who will be full members or hired workers in the new company.[14]

The fourth is widespread bribery in connection with privatization. An expert of the State Property Management Committee received 200,000 rubles for understating an enterprise's assets. In the *oblast'* of Orlovsk, the vice-chairman of a local State Property Management Committee was arrested for accepting 1 million rubles after rendering the same service. The chairman of an asset fund belonging to the district soviet of St. Petersburg pocketed 20 million rubles for artificially depressing asset prices in privatization auctions.

The fifth type of privatization crime is the embezzlement, theft, forgery, and reuse of privatization vouchers.

Other crimes are also reported. In summary, A. Bykov concludes that a new class of asset owners and entrepreneurs is likely to emerge from among these operators in the underground economy. The fact that Russian privatization is accompanied by widespread crime and fraud may undermine the legal basis of the fragile property ownership.[15]

Concluding remarks

From above, six points which characterize Russian privatization can be listed. First, privatization voucher schemes and preferential treatment of managers and employees, strategies which were supposed to distribute state assets equally among citizens, in fact work as an "enclosure" mechanism that transfers wealth from the poor to the rich, and from pensioners and state workers (public servants, teachers, doctors, etc.) to enterprise manager–employee groups. Second, as shown by the distribution of stock, the control of enterprises is increasingly dominated by insiders, namely, managers and employees of the enterprise. However, even among enterprise employees, a division between owners and non-owners is occurring. Third, "nomenclatura" privatization by former managers and state officials is widespread. Fourth, privatization is proceeding amid rampant crimes and fraud. Fifth, as the crisis of privatization voucher investment funds indicates, new owners are facing financial difficulties and may lose their asset holdings in the near future. Sixth, the progress of any scheme for marketization depends on compatibility with the interests of the majority of people involved. It is interesting to observe that the second preferential option in privatization, which met the needs of managers and employees, was rapidly accepted, while investment funds are facing difficulty in purchasing stocks and receiving dividends from enterprises.

Deep problems lie behind Russian privatization. Most important among them is the fact that the basic question in privatization has not been adequately addressed. Privatization is a complicated process because ownership is not just a matter of economic activity but also closely related to people's consciousness which in turn depends on will and ideology. Ownership – private ownership in particular – is a social order of will domination over physical assets. Economic activities such as production, sales, and consumption must be carried out under such an order in the will to control physical assets. Through these activities, the order is maintained and reproduced. It is critically important that people who are granted control over physical assets have the will and ability to use them for productive purposes and feel enriched by it.

Thus, privatization in the true sense may not be achieved for the following two reasons. The first is the case when the ownership relationship is not repro-duced through economic activities. If the economy declines or stagnates for a long time under a certain ownership relationship, such a relationship becomes irrelevant and difficult to sustain. In today's Russia, where an irreversible erosion of production capacity continues, there exists a serious risk of productive capital becoming a heap of scrap. For example, while real wages rose in 1993, the share of depreciation allowances in the production cost of the mining and manufacturing sector declined from 7.5 percent in 1990 to 3.0 percent in 1991, 2.6 percent in 1992, and 1.0 percent in 1993. Investment no longer covers even the physical wear and tear on the existing capital stock. Nearly 60 percent of industrial fixed assets are now obsolete, and some enterprises are unable to fulfill their function as production units. Apart from the 18 percent of state enterprises which are reported to be deficit-ridden, many more suffer from inter-enterprise arrears aggravated by macroeconomic tightening and face the danger of mass bankruptcy. Under liberalized trade, the financial woes of uncompetitive Russian enterprises are deepening. Should some or all of the dangers mentioned here become reality, ownership based on joint-stock companies would become almost irrelevant. In the absence of effective economic policies to restore the Russian economy, the likely result would be prolonged economic chaos without the substance of private property ownership.

Behind this unfortunate situation lies the problem of non-ownership and lack of responsibility of management units in the transition process from state ownership to private ownership. Difficulty arises because no economic agent is interested in or capable of the efficient use and maintenance of enterprise assets. Managers and employees take advantage of production equipment and enterprise assets – not because of interest in the development of their enterprise as a production unit but for personal gains and misappropriation. While Russian enterprises suffer from obsolete equipment and lack of international competitiveness, many enterprises increasingly turn to raising real wages and reducing depreciation allowances or profits. This is totally irrational. A class of managers with a strong stake and knowhow in operating and managing existing enterprises normally is desperately needed.

In a sense, the choice of most enterprises to install insider control is a step forward from the situation of no-ownership and no-responsibility. This is also inevitable since no one except the current management has the knowledge to manage Russian enterprises at present. On the other hand, the efficient management required of these enterprises is hardly possible if they are controlled by managers and employees themselves. V. Rutgaizer (1993b: 62) seems to favor the emerging system which resembles the American ESOP (employee stock ownership plan), but this is too optimistic. In a quasi-private company owned predominantly by its managers and employees and partly by the state and outside private-sector agents, employees' demand for higher wages and dividends and guarantees against layoffs would be too strong to carry out capital accumulation and downsizing. This internal force would thwart a shift to efficient management. It must be recalled that employees abhor external intervention primarily due to fear of job reduction. An additional claim to profit is made by the demand for dividends by general stockholders who invested in investment funds. Whether the new class of management is able to effectively resist these demands from employee-owners and general stockholders is a moot point. When 80 percent of enterprises are faced with severe need to upgrade equipment and technology, this is a serious problem (Volkov 1993: 9). Furthermore, if a large number of monopolistic enterprises are to simultaneously satisfy the demand for income and dividends on the one hand and the requirement for capital investment on the other, they may resort to raising output prices and cause serious inflation.

The second reason for possible failure of privatization is that the ownership system can be sustained only when people mutually accept the status and legitimacy of control over physical assets. A capitalist market economy is also a community based on mutual acceptance of each other's ownership. Thus, ownership is critically dependent on people's consciousness, including their ideology and the legal framework. From this point of view, two problems can be noted in today's Russia.

First, the mounting popular discontent fueled by the rapidly widening income gap, disintegration of the middle class, and mass impoverishment, is a big problem. A public opinion poll by the European Commission found that the percentage of people in European Russia who did not think that the market economy was a good option for Russia increased from 44 percent in December 1992 to 53 percent in December 1993 just prior to the election, and to 58 percent after the election (*Asahi Shimbun*, evening edition, March 19, 1994). Thanks to the transferability of privatization vouchers, misappropriation of state assets by the few and the division of society into haves and have-nots are spreading rapidly. It is a matter of time until people feel betrayed by investment funds which had amassed vouchers with an illusion of a 1,000 percent dividend return after one year. Privatization is encouraging concentration of assets in the hands of a small group of citizens amid rampant crimes. If this situation continues, the emerging ownership relationship will win neither popular support nor social legitimacy. If dissatisfaction leads to social explosion, the new ownership relationship will be considered unjust and remain unstable, even if the total rejection of private ownership is averted. Many questions will likely be raised about the past privatization process, including the appropriateness of procedures for state asset sales. There will be calls for investigation, and the issue will surely be politicized.

Second, despite the importance of the legal framework in stabilizing ownership, government at all levels remains unable to enforce the large number of laws and presidential decrees that are issued (Shatalin 1994: 2; Savvateeva 1994: 2). In 1993, privatization law itself remained uncertain due to the political feud between the president and Parliament. The Federal Property Fund unsuccessfully tried to impose a fourth preferential option for privatization – managers and employees were to purchase 90 percent of the stocks in installments using enterprise profit. The presidential decree which accelerated privatization was annulled by the Supreme Soviet, whereupon the president responded with another decree. Legal uncertainty coupled with the non-enforcement of existing laws militate against the stability of ownership relations.

Russian privatization is proceeding amid lawlessness and economic confusion brought about by the collapse of the state. At the same time, in this desperate situation, people are surely acting rationally in pursuit of their own personal interest. What is required today is additional privatization measures which will direct such behavior to the realization of efficient management with proper economic incentives.

Notes

1 This paper originally appeared in *Keizai Kenkyu* (Economic Review), vol. 45, no. 3, Institute of Economic Research, Hitotsubashi University, July 1994, pp. 203–17 [Editors].

2 In the third option, the privatization implementation group selected by both managers and employees could buy common stocks equivalent to 20 percent of statutory capital, and managers and employees (including the privatization implementation group) could purchase 20 percent of the remainder at a 30 percent discount from the face value. This option applied only to enterprises with more than 200 employees and fixed capital of 1 million to 50 million rubles at book value [Editors].

3 This often quoted sum, based on the total population of the Russian Federation, over-states the number of issued vouchers since some local governments – for instance, Tatarstan with a population of 3.6 million – introduced personal registered accounts which reduce actual voucher circulation. See Rutgaizer 1993a: 119.

4 Thus, the conditional prediction by G. Mikhailov that 60 million privatization vouchers would be redeemed by October 1993 did not materialize. See Mikhailov 1993: 73.

5 Not all of the remaining 55 million people redeemed privatization vouchers for cash, since some are known to have exchanged them for assets other than enterprise stocks.

6 The time of this observation is not clearly stated, but is likely to be around summer 1993 from the overall context of the paper. See Mikhailov 1993: 72.

7 Article 8, Russian Privatization Law, quoted in *Japan-Russia Economic Research Data*, October 1991, p. 40. This article was not affected by the Amended Russian Privatization Law of June 11, 1992.

8 In addition, Novosibirsk and Primopskii Province of Siberia also report the dis-continuation of auctions. See Pashkov 1993: 2; Berezhnaia 1993; 5.

9 The wait-and-see attitude of Siberian investment funds awaiting enterprise privatiza-tion in European Russia is exerting another negative influence.

10 Article 24 of the Russian Privatization Law provides preferential treatment for managers and employees at the time of acquisition of their enterprises. It includes the right to installment payments for up to three years and the partial use of the enterprise's economic stimulation fund for the purchase in proportion to the number of employees who participate in the fund.

11 In one case in Ekaterinburg, managers sold a bakery attached to an enterprise without the knowledge of employees, who reported to work the next morning to discover that their jobs had been given to other workers. Hundreds of similar cases are also reported. See Barsukova 1993b: 80; Dmitrieva 1992; Babaeva and Nelson 1993: 108.

12 For more cases of misappropriation by state officials, see Pushkal' 1992: 2, and Keizerov 1993: 8.

13 In another case, a company with limited liability was set up by insiders to purchase an enterprise through auction, but the origin of its capital, amounting to 50 million rubles, remains unidentified. An illegal tie with an outsider is suspected. In this incident, six people with no intention of buying the company ceremonially partici-pated in the auction to meet the required formality. See Kariakina 1992: 3.

14 See note 11 for the episode in Ekaterinburg. The business conference reported in the

Economy and Life, no. 17, April 1992, p. 6, attributes the pervasiveness of such malfeasance to the disproportionate power accorded to the Property Management Committee in Moscow.

15 See Golubev 1992: 3, for government officials' bribe-taking and purchases of real properties with large injections of mafia-related funds.

References

Babaeva, L. and Nelson, L. (1993) Privatizatsiia: sotsial'naia baza podderzhki i sopro-tivleniia, *EKO* No.1.

Barsukova, S. (1993a) Malaia privatizatsiia: sponsory i trudovye kolletivy, *EKO* no. 7.

—— (1993b) Malaia privatizatsiia: kto, chto, zachem i pochemu, *EKO* no. 11.

—— (1993c) Dirktorskaia privatizatsia, *EKO* no. 12.

Berezhnaia, O. (1993) Goskomimushchestvo ne pozvolit predpriiatiiam svoevol'nichat', *Moskovskie novosti* 12, December.

Boiko, T. (1993) Chekovye auktsiony: pervye rezul'taty, *EKO* no. 10.

Bolkin, A. (1993) Otsenka privatizatsionnogo cheka na 1993 god, *Ekonomika i zhizn'* no. 4, January.

Bulantsev, V. (1993) Ekonomika Rossii v pervoi polovine 1993 g.: privatizatsia, *EKO* no. 10.

Bykov, A. (1994) O narusheniiakh zakonodatel'stva pri privatizatsii federal'noi sobstvennosti, *Ekonomika i zhizn'* no. 7, February.

Dmitrieva, L. (1992) Privatizatsiia, kto proigraet v kommercheskom konkurse, *Rossiiskie vesti* 27, June.

Ekonomika i zhizn' (1992a) Privatiizatsiia: pervye shagi, *Ekonomika i zhizn'* no. 14, April.

—— (1992b) Otdel ekonomicheskovo analiza i koniunktury rynka RFFI, Otsenka stoimosti vaucherev cherez balansovuiy stoimost' osnovnykh fondov, *Ekonomika i zhizn'* no. 47, November.

—— (1992c) Privatizatsionnye cheki: problemy realizatsii, *Ekonomika i zhizn'* no. 51, December.

—— (1994) Svodno-analiticheskii otdel RFFI, Osnovnye pokazateli khaoda privatizatsii v Rossiiskoi Federatsii na 1 XI 1993 g., *Ekonomika i zhizn'* no. 2, January.

Gel'vanovskii, M. (1993) Privatizatsiia cherez vauchrizatsiiu: obeshchaniia i real'nost', *Voprosy ekonomiki* no. 10.

Golubev, A. (1992) Prestupnyi kapital otsrochki ne daet, *Possiiskaia gazeta* 28, July.

Gorbatov, L. (1993) Chekovye fondy razopit'sia ne dozhdavshis' dividendov ot kuplen-nykh aktsii, *Finansovye izvestia* 19–25, June.

Goskomstat (1993a) *O razvitii ekonomicheskikh reform v Possiiskoi Federatsii v 1992 godu*, Moscow: Goskomstat.

—— (1993b) *Sotsial'no ekonomicheskom polozhenii Rossii v 1993 g.* Moscow: Goskomstat.

—— (1994) O sotsial'no ekonomicheskom polozhenii Rossii v 1993 g., *Ekonomika i zhizn'* no. 6, February.

Iakovlev, A. (1993) Gosydarstvennye predpriiatiia prodaiut deshevle, chem oni stoiat, *Finansovye izvestia* 13–19, March.

Izvestia (1992) Predpriiatiia prodolzhaiut skupat' vauchery, *Izvestia* 22, 23, December.

—— (1994) Vygodno li perezhidat' v okopakh chekovuiu privatizatsiiu? Na etot vopros *Izvestii* otvechaet A. Chubais, *Izvestia* 6, March.

Kariakina, T. (1992) Bankrot vykladyvaet milliony, *Possiiskaia gazeta* 29, July.

Keizerov, N. (1993) Chastnaia sobstvennost' nuzhdaetsia v zashchite, *Izvestia* 22, May.

Kolan'kov, A. and Grabarnik, V. (1993) Chastnoe litso mozzhet zarabotat' na bystrom oborote vauchera, *Finansovye izvestia* 12–18, June.

Kornev, V. (1994) 900% godovykh poluchat vladel'tsy aktsii, priobretennykh na chekovykh auktsionakh za vauchery, *Izvestia* 6, May.

Kotel'nikova, E. (1994a) Prezident legitimiziroval politiku goskomimushchestva, *Kommersant'-Daily* 11, January.

—— (1994b) Aktsionery ne poluchat obeshchannykh dovidendov, *Kommersant'-Daily* 20, January.

Mikhailov, S. (1993) Dvizhenie privatizatsionnykh chekov, *Voprosy ekonomiki* no. 10.

Pashkov, A. (1993) Razvedka boem, *Izvestia* 17, April.

Pushkal', A. (1992) Provintsial'naia nomenklatura rvetsia v millionery, *Izvestia* 24, April.

Rutgaizer, V. (1993a) Privatizatsiia v Rossii: dvizhenie "na oshchup"', *Voprosy ekonomiki* nos. 10–12.

—— (1993b) Privatizatsiia v. Rossii: dvizhenie "na oshchup"', *Voprosy ekonomiki*, no. 11.

Rutgaizer, V. and Shoiko, S. (1992) Privatizatsionnye cheki, *Ekonomika i zhizn'* no. 30, July.

Savvateeva, I. (1994) Zakrytsyi SOVMIN: vse tainoe stanovitsia iavnym, *Izvestia* 7, May.

Shatalin, S. (1994) Rynok trebuet upravleniia, *Ekonomica i zhizn'* No.5, February.

Shimov, Ia. (1993) Skol'ko stoit vaucher pensionera? *Izvestia* 21, December.

Skatershchikov, S. (1993) Investionnye fondy spkuliruiut radi vyzhivaniia, *Finansovye izvestia* 13–19, March.

Vestnik ekonomiki SSSR (1991) Russian Privatization Law, *Vestnik ekonomiki SSSR* October.

Volkov, V. (1993) O protsesse privatizatsii v Rossii, mimeo.

14

COUNTRY STUDY FOR JAPAN'S OFFICIAL DEVELOPMENT ASSISTANCE TO THE SOCIALIST REPUBLIC OF VIET NAM[1]

Japan International Cooperation Agency

I Introduction

This paper presents the findings of the Committee on the country study for Japan's Official Development Assistance to the Socialist Republic of Viet Nam. The findings are divided into three broad topics, namely, development conditions and issues, development scenarios, and aid strategies. This format basically follows the six-step aid strategy approach of the "Country Study for Japan's Official Development Assistance to the Arab Republic of Egypt" (April 1992).[2] Each topic is further broken down into three analytical dimensions: macro-economic stabilization, structural adjustment (policy and institutional reforms), and long-term development (which is an area of high relevance to current loan and grant aids).

II Summary of conclusions

A Long-term development

The Committee considers the chief issues and aid priorities for long-term development in Viet Nam to include rural economic restoration, rural industrialization, industrial policy formulation and implementation (including the provision of economic infrastructure), and human resource development.

In agriculture, the biggest issues confronting Viet Nam are the impoverishment of its rural economy and a lack of stable food supply. Rural impoverishment results from a combination of rapid population growth and a breakdown in basic infrastructure stemming from several decades of war. Stable food supply is put at risk by the fragile rice exports which, despite sustained surplus production in the south, are endangered any time harvests in the north and central regions are poor.

Solutions to these two issues are prerequisites to any improvement in social or political stability. We believe that the agricultural and rural issues confronting Viet Nam today command more urgency than similar agricultural and rural problems commonly witnessed elsewhere in the developing world.

The country's efforts at rural industrialization have just begun to get off the ground. Were Viet Nam to emulate China, rural industrialization could trigger heightened activity across the economy at large. In the short run, it could also be a means to rescue the country's beleaguered rural economy. The driving force for rural industrialization must be breakthroughs in productivity backed by institutional reforms and technological innovations in the agricultural sector. Owing to the exceptionally small acreage in cultivation on a per-farmer basis, especially in the north, those breakthroughs will not be easy. Therefore, policy supports and innovations within the rural sector itself will be critical in order to promote rural industrialization and revitalization in Viet Nam today.

Industrial policy recommended in this report refers to more than the maintenance and expansion of infrastructure in such areas as power generation, transportation, and communications. It also has to do with the selection of industrial sectors deserving priority development with strong government support, in the form of resources and policies. In policy documents released to date, Viet Nam has not articulated its development policies on an industry-by-industry basis, except in the area of infrastructure restoration. That silence appears to be in deference to the position of the IMF and the World Bank, namely that the market mechanism should guide the selection and operation of production activities unless increasing returns and other special causes warrant public investment in social overhead capital.

However, we believe it is essential that industrial priority lists for domestic and foreign-led investment be drawn up in developing countries where the market mechanism has yet to fully manifest itself. This is especially true in countries like Viet Nam that face an uncertain outlook in their trade balances. Viet Nam in particular has to decide how much promotion should be accorded to skill- and capital-intensive industries as an export base, in addition to textile and electrical and electronic product assembly which are labor-intensive. If entirely new industries are to be created which will use domestic oil and gas as inputs, proper development planning for these industries will become crucial. Viet Nam today seems to have limitless demand for investments in infrastructure. It is important, though, to balance available resources between infrastructure development needs and the need to cultivate the direct production sector in fields cited above. Attention to industrial policy has become increasingly apparent in policy making resolutions passed by major Communist Party assemblies since the start of 1994 (hence, the new popularity of terms such as "industrialization and modernization" in party slogans). Accordingly, it has become much easier to engage in a dialogue with the Vietnamese government on these issues.

Human resource development is an extremely serious issue spanning practically every dimension of economic and social endeavor. Its broad scope makes it difficult to set priorities for action, and additional studies are required for narrowing the policy targets in this area. Given widespread compulsory education and the comparatively high literacy rate, efforts at vocational training, and the education and training of mid- and high-level managers, are probably more urgent [than additional attention to primary education]. During the war years, opportunities for higher education and vocational training were poor and quality was low. Further, Viet Nam has not been fast enough in training its labor force in the skills needed to adapt to the rapid transition from a centrally planned economy to a market-driven economy. Measures to deal with these disparate issues will naturally demand different approaches.

B Macroeconomic stabilization

At first glance, it would appear that Viet Nam has shown significant success in the arena of macroeconomic management following the broad-based price liberalization introduced in 1989. At least on paper, the IMF and World Bank alike have showered Viet Nam with praise in this area. Those reforms compared closely with the "shock therapy" model of price liberalization which Russia launched in 1992. Especially noteworthy are the improvements witnessed in GDP growth and inflation. GDP growth declined only to about an annual 5 percent following the 1989 reforms, then recovered to run in the 8 percent range today. Also, though with some volatility, inflation has since fallen steadily from a high annual rate of close to 100 percent to the present 5 percent range. In tandem with these stabilizing trends, the domestic savings rate has risen substantially from the conspicuously low level it traced through the 1980s.

These accomplishments were an outcome of state policies pursued from 1990 to 1991 to rein in aggregate demand chiefly through cutbacks in fiscal expenditures (e.g., cuts in public investment and real cutbacks in civil servant pay). It was feared, however, that those policies exacted a heavy price on the country's potential for sustainable growth. To remedy the situation, in 1993, the government sought fiscal expenditure increases aimed at lifting the levels of public investment and improving civil servant pay. The hastiness of that policy reversal, however, contributed to a sharp surge in the fiscal budget deficit in the same year. In addition, the current account deficit began expanding again and consumer prices moved back up (Table 14.1). What these developments suggest for extremely low income countries like Viet Nam is that stabilization policies cannot take root without a steady rise in per capita GNP and real increases in savings and investment rates. (Prior to 1992 when foreign savings became readily available, this implied the need to increase *domestic* savings.)

One factor of relevance to the stabilization process is the dual nature of Viet Nam's economic structure, which consists of a dong economy and a dollar-and-gold economy. According to a survey of household income, savings, and credit conducted jointly by the United Nations Development Program (UNDP) and the State Planning Committee (SPC) in 1994, Vietnamese households maintained

Table 14.1 Viet Nam: key macroeconomic indicators

	1986	1987	1988	1989	1990	1991	1992	1993
GDP								
Nominal GDP (billion dong)	636	3,099	13,266	28,135	41,848	76,707	10,535	125,076
(annual % change)	385	387	328	112	49	83	44	24
Real GDP (annual % change)	3.4	3.9	5.1	8.0	5.0	6.0	8.6	8.1
Inflation (%)								
GDP deflator	370.0	370.0	310.0	70.0	49.7	73.0	35.0	13.2
Consumer prices	387.2	301.0	308.2	95.8	36.4	83.1	37.8	8.3
Sectoral share of GDP (%)								
Agriculture and forestry	...	...	...	40.8	37.3	39.5	33.0	29.3
Mining and manufacturing	...	...	...	22.9	24.1	23.8	27.1	28.4
Services	...	...	...	35.1	37.9	35.7	34.6	41.2
Labour (thousands)								
Population	60,249	61,750	63,263	64,774	66,233	67,774	69,405	70,918
Employment	27,399	27,968	28,477	28,941	26,915	31,094	31,815	32,718
Public sector	4,028	4,091	4,052	3,801	3,418	3,144	2,975	2,923
Private sector	23,371	23,877	24,425	25,140	26,197	27,950	28,840	29,793
External trade (US$ million)								
Trade balance	−627	−575	−679	−350	−41	−63	−60	−655
Exports	494	610	733	1320	1,731	2,042	2,475	2,850
Imports	1,121	1,184	1,412	1,670	1,772	2,105	2,535	3,505
Current account	−655	−624	−751	−586	−259	−132	−8	−869
Money (billion dong)								
Currency in dong	55	205	1,024	2,352	3,735	6,419	10,579	14,218
Bank deposits in dong	54	237	1,303	4,127	3,943	5,528	8,352	10,665
Demand deposits	...	...	...	1,615	1,578	2,707	4,232	4,870
Time deposits	...	...	...	1,357	2,365	2,821	4,120	5,794

Table 14.1 continued

	1986	1987	1988	1989	1990	1991	1992	1993
Foreign currency deposits	1	29	242	2,096	3,680	8,354	8,213	7,406
M₁	...	...	...	3,967	5,313	9,126	14,811	19,088
M₂	111	471	2,569	8,575	11,357	20,301	27,144	32,289
Exchange rate (dong/US$)	80	368	3,100	4,415	6,689	13,252	10,717	10,845
Budget (% of GDP)								
Revenue (incl. grants)	13.2	12.2	11.3	13.8	14.7	13.5	19.0	22.3
From state enterprises	9.5	9.2	7.2	8.0	8.7	8.1	10.8	11.8
Oil revenue	...	...	...	1.0	2.0	2.8	3.8	3.8
Expenditure	19.0	16.7	18.6	24.1	22.8	17.2	22.7	28.5
Current (excl. interest)	12.9	12.7	14.0	15.4	14.7	11.4	14.0	18.8
Capital	5.9	3.9	4.4	5.8	5.1	2.8	5.8	7.0
Interest payments	0.2	0.1	0.2	2.9	3.0	3.0	2.9	2.7
Primary balance	−5.7	−4.3	−7.0	−7.2	−5.1	−0.7	−0.8	−3.5
Overall balance	−5.8	−4.4	−7.2	−10.2	−8.1	−3.8	−3.7	−6.2

Sources: World Bank, *Public Sector Management and Private Sector Incentives*, 1994; and IMF data.

Note: Vietnamese statistics have long been MPS-based; the availability of SNA-based data is therefore highly limited. Moreover, data are often subject to large revisions. For instance, nominal GDP for the period prior to 1989 was revised significantly upward in 1994 in the statistics reported by the World Bank. As a result, the ratios to GDP of fiscal and monetary figures were revised downward.

47.5 percent of their real and financial assets in gold and dollars (of which 44 percent was in gold), and only 10.1 percent in domestic currency and 12.2 percent in dong-denominated bank deposits, stocks, and bonds.[3] Estimates are that the total amount of dollar currency in circulation has reached an equivalent of 8 trillion dong, or roughly half the amount of dong in circulation (16 trillion dong).

As these statistics demonstrate, gold and dollars play a vital role in the Vietnamese economy as units of account, means of payment, and – even more effectively – as stores of value. We as yet do not have an adequate understanding of how these features of the dollar-and-gold economy and the dong economy manifest themselves in the real economy, nor how they interact with each other. The data do suggest, however, that the gold-and-dollar side of the economy could in reality be supporting the stabilization trends that have surfaced on the dong side. They also indicate that current monetary policies will have limited effectiveness on the total economy should monetary authorities concentrate their efforts on the dong side of the economy alone. Furthermore, there is a large amount of evidence to suggest that Viet Nam's financial markets are still in the earliest stages of development.

In September 1994, the World Bank, IMF, and Vietnamese government struck an accord on a policy framework paper for the formulation of a medium-term program of stabilization and structural adjustment (1995–97). This agreement appears to be aimed at offsetting the structural weaknesses we described above and at placing the country on a path of sustainable growth. In tandem with prescribed structural adjustment measures discussed in the next section, it calls for annual GDP growth of 8 percent through the program period, conditioned on holding the annual inflation rate to 6 percent (equivalent to the expected inflation rate among Viet Nam's key trading partners) or less. To that end, the government is required to maintain the current fiscal surplus at 3.75–4.25 percent of GDP (and the overall fiscal deficit at 4.25 percent of GDP), and to keep the external current account deficit within a level equivalent to the inflows of concessional foreign financial assistance. Based on these targets, the World Bank in October 1994 agreed to furnish with Viet Nam $150 million in structural adjustment credit (SAC) as support for its medium-term program. The following month Viet Nam also reached agreement with the IMF on an enhanced structural adjustment facility (ESAF) worth $535 million, for a combined total of $685 million in new capital.

C Structural adjustment

In the arena of structural adjustment, also, at first glance it would appear that Vietnamese policies since 1989 have produced favorable results. In particular, success has been seen with the ban on fiscal-deficit financing through extension of central bank credit to the government (i.e., through the so-called process of "monetization"); the protection of central bank autonomy in the issuance of bank notes; ceilings on total lending to enterprises by state-owned banks; a ban on lending to enterprises with operating deficits; and the dismissal of redundant employees at state-owned enterprises. These measures have been implemented with a degree of determination unparalleled even in China. Despite their effectiveness to date, though, they could face immediate retraction depending on trends in the macroeconomic indicators discussed earlier.

As structural adjustment conditionalities attendant to the provision of abovementioned credit facilities, the World Bank and IMF prescribed tax reform, budget management, state enterprise reform, financial sector reform, and the liberalization of foreign trade. Further, as targets that should be achieved through the satisfaction of these conditionalities, the World Bank has called on Viet Nam to raise levels of national savings and domestic investment in the overall economy. These targets are consistent with our own views presented above and a position with which we concur. Nonetheless, as a complementary strategy toward raising savings and investment, we recommend that the scope of action be extended from structural adjustment to long-term development, that the Vietnamese government assume a leadership role in this enlarged strategy, and that Japan provide assistance to that end.

III Basic research stance behind study conclusions

The next three sections will present the basic research stance that supports our conclusions summarized above.

A A comparison of transition economies: Viet Nam, China, and Russia

This three-country comparison of economies in transition provides the broad foundation for our research. The term "transition economies" generally refers to those countries in the process of moving from centrally planned to market-oriented economic systems. Three dimensions shape the cross-country comparison outlined here.

1   First, it deserves noting that whereas Russia was already a fully industrialized and mature socialist state, Viet Nam and China entered the economic transition process as developing countries, which for the most part were still focused heavily on agriculture. (As Table 14.2 illustrates, the public sector, led chiefly by state-owned enterprises, accounted for 86 percent of total employment in Russia, compared to only 18 percent in China and 10 percent in Viet Nam.) In Russia's case, the challenges of transition have been limited to systemic reforms and stabilization efforts along the way. For China and Viet Nam, on the other hand, the demand of systemic reform has been compounded by the challenge of economic development itself. In addition, macroeconomic problems also existed in each country in varying degrees.

Table 14.2 Russia, China and Viet Nam: share of employment by type of employer and sector (percent)

	Russia (1988)	China (1992)	Viet Nam (1991)
A By type of employer			
1 Public sector	86.1	18.3	10.2
Government	. . .	5.4	4
State-owned enterprises	. . .	12.9	6.2
2 Cooperatives	5.3	23.9	58.7
Township and village enterprises	. . .	17.8	. . .
3 Private sector	8.6	57.8	31.2
B By sector			
Industry	25.9	17.2	11
Agriculture and forestry	20.2	58.6	73

Sources: Jeffrey Sachs and Wing Thye Woo, "Reform in China and Russia," Economic Policy, April 1994; *China Statistical Yearbook* 1993; and General Statistical Office, *Viet Nam Statistical Yearbook*.

Note: For China, the cooperative sector is the sum of urban collectives and township and village enterprises. Its private sector is the sum of urban and rural individual workers and workers of other units. Employees of township and village enterprises are deducted from rural individual workers to avoid double counting.

For Russia, the development process has essentially ended. That is to say, Russia's social division of labor in production[4] is already well advanced and its distribution infrastructure is sufficiently developed, albeit under a centrally planned economic system. In other words, it has already satisfied latent conditions for adoption of a more advanced market economy. Viet Nam and China, though, have not met those conditions yet, and to do so they still have to make further progress in industrialization. Institutional reforms alone would not prepare Viet Nam for that requisite step toward marketization. As noted earlier, Viet Nam's financial markets are still underdeveloped. Remedying that situation will be exceedingly difficult in the absence of parallel development efforts on the real side of the economy. This is one reason for our earlier assertion that the problems of systemic transition are often superimposed on the challenges of economic development.

2   Next, there are also certain advantages to facing lingering development problems in the transition to a market economy. Full development under a centrally planned system places most of the economy in the hands of state-owned enterprises, leaving few non-state sectors (Table 14.2). In a centrally planned economy, there are vast differences in the degrees of economic control over state-owned and non-state-owned sectors. In the state-owned sector, control is stern in the form of directed plans, affecting the enterprise's internal organization and modes of conduct. In the non-state sector, by contrast, control is limited mainly to regulations on distribution and pricing; typically, it does not extend to internal organization or modes of conduct. In

moving to a market economy, state-owned enterprises will therefore face more difficulties in changing their behavior even after they are privatized, compared with non-state businesses which tend to perform well once regulations are removed. This is the reason why reforms have failed to show much success in Russia, where state-owned enterprises dominated, but are working effectively overall in China and Viet Nam, where such enterprises represent a smaller share of the economy.[5]

3   A further comparison between Viet Nam and China is possible within the general context outlined above. As already noted, the non-state sector is relatively large in both countries. For both, introducing market-oriented economic reforms into the non-state sector can help achieve a critical mass to spur a leap in productive activity throughout the economy. China, in fact, has already translated this potential into reality, and since 1991 has continued to register annual GDP growth averaging 13 percent. For the Chinese, the process went as follows. First, institutional reforms and innovations in production technology sparked breakthroughs in agricultural sector productivity. That triggered a boom in rural industrialization, led by township and village enterprises. This boom, in conjunction with foreign direct investment, provided the catalyst for a sharp expansion in the production of labor-intensive export goods.

Viet Nam, however, has yet to harness its potential. The extremely small scale of per-farmer acreage under cultivation has been cited as one reason, but China faced essentially the same conditions in districts that today have demonstrated dramatic increases in agricultural productivity. On this point, therefore, more intensive research is needed to determine whether another more decisive constraint has been in play in Viet Nam, and if not, to ask what lessons Viet Nam can glean from the Chinese experience.

4   It must also be noted that Viet Nam, China, and Russia are also distinguished by differences that the above comparative framework cannot explain. For one thing, Viet Nam stands out as a country heavily impacted by war on its territory for over three decades, from the closing days of World War II to 1975. To be sure, China and Russia too have been disadvantaged. In Russia, for instance, the unproductive defense sector accounted for 60 percent of total industrial production. Farmer ignorance of market-oriented management practices throughout Russian history has been blamed, moreover, for the languishing state of Russian agriculture. Collective farms were long divorced from ownership of farm machinery under the state-run machine tractor station (MTS) system established under Stalin's rule. Further back, the emancipation of Russian serfs in 1861 furnished the institutional framework for Russian agriculture prior to the debut of collective farms. Even then, land ownership was a right accorded only to rural communities and not individual farmers.

B Development assistance strategies for low-income countries

Drawing on comparisons with Russia and China, the foregoing presented perspectives that should help in understanding Viet Nam's development challenges as an economy in transition. But while Viet Nam is an economy in transition, it is also a developing country – a typical "low-income" economy by the classification of the World Bank.[6] With this in mind, we now turn to an explanation of a view gradually gaining broader support as the Japanese position on economic development strategy, a view that seems particularly applicable to Viet Nam as a low-income country.

(1) Economic system reform

Market economies are underdeveloped in most developing countries. Dirigiste economic systems,[7] of which centrally planned economies are one variety, are one factor distorting the market economy in these countries. However, removing that factor alone will not cure the underdevelopment of the market economy when other pre-existing distortions are present. We term these "innate distortions" and distinguish them from "artificial distortions" attributable to state control. In such instances, efforts must be made to create and enhance the market economy itself, if that system is to take root. But what exactly should be done? Development of a market economy requires work to promote the social division of labor, and to establish physical infrastructure (including networks for trade and commerce, transport, and communications) as well as institutional infrastructure (including emergence of entrepreneurs and the rules for protecting contracts and the right of ownership).[8] In addition to infrastructure building, efforts must be made to bolster productivity, primarily through industrialization, in order to deepen the social division of labor and realize the goal of marketization.

(2) Bolstering productivity

Apart from systemic transition, boosting national vitality and production is itself a legitimate policy objective of developing countries. Steps to raise savings and investment levels will be an essential element of such policies, but high savings and investment alone will not achieve economic development if the market economy of that country remains underdeveloped. Industrial policy is often used to remedy this situation. In the execution of industrial policy, the most important thing is to identify the development path suited to a country's resource endowment and stage of development, and to steer savings and investment flows in that direction. Models based on the experience of other countries are useful in selecting suitable development paths.

One such model is the dual-economy development model, which calls for creating a new industrial sector and supplying it with labor from the agricultural sector, an approach particularly suitable for countries where heavy population densities effectively leave no more farmland available for cultivation. Another model of vent-for-surplus addresses economies driven by the export of primary commodities, as patterned on development in countries that have substantial uncultivated land but suffer shortages of labor supply. In the process of successful development, the situation of a shortage of one primary factor of production (land or labor) coupled with a surplus of the other is rectified by proper investment in capital, an "artificial" factor of production, in a manner that puts the surplus factor to productive use while compensating for the deficiency of the other. Consider, for example, the differences behind investments in flood control and irrigation [which augment land in densely-populated, land-scarce countries] on the one hand and in tilling and threshing machinery [which augment labor in sparsely-populated, land-abundant countries].

However, both the dual-economy and primary-commodity-export models of development are abstractions from historical experience. These models need to be modified or extended to fit the circumstances of contemporary developing countries. For instance, under the dual-economy model, this would include the addition of a substage characterized by an increase in agricultural productivity and rural industrialization, and the experience of domestic economic development accompanied by foreign trade and investment. Under the primary-commodity-export model, it would include experience in shifting to intensive agriculture after the arable frontier has been fully exploited, and then pursuing industrialization through the new cross-industrial linkages. Below, references to such development models will be concerned with extended variants that take these factors into account.

(3) Policy tools for systemic transition

The World Bank and IMF refer to the transition in a developing country from a state-controlled economic system to a market-driven one as "structural adjustment." In implementing structural adjustment policy, the Bank and the Fund strive to replace the mechanisms for state control by various systems imported from countries with highly developed market economies. Though we regard it as obvious, World Bank surveys of countries undertaking structural adjustment reforms, in 1988, 1990, and 1992, show that structural adjustment measures that are effective in middle-income countries tend to be of little help in low-income countries.

Developing countries, and especially low-income countries, do not necessarily have to rely on the market mechanism in order to strengthen market economies. Such countries should utilize state intervention in line with appropriately designed programs for action. Assistance from the industrialized world should be used to support state intervention of this kind.

The above three points form the basis for our position in the formulation of economic development strategy of Viet Nam, expounded in the main report [not included here]. Here, we shall offer some additional remarks on the first and second points in the context of Viet Nam.

On the first point regarding economic systems reform, it should be under-scored that Viet Nam's market economy is one of the least developed in the world, as should be evident from its per capita GDP of $150. Another indicator of this is Viet Nam's low M_2-to-GDP ratio[9] at only slightly above 20 percent, a ratio that expresses the degree of monetization and financial intermediation in the economy. Barter exchange is said to be the dominant form of commerce in the central highlands and northern flood plains. What is more, bank deposits and check-based methods of settlement (especially between separate regions) have yet to take root even in transactions among state-owned enterprises. The main report draws on historical observations to further highlight the backward-ness of Viet Nam's market economy.

On the second point regarding development models, the distinction between the northern delta which has been densely populated and intensively cultivated throughout history and the southern delta which was opened more recently should be noted. Given these differences, it would appear that the dual-economy model is more appropriate to the north and the primary-commodity-export model to the south. However, as we shall argue in the main report, agricultural con-ditions are not uniformly good in the south; intensive multi-season agriculture on new delta farmland exists side-by-side with extensive lowland tracts of reclaimed farmland still plagued by poor soil quality and poor drainage. Agricultural support measures in the south should include a modernization drive through expanded infrastructure investment in the areas where intensive agriculture is already established, together with large-scale projects in farmland improvement and a shift to intensive agriculture in the lowland regions. If these efforts in agrarian development are undertaken, the challenge of industrialization will also emerge. Given that prospect, we believe that it is appropriate to adopt the dual-economy model as an approximate guide for a study of the overall economic development of Viet Nam.

C The distant shape of Viet Nam's market economy

Vietnamese economic policy documents are notable for their frequent use of "state-regulated" and "socialist" as modifiers for the phrase "market economy" when discussing the objectives of government transition policies. It is perhaps best not to read too much into such expressions. Viet Nam is still a communist-ruled country. No doubt, its Communist Party faced various hurdles in making market orientation the centerpiece of official economic policy. To ensure a smooth transition, perhaps party leaders needed to explain to other party officials that the shift was not a break with past policy, but rather a continuation. If there was any internal controversy over the issue, the party likely would have faced the need to resolve it through compromise, not confrontation. To be sure, it is important to pursue the meaning of such phrasing through analysis of available literature, and we would respect any responsible conclusions drawn therefrom. Nonetheless, our present intention is to focus on the market economy itself from the perspective of economic analysis. This is also the guiding principle behind our interest in policy documents in general. Accordingly, in this report, we intend to limit our observations to the purview of development economics and political economy of development.

As to the design of the market economy which Viet Nam is now working to build, we see no reason to be concerned with how the design differs from systems based on *laissez-faire* capitalism, whether such differences are good or bad, or about the shape the economy could take at some point in the future. At present, Viet Nam's leaders appear to be doing their best to understand and realize the model of the market economy proposed by the IMF and World Bank. It is impossible at this juncture to predict what shape Viet Nam's market economy will take after it has undergone the test of reality for an extended period of time. Three types of market economies are widely recognized in the industrialized world: the U.S. *laissez-faire* model, the strongly interventionist Japanese model with its emphasis on industrial policy, and the continental European model which fits somewhere in between the U.S. and Japanese models. Which of these – or any other – models Viet Nam's market economy ultimately emulates is not a question demanding serious concern at this time.[10]

D A broader perspective in economic assistance

In contemplating aid strategy for Viet Nam, apart from studying the Vietnamese economy itself, we must also be aware of the basic goals of Japanese aid to that country. We believe that economic aid to Viet Nam is consistent with the goal of promoting economic cooperation with the countries of Southeast Asia, a cornerstone of Japan's international economic policy. At present, the most important objective in this region should be providing assistance aimed at helping Indochina achieve lasting peace and prosperity. Hence, it is desirable to extend our focus to Viet Nam's relationships with its two Indochinese neighbors and with other countries in Southeast Asia, and consider aid for Viet Nam in that broader context. Among them, China and NIEs warrant special attention because of their key roles in the history of Viet Nam and in today's international economy. These external relations of Viet Nam provide the background for our study. However, in the substance of the following report, we will concentrate on the analysis of the Vietnamese economy itself.

Notes

1 This official report dated March 1995 was prepared by the Committee mentioned in the text, a study group organized by the Japan International Cooperation Agency. The "Introduction with the Summary of Conclusions" (i.e., executive summary) of this report was drafted by Shigeru Ishikawa, chairperson of the study group. The present chapter reproduces the first half of this executive summary [Editors].

2 The study group which produced the report on Egypt was also headed by Ishikawa [Editors].

3 UNDP and State Planning Committee, *Reports on Income, Savings and Credit for 1994 in Viet Nam*, Hanoi, 1994.

4 Social division of labor means an expansion of the physical domain of production and exchange, that is to say, the web of input–output linkage and merchandise distribution is expanded to encompass the entire country (and beyond) so that each economic unit or region produces mainly for others and not for self-sufficiency. This process is normally accompanied by rising productivity. Ishikawa cites (1) social division of labor, (2) infrastructure for merchandise distribution, and (3) acceptance of rules for market exchange, as the three basic conditions for the development of a market economy – see Chapter 6 of this volume [Editors].

5 Harvard University Professor Jeffrey Sachs, who supports Russia's shock-therapy program, draws the same distinction in explaining the divergent Russian and Chinese track record in economic reform.

6 The World Bank classifies any country with a per capita GNP equal to or less than $675 in 1992 dollars as a low-income economy.

7 Ishikawa defines dirigisme as a system where the existing market economy remains seriously underdeveloped and subject to vigorous state intervention – see Chapter 6 of this volume [Editors].

8 See note 4 above [Editors].

9 M_2 is defined as the sum of currency in circulation and demand and time deposits at banks.

10 It is interesting to compare Ishikawa's argument on the *irrelevance* of the ultimate shape of the market economy with Aoki's assertion that a multi-pronged approach should be taken in building institutions in a transition economy, since the most appropriate type of market economy is *uncertain* at the outset (Chapter 8 of this volume). While both remain open to the distant shape of the economy, their reasons for remaining neutral about future institutions are different [Editors].

15

OWNERSHIP, PERFORMANCE, AND MANAGERIAL AUTONOMY

A survey of manufacturing enterprises in Viet Nam[1]

Izumi Ohno

The purpose of this paper is to examine complex questions on the relations between ownership, performance and managerial incentives and draw implications for transition strategies in Viet Nam, by conducting empirical analyses drawn from a survey of 200 manufacturing enterprises in Viet Nam. Viet Nam's experience in state enterprise reform is unique in several aspects: (1) official statistics indicate that the state enterprise sector is a major contributor to the rapid growth in industrial production; and (2) Viet Nam, like China, has been cautious about implementing a program of large-scale privatization. Instead, priority has been placed on expanding managerial autonomy of enterprises and hardening the budget constraint on state-owned enterprises.

The results of our empirical analysis of roughly 200 Vietnamese manufacturing enterprises do not support the standard view held by "big bang" economists that private ownership is necessarily superior to state or public ownership, or that state enterprises are resistant to restructuring and thus associated with inefficiency. Rather the evidence suggests that: (1) factors specific to each enterprise (such as managerial autonomy, size, industrial sector, and degree of competition) are more strongly associated with performance; and (2) Vietnamese state enterprises have sufficient supply–response capacity and adaptability to adjust to the new market environment. In fact, during 1991–94, many state enterprises improved their performance and made a difficult adjustment to new conditions by shedding redundant labor. All enterprise managers now perceive that the market is competitive. These findings suggest that a two-track approach has been working in Viet Nam and that the absence of immediate privatization has not prevented restructuring in Vietnamese enterprises.

At the same time, the evidence suggests the need for continued efforts to improve the business environment for private enterprise, particularly through financial sector reforms. It is essential to analyze the major weaknesses in the present banking system and take measures to improve the system's efficiency. Parallel efforts should be also made to expand private sector access to bank financing.

I Problem setting

There is a lively debate concerning the pace and proper sequencing of systemic transition. The "big-bang" approach, supported by many Western economic advisors, recommends a package of rapid liberalization measures that covers both state and new non-state enterprises, accompanied by comprehensive privatization of state industry over the course of a few years (Sachs and Woo 1993, 1994a, 1994b).[2] In contrast, "gradualists" advocate a "two-track" approach, in which the government liberalizes the non-state sector of the economy while retaining control of the state sector until certain basic institutions in support of a market economy are put in place. The gradualists argue that market institutions cannot be created overnight and that there are potentially large risks of institutional breakdown (e.g., a drastic loss of government revenues, unemployment, and disruption in productive activities), if the old system is shattered without the establishment of an alternative system.[3]

Among other issues, the two approaches differ sharply in the supposed proper steps to reform state-owned enterprises (SOEs). Big-bang supporters argue that the transfer of ownership from the state to private hands is a prerequisite for improving enterprise performance; unless rapidly privatized, state enterprises would not have managerial incentives to restructure. Their argument finds theoretical backing in the Coase Theorem, which states that if property rights are assigned clearly, individuals have incentive to work out efficient economic arrangements. The essential problem with socialism is the inherent ambiguity of property rights because when property is owned by the "state" everyone wants a claim to it but no one is willing to bear the burden of maintaining it. On the other hand, gradualists argue that a solution other than immediate privatization exists for reforming SOE activities. They often cite the example of China, where Township and Village Enterprises (TVEs), although mostly under public owner-ship, have enhanced their performance under expanded managerial autonomy and have become a dynamic element in China's economic development.[4] The recent theory of information economics also stresses that in large organizations, ownership may be less important than designing good incentive structures, i.e. corporate governance (Stiglitz 1994).

Can enterprise reform work without a change in ownership? Is private owner-ship necessary – or sufficient – to improve efficiency? What are the relations between ownership, performance, and managerial incentives? Our review of developing countries experiences and of the progress of reform in Russia, Poland, and China suggest that: (1) the privatization of state enterprises requires far greater effort and much more time than was originally anticipated; (2) the speed of privatization should not be the only criterion for judging reform success, and greater attention must be paid to how to establish effective corporate governance; and (3) as shown in the commercialization of China's TVEs, immediate privatization may not be necessary for successful reform – but diversifying ownership, providing financial incentives, and encouraging entry are very important; at least in the case of China, the more gradual approach aimed at a "soft landing" for state enterprise reform appears to be working.

The purpose of this paper is to shed light on these complex questions and verify the above preliminary findings, based on empirical analyses of survey data on 199 manufacturing enterprises in Viet Nam. It will also draw implications for reform strategies in Viet Nam and other transitional economies. The survey was conducted by the Planning Department of the State Planning Committee[5] during November–December 1994, with financial assistance from the Research Institute of Development Assistance (RIDA) of the Overseas Economic Cooperation Fund (OECF).

Although the survey has several limitations (e.g., limited availability of detailed quantitative information on costs and profits – due partly to managers' unfamiliarity with basic business concepts and weak SOE accounting systems as well as our resource constraints), we believe that our investigation deserves special attention for the following four reasons:

1   This is the first, major empirical work to examine the relationships among ownership, performance, and managerial incentives regarding Vietnamese enterprises. Although several firm surveys have been conducted in Viet Nam in recent years, they did not deal with these theoretical issues directly.[6]

2   According to official statistics, the SOE sector is a major contributor to the recent rapid growth in industrial production (see Figures 15.1 and 15.2). The evidence also suggests that SOEs, particularly those that are centrally-owned, have been growing faster than non-SOEs. It is worthwhile to verify this observation and analyze its causes based on firm-level micro data.

3   Viet Nam's unique experience in SOE reform, if successful, can offer useful lessons to other transitional economies. Viet Nam, like China, started SOE reforms in the early 1980s by expanding managerial autonomy and introducing competition while retaining state ownership. However, the reforms have accelerated since the adoption of Doi Moi [meaning renovation, a policy of economic liberalization and openness] in 1986 and particularly from 1989 onwards. Also, measures aimed at hardening SOE budget constraints were introduced far more rapidly than in China.

4   Because SOE reform is high on the government's agenda, in-depth analysis of the survey results may contribute to current policy debates, including the drafting of State Enterprise Law and related regulations, a pilot equitization program, a pilot program for enterprise grouping, strengthening of SOE financial management, and reducing intermediary institutions such as unions and corporations.

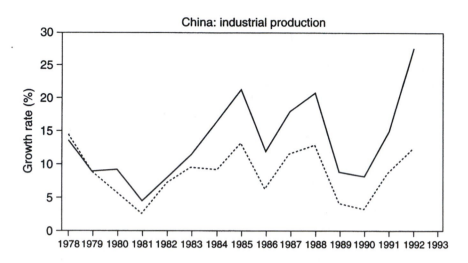

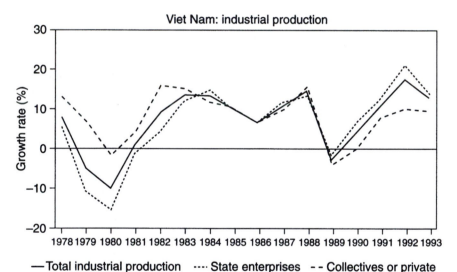

—Total industrial production ···· State enterprises − − Collectives or private

Figure 15.1 China and Viet Nam: growth rates of industrial production

This paper is organized as follows. First, to clarify the motives for reform and put them in the broader context of the Vietnamese economy, section II outlines recent industrial development and SOE reforms in Viet Nam. Section III presents the survey methodology and results of empirical analyses. Special effort has been made to identify key determinants of enterprise performance. Section IV discusses implications of the analysis as well as policy issues relevant to Vietnamese reform strategies. Section V is the conclusion.

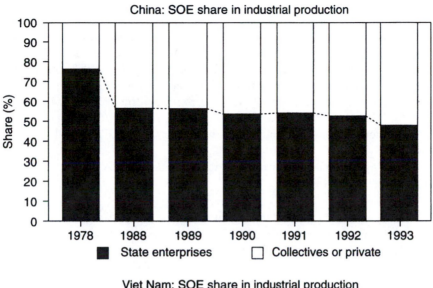

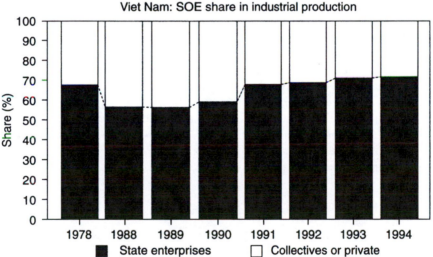

Figure 15.2 China and Viet Nam: shares of state-owned enterprises in industrial production

II Industrial development and SOE reform in Viet Nam

Industrial development

Over the past fifteen years, Viet Nam has been making a transition to a market economy, although its path has not always been smooth. Initial structural reforms, such as the decollectivization of agriculture and the encouragement of small private businesses, laid the foundation for a comprehensive program of macroeconomic reforms and development of market institutions in later years. These reforms produced notably good results by the early 1990s. Real GDP growth accelerated from 5–6 percent during 1990–91, to 8.6 percent in 1992, 8.1 percent in 1993 and 8.5 percent in 1994. Industry (together with construction) has been a major contributor to rapid economic growth. Real GDP growth in industry increased from 2.5 percent in 1990, to 9.9 percent in 1991, 14.6 percent in 1992, 12.1 percent in 1993, and 12.9 percent in 1994. It is estimated that industry alone accounted for more than 30 percent of real GDP growth in 1993 and 1994.

According to official statistics, recent industrial development in Viet Nam can be characterized as follows:

- Heavy industry – particularly the oil and gas sector – was the driving force behind industrial growth until 1991, contributing about 70 percent of the change in industrial GDP in 1991 (44 percent in the case of oil and gas). However, in recent years, there has been rapid growth in light industry, including textiles and garments, electrical machinery, food processing, paper, wooden products, and construction materials.
- In industry, SOEs continue to dominate, with their share in total industrial production rising from 56 percent in 1986 to 70 percent in 1992. The emerging private sector remains concentrated in service and trading activities, and its involvement in production is limited.
- SOEs have been growing faster than non-SOEs, at 11.2 percent (1993) and 11.0 percent (1994) compared with the non-SOE growth of 5.6 percent and 7.0 percent respectively.[7] However, the performance gap has narrowed recently. Available data also suggest that, on average, centrally-owned SOEs have performed better than locally-owned SOEs.

State-owned enterprise reforms

Vietnam's SOE reforms date back to 1981. Like China, Viet Nam has been cautious about implementing a program of large-scale equitization (or privatization). Instead, the authorities have placed priority on: (1) improving enterprise governance through increased managerial autonomy (phase 1: 1981–86, and phase 2: 1987–89); (2) hardening budget constraints through various measures: the elimination of operating subsidies, interest rate reforms, tight monetary policy, and increased competition through trade liberalization and deregulation of private businesses (1989–90); and (3) reducing the number of SOEs from 12,000 to 7,000 by launching a re-registration program, where loss-making enterprises were liquidated or merged with other SOEs (1991–94).

Furthermore, the following new initiatives have been introduced, in order to help SOEs adapt to a market-oriented mechanism:

- a pilot equitization program aimed at transforming a limited number of medium-scale and non-strategic SOEs into shareholding companies (Prime Minister's Decisions 202: 1992 and 84: 1993);
- strengthening financial management of SOEs by improving accounting, auditing, and monitoring, and by taking measures to settle SOE overdue debts;
- a pilot program for the establishment of enterprise groups, aimed at strengthening international competitiveness via concentration and separating management from ownership through the introduction of a modern corporate system (Decision 91: 1994);
- the preparation of a State Enterprise Law and related regulations, aimed at establishing clear criteria for identifying "strategic" firms that provide essential public services, and specifying the management and operational structure of these firms (The State Enterprise Law was approved in the National Assembly in late April 1995).

As a result, it is estimated that the number of loss-making SOEs has declined from 30–40 percent to below 20 percent during the past few years. Major labor adjustment also took place, and employment in SOEs decreased from 2.1 million to 1.7 million during 1990–93 (World Bank 1994).[8]

The following sections attempt to verify these positive developments through firm survey data, examine the key determinants of enterprise performance, and draw implications on strategies for transitional reforms for both Viet Nam and other countries.

III Methodology and survey results

Sample and methodology

A sample of 208 enterprises was selected randomly from a list of manufacturing enterprises (centrally-owned SOEs, locally-owned SOEs, and private enterprises) registered at the Planning Department of the State Planning Committee (SPC).[9] Due to time and budget constraints, the sample was restricted to the two big cities of Hanoi and Ho Chi Minh City where about 27 percent of the total Vietnamese enterprises, both state-owned and private, are located. Enterprises were chosen from seven manufacturing sectors: textiles and garments; chemicals; food processing; metallurgy; non-electrical machinery; electrical machinery; and other miscellaneous light manufacturing (such as paper, printing, leather, wooden products).

Special efforts were made to ensure a fair representation of enterprise structure in the two cities (1) by including at least ten enterprises per city from each sector (to allow for balanced analysis at the sector level) and reflecting the actual sectoral composition of enterprises in the two cities; and (2) by reflecting the actual ownership composition of enterprises in the two cities. The 208 enterprises consist of: 85 centrally-owned SOEs, 63 locally-owned SOEs, and 60 private enterprises. A total of 101 enterprises are drawn from Hanoi, and 107 enterprises are from Ho Chi Minh City. The SOEs in this sample account for 24–43 percent of the above seven manufacturing sectors in the two cities, and the private enterprises in the sample represent more than 10 percent of such manufacturing firms registered in the two cities.[10]

The survey methodology and questionnaires were designed by OECF's RIDA, and the actual survey – in the form of questionnaires and follow-up interviews – was conducted by the Planning Department of SPC simultaneously in Hanoi and Ho Chi Minh City during November–December 1994. The questionnaire contains comprehensive questions (83 items) on: basic enterprise information, production, employment, management, financing, physical assets, raw materials and inputs, sales/marketing/distribution, and competition. The empirical analysis in this paper deals with 199 enterprises because nine enterprises are judged to have completed the questionnaire incorrectly.

It should be noted that the survey has several limitations. First, due to resource constraints, it was not possible to obtain detailed quantitative information on costs and profits at the sample enterprises. Weak accounting systems in target enterprises also made quantitative analysis difficult. Second, some managers did not understand fully certain basic concepts such as capacity utilization, profits, and joint ventures. Thus, it is possible that survey questions were not answered according to the same objective criteria. Third, it was found that many enterprises have diversified their product mixes during 1991–94 in response to changing market conditions. While this is sensible firm behavior, it complicated sectoral analysis.

Analytical framework

The empirical analysis is conducted in the following steps. First, to obtain a reliable performance measure of the 199 enterprises, the Performance Index (PI) is generated by combining five indicators: capacity utilization rate (1994), changes in nominal profits (1993–94), the ratio of redundant labor to total labor (1994), and perceived competitiveness against domestic products, as well as imports (1994). The weights are devised from the first principal component of the covariance matrix. It is statistically confirmed that the factor loadings of this component carry reasonable signs and sufficient explanatory power. The PI is further normalized to have a minimum of 0 (worst) and a maximum of 1,000 (best). (See Appendix) The use of the PI is considered necessary because ranking performance of the sampled enterprises by a single indicator carries risks. (For example, managers are not yet familiar with basic business concepts as explained above; and half of the private enterprises in the sample were created only after 1991.) Through principal component analysis, we can obtain a more robust performance index while ascertaining the reliability of each individual indicator.

Second, to measure the degree of managerial autonomy, the Control Index (CI) is formed by counting the number of management decisions controlled by public authorities: annual production targets, investment levels, allocation of retained profits, worker recruitment, worker lay-off, appointment of top managers, and the recruitment base of top managers. A large CI indicates less managerial autonomy.

Third, to explain PI variations among the 199 enterprises, performance equations are estimated by including some or all of the following explanatory variables: CI, ownership, sector, location, merger, joint venture, excess competition, labor size, access to subsidy, access to bank financing, and degree of market access (i.e., input purchase and output sales at market). Most of these variables are in dummy forms. Correlations among these variables are also examined. Diagrams are also produced to supplement regression results.

Empirical results

Performance and ownership

Figure 15.3 indicates the distribution of the performance index (PI) by ownership. No simple relations are found between the two variables. It appears that SOEs, particularly centrally-owned SOEs, are doing better than is generally assumed. The average PI is highest for centrally-owned SOEs (616) and lowest for locally-owned SOEs (566), with private enterprises falling in between

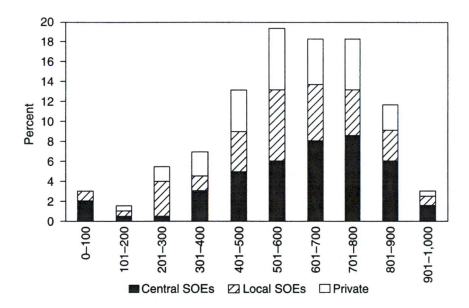

Figure 15.3 Viet Nam: performance index distribution

287

(582). The mode (highest occurrence) is found in the category of 701–800 for centrally-owned SOEs and in 501–600 for both locally-owned SOEs and private enterprises. We found no private enterprises with a PI below 100, while four centrally-owned SOEs and two locally-owned SOEs are found in this worst category.

Moreover, performance varies significantly within each ownership type. As Table 15.1 shows, some enterprises are doing well while others are not. This implies that factors specific to each enterprise, other than ownership, are important in determining performance. These findings are also confirmed by analysis of individual performance indicators such as nominal sales growth, change in nominal profits, change in capacity utilization, and perceived competitiveness against both domestic products and imports (Figures 15.4 to 15.8).

Table 15.1 Viet Nam: performance index distribution

	Total	Central SOEs	Local SOEs	Private
0–100	6	4	2	0
101–200	3	1	1	1
201–300	11	1	7	3
301–400	14	6	3	5
401–500	26	10	8	8
501–600	38	12	14	12
601–700	36	16	11	9
701–800	36	17	9	10
801–900	23	12	6	5
901–1000	6	3	2	1
Total	199	82	63	54

The degree of managerial autonomy

There has been considerable progress in the expansion of managerial autonomy in SOEs, except for the appointment of top managers. Almost all SOEs indicated that public authorities decide their top managers. This finding is consistent with Decision 217–HDBT and related managerial reforms undertaken by the Vietnamese government during 1987–89.[11] Other than this, nearly half of SOEs answered that they are subject to one of the six remaining control indicators. About 30 percent of SOEs replied that they are subject to two controls (including top appointment). Only 20 percent are subject to more than three controls (including top appointment). Needless to say, there is very little government intervention in the management of private enterprises (Figure 15.9).

More importantly, the number of management decisions controlled by public authorities is inversely related to SOE performance (Figure 15.10). In other words, SOEs tend to perform better when they are given greater managerial

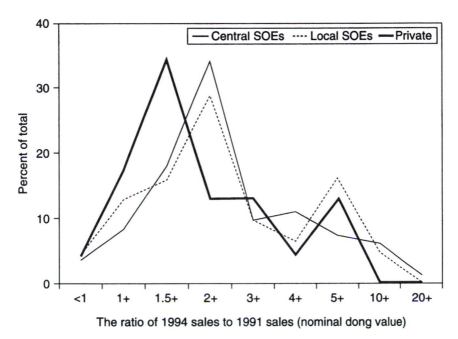

Figure 15.4 Viet Nam: distribution of nominal sales growth, by ownership

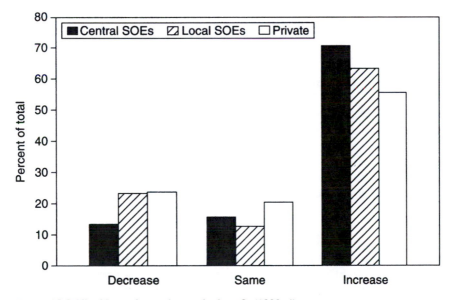

Figure 15.5 Viet Nam: change in nominal profit (1993–4)

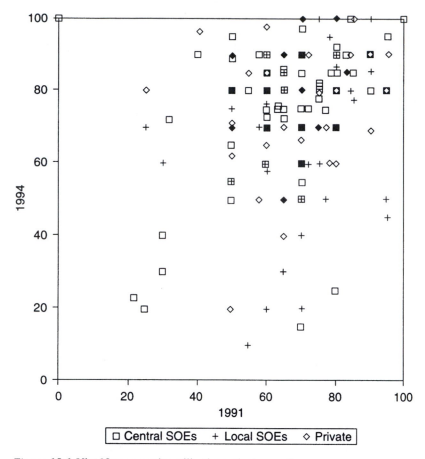

Figure 15.6 Viet Nam: capacity utilization ratio (percent)

autonomy. The importance of managerial autonomy is confirmed by another question included in the survey, where about one-third of the SOEs indicated a desire for the government to adopt one or more of the following measures: simplifying administrative formalities, defining the responsibility of ministries or provincial governments more clearly, abolishing intermediary institutions, and/or strengthening enterprise autonomy (SPC 1995a, 1995b).

Labor redundancy

All private enterprises answered that there was no redundant labor in either 1991 or 1994, which is quite normal for private businesses during a period of vigorous economic growth. What is more striking is the fact that considerable labor shedding has already occurred in many SOEs. As a result, about 80 percent of SOEs answered that they have no excess labor as of end-1994 (Figure 15.11).

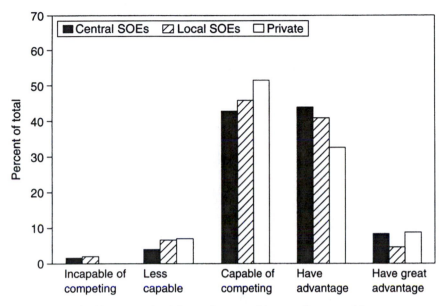

Figure 15.7 Viet Nam: perceived domestic competitiveness, by ownership

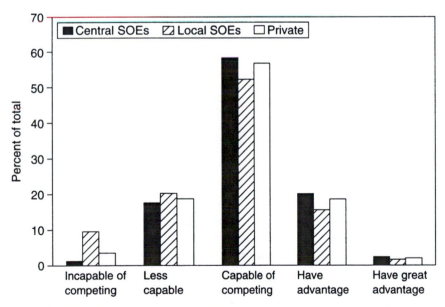

Figure 15.8 Viet Nam: perceived competitiveness against imports, by ownership

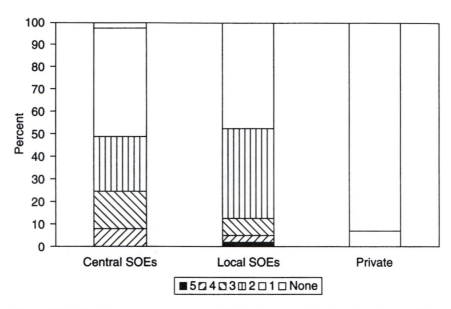

Figure 15.9 Viet Nam: government control index, by ownership (number of controlled decisions)

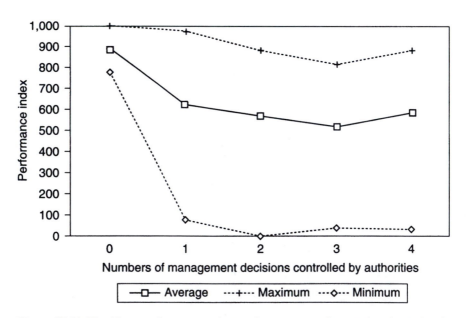

Figure 15.10 Viet Nam: performance and control – state-owned enterprises (central and local government)

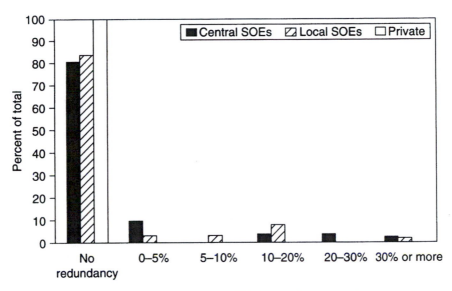

Figure 15.11 Viet Nam: labor redundancy in 1994 (ratio of excess workers to total workforce)

The drastic labor adjustment within SOEs is well documented in a report prepared by the Planning Department of SPC. During 1991–94, in Hanoi the number of redundant workers per enterprise decreased from 59 to 14 persons in centrally-owned SOEs, and from 39 to 15 persons in locally-owned SOEs. Similarly, in Ho Chi Minh City, the number decreased from 10 to 1 person in centrally-owned SOEs, and from 4 to almost zero in locally-owned SOEs. During the three-year period, in Hanoi the percentage of redundant labor in the total labor force declined from 8 percent to 2 percent in centrally-owned SOEs, and from 9 percent to 4 percent in locally-owned SOEs. In Ho Chi Minh City, this ratio declined from 1 percent to almost zero in both types of SOEs (SPC 1995a). Judging from the generally improved performance in SOEs, it is possible to conclude that such labor shedding has led to increased labor productivity in SOEs.

Performance by sector

Sectoral factors are accountable for at least part of the performance differences. As Figure 15.12 shows, the food processing and non-electrical machinery sectors are performing poorly compared to the other five manufacturing sectors. In terms of the average PI, the metallurgy sector scores the highest (672), followed by textiles and garments (643), miscellaneous light manufacturing (628), electrical machinery (617), and chemicals (596). However, the good performance of the metallurgy sector needs careful interpretation because of its small sample size. (Only eight metallurgy enterprises are located in Hanoi and Ho Chi Minh City, of which three are included in the sample.)

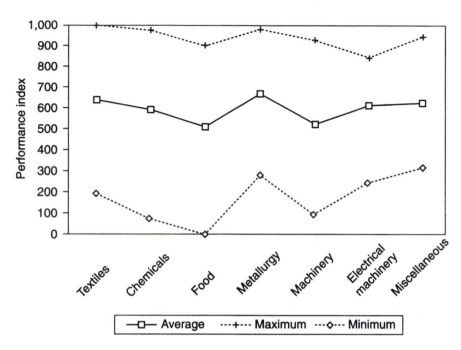

Figure 15.12 Viet Nam: performance by industry (all enterprises)

Sectoral differences in the PI are even more clear, when the sample is limited to SOEs (Figure 15.13). Moreover, it is striking that the non-electrical machinery sector records the highest PI, when only private enterprises are included in the sample (Figure 15.14). This is a sharp contrast with the dismal performance of the public machinery industry. Further studies are necessary to correctly evaluate these performance differences by sector.

Key determinants of performance

To identify the key determinants of good performance, a regression analysis of performance equations has been conducted. Equation 3 in Table 15.2 confirms the above findings and indicates, at 5 percent of significance: (1) the degree of authorities' control, the presence of "excessive" competition, and the two sector dummies (namely, food processing and non-electrical machinery) are negatively related to performance; and (2) the size of the labor force, which also indicates enterprise size, is positively related to performance. The ownership dummy for central government is also positive and significant at the 10 percent level. The addition of other variables (such as location, joint ventures, access to subsidies) does not significantly change these parameter estimates, except that the ownership dummies lose explanatory power (Equations 1, 2). None of the other variables has a significant explanatory impact on performance.

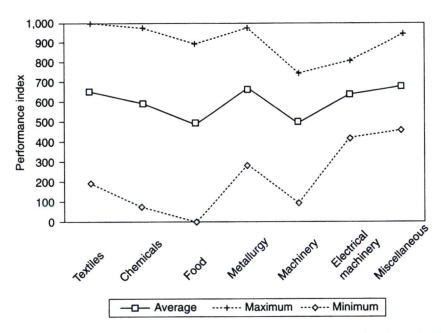

Figure 15.13 Viet Nam: performance by industry – state-owned enterprises (central and local government)

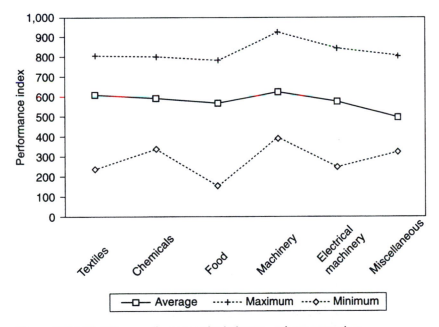

Figure 15.14 Viet Nam: performances by industry – private enterprises

Table 15.2 Viet Nam: performance equations

Dependent Variable: Performance Index, i.e., weighted average of 5 variables, ranging from 0 (worst) to 1,000 (best)

	(1) All N=199		(2) All N=199		(3) All N=199		(4) SOEs N=145		(5) Private N=54	
CONSTANT	634.4	(7.96)	633.7	(7.72)	655.4	(17.88)	630.9	(6.01)	485.6	(3.17)
STATE	53.8	(0.97)	71.1	(1.28)	84.6	(1.85)*				
LOCAL	31.9	(0.58)	34.9	(0.63)	53.6	(1.20)				
CONTROL	-38.6	(-2.19)**	-42.4	(-2.37)**	-39.5	(-2.37)**				
LOCATION	15.8	(0.53)	9.0	(0.30)			29.4	(0.82)	-0.1	(-0.00)
MERGER	28.2	(0.78)	7.7	(0.21)			-8.2	(-0.21)	-110.4	(-0.90)
JV	8.4	(0.19)	-2.8	(-0.06)			-26.3	(-0.50)	59.6	(0.69)
JVfin	-18.7	(-0.37)	21.0	(0.41)			-14.1	(-0.17)	16.9	(0.25)
EXCOMPET	-85.5	(-2.50)**	-75.2	(-2.29)**	-80.6	(-2.57)**	-72.4	(-1.82)*	-162.1	(-2.59)***
LABRSIZE	0.038	(2.50)**	0.028	(1.66)*	0.032	(2.29)**	0.043	(1.94)*	0.035	(1.49)
SUBSIDY	3.4	(0.08)	35.7	(0.82)			39.3	(0.85)		
BANKACCS	4.0	(0.11)	0.5	(0.01)			-61.1	(-1.19)	94.3	(1.75)*
MKTINPUT	-8.0	(-0.70)	-6.6	(-0.58)			-4.5	(-0.34)	18.2	(0.71)
MKTOUTPUT	6.1	(0.53)	10.8	(0.92)			11.5	(0.77)	19.3	(1.02)
CHEM			-41.3	(-0.82)			-18.9	(-0.30)	-2.0	(-0.02)
FOOD			-93.4	(-1.84)*	-79.5	(-1.99)**	-122.5	(-1.88)*	20.2	(0.25)
METL			34.7	(0.29)			24.2	(0.19)		
MACH			-108.8	(-2.22)**	-97.0	(-2.56)**	-129.7	(-2.12)**	50.0	(0.60)
ELEC			1.2	(0.02)			43.7	(0.58)	-59.4	(-0.77)
MISC			14.0	(0.29)			74.2	(1.21)	-116.9	(-1.53)

Table 15.2 continued

R-squared	0.124	0.168	0.156	0.196	0.358
SE	198.8	197.0	192.1	204.6	166.1
Mean	590.8	590.8	590.8	594.2	581.4

t-statistics are in parentheses
*** significant at the 1% level
** significant at the 5% level
* significant at the 10% level

Variables

STATE: dummy for central SOEs
LOCAL: dummy for local SOEs
CONTROL: the number of controlled management decisions
LOCATION: dummy for city, Hanoi (0), Ho Chi Minh (1)
MERGER: dummy for merger, no (0), yes (1)
JV: dummy for joint venture, no (0), yes (1)
JVfin: dummy for joint venture as main financing source, no (0), yes (1)
EXCOMPET: dummy for 'excessive' competition, no (0), yes (1)
LABRSIZE: the number of total workers
SUBSIDY: dummy for subsidy, no (0), complementary source (0.5), main source (1)

BANKACCS: dummy for access to banks, no (0), yes (1)
MKTINPUT: dummy for the degree of input purchase from market
(1<20%, . . . , 80%<5)
MKTOUTPUT: dummy for the degree of output sales at market
(1<20%, . . . , 80%<5)
CHEM: dummy for chemical industry
FOOD: dummy for food processing industry
METL: dummy for metallurgy industry
MACH: dummy for nonelectrical machinery
ELEC: dummy for electrical machinery
MISC: dummy for other light manufacturing industry

Note: The textile garment industry is represented by all industry dummies being zero (0).

It is also notable that when the sample is restricted to private enterprises, the "excessive" competition dummy increases its statistical significance (to the 1 percent level), and the bank access dummy becomes positive and significant (at the 10 percent level). The bank access dummy is negative when only SOEs are included the sample, although it is not statistically significant (Equation 4). Size of the labor force (or enterprise size) continues to be positively associated with performance but it is no longer significant. Sector dummies lose their explanatory power (Equation 5).

What are the quantitative effects of the above variables on performance? According to Equation 3, if the number of controlled managerial decisions increases by one, the PI drops by 40 points on a scale of zero to 1,000. If the number of workers increases by 1,000 persons, the PI rises by 32 points. The PI of the enterprises facing "excessive" competition is 81 points lower than other-wise. (All enterprises answered that they are currently facing competition. No enterprises responded that there is "no" or "too little" competition.) Furthermore, the PIs of the enterprises in food processing or non-electrical machinery are 80 points and 97 points lower, respectively, than the enterprises in the other sectors.

In sum, the profile of well-performing enterprises in Viet Nam includes: (1) great managerial autonomy; (2) large scale; (3) absence of "excessive" competition; (4) not being in the food processing sector; (5) not being in the non-electrical machinery sector (only for SOEs); and (6) access to bank financing (only for private enterprises).

IV The implications for Vietnamese reform strategies

The findings of Section III provide useful implications for the transition to a market economy in general, as well as for the design of a Vietnamese reform strategies in the future.

General issues

The data on the Vietnamese manufacturing enterprises do not support the standard view held by big-bang economists that private ownership is necessarily superior to state or public ownership, or that SOEs are resistant to restructuring and thus associated with inefficiency. Rather, the evidence suggests that: (1) factors specific to each enterprise (such as managerial autonomy, sector, size, and degree of competition) are more strongly associated with performance; and (2) Vietnamese SOEs have the supply–response capacity and ability to adapt to the new market environment. In fact, during 1991–94, many SOEs improved their performance and made difficult adjustment by shedding redundant labor. All enterprise managers now perceive that the market is competitive. These results suggest that a two-track approach has been working in Viet Nam and that the absence of immediate privatization has not prevented Vietnamese enterprises from restructuring.

Moreover, our findings reject commonly held beliefs such as: "large enterprises are difficult to restructure" and "the greater the competition, the more efficient the industry". The fact that even large enterprises can be reformed is consistent with the findings of recent firm surveys in other countries. For example, Brian Pinto *et al.* have concluded from data on 64 large Polish SOEs that these SOEs have taken painful measures to improve their long-term profitability and that at least half of them have started to recover from the 1990–91 decline (Pinto *et al.* 1993, Pinto and Wijnbergen 1994). In their analysis of 111 Chinese garment enterprises, Liu *et al.* and Otsuka found that large-scale TVEs which have joint ventures with SOEs are as efficient as joint ventures with foreign firms and that they are performing much better than other types of enterprises.[12] They point out the possibility that large TVEs linked with SOEs could benefit from the double merits of: (1) being TVEs (managerial autonomy), and (2) being SOEs (access to financial, physical, and other necessary resources) (Liu *et al.* 1994). The negative impact of "excessive" competition on performance may suggest a need for "compartmentalized competition," particularly in the case of industries with scale economies.[13]

It should be noted, however, that the empirical analysis in this paper does not directly prove any causal relationship among variables. For example, in interpreting the inverse relationship between "excessive" competition and performance, it is not clear whether enterprises are really suffering from "excessive" competition, or they are simply using it as an excuse for their poor performance. Other relationships are also subject to similar causal ambiguity and thus must be interpreted with care.

Issues specific to Vietnamese reform strategies

From the above evidence, we draw the following five implications, which are specific to Vietnamese SOE reform.

First, the positive relationship between significant managerial autonomy and performance implies that government efforts to reform SOEs have so far produced good results. It also means that ongoing or planned reforms – redefinition of the governance structure within SOEs as well as the relationship between SOEs and supervisory institutions (which are broadly outlined in the recently promulgated State Enterprise Law and to be stipulated in more details in related regulations), strengthening of financial management, and the move toward reducing intermediary institutions and simplifying administrative procedures – are moving in the right direction.

Second, the weak relationship between ownership and performance may pose the question of the desirable pace and timing for implementing a full-fledged equitization (or privatization) program. In this connection, the government's current strategy of starting with a pilot equitization program and learning lessons for further refinement is sensible and should be supported. Because a functioning market economy based on private property requires a number of well-developed market institutions (e.g., financial institutions, legal framework, entrepreneurship, and intra-firm labor market) and human resources (equipped with accounting, auditing, and management skills), it is necessary to decide carefully how to proceed with the larger equitization program, monitoring progress in related reforms and evaluating continuously the results of the pilot program.

These two issues raise the important question of why in Viet Nam, SOE managers had incentives to restructure and positively responded to the new market environment – even though the change in ownership lagged behind. Answering this question properly will require additional detailed firm surveys, and thus is beyond the scope of this paper. However, it is possible to infer from the Chinese experience of TVEs that hardened budget constraints and increased competition in Viet Nam (particularly during 1989–90) exerted adjustment pressure on SOE managers to turn to profit-maximization objectives and that expanded managerial autonomy facilitated behavioral changes. This is also consistent with the results of the Polish firm survey (Pinto *et al.* 1993).

Third, the positive relationship between large-scale enterprises and performance may suggest: (1) the desirability of exploring scale economies in certain industries; and (2) the need for enhanced efforts in promoting small- and medium-scale enterprises, at the same time. In this sense, the government's recent decision to form enterprise groups or General Corporations deserves attention. However, further work is necessary to find out why large enterprises have advantages over smaller ones (after controlling for ownership, sector, and other attributes). The degree of scale economies must be evaluated industry by industry, and it should not be used as an excuse to justify monopoly or oligopoly, especially in consumer-goods manufacturing industries.

Fourth, the observed association between sectors and performance may imply the need for sector-specific policies. The survey indicates that the textile and garment industry and the electrical machinery industry are growing rapidly by making use of the comparative advantage afforded by current Vietnamese resource endowments (abundant and cheap labor). On the other hand, food processing (in general) and non-electrical machinery (SOEs only) are found to have been facing difficulties. It is important to identify the reasons for their poor performance and determine whether a certain type of industrial policy is needed (for example, measures to facilitate a fade-out adjustment).

It should be noted that the poor performance of the food processing industry is at odds with macro data, which indicate the sector's rapid growth in recent years. (Gross production of food and food stuffs grew at about 14 percent in both 1992 and 1993.) One of the possible interpretations for the mismatch between firm-based and macro data would be that increased new entrants in the food processing industry, while contributing to sector-wide industrial growth, have intensified competition and negatively affected profitability at the enterprise level. In fact, almost all enterprises in the food processing industry (30 out of 32) answered that the market is "too competitive" (including competition against smuggled imports). This implies that "excessive" competition accounts for part of the sector's poor performance. Regarding the non-electrical machinery industry, preliminary findings indicate that outdated equipment and technology are at least partly responsible for its poor performance.

Fifth, the positive relationship between access to bank financing and performance of private enterprises highlights the importance of continued reforms in the financial sector, including the need to create a level-playing field in terms of access to capital for SOEs and private enterprises. According to the survey, more than 70 percent of private enterprises answered that their operations and investments are primarily self-financed and that they have never borrowed long-term capital from banks. The survey also shows that private enterprises continue to face disadvantages relative to SOEs, such as the traditional state bank practice of favoring SOEs (despite some improvements in recent years) and the difficulty in providing sufficient collateral (which is in turn related to limited physical assets, e.g., land, building, and equipment).[14]

It should be noted that limited access to formal finance is regarded as the major constraint on production by all types of enterprises in Viet Nam. The survey reveals that this is the most serious problem for 46 percent of the sampled enterprises and is one of the three most serious problems for nearly 80 percent of the enterprises. A number of factors might be accountable for this weakness, including the shortage of capital (partly due to low capital accumulation, the perverse term structure between short- and long-term interest rates etc.), inefficient banking services (e.g., cumbersome paper work, low quality of services), and lack of human resources trained in loan appraisal, monitoring, and accounting.

At the same time, as the seemingly negative relationship between access to bank financing and SOE performance suggests, it should be warned that the simple expansion of financial access may not help enhance enterprise performance – unless the financial system itself functions effectively and unless enterprises are disciplined to use scarce resources efficiently. It is necessary to examine thoroughly the weaknesses in the existing financial system in Viet Nam, find ways to address them, and continue efforts to improve enterprise financial management.

V Conclusion

Empirical evidence from Vietnamese manufacturing enterprises indicates that Vietnamese SOEs have supply-response capacity as well as the ability to adapt to a new market environment. At least in Viet Nam, but also in a few other countries, immediate privatization is not a necessary ingredient of transition strategies. Policies for hardening budget constraints, bestowing managerial autonomy, and fostering competition appear to be more important in the early period of transition and contribute to improving managers' incentives. These findings support the conclusion that the government's efforts in SOE reforms have so far been in the right direction.

At the same time, the evidence suggests the need for continued efforts to improve the business environment for private enterprises, particularly through financial sector reforms. It is essential to analyze the major weaknesses in the present banking system and take measures to improve its efficiency. Parallel efforts should be also made in expanding private sector access to bank financing.

Lastly, further work is needed to find out why large-scale enterprises are faring well and why industries in the public domain facing "excessive" competition, including food processing and non-electrical machinery, are not doing well. These issues may have important bearing on the direction of future reforms, especially in the areas of establishing enterprise groups, and implementing "compartmentalized competition" for sectors exhibiting scale economies, as well as in industrial policy in general.

Appendix

A note on the Performance Index

To obtain a reliable performance measure, five indicators are combined to form the Performance Index (PI), using data on 199 public and private enterprises. The weights are devised from the first principal component (eigenvector) of the covariance matrix. This component carries reasonable signs and accounts for 42 percent of the total variance. The PI is further normalized to have a minimum of zero (worst) and a maximum of 1,000 (best).

Use of six indicators was also attempted, adding nominal sales growth from 1991–94 to the above five; however, this produced little change in the ranking of enterprise performance ($R^2 = 0.388$). The number of data was also reduced to 164 because half of the private enterprises did not exist in 1991.

Five indicators	*Factor loading (=weight)*
Capacity utilization (current rate %)	0.61813
Profit change 1993/1994 1–3 (less, same, more profitable)	0.66161
Labor redundancy redundant workers/total workers (%)	–0.39111
Perceived competitiveness vs. domestic products 1–5 (incapable, less capable, capable to compete, have advantage, have great advantage)	0.76599
Perceived competitiveness vs. imports 1–5 (incapable, less capable, capable to compete, have advantage, have great advantage)	0.73215

Explanatory power of the first
principal component =   41.9%

Notes

1 This is the entire chapter IV of *Transition Strategies and Economic Performance: "Gradualism" Revisited*, OECF Discussion Papers no. 8, September 1995. It was also published in *OECF Journal of Development Assistance*, vol. 1, no. 2, March 1996. [Editors] This chapter is a revised version of a paper presented at the workshop, "Assessment of Firm Response to a New Economic Environment," sponsored jointly by the State Planning Committee, Viet Nam, and the Overseas Economic Cooperation Fund, held in Hanoi on May 31, 1995. For the summarized results of the firm survey, see *OECF-SPC Proceedings of the Workshop*, July 1995.

2 See also Blanchard *et al.* (1991).

3 See McKinnon (1993, 1994), Naughton (1994), and Rana and Paz (1994).

4 The concept of ownership remains ambiguous in China. However, it is often pointed out that TVEs operate as if they were private firms. This is primarily due to hardened budget constraints (heavy dependence on internally-generated profits to fund operating budgets), performance-based incentive systems (reward and punishment), competitive business environment, and managerial autonomy (Nellis 1995). Ishikawa argues that non-material incentives such as communal bonds and societal pressure are critically important in making TVEs behave as if they were private firms (Ishikawa 1995).

5 As part of government reorganization in fall 1995, the State Planning Committee became the Ministry of Planning and Investment [Editors].

6 Other firm surveys include: Ministry of International Trade and Industry and International Development Center of Japan, *Dynamic Viet Nam: Toward Cooperation for Industrial Development and Investment Promotion* (November 1993; in Japanese), and International Labor Organization, Asian Regional Team for Employment Promotion (ARTEM), *Small Enterprises in Viet Nam*, report prepared for the Ministry of Labor, Invalids and Social Affairs, Government of the Socialist Republic of Viet Nam (September 1992). The Central Institute of Economic Management (CIEM), under the Ministry of Planning and Investment has also conducted a series of firm surveys.

7 These figures indicate the overall growth rates of both SOEs and non-SOEs and are not restricted to industry.

8 According to a World Bank report, it is estimated that previously about 20 percent of centrally-run SOEs and 60 percent of locally-run SOEs were loss-making (World Bank 1994). SPC officials claim that only 11 percent of SOEs are loss-makers at present.

9 The Planning Department of SPC is responsible for the re-registration of SOEs, which started in 1991, and has been also responsible for the registration of private businesses since 1994. The Planning Department also carried out a household survey (or Living Standard Measurement Survey) at the national level during 1992–93, supported by the World Bank, UNDP, and SIDA.

10 The only exception is the metallurgy sector, where only three enterprises out of eight were selected. As of mid-1994, there were about 1,700 SOEs in Hanoi and Ho Chi Minh City, and 436 SOEs were engaged in production of the six sectors (excluding the miscellaneous sector). The sample draws 118 enterprises from the six sectors. There are about 4,000 private enterprises in the two cities, and only 10 to 15 percent are estimated to be engaged in productive activities. The sample covers 60 private enterprises in seven manufacturing sectors. For details, please see the report by the Planning Department of SPC (SPC 1995a, 1995b).

11 Decision 217-HDBT (1987) marked a turning point in SOE managerial reforms. Except for the one target of "contribution to the state budget," SOEs were given managerial autonomy in production and business in the areas of planning, pricing, input purchase, output sales, allocation of retained profits, wage setting, investing own resources, asset acquisition, etc. There management reforms at the micro level were followed by a drastic macroeconomic adjustment in 1989.

12 The survey data cover various types of enterprises – SOEs, collectives, TVEs having joint ventures with SOEs, TVEs without joint ventures, and joint ventures with foreign firms – in Beijing, Shanghai, and Guangzhou.

13 Some economists argue that in post-war Japan the Ministry of International Trade and Industry implemented industrial policy for the purpose of promoting scale economies while avoiding destabilizing "excessive" competition.

14 The private sector's share in total bank lending increased substantially from 10 percent in 1991 to 27 percent at end-1993 (mainly in the agricultural sector). But the overwhelming majority of this is short-term. The absence of medium- and long-term finance is considered a general constraint in Viet Nam, especially for the industrial private sector. At end-1993, the non-SOE sector accounted for only 14.4 percent of the total medium- and long-term credit (the private sector less than 10 percent) (World Bank 1995).

References

Blanchard, Olivier, Rudiger Dornbusch, Paul Krugman, Richard Layard, and Lawrence Summers (1991) *Reform in Eastern Europe*, Cambrige, MA: MIT Press.

Ishikawa, Shigeru (1995) "The Issues on Vietnamese Enterprise Reform: Lessons from the Chinese Experience", paper presented at the OECF-SPC workshop held in Hanoi on May 31, 1995.

Lee, Chung H. and Helmut Reisen (eds) (1994) *From Reform to Growth: China and Other Countries in Transition in Asia and Central and Eastern Europe*, Paris: OECD.

Liu, T., Naoki Murakami, and Keijiro Otsuka (1994) "The Emergence of Township Village Enterprises in China and the Development of Apparel Industry," in *Keizai Kenkyu* [Economic Review], vol. 45, no. 2, April.

McKinnon, Ronald I. (1993) *The Order of Economic Liberalization*, 2nd edn. Baltimore, MD: Johns Hopkins University Press.

—— (1994) "Financial Control in the Transition from Classical Socialism to a Market Economy," *Journal of Economic Perspective*, vol. 5, no. 4, Fall.

Naughton, Barry (1994) "Reforming a Planned Economy: Is China Unique?" in Chung H. Lee and Helmut Reisen (eds) *From Reform to Growth: China and Other Countries Transition in Asia and Central and Eastern Europe*, Paris: OECD, pp. 49–74.

Nellis, John (1995) "Public Enterprise Reform: Key Lessons of International Experience," paper for the workshop on "Alternative Approaches to Improving SOE Efficiency," January 17–18, 1995, in Hanoi, Viet Nam.

OECF and SPC (1995) *Proceedings of Workshop: Assessment of Firm Response to New Economic Environment* Hanoi: Overseas Economic Cooperation Fund and State Planning Committee.

Pinto, Brian and Sweder van Wijnbergen (1994) "Ownership and Corporate Control in Poland: Why State Firms Defied the Odds," Policy Research Working Paper 1308, International Finance Corporation, June.

Pinto, Brian, Marek Belka, and Stefan Krajewski (1993) "Transforming State Enterprises in Poland: Evidence on Adjustment by Manufacturing Firms," *Brookings Papers on Economic Activity*, 1: 1993: 213–70.

Rana, Pradumna B., and Malcolm Dowling, Jr. (1993) "Big Bang's Bust," *International Economy*, September/October.

Rana, Pradumna B., and Wilhelmina Paz (1994) "Economies in Transition: The Asian Experience," in Chung H. Lee and Helmut Reisen (eds) *From Reform to Growth: China and Other Countries in Transition in Asia and Central and Eastern Europe*, Paris: OECD, pp. 119–140.

Sachs, Jeffrey and Wing Thye Woo (1993) "Big Bank Smear Job", in *International Economy*, November/December.

Sachs, Jeffrey and Wing Thye Woo (1994a) "Understanding the Reform Experiences of China, Eastern Europe and Russia," in Chung H. Lee and Helmut Reisen (eds) *From Reform to Growth: China and Other Countries in Transition in Asia and Central and Eastern Europe*, Paris: OECD, pp. 23–48.

Sachs, Jeffrey and Wing Thye Woo (1994b) "Structural Factor in the Economic Reforms of China, Eastern Europe and the former Soviet Union", *Economic Policy*.

SPC (Planning Department of the State Planning Committee in Viet Nam) (1995a) *Firm Survey: Assessment of Firm Responses to the New Economic Development*, March 1995.

—— (1995b) "Brief Outcomes of the Firm Survey", paper presented at the OECF–SPC workshop held in Hanoi on May 31, 1995.

Statistical Publishing House of the Government of Viet Nam (1994a) *Economy of Viet Nam: Reviews and Statistics*, Hanoi: Statistical Publishing House.

—— (1994b) *Industrial Data 1983–1993*, Hanoi: Statistical Publishing House.

Stiglitz, Joseph E. (1994) *Whither Socialism?*, Cambridge, MA: MIT Press.

Svejnar, Jan (1990) "Microeconomic Issues in the Transition to a Market Economy", *Journal of Economic Perspectives*, vol. 5, no. 4, Fall.

World Bank (1994) *Viet Nam: Public Sector Management and Private Sector Incentives*, September, Washington, DC: World Bank.

—— (1995) *Viet Nam: Financial Sector Review: An Agenda for Financial Sector Development*, March.

AFTERWORD

Since the early 1990s when most of the essays in this book were written, there has been increased intellectual exchange between the World Bank and the Japanese government over economic development and systemic transition strategies. On one crucial point, the views of the Bank and Japan are coming closer. Both now agree that each developing country is *unique* and that development strategy should reflect this diversity. The Bank's *World Development Report 1997* rejects the one-size-fits-all approach and declares that development without an effective state is impossible. This is a welcome departure from the 1980s, when development was all about putting free markets first and reducing government involvement in the economy.

Furthermore, new elements have recently been added to the Bank's development paradigm. Environment, gender, and other social dimensions are among the new concerns. But the most notable addition to the Bank's analytical toolbox, from the viewpoint of strengthening the role of the state, is the increased emphasis on "institutions." The Bank is currently engaged in a large number of projects to help member countries ensure the rule of law, improve the efficiency and accountability of the public sector, and promote good governance. (The Bank's working definition of institutions is narrower than that contemplated by Aoki in Chapter 8 of this volume, and confined mostly to the government's ability to design and implement appropriate policies.)

The Bank's interest in institutions has both empirical and theoretical grounds. On the empirical side, there is wide recognition that the recipe of the 1980s provided perhaps necessary, but not always sufficient, ingredients for sustainable growth in less developed economies. Internal reviews of the Bank's adjustment lending candidly admit that the developmental impact of free-market reforms has been mixed. Reforms worked relatively well in middle-income developing countries, and private capital is flowing into emerging markets of East Asia and Latin America. However, many low-income countries, particularly in Africa, have failed to attract private capital, domestic or foreign, despite repeated attempts at bold free-market reforms. The Bank wants to know why some governments are able to reform and others not, and why reform, once implemented, works better in some countries than in others.

To answer these questions, new institutional economics has made important contributions on the theoretical front. Applying principal–agent theory and emphasizing imperfect and asymmetric information, the new theory has shown that, for markets to work well, an economy requires a complex web of effective institutions, from basic property rights and well-run legal systems to effective and uncorrupted bureaucracies.

Does this shift in the Bank's development paradigm bridge the existing gap between its and Japan's position on development and transition? We applaud the increased concern with institution-building as a right step toward more productive discussions on how to achieve an appropriate blend of market and government, taking the specific factors of each country into consideration. Nevertheless, we still feel that the Bank's new institutional focus is not quite on the mark. It misses what Japanese development economists believe is the most important task in economic development.

Each developing country is *unique* at least in two distinct aspects: the state of underdeveloped markets and the strength of institutional capacity. The first deals with how the private sector functions in the real economy, while the second relates to the effectiveness of the public sector. Japanese development economists are almost exclusively concerned with the first type of uniqueness. As all chapters of this volume clearly demonstrate, we are primarily interested in drawing up a tailor-made action plan to create a viable market economy in the diverse setting of each country. In our view, market creation is the substance of economic development. Moreover, it is through the process of designing and implementing a comprehensive and concrete long-term development strategy that necessary institutions are identified and government resolve to carry out reform hardens.

In contrast, the Bank's idea of institution-building is highly abstract. Terms such as accountability, transparency, governance, anti-corruption, and contract and law enforcement capacity which adorn Bank documents speak of the general principles under which ideal, efficient public-sector institutions should function. While these principles are undoubtedly important, they do not directly link capacity building to each developing country's specific need to overcome formidable problems in employment, production, investment, trade, and technology. Virtually all of the Bank's institution-supporting projects implemented around the globe are based on a common policy agenda. In other words, institution-building is advocated in isolation, project by project, without being embedded in the concreteness of diverse reality. Here again, we are reminded of Yanagihara's distinction between the neoclassical "framework approach" versus Japan's "ingredients approach" (Chapter 4 of this volume). The World Bank sets out universally applicable rules and monitors the progress of each game as an impartial referee, while Japan advises like a coach who is eager to improve the skills of each player and design a winning strategy for the next game.

World Development Report 1997 (WDR97) offers a good example of how the Bank perceives institutions. Its central theme is the role and capabilities of the state. The report offers a two-part approach: (1) match the state's role to its current capabilities; and (2) enhance its capabilities over time by constructing incentive mechanisms that drive behavior (effective rules and restraints, increased citizen voice and partnership, and greater competitive pressure). Thus, the report argues generally that governments with weak institutions should refrain from intervening heavily in the economy, and instead concentrate on fostering sufficient capabilities. If the operational criteria for a "strong" state are very demanding (no such criteria currently exist), the message becomes essentially the same as that of the 1993 *East Asian Miracle* report, that is, industrial policy is too difficult for virtually all countries, which disappointed Shiratori (see Chapter 5 of this volume). In a recent informal OECF–World Bank meeting, an eminent Japanese development economist complained that WDR97 was full of institutions but lacked any analysis of underdeveloped markets. In reply, a World Bank vice-president agreed with the Japanese economist that each embryonic market economy was unique, but admitted that this recognition had not so far been incorporated in the Bank's actual lending operations.

So what should be done? In addition to the well-deserved research on institutions, we believe that attention of development economists should be redirected to the heart of the developmental problem – intrinsic difficulties in the real economy – that plagues different developing countries differently. Institution-building should be an important but supplemental component of a comprehensive and concrete long-term development strategy. To this end, we offer three proposals.

First, *establish a common methodology to diagnose the diversity of underdeveloped markets*. There is an acute need to improve the analytical and operational tools of the international financial institutions to allow for a systematic analysis of real-sector problems in low-income countries. What are the preconditions for a market economy to function and develop? What should the governments of latecomer countries do to prepare these preconditions? How do these preconditions and the government's proper role differ from one developing country to another? To answer these important questions, researchers must examine a large number of topics in the context of each country: when and how integrated labor and financial markets emerge, how to identify and support key market players (merchants, entrepreneurs, bankers, etc.), what hurdles thwart productivity breakthrough, how to selectively use or create various "networks" (subcontracting, enterprise groups, government–business relationships, commercial and trade guilds, etc.), and so on. A suitable development model should be chosen, with revisions if necessary to reflect the stage of development, factor endowment, social segmentation, and cultural and historical peculiarities of each country. The best minds on Washington's 19th Street should be assigned to these challenging tasks, not to endless number crunching for the next Paris Club meeting. Ultimately, the analytical procedure should be formalized within each institution in standardized reports, similar to the IMF's

Recent Economic Development and the World Bank's Country Assistance Strategy, Country Economic Memorandum, and Public Expenditure Review.

Second, *conduct in-depth case studies of the institution-building experience of countries that succeeded in catching up with the West.* How did countries that have succeeded in economic development (Japan, Singapore, Taiwan, Korea, Malaysia, Chile, etc.) build up their institutional capacity in the early stage of development? What was the role of political leadership in this process? How were the reform of public administration and key institutional innovation linked to the design and implementation of national development strategies at that time? In this connection, it is also crucial to deepen the analysis of East Asian authoritarian developmentalism. We are not entirely satisfied with past research on the relationship between political regimes and economic development, which tended to make simple generalizations by failing to distinguish different types of autocratic regimes. Authoritarian developmentalism, as defined by Watanabe (Chapter 11 of this volume), is a very special type of authoritarianism. It should not be confused with Stalinism or Maoism, or the personal fiefdom of a badly-run African state. Those who actually lived through the period of East Asian high growth know in their blood that this regime made an enormous difference. It is true that East Asia's authoritarian developmentalism may not be easily copied by other countries. But what we need is not another ideological battle over authoritarian developmentalism. Instead, we should conduct more in-depth theoretical and empirical analyses of East Asian political regimes from which other latecomer countries can draw practical lessons.

Third, *revisit non-neoclassical development economics, which once addressed the unique characteristics of underdevelopment.* To design the future, we recommend a journey into the past – to the era before the neoclassical influence became so pervasive. Development economics was born after World War II, driven by enthusiasm to assist newly independent ex-colonial states attain economic autonomy. Enormous analytical and operational efforts were made to identify and relieve the bottlenecks of economic development. Economists of the 1950s and 1960s left us a rich literature which should not be forgotten. Confronted with concrete problems, they had little time for fantasizing either market or government. In the process of preparing the present volume, we came to be greatly impressed by Alexander Gerschenkron's historical perspective, Albert O. Hirschman's argument on the linkage effect of industrialization, W. Arthur Lewis's famous model of rural–urban migration, Hla Myint's concern on the structural segmentation of the national economy, Harry T. Oshima's insight into the patterns of Asian development, just to name a few. (We would also like to mention the more recent contribution by Lance Taylor on neo-structuralism.) It would be a serious mistake to dismiss those non-neoclassical works of the past by simply stating that excessive state involvement in the early postwar period resulted from some of these studies. Of course, this does not mean that every old theory should be resurrected. While we must certainly be selective, it would be a very good idea to take a fresh look at classical development literature.

Confucius (551?–479 BC) once said, "study the past, understand the new" (*onko chishin*, in Japanese transcription). We are simply trying to follow this old East Asian tradition.

Editors

INDEX

Printed in the United States
133184LV00003B/34/A